GOOD RETIREMENT GUIDE

1987

Save & Prosper

GOOD RETIREMENT GUIDE

1987

Rosemary Brown

R£WARD RETIREMENT SERVICES

Duckworth

First published in 1986 by
Gerald Duckworth & Co. Ltd.
The Old Piano Factory
43 Gloucester Crescent, London NW1

© 1986 by Rosemary Brown

ISBN 0 7156 2106 8 (cased)
ISBN 0 7156 2107 6 (paper)

Photoset in North Wales by
Derek Doyle & Associates, Mold, Clwyd.
Printed in Great Britain by
Redwood Burn Limited, Trowbridge

Contents

8. Starting Your Own Business

9. Looking for Paid Work 223

12. Holidays   295

Preface

Retirement has never offered as much scope or as many opportunities as it does today. Whether your prime concern is finance, your home, developing new leisure interests, starting a business, finding paid or voluntary work, staying fit or caring for elderly parents, the choice of possibilities is enormous. The aim of the *Good Retirement Guide* is to highlight the various options that are available together with the information ... including price guides, sources of advice and useful names and addresses ... to enable you to decide what is best for you. I am extremely grateful to the hundreds of people who generously gave their time in helping us to track down the facts. While it is impossible to mention everyone by name, my special thanks are due to my assistant editor, Annabelle Campbell; our researchers Deborah Manley, Vicki Males and Terry West; Alec Morrison and Peter Brown; the Volunteer Centre for their help with Chapter 10; and KMG Thomson McLintock for their assistance in checking the tax information. I should like to thank Duckworth for publishing a much bigger book than they had anticipated and for producing it in record time. Finally, my very special thanks to Pauline Bessell who did a magnificent job in typing the manuscript and without whose help and enthusiasm this book would never have been possible

R.B.

Introduction
Preparing for your Retirement

Just as there are some people who become engaged within three hours of meeting and live happily ever after, there are others who without any apparent planning enjoy a totally fulfilled retirement, clearly relishing everything it has to offer. But for most of us life does not work like that. Important events require some preparation if we are to make the most of them and arguably this is more true of retirement than any other stage.

Glancing through a book I wrote for the *Daily Telegraph* in 1970, I was struck by the gloom with which many men and women – but especially men – viewed the prospect of what could be their happiest and most satisfying years. Far from welcoming the new challenges and opportunities, many saw retirement as a kind of bogeyman who trailed in his wake the threats of a lower standard of living, boredom and impending old age. Small wonder perhaps that many buried their heads in the sand and refused even to think about the event until the last possible moment.

Happily over the last decade attitudes have been radically changing. Not only are a majority of those retiring today fitter, more skilled and better off financially than any previous generation but with early retirement increasingly becoming the norm, a great many of us can realistically look forward to 25 years or more of active life ahead.

As a result, planning the future has become even more critically important. *The Good Retirement Guide* is not designed to offer you a ready-made philosophy or a few rose-tinted blueprints on the theme 'Life Begins in Middle Age'. Its sole aim is to set you thinking along constructive lines, to indicate what is possible, to advise on the best sources of information and to help you avoid the pitfalls that can trap the unwary. Key concerns are likely to be the question of money and how you will occupy your time. Others may well include: where you live, how best to keep fit, the effect of your retirement on close personal relationships and perhaps new responsibilities such as the care of elderly parents.

You don't need to be an accountant to know that once you stop earning your income will drop. However, if you complete the Budget Planner at the end of Chapter 5, you may be pleasantly surprised to find that the difference is far less than you feared. On the plus side, you will be saving on travel and other work-related expenses as well as enjoying a welcome reduction in tax.

As with all questions affecting retirement, it is sensible if possible to plan ahead. Assess your likely savings including the lump sum from your pension and any insurance policies you may have. Then draw up a plan as to how you can maximise their value. Should you invest your money in a building society, unit trust, stocks and shares or government securities? Does it make sense to buy an annuity? What are the tax angles for someone in your position? Should you consider consulting a good accountant, stockbroker or other professional adviser? If you are unsure of the answers, then Chapter 5 may help to clarify your thinking.

Your retirement income may well depend on whether you start a third career. Though with unemployment at its present level we are not pretending this is easy, a great many men and women do in fact find rewarding work when they are well into their sixties. While some turn their talents to something entirely new, others go freelance or become consultants in their existing area of expertise.

An increasing number are taking the heady step of starting their own business. This is not a decision to be entered into lightly. The risks are legion and most budding entrepreneurs find that they have never worked as hard in their lives. In the early days at least, being your own boss means sacrificing your social life, foregoing a salary and going out in the rain to post your own letters. Moreover, if you are married, then unless your partner is solidly behind you there are liable to be domestic tensions – especially if you run the business from home.

Against this, many who take the plunge derive enormous satisfaction from building up a family enterprise. If you are seriously flirting with the idea Chapter 8 provides a lot of the detail you will need to know.

A worthwhile alternative to becoming a business tycoon is to devote your energies to voluntary work. There are literally scores of opportunities for retired people to make a valuable contribution within their own community.

You might visit the elderly in their own homes, drive patients to hospitals, run a holiday playscheme, help out in your citizens advice bureau or become a Samaritan. Other ideas which might appeal are conservation work or playing a more active role in politics by joining your local party association. Whether you can only spare the occasional day or are prepared to help on a regular basis Chapter 10 lists a fund of suggestions you might like to consider.

A prime requirement whether you are thinking of paid or unpaid work, or for that matter simply planning to devote more time to your hobbies, is to remain fit and healthy. Good health is the most valuable possession we have. Without it, energy is lacking, activities are restricted and the fun goes out of life. No amount of money can compensate for being bed-ridden or a semi-invalid. While anyone can be unfortunate enough to be struck down by an unexpected illness, your future good health is largely in your own hands.

The reason why the seventies are so often dogged by aches and pains is that sufficient care has not been taken during the fifties and sixties.

As well as all the obvious advice about not smoking, becoming too fat or drinking to excess, there is the important question of exercise. While you could of course do press-ups and go for walks, you will probably have a much better time if you join the new keep-fit brigade. Thanks to the Sports Council there are opportunities around the country for almost every kind of sport, with 50 plus beginners especially welcome. Additionally dancing, yoga, keep-fit-to-music and relaxation classes are readily available through most local authorities as well as being offered by the many specialist bodies listed in Chapters 7 and 11.

The only problem is likely to be fitting everything in. The choice of organised leisure pursuits is little short of staggering. If you have ever wanted to learn about computers, take a degree, join a choir, become proficient in a craft, play competitive scrabble, start coin collecting or become a beekeeper, you will find an organisation that caters for your enthusiasm.

The type of activities you enjoy could be an important consideration in choosing where you will live. Because we are conditioned to thinking of retirement as a time for settling in a new home, many people up sticks without perhaps giving enough thought to such essentials as proximity to family and friends and whether a different area would provide the same scope for pursuing their interests.

A fairly common mistake is for people to retire to a place where they once spent an idyllic holiday, perhaps fifteen or twenty years previously, with only a minimum of further investigation. Resorts that are glorious in mid-summer can be bleak and damp in winter as well as pretty dull when the tourist season is over. Equally, many people sell their house and move somewhere smaller without taking account of the fact that when they are spending more time at home they may actually want more space, rather than less. This is particularly true of anyone planning to work from home or who has a hobby such as carpentry which requires a separate workroom.

While moving may be the right solution, especially if you want to realise some capital to boost your retirement income, there are plenty of ways of adapting a house to make it more convenient and labour-saving. Likewise, for example with insulation, you may be able to cut the running costs These and other possibilities, including taking in a lodger and creating a granny flat are explored in Chapter 6.

While on the subject of granny flats, if you are caring for elderly parents there may come a time when a little bit of outside help could make all the difference. The range of organisations that can provide you with back-up is far more extensive than is generally realised. For single women especially, who may feel that they have to give up a career, knowing what facilities are available could prove a veritable godsend.

While there may be pressure if a parent, however much loved, requires an undue amount of attention, a more commonplace problem is the effect of retirement on a couple's relationship. Many husbands are puzzled, and sometimes hurt, by their wife's attitude to the event. For years she has been complaining 'I never see anything of you darling' and 'Why can't you spend a little more time with the family?' – so naturally you expect her to be delighted to have you at home. But, apparently, not a bit of it. Before you have even had time to visit your old haunts, she is wishing that you were back at work – even urging you to go out and find something to do.

The reverse situation can also apply, especially if the wife had a high-powered career and retires a year or so after her husband, although in general the evidence suggests that it is usually the man's retirement that provokes most friction. This may change as more of today's working wives turn sixty and find themselves facing the same need to make difficult adjustments.

Either way, the point is that after years of seeing relatively little of each other, retirement suddenly creates the possibility of much more togetherness. Put in blunt terms, from a wife's point of view, having a husband at home during the day means an extra meal to cook and inevitable disruption to her normal routine.

If he stays in bed longer in the morning, the chores will be finished later which can be an irritation. But an even greater cause for resentment is that she may feel guilty about meeting her friends or pursuing her usual weekday activities unless her partner is also busy. If she is still at work, the situation can be even more fraught as, apart from the extra housework, she may find her loyalties uncomfortably divided. Furthermore, quite irrationally, some retired husbands begin to harbour dire suspicions about their wives' working colleagues, imagining romantic entanglements that had never crossed their mind before.

Sometimes too, retired people subconsciously label themselves as 'old' and start denying themselves and their partner the pleasures of a happily fulfilled sex life. It is difficult to know whether this is more ludicrous or tragic. As studies in many parts of the world show, the sexual satisfaction of both partners continues in a high proportion of cases long after the age of seventy and often well into the eighties.

Usually all these problems can be fairly simply overcome by willingness to discuss them frankly and to work out a solution that suits both. The situation is very much easier today than even ten years ago when male/female roles were far more stereotyped and many couples felt that they had to conform to a set pattern for the sake of convention.

Talking to other people to find out how they plan to tackle the challenges as well as the opportunities of retirement can be immensely helpful.

Many companies recognise this need by providing pre-retirement courses. If you are unlucky enough to be in a firm where this is not yet done, or if you are self-employed, there are a number of organisations to which you can turn for advice and help.

Before deciding on a particular course, it is worthwhile giving a little thought to the best time to go and the subjects which the counselling should cover. The traditional view is that the ideal time is somewhere between one or two years before you are due to retire. While this is probably true for most people, it is also important to remember that preparing for retirement really has to be a staged process.

Some financial decisions, such as those affecting company or personal pension planning, need to be taken as early as possible. Others, such as whether to move house, can probably only be made much later. The basic subjects that the best courses address are finance, health, activity, leisure, housing and the adjustments which will need to be made by both you and your family when you retire. The crucial test however is not the amount of factual information that is contained but the extent to which the course helps to focus and stimulate your own thoughts on the various issues and to lead to discussion with your partner and others in the same position.

Pre-retirement courses

The following is a list of the best known courses available to individuals enrolling independently of company sponsorship.

The Pre-Retirement Association, 19 Undine Street, London SW17, T:01-767 3854.

Although they no longer run courses themselves, the PRA will be able to put you in touch with the nearest Pre-Retirement group who should in turn be able to advise you on courses in your area. They can also supply reading lists of relevant material.

Choice Publications Ltd., 12 Bedford Row, London WC1R 4DV, T:01-404 4320.

Choice now administers all the courses for the PRA. These range from week-long courses for about £100 a head at Pontins or Warners Holiday Camps to a number of week-end and day seminars. Contact John Kemp at the address above.

Adult education centres

(See local telephone directory under your local council listing). As interest in this area increases a growing number of Adult Education Centres are running both day and evening courses. Standards vary but you should be able to get a good idea of the approach from the syllabus.

Workers Educational Association, 9 Upper Berkeley Street, London W1, T:01-402 5608.

Many of the 900 branches of the WEA run local courses. Check your telephone directory for the nearest branch or contact the London HQ for further information.

The Open University, The Learning Materials Service Office, The Centre for Continuing Education, The Open University, P.O.Box 188, Milton Keynes MK7 6DH.

The OU produces a study pack called 'Planning Retirement' which covers all the important areas and provides a useful starting point for thought and discussion. The price, which includes an audio cassette, is £20. This can be supplemented by written exercises which will be computer assessed. This costs £10 as a separate item but the two parts together come for £29.50.

Financial organisations

Pensions and pensioners are a big market as is reflected in the wide range of financial institutions offering pre-retirement courses. The very largest like the Prudential and Legal and General are able to offer these as a genuinely independent extension of their huge pension businesses but many of the smaller firms obviously see them as commercial marketing opportunities. It is, therefore, important to be aware of this if you do go on such a course.

Legal and General Assurance Society Ltd., Grosvenor House, 125 High Street, Croydon, Surrey CR9 3UA, T:01-681 5177.

Legal and General, who administer more pensions than any other company in Europe, were the first in this field. They now run a number of open courses and free evening roadshows. While the shorter ones inevitably concentrate largely on financial matters, the longer courses also cover health, leisure activities and the psychological aspects of retirement. Prices start at £25 a head but will depend on the nature and level of the course. The company has recently produced a video presentation kit which may be hired for £25 plus VAT and could be used either by an individual or a group. Contact Keith Hughes, Retirement Counselling Manager at the above address.

Prudential Assurance Company Ltd., 142 Holborn Bars, London EC1, T:01-405 9222.

The Prudential are planning to run about a dozen two-day non-residential courses across the country in 1987. Financial advice is completely impartial and a wide range of other subjects is also covered. The price is £100 a head, including lunch, plus VAT. Contact Roy Elms, Retirement Counselling Manager at the above address.

Godwins Ltd., Briarcliff House, Kingsmead, Farnborough, Hants. GU14 7TE, T:0252-544484.

Godwins are probably the best known of the number of insurance brokers who are concerned with pre-retirement. They give two-day, non-residential courses at their Farnborough headquarters. Cost is £50 per person, £85 per couple plus VAT.

Other commercial organisations

Saga Holidays plc, Saga House, Enbrook House, Sandgate Hill, Folkestone, Kent CT20 3SG, T:0303-47654.

Saga have for long specialised in holidays for older people and they are now branching out into retirement planning holidays. These are currently planned to last a week and to take place at the University of Dundee. This year the cost is a basic £162 per person. Contact Mrs Ruth Dawson at the Folkestone office.

Finally two organisations which cater specifically for senior executives.

DPS Consultants Ltd., 27 Preston Street, Faversham, Kent ME13 8PG, T:0795-531472.

Three-day courses held at Leeds Castle near Maidstone, in Kent, and Ballathie House near Perth. Groups are small with very good independent coverage of financial matters, a lot of emphasis on the emotional adjustments that the couple may need to make, and much practical advice on different ways of staying active and involved. The course fee is £225 per person, £375 per couple. Accommodation which is extra costs £270 single, £465 double, at Leeds Castle for the three days. At Ballathie House, the price is £210 and £390. All prices are quoted exclusive of VAT. Two-and-a-half-day week-end courses are also held in hotels. The approach is identical to the above but the financial advice is tailored especially to the £15,000 – £20,000 a year bracket. Cost, inc accommodation, is £275 single, £450 double plus VAT.

Millstream Ltd., Mill House, South Harting, Petersfield, Hants. GU13 5LF, T:0730-85711.

Millstream two-day courses are held at The Royal Yacht Squadron, Cowes, the Manor House Hotel in the Cotswolds and Cumberland Lodge in Windsor Great Park. They give excellent, completely independent financial advice with a follow-up service if required and a very positive and stimulating approach to the new opportunities that retirement can offer. The cost is £440 plus VAT (accompanying husband or wife £320 plus VAT).

Chapter 12 also contains the names of one or two organisations that run pre-retirement courses as part of their holiday programme.

1. Money in General

For most people approaching retirement, the major concern is money. Some individuals have no worries; they have planned the event for years, made maximum pension contributions, carefully invested their savings, covered themselves and family in insurance policies, budgeted ahead and can even gleefully tell you about the exotic round-the-world trip they intend to take just as soon as their new life begins.

But for a majority of people, however, it is not like that. After years of hardly giving a thought to their pension, panic suddenly sets in as they consider the prospect of no longer drawing a regular salary. The fact that most of their friends who have already retired seem to manage pretty well is of little comfort. Even quite wealthy individuals confess to conjuring up images of going cold and hungry.

Happily, the reality is far rosier than many people imagine. For a start, those retiring today are better off financially than any previous generation. Equally to the point, the spectre of drastic economies that haunts so many men and women is often the result of their having only the haziest idea as to their likely income and expenditure.

Doing the sums

Knowing the facts is the first priority. To make a proper assessment, you need to draw up several lists:

- Expected sources of income on retirement
- Unavoidable outgoings
- Normal additional spending (including holidays and other luxuries).

Stage two, you need to consider a number of options under the following headings:

- Possible ways of boosting your retirement income
- Spending now for saving later
- Cherished plans, if affordable.

Most difficult of all, you will require a third list of variables and unknowns which, while impossible to estimate accurately, must as a matter of prudence be taken into account in any long term budget planning. The two most important are tax and inflation. Additionally, there are all the possible emergency situations, such as your health, for which if this ever were to become a problem you might want to make special provision. Your life expectancy is another consideration, as is that of your partner and any dependants.

Ideally, you should start thinking about at least some of these points, especially those that relate to your pension and to any savings or investment plans, five or even ten years before you retire.

When doing the sums, aim to be realistic. Many people make the mistake of basing their calculations on their current commitments and expenditure, without properly realising that some of their requirements will change. To get the figures into perspective, it is a good idea to imagine yourself already retired. The good news is that, while some items will probably take a heftier slice of your budget, others will certainly be cheaper or no longer cost you anything at all.

Possible savings and extra outgoings are discussed below. The most practical way of examining the list is to tick off the items in each column that you expect definitely to apply and, where possible, to write down the expenditure involved (see Budget Planner at the end of Chapter 5). While inevitably this will be a somewhat rough-and-ready exercise – and obviously there will be gaps – the closer you are to retirement, the more worthwhile it will be.

Possible savings

Going out to work generally involves a fair number of expenses. When you leave your job, you will probably save at least several pounds a week. Items for which you will no longer have to pay include: your travelling costs to work, bought lunches, special clothes plus all the out-of-pocket incidentals such as drinks with colleagues, trade magazines and collections for presents or the Christmas party.

You will not have to pay any more national insurance contributions and, unless you choose to invest in a private plan, your pension payments will also cease. Additionally, when you retire, you may be in a lower tax bracket.

At the same time you may have reached the stage when your children are now independent, your mortgage is substantially paid off and you have stopped subscribing to a life assurance policy.

Moreover, one of the gratifying aspects of attaining state retirement age is that you become eligible for a variety of benefits, for example: concessionary travel, free national health service prescriptions, cheaper theatre tickets (usually matinees), reduced entrance charges for exhibitions and a wide choice of special holiday offers.

Another point worth remembering is that many insurance companies give substantial discounts to mature drivers. In some instances, discounts apply to those aged 50; other companies restrict eligibility to those aged 55 or even 60. Normally, but again this varies, the scheme is terminated when the policy holder reaches 75. Most companies, but not all, extend the cover to a spouse or other named person with a good driving record. As to the discounts, these appear to range in generosity from 5 per cent to over 60 per cent. Best advice is first approach your existing insurance company and ask what terms they will give you. If these appear dullish, it could pay to shop around. Among those that offer special rates for mature drivers are: Sun Alliance, the Royal, the Provincial, Guardian Royal Exchange and Legal & General.

Extra outgoings

There is no escaping the fact that when you retire some of your expenses will be heavier than at present.

Firstly, you will probably be spending more time at home, so items like heating and lighting are liable to be costlier. If you received any perks with your job, such as a company car or health insurance, then unless you have a very generous employer these will have to come out of your own pocket in future. Equally, any business entertaining you enjoyed will largely cease, so any free lunches and the like will have to be substituted instead from the domestic housekeeping.

Another very important consideration is your extra leisure. With more time available, you will understandably be tempted to spend more on outings, your hobbies and longer holidays from home. To avoid having to stint yourself, these need to be budgeted for in advance. Most people say that in an ideal world they would assume to be spending roughly double on entertainment of all kinds, compared with when they were working.

Even voluntary activity is not without its hidden expenses, for example: more use of the telephone, petrol costs, raffle tickets, support of fund-raising occasions and so on.

Looking ahead, as you get older you may want more home comforts. Likewise, you may have to pay other people to do some of the jobs, such as the decorating, that you previously managed yourself.

Anticipating the areas of additional expenditure is not to be pessimistic. On the contrary, it is the surest way of avoiding future money worries. Moreover, when you have sat down and worked out your retirement income in detail, you may even be pleasantly surprised.

Expected sources of income on retirement

Your list will include at least some of the following. Once you have added up the figures in the Budget Planner, you will have to deduct income tax to arrive at the net spending amount available to you.

- State basic pension
- State graduated pension
- Serps
- Occupational pension
- State benefits

Additionally, you may receive income or a capital sum from some of the following:

- Company share option scheme
- Endowment policy
- Investments (stocks and shares, building society etc.)
- Bank deposit account
- National Savings interest
- Other existing income (from a trust, property, family business)
- Sale of business or personal assets

You might also be in receipt of income from an annuity. However, since at this stage you will be unlikely to have purchased one, this really belongs in the category of investment decisions.

Unavoidable outgoings

One person's priority is another person's luxury – and vice versa. For this reason, the divide between 'unavoidable' and 'normal additional spending' (see next section) is fraught with obvious difficulty. For example, readers who do not possess a pet would never include pet food among the essentials, whereas a dog or cat owner unquestionably would.

Almost everyone will want to juggle some of the items between the two lists; or add their own particular commitments or special enthusiasms, omitted by us. Our suggestions are simply intended as memory joggers – and emphatically not as a guide as to what should, or should not, constitute a luxury. What matters is the basic principle behind the exercise. If at some stage budgeting choices have to be made, decisions will be very much easier if you already know: your total outgoings, what you are spending on each individually and those you variously rate as important or marginal.

Whatever your own essentials, some of the following items will certainly feature on your list of unavoidable expenses:

- Food
- Rent or mortgage repayments
- Rates
- Repair and maintenance costs

- Heating
- Lighting and other energy
- Telephone
- TV licence/rental
- Household insurance
- Clothes
- Domestic cleaning products
- Laundry, cleaners' bills, shoe repair
- Misc. services, e.g. plumber, window cleaner
- Car, including licence, petrol, AA, etc.
- Other transport
- Regular savings and life assurance
- HP/other loan repayments
- Outgoings on health

Normal additional expenditure

This may well include:

- Gifts
- Holidays
- Newspapers/books
- Drink
- Cigarettes/tobacco
- Hairdressing
- Toiletries/cosmetics
- Entertainment (hobbies, outings, home entertaining etc.)
- Misc. subscriptions/membership fees
- Charitable donations
- Expenditure on pets
- Other

Work out the figures against these lists. Then, in order to compare your expenditure against likely income, jot them down on the Budget Planner (end of Chapter 5).

Possible ways of boosting your retirement income

Other than luck – winning the football pools or coming into a legacy – there are three main possibilities for providing you with extra money: your home, work and investment skill.

Your home

Your home offers several different options.

Moving somewhere smaller. You could sell your present home, move into smaller accommodation and end up with the double bonus of pocketing a lump sum and reducing your running costs.

Leaving aside such considerations as whether you would still be able to have your grandchildren to stay and looking at the matter strictly in financial terms, it is as well to realise from the outset that the cash difference on the exchange – in other words, your profit – is invariably less than you expect. What with removal charges and lawyers' fees, moving house is a very expensive business. Additionally, you will probably have some decorating expenses and there is bound to be a period of overlap when you will be paying double rates, two lots of telephone rental, extra electricity bills and so on. This is not to say that moving may not be an excellent decision; simply that, if money is the main criterion, you need to be thoroughly realistic when calculating the gains.

If you do decide to move, you should consider very seriously transferring an existing mortgage to your new property or getting a new one, even if you could afford to buy it outright. Providing the total amount borrowed qualifies for tax relief on the interest, it will probably pay you. Too old? Not at all. In contrast to ten years ago, mortgages are commonly available to people of 65. However, there may be reasons why a mortgage would not be sensible for you. You should consult an accountant or solicitor who will help you work out the various after-tax and other angles.

Taking in lodgers. If your children have left home and you have more space than you need, you could consider taking in lodgers: either as paying guests or, if your property lends itself to the creation of a separate flatlet, in a tenancy capacity.

When assessing the financial rewards, it is wise to assume that there will be times when the accommodation is empty - so you will not be receiving any rent. Also remember that any rental you do receive will be part of your taxable income, so the amount you pocket will be reduced accordingly.

Raising money on your home. A third option is to part-sell your home either for a capital sum or regular payments, under a home reversion scheme, and continue to live in it for as long as you wish. Sounds wonderful? As with mortgage annuities, which operate on a slightly similar principle but with the important difference that these are only suitable for people who are at least 70, there are both attractions and drawbacks which need to be considered carefully.

All these possibilities are explored in greater detail in Chapter 6. If you think any of the ideas sound interesting, see the sections 'Moving to a new home',

'Paying guests or lodgers', 'Home reversion plans', 'Mortgage annuity schemes'.

Work

If you would like to continue working, arguably the easiest solution if your employer is agreeable is for you to remain where you are and to defer your pension. See Chapter 2. Alternatively, as many people do, you may look on retirement as the opportunity for a job switch (with perhaps a reduction in hours) or the chance you have always wanted of setting up on your own.

When assessing your budget plans, it is as well to err on the cautious side as regards the additional income you will be likely to earn. Not only are many so called 'retirement jobs' notoriously badly paid but there is also a nasty provision, known as the earnings rule, which has the effect of reducing your basic pension if your earnings exceed £75 a week. The rule only applies to men between the ages of 65 and 70; and to women between the ages of 60 and 65. After that, quite illogically, you can earn as much as you like without any penalty.

If instead of paid work, you are thinking of becoming self-employed or setting up a business, you will not only have the start-up costs but, as you are probably well aware, very few new enterprises make a profit during the first two or three years.

On the other hand – again, just looking at the economics – while you are working, you will not be spending money on entertainment. Also, particularly if you are self-employed or own a business, there may be certain tax advantages as well as possible scope for improving your pension. Lastly, of course, you may be one of the lucky ones for whom work after retirement really pays.

Quite apart from the money, work can be thoroughly enjoyable and rewarding in its own right. For ideas and information, see Chapters 10 and 11.

Investment

Contrary to what some people believe, you do not need to be very rich; nor for that matter is it too late to start thinking about investing once you are over the age of 55.

As the 'investment and savings' section of this chapter shows, investment can take many different forms and among the list of different options there should be something to suit almost everyone.

Although you may consider this to be specialist reading, we do suggest that you at least look at it, since maximising your income in retirement could make all the difference between being able to enjoy life or worrying about money.

Spending now for saving later

Although you may normally take the view that there is never a best time for spending money, retirement planning is different in that sooner or later you will need, or want, to make certain purchases – or pay off outstanding commitments, such as a mortgage.

Most people's basic list – at least to think about – under this heading includes one or more of the following:

● expenditure on their home
● the purchase of a car
● the termination of HP or other credit arrangement

Additionally, there may be a number of general domestic or luxury items which you had been promising yourself for some time and the only question is one of actual timing, i.e. determining the right moment to buy. Typical examples might include: a duvet, gardening equipment, a video recorder, a home computer, hobby materials and so on.

To help you decide whether a policy of 'spending now' is sensible, or possibly self-indulgent, there are two very simple questions you should ask:

● can I afford it more easily now – or in the future?
● by paying now rather than waiting, shall I be saving money in the long run?

True, the issue may be complicated by tax and other considerations but for most choices this very basic analysis helps greatly to clarify the financial arguments on both sides.

Home improvements. If you plan to stay where you are, the likelihood is that at some point you will want to make some changes or improvements: install central heating, insulate the loft, modernise the kitchen or perhaps convert part of the house to a 'granny flat' for an elderly parent who is becoming too frail to live alone.

Conventional wisdom has it that any significant expenditure on your home is best undertaken several years prior to retirement. However, in our experience the matter is less clear-cut and what is right for some is not the solution for others.

As with many other important decisions, the question largely depends on individual circumstances. Some people find it easier, and more reassuring, to pay major household bills while they are still earning. Others specifically plan to use part of the lump sum from their pension to create a dream home.

To arrive at the answer that makes best financial sense, present commitments have to be weighed against likely future expenditure (together with what money you will have available). Equally, as with insulation for example, you will need to work out what long term savings you could effect by taking the plunge now. There is also the safety aspect: if you have bad lighting or dangerously worn carpet on part of the staircase, waiting for a few years to tackle the problem because it is all part of the grand plan could prove very false economy indeed.

Another very important consideration is how certain you are that you intend to stay in your present home. Investing a fortune and then upping sticks a couple of years later is generally a recipe for being out of pocket. Despite what one or two people may have told you, it is very unusual to recoup all your expenditure by reaping a vast profit when you come to sell.

Though it involves a few minutes' paperwork, a worthwhile exercise is to jot down your own personal list of pros and cons, under the headings: 'spending now' and 'spending later'. If still in doubt, then waiting is normally the more prudent course.

Purchasing a car. There could be two good reasons for buying a new car ahead of your retirement. One is that you have a company car that you are about to lose. The other is that your existing vehicle is on the old side and is beginning (or will probably soon start) to give you trouble. If either of these apply, then it probably makes sense to buy a replacement while you are still feeling relatively flush.

However, on the principle of 'look before you leap', company car owners should first check whether they might be entitled to purchase their present car on favourable terms: although not very widespread, the practice seems to be growing. Also, dreary suggestion as it sounds, if economies look like being the order of the day, two car families might assess whether, come retirement when perhaps husband and wife will be doing more things together, two cars are really such an essential as before.

Paying off HP and similar. In general, this is a good idea since delay is unlikely to save you any money – and may in fact actually cost you more. The only precaution is to check the small print of your agreement, to ensure that there is no penalty for early repayment.

A further exception to the rule could be your mortgage. As already discussed, there could be tax advantages in retaining a mortgage especially if you are a higher rate taxpayer. Since quite a lot of money may be involved, you would be well advised to consult an accountant; or, if you are thinking of moving (and the issue is really whether to transfer an existing mortgage – or possibly acquire a new one), include this among the points to raise with your solicitor.

Cherished plans, if affordable

The Budget Planner (end of Chapter 5) may help you to work out whether the various luxuries and plans of which nearly all of us dream could be affordable or are destined to remain as fantasies.

Fun as it might be to imagine what a 'top twenty' list might include, there would be little real purpose in discussing the practicalities, or otherwise, of going on a cruise, owning a race horse, buying a caravan, flying Concorde or whatever, since not only – even among married couples – would there be wide variations in choice but more particularly, since normal budget wisdom does not apply, any advice would risk being grossly misleading.

This does not mean that you should promptly forget the whole idea of noting items which come into this category; but that, as this is such a very personal decision area, only you can really make the assessments.

As a general point, however, if you plan your finances with a specific objective in view, you may find that against expectations a notion that first seemed impossible is actually affordable. Or possibly, when you really think about the choices, some of your earlier priorities will seem less important.

One subject of interest to many grandparents, where some broad factual information could be genuinely useful, is helping with the payment of school fees. In most cases, the preferred method is to take out a covenant.

Making a deed of covenant

Making a deed of covenant to pay for grandchildren's education has become increasingly popular in recent years. One reason is alleged falling standards in state schools. Another is that a covenant is a particularly tax efficient way of giving money, care of their parents, to children and young people.

Provided the youngster is a non-taxpayer, basic rate tax can be reclaimed on his/her behalf on the covenanted payments. In other words, for every £100 contributed by grandparents, a further £40.85p can be recovered from the Inland Revenue.

Before describing the procedure, there are two fundamental points that should be mentioned. One is that, contrary to what some people think, covenants are not simply a device for the very privileged: quite small sums of money can make a notable contribution. The other is that making a deed of covenant, far from being complex, is actually very simple. It does however involve a commitment to make payments for at least 7 years.

All that is required is the completion of two very straightforward forms, both obtainable from the Inland Revenue.

- Form R 111, which serves in effect as the contract document
- Form 185 (RP) which, after grandparents have completed it
  every year, goes to the child's parents who can then claim
  back the tax.

Parents can also make covenant arrangements for their children, but *only once* their offspring have reached the age of 18.

There are two main types of scheme: one, involving regular payments; the other, a lump sum. In the latter case, the money would probably either be paid into a capital scheme and the tax reclaimed on a year by year basis; or into an educational trust which would purchase annuities, guaranteeing a certain amount a year for a set period towards the school fees.

If a covenant starts several years ahead of a child starting school, or if the money is specifically intended to pay future secondary school fees, both the covenanted payments and the tax refunds can be invested on the child's behalf.

Because of these and other options, it is sensible to talk to a specialist before entering into a scheme. An accountant could advise you. Or it could be a good idea to approach the Independent Schools Information Service who, as well as maintaining a list of expert advisers, can send you a leaflet *How Grandparents Can Help With School Fees* (enclose two 1st class stamps to cover postage). Contact: ISIS, 56 Buckingham Gate, London SW1E 6AG.

Covenants in respect of charities. These operate on much the same principle as school fees. In order to encourage charity giving, the government has reduced the length of commitment to four years. For further information plus details of their own very flexible scheme, contact: **Charities Aid Foundation**, 14 Bloomsbury Square, London WC1.

Alternatively, as most of the larger charities will have covenant forms, you can approach the charity you wish to help direct.

Budget change note. If you make payments under deed of covenant you may need to amend your payments to take account of the change in the basic rate of tax from 30 per cent to 29 per cent.

Extra income

There are a great many state benefits and allowances available to give special help to people in need.

Definition of need covers a very wide range and applies, among others, to problems connected with: health, housing, care of an elderly or disabled relative, as well as widowhood and problems encountered by the frail elderly who for example may require extra heating during the winter.

While many of these benefits are 'means-tested', in other words are only given to people whose income is below a certain level, some, such as mobility allowance, are not dependent on how poor or how wealthy you are. Moreover, even when 'means-testing' is a factor, for some of the benefits income levels are nothing like as low as many people imagine. Because this information is not widely enough known, many individuals or families are not claiming help to which they are entitled and for which in many cases they have actually paid through their national insurance contributions.

The main benefits and allowances are listed in their appropriate chapters: for example, housing benefit appears in Chapter 6, invalidity benefit is briefly described in Chapter 13.

For further information about these and some others, such as criminal injuries compensation, obtain a copy of DHSS booklet FB2, 'Which Benefit?', available from any Social Security Office.

Also useful reading is *Your Rights for Pensioners* published by Age Concern.

A number of voluntary organisations also provide assistance to individuals: sometimes in cash or sometimes with facilities, such as special equipment for the disabled. Details are given in the relevant chapters.

For further advice and information, contact your local social services department or Citizens' Advice Bureau. Another very useful source of help is your local Age Concern branch.

The national addresses of these organisations are as follows:

Department of Health and Social Security

England: Alexander Fleming House, London SE1 6BY, T: 01-407 5522.

Northern Ireland: Dundonald House, Upper Newtornards Road, Belfast BT4 3ST, T: 0232-650111.

Scotland: 3 Lady Lawson Street, Edinburgh HE3 9SH, T: 031-229 9191.

Wales: Government Buildings, St. Agnes Road, Gabalfa, Cardiff CF4 4YJ, T: 0222-693131.

Freephone: Dial 100 and ask for DHSS; operates between 9-4.30 Monday to Friday.

National Association of Citizens Advice Bureaux, 115-123 Pentonville Road, Kings Cross, London N1 9LZ, T: 01-833 2181.

Age Concern England, 60 Pitcairn Road, Mitcham, Surrey CR4 3LL, T: 01-640 5431.

Age Concern Northern Ireland, 128 Great Victoria Street, Belfast BT2 7BG, T: 0232-245729.

Age Concern Scotland, 3 Castle Street, Edinburgh EH2 3DN, T: 031-225 5000.

Age Concern Wales, 1 Park Grove, Cardiff CF1 3BJ, T: 0222-371821.

2. Pensions

Those retiring from the mid-eighties can count themselves lucky. In contrast to the high inflation years, state pensions are more than keeping pace with the cost of living. Additionally, thanks to an increasingly enlightened climate, occupational pensions are not only becoming more widespread, but most schemes have been steadily improving.

Because pensions come in a variety of forms, many even sophisticated people fail to collect all their entitlements or do not understand all the options that are available to them. Since, next to your home, your pension is almost certainly your most valuable asset, it is important to check all the angles well ahead of time to ensure that when you retire you receive the maximum benefit. Incidentally, this applies even to young men and women in their thirties!

State pensions

You can get a pension if you are a man of 65 or a woman of 60, providing you have retired from regular employment and have paid (or been credited with) sufficient National Insurance contributions.

Your right to a state pension

Your right to a State pension depends on your (or your spouse's) National Insurance contributions. Most people have to pay contributions into the National Insurance scheme while they are working.

If you are an employee, your employer will have automatically deducted Class I contributions from your salary, provided your earnings were above a certain limit (currently £38 a week).

If you are self-employed you will have been paying a flat rate Class 2 contribution every week and possibly the earnings-related Class 4 contributions as well.

You may also have paid some Class 3 voluntary contributions at some point in your working life in order to maintain your contributions record.

If you are over retirement age (65 for men and 60 for women) you do not need to pay National Insurance contributions.

There may have been times during your working life when you have not, either knowingly or unwittingly, paid National Insurance contributions. This may mean that you are only entitled to a reduced rate of pension. *However, your NI contributions record will have been maintained in the following circumstances:*

If you have lived outside Great Britain. If you have lived in Northern Ireland or the Isle of Man, any contributions paid there will count towards your pension.

If you have lived in a European Community country or any country whose social security system is linked to Britain's by a reciprocal agreement,* any contributions you have paid while abroad may be counted towards your pension.

If you have any doubts, you should enquire what your position is at your local social security office.

* Countries with reciprocal agreements are: Australia, Austria, Bermuda, Canada, Cyprus, Finland, Israel, Jamaica, Jersey, Guernsey, Malta, Mauritius, New Zealand, Norway, Portugal, Spain, Sweden, Switzerland, Turkey and Yugoslavia.

If you have received Home Responsibilities Protection (HRP). If you have not worked regularly since 1978 because you have had to stay at home to care for either a child or an elderly person you may have protected your right to a pension by claiming HRP. This benefit allows you to deduct the years when you were required to give up work from the normal qualifying period for a basic pension and so, in effect, shorten the number of years when you would otherwise have been required to make contributions.

While HRP can be claimed by both sexes, it predictably applies more frequently to women. For more information, see below 'Pensions for women' or obtain leaflet NP.27 from your local social security office.

If you have been in any of these situations. You will have been credited with contributions (instead of having to pay them) in the following circumstances:

- if you were sick or unemployed (provided you sent in sick notes to your social security office or signed on at the Unemployment Benefit Office);
- if you were entitled to maternity allowance, invalid care allowance, or unemployability supplement;
- if you were taking an approved course of training (see leaflet NI 125 from the DHSS);
- when you left education but had not yet started working.

Married women and widows who do not qualify for a basic pension in their own right can also be entitled to a full basic pension on their husband's contributions (see below, 'Pensions for women').

Reduced rate contributions note

Many women retiring today may have paid a reduced rate contribution under a scheme which was abolished in 1978. Women who were already paying a reduced rate contribution were however allowed to continue doing so (see below 'Pensions for women'). These reduced rate contributions *do not count* towards your pension and you will not have had any contributions credited to you.

How your pension is worked out

Your total pension can come from four main sources: the basic pension, the additional pension, the graduated pension, and other additions.

Anyone wanting to work out what they are due can write to their local DHSS office for a 'pension forecast'. This is normally expressed in percentage terms so, for instance, someone with full contributions will get 100 per cent of pension.

It is worth getting an early estimate of what your pension will be, as it may be possible to improve your National Insurance contribution record by making additional Class 3 voluntary contributions.

Basic pension

The full basic pension for a man or woman is £38.70 a week, £61.95 for a married couple (unless your spouse is entitled to more than the £23.25 spouse's addition on his/her own contributions, in which case you will receive more).

Pensions are uprated in April each year. Up-to-date rates are contained in leaflet NI. 196 from your local social security office.

All pensions are taxable, other than supplementary pension and one or two special categories, such as war widows and the victims of Nazism.

The rate of basic pension depends on your record of NI contributions over your working life. To get the full rate you must have paid (or been credited with) NI contributions for roughly nine-tenths of your working life, although widows can also be entitled to a full basic pension on their husband's contributions.

Your working life, for this purpose, is normally considered to be 44 years for a woman and 49 years for a man (i.e. age 16 until pension age), but it may be less if you were born before July 5 1932 and were therefore over 16 when the National Insurance Scheme started in 1948.

Reduced rate pension

If you do not have full contributions but have maintained your contributions record for between a quarter and nine-tenths of your working life, you may get a pension at a reduced rate. The amount is calculated according to the number of years for which you have paid contributions. However, to get *any* basic pension you must actually have paid enough contributions in any *one* tax year, from April 6 1975, for *that* year to count as a qualifying year; or have paid 50 flat rate contributions at any time before 6 April 1975.

Additional pension

This is also known as SERPS, short for the State Earnings Related Pension Scheme. It is worked out on earnings since April 1978 on which you have paid Class 1 contributions as an employee. It is not applicable to the self-employed.

Class 1 contributions are paid as a percentage of earnings between a 'lower' and an 'upper' limit (currently £38 and £285 a week respectively). The lower earnings limit is roughly the same level as the basic retirement pension.

How much additional pension you get depends on the amount of your earnings over and above the lower earnings limit for each complete tax year since April 1978.

These earnings are then revalued to allow for inflation over the interim period and added together to produce the total earnings figure on which your additional pension depends.

The *annual* additional pension is calculated as 1/80th of the total earnings figure. This is then divided by 52 to provide a weekly rate which is added to your basic pension.

Since the scheme only started in 1978, the amount of additional pension to which you would be entitled is likely to be small.

Although there are plans to scale down the additional pension, this will not affect anyone retiring before 1998. However, the government is planning to introduce new optional individual pension policies called personal pensions during 1988. At the time of writing, the details have not been finalised.

If you are a member of a contracted-out occupational pension scheme, you are legally entitled to a guaranteed minimum pension which must be at least as much as you would have got under the State scheme (i.e. the additional pension).

Graduated pension

This pension existed between April 1961 and April 1975. The amount you receive depends on the graduated NI contributions you paid during that period.

Anyone over 18 and earning more than £9 a week at that time will probably be entitled to a graduated pension. This includes married women and widows with reduced contribution liability. A widow or widower whose spouse dies when they are both over pension age can inherit half of the graduated pension based on their late spouse's contributions.

Other additions

Invalidity addition: your pension will automatically be permanently increased if you were getting invalidity allowance with invalidity benefit within eight weeks and a day before reaching retirement age. The amount you get will be the same as the invalidity allowance you are already receiving (lower rate £2.60; middle rate £5.20; higher rate £8.15) but any additional pension (SERPS) and/or occupational pension will be subtracted from your invalidity allowance with only the balance (if any) being paid to you as invalidity addition.

Age addition: your pension will be automatically increased when you are aged 80 or over. The current rate is 25p a week.

Other ways to increase your pension

Deferring your pension
Your pension may be increased if you delay claiming it and instead continue working after normal retirement age. This applies between the ages of 65 and 70 for a man and from 60 to 65 for a woman. For every year that you defer retirement, approximately another 7.5 per cent a year will be added to your pension. This extra pension is paid when you reach 70 (65) regardless of whether you have retired from work or not. For further details obtain leaflet NI.92 from your local Social Security Office.

Increases for dependants
Your basic pension may be increased if you are supporting a dependent spouse or children. Most typically, this applies in respect of a non-working wife (or one whose earnings are very low) who is under 60 when her husband retires. However, this also applies for a retired wife supporting a dependent husband. The current rates are £23.25 a week for a spouse and £8.05 for each dependent child. See leaflet NI.196 for up-to-date rates.

Supplementary pension
If your pension is inadequate, you may qualify for supplementary pension. This is an addition, similar to supplementary benefit, designed to provide those with insufficient means with enough money to live on. You can claim it to bring your total income up to £37.50 a week for a single person, £57.10 for a married couple. As it is a fairly modest sum, it is not taxable.

You cannot claim supplementary pension if you have savings of more than £3000.

For further information, and a claim form, see leaflet SB 1 obtainable from your local Social Security Office or from any Post Office.

Working after you start getting your pension

If you wish to continue working *and* draw your basic pension, this is allowed providing you do not earn more than the earnings rule limit, which is currently £75 a week. If your earnings exceed this amount, then your pension will be reduced on a graduated scale. If you are at risk of losing most of your pension due to your earnings, there could be a strong argument for delaying drawing it. You should work out the sums carefully.

The earnings rule only applies to men between the ages of 65 and 70; and women between the ages of 60 and 65. After that, you can earn any amount without reducing your pension.

A widow over 60 can get a pension from her late husband's contributions, whether or not she has retired.

Early retirement and your pension

Because so many people now retire early, there is a widespread belief that it is possible to get an early pension. While the information is correct as regards a growing number of employers' occupational pension schemes, *it does not apply to the basic State pension.*

If you take early retirement before the age of 60, it may be necessary for you to pay voluntary Class 3 National Insurance contributions in order to protect your contributions record for pension purposes. If you are a man over 60, however, you will automatically get contribution credits from the tax year in which you reach 60.

You can opt to go on the Job Release Scheme. This does not entitle you to an early pension but instead you will receive an allowance. For details see below.

How you get a pension

You should claim your pension a few months before you reach state retirement age. Normally, the DHSS office will send you a claim form at the proper time but if this does not arrive, then it is *your* responsibility to contact them. You should apply for the form about 3 months before you are due to retire. If you claim your pension late, you could lose some of the money.

After you claim, you are told in writing exactly how much pension you will get. You will also be told what to do if you disagree with the decision. The information you are given should include the name and address of the organisation responsible for paying you any guaranteed minimum pension.

How your pension can be paid

If you live in the UK, you can choose to have your pension paid either by credit transfer or in order book form.

Credit transfer. This method gives you the choice of having your pension paid direct into a bank or National Giro account; or, alternatively, into an investment account with either the National Savings Bank or with most building societies. Payment will be made in arrears every 4 weeks or quarterly, whichever you prefer.

Order book. You receive a book of orders (or pension book) which you can cash at a post office of your choice. Each order is your pension entitlement for one week and is valid for 12 weeks after the date shown on the voucher. If it is difficult for you to get to the post office, the coloured pages in the book explain how someone else can draw the payment for you.

Other situations. If your pension is £1 a week or less, it will normally be paid once a year in arrears by a crossed order which you can pay into a bank or building society account. Payment is made each year shortly before Christmas.

Pensions can be paid to an overseas address, if you are going abroad for 3 months or more. Contact your local Social Security Office. If you are in hospital, your pension can still be paid to you. You will receive a reduced amount if you are in hospital for more than 8 weeks. Leaflet NI 9 (obtainable from your local Social Security Office) provides full information.

Christmas bonus

Pensioners usually get a small tax free bonus shortly before Christmas each year. The amount and due date will be announced in advance. The bonus is combined with your normal pension payment for the relevant week, so if you have not received it by the end of December ask at your local Social Security Office.

Advice

If you have any queries or think that you may not be obtaining your full pension entitlement, you should contact your local DHSS office as soon as possible. If you think a mistake has been made, you have the right to appeal and can insist on your claim being heard by an independent social security tribunal. Before doing so, you would be strongly advised to consult a solicitor at the Citizen's Advice Bureau.

If you are writing to your local Social Security Office with a query you should quote either your National Insurance number (or your spouse's) or your pension number if you have already started receiving your pension.

DHSS Freefone: for free advice on your pension, dial 100 and ask for Freefone DHSS.

Job release scheme

This is a government supported scheme, designed to enable people to give up work a little earlier than normal, providing that a currently unemployed person is recruited to take their job.

The scheme is available to: women aged 59; men aged 64; and disabled men, aged between 60 and 63. To qualify, individuals must have been in full time employment (i.e. at least 30 hours a week) for a minimum of twelve months, with their present employer.

The scheme is entirely voluntary and both employer and employee must agree to the conditions.

'Released' individuals are then paid a weekly allowance. *This is not an early pension* and does not entitle the recipient to the various concessions, such as free national health service prescriptions, that an officially retired person enjoys.

There are several different rates of allowance, as follows:

For men aged 64 and women aged 59: there is a lower and a higher rate:

● the *lower rate* is paid either to single people; or to married applicants, whose partner's income is more than £13 a week. The allowance is £51.95p.
● the *higher rate* is paid to married people, whose partner's income is less than £13 a week. The allowance is £65.50p.

These payments are tax free

For disabled men aged 60 to 63: again, there are two different rates, which are determined exactly as above:

● the *lower rate* is £60.65p.
● the *higher rate* is £74.

The allowances for disabled men are higher. Payments made for more than one year are, however, taxable.

Other income. An occupational pension or any other income does not stop you receiving the allowance. But if you are receiving some social security benefits, you will have to choose between them and the allowance. You cannot receive both.

A further point is that you are not allowed to earn more than £4 a week, without forfeiting the whole allowance for that week.

If having given up work to go on to the scheme, you subsequently decide you want to take another job, you *must* inform: the Payments Manager, Job Release Scheme, P.O.Box 12, East Lane, Halton, Runcorn WA7 2DN. Your job release allowance will then be stopped.

Before you go on the scheme. You should read leaflet *Job Release Scheme*, PL 761, which you can get from any Department of Employment office or Jobcentre. This gives full details of the scheme and its provisions. You should then discuss it with your employer. You will need his agreement and help.

Joining the scheme will *not* affect your basic state pension rights but it *may* affect your occupational pension, if you have one. Once again, check this with your employer.

You will not earn any additional state earnings related pension (SERPS) while you are receiving the allowance. Leaflet NP 32, available from DHSS offices, has more information on this point.

Private pensions

The importance of persuading individuals to save for their own pension instead of just relying on the State has been recognised by successive governments. Encouragement has been made through tax incentives, so that pension savings are now one of the most tax effective investments available.

- You get income tax relief on contributions at your highest tax rate
- The pension fund is totally exempt from income tax and capital gains tax, providing excellent growth prospects for your money
- Part of the pension can be taken as a cash sum when you retire and that too is tax free

Private pension schemes fall into two categories: those arranged by employers, e.g. company pension schemes, and those you can arrange for yourself.

Company pension schemes

About 11 million people, roughly half the employed population, are now participating in company schemes. While these can vary considerably, the following basic features apply to them all.

Pension fund. Pension contributions go into a pension fund which is quite separate from your employer's company. It is set up under trust and run by trustees, appointed from management and sometimes from staff. It is the job of the trustees to manage the fund and its investments and to ensure that the benefit promises are kept.

Payments into the fund. Your scheme may or may not ask for a contribution from you. For this reason, schemes are known as 'contributory' or 'non-contributory'. If you are required to make a contribution, this will be deducted from your pay before you receive it.

Your employer's contributions to the scheme represent the 'deferred' pay he is setting aside for your pension and other benefits. The amount needed is estimated by the scheme actuary and this can vary from year to year, according to how much money is accumulated and how much the scheme is likely to have to pay out in benefits.

Benefits from the scheme. You can ask the person in your company responsible for the pension scheme – this is often the personnel manager – for a booklet describing the scheme's benefits. The main ones are generally as follows:

● a pension due at retirement age, usually still 65 for men and 60 for women
● lump sum life assurance, paid out if you die before retirement age
● a widow's pension (and sometimes, a widower's pension), paid for life no matter when you die.

Benefit limits. The Inland Revenue sets limits on pension benefits which members of company schemes can receive. The main ones are:

● the maximum pension you are allowed is two-thirds of your final pay (excluding state pension)
● if you die, the pension can be passed on to someone else but no one beneficiary can receive more than two-thirds
● the tax free lump sum, if you choose to take it, cannot be more than one and a half times salary.

Types of scheme

There are four main types of scheme, as follows:

Final pay scheme. This is the most common. Your pension is calculated as a proportion of your final pay, which could mean literally the last year you work or the average of the last two or three years.

The amount you receive depends on two factors: the number of years you have worked for the organisation plus the fraction of final pay on which the scheme is based, typically 1/60th. So if you have worked 30 years for a company that has 1/60th pension scheme, you will receive 30/60ths of your final pay – in other words, half.

Final pay schemes can be contracted into or out of SERPS. If a scheme is contracted out of SERPS, it must provide a guaranteed minimum pension that is at least as good as its SERPS equivalent.

Average earnings scheme. As its name implies, this scheme is based on your average earnings over the total period of time that you are participating in the scheme.

Every year, an amount goes into the scheme on your behalf, calculated in accordance with your level of earnings. As your salary increases, so too do your potential benefits. Each year, your 'profits' from the scheme are worked out from a formal table and the total of all these annual sums constitutes your pension.

Flat rate pension scheme. Your level of pay is not a factor. Instead, the same flat rate applies to everyone, multiplied by the number of years in which they have been participants of the scheme. So, for example, if the flat rate is £10 a year of pension and you have been a member of the scheme for 20 years, your pension will be £200 a year.

Money purchase scheme. This has been increasing in popularity in recent years, especially among smaller companies. Unlike the other three schemes described above, the amount of pension you receive is not based on a fixed formula but is dependent on the investment performance of the fund into which your own and your employer's contributions on your behalf have been paid.

Although there is a slight element of gamble with money purchase schemes, in that no one can forecast with certainty how well or badly a pension fund might do, in practice most trustees act very conservatively.

Different schemes have different ways of determining how members' pension entitlements are calculated. You should enquire what the rules are and additionally, to give you a better idea of what size pension you might realistically expect, you could ask for some practical examples – say, over the last five years – of retired individuals in a similar earnings bracket to your own.

Additional or other schemes. There may be one scheme that applies to everyone in the organisation or there may be a variety of schemes for different grades of employees. For example, there may be a works scheme and a staff scheme operating side by side. It is also quite common for there to be a special pension scheme for executives and directors.

Executive pension plans

These are individual pension plans arranged by an employer for the benefit of some or all executives above a certain grade. In some companies, executive pension plans only apply to directors; in others, they may also include senior and middle management. Equally, there may be a separate policy for each individual; or a master policy, covering everyone in the scheme.

One of the attractions of the executive pension plans is their potential flexibility. They can be tailored to cater for differing retirement ages as well as for varying contribution levels, which explains why some organisations are able to offer early retirement on very attractive terms.

Historically, executive pension plans are of the money purchase type. Because they are provided by the employer, the maximum benefit allowed is two-thirds of final salary. Normally, one of the following four types of investment policy are used: with profits, unit linked, deposit administration and non profit. These are described below under 'Individual pension schemes'.

Additional voluntary contributions (AVCs)

If, as you approach retirement, you become aware that you are not going to have a big enough pension to live as comfortably as you would like, it may be possible to make additional voluntary contributions. This facility is not yet offered by all schemes, but they will be obliged to do so from 1988.

If you have the option, you should certainly consider it seriously as AVCs are a very attractive way of making extra savings for retirement. Firstly, as with other contributions, AVCs – as well as the growth of the plan – are tax free, so for basic rate tax payers the Inland Revenue is in effect paying £29 for every £100 you invest. Additionally, if you choose to take a lump sum on retirement, this too will be tax free.

For some people, the key advantage of AVCs is that they allow individuals to purchase 'added years', to make up any shortfall in their entitlement to benefit under the company scheme.

Inevitably, there are one or two rules. The total of AVCs plus other contributions to the pension plan is not allowed to exceed 15 per cent of your earnings. A more important consideration is that normally you cannot stop paying AVCs once you start, so before committing yourself you must make sure that you will be able to afford to continue. A requirement is that you must contribute for at least 5 years. (If you change jobs or can prove that you are undergoing serious financial hardship, however, it may be possible to stop payments.)

Early leavers

In the past, the big problem as everyone knows is that early leavers have tended to do very badly, due to the heavy financial penalties of withdrawing from a scheme in mid-term. The Government has recently introduced new rules, which should improve the situation considerably.

There are three choices available to people who leave to switch jobs.

Leaving the pension with the scheme. Whereas previously most pensions got frozen, the Social Security Act 1985 obliges companies to increase deferred pensions by 5 per cent a year or the rate of inflation whichever is lower. If you choose to stay in the scheme, you may also share in its benefits – such as any additional increases that may be given. These new provisions are not retrospective and only apply to job leavers after 1st January 1986.

Taking your pension to a new scheme. Early leavers now have the right to move their pension – or more precisely, its transfer value – to a new employer's scheme. The transfer value is the cash value of your current pension rights. Calculating this, however, is fraught with difficulties and early leavers are usually at a disadvantage compared with those who remain in the scheme. For example, if the job change has meant a salary increase, the new scheme will be more expensive to buy into as it will be earnings-related. Any added years will also be calculated in relation to your new salary, so these too will be more expensive.

Your new employer might appear to place a disconcertingly low valuation on your old company pension rights. However, even if ten years' worth of rights from an old company pension scheme are commuted to no more than two years' worth in your new one, it could still be worth accepting, particularly if your new job is likely to produce rapid pay rises. As your pension is ultimately based on the size of your salary when you retire, the two years' worth of added rights could still be worth a tidy sum.

Taking your pension to an insurance company. If neither of the two previous options appeal, or your new company will not accept your old pension value into its own scheme, you can go independent and pay the transfer value of your pension into an insurance company bond. This is called a Section 32 contract and is a single premium investment. It is very similar in fact to self employed pension plans, with the same choice of vehicles: unit linked, deposit administration, with profits and non profit. See below under 'Individual pension schemes'.

Advice

Deciding on your best option is not easy, so before taking action you should at least consult your company pension scheme manager. If a large sum of money is involved, it could pay you to get the advice of a pension consultant. For a list of those operating in your area, contact the **Society of Pension Consultants**, Ludgate House, Ludgate Circus, London EC4A 2AB.

Becoming self employed

If as opposed to switching jobs, you leave paid employment to start your own enterprise, you are allowed to transfer your accumulated pension rights into a new fund. You may have a choice of two options.

The more obvious solution is to invest your money with an insurance company, as mentioned above.

Alternatively, you might very usefully consider the advantages of setting up a limited company, *even if you are the only salaried employee*, rather than launching the same business as a self-employed individual.

The company could set up a self-administered pension scheme with 50 per cent loan-back facilities plus other advantages that are not available to individuals who are self-employed.

This is rather a complex area, so before taking any action you are strongly advised to consult an accountant.

Questions on your pension scheme

Most people find it very difficult to understand how their pension scheme works. However, your pension may be worth a lot of money and, especially as you approach retirement, it is important that you should know the main essentials, including any options that may still be available to you.

If you have a query (however daft it may seem) or if you are concerned in some way about your pension, you should approach whoever is responsible for the scheme in your organisation. If the company is large, there may be a special person to look after the scheme on a day-to-day basis: often this is someone in the personnel department. In a smaller company, the pension scheme may be looked after by the company secretary or managing director.

The sort of questions you might ask will vary according to circumstance, such as: before you join the scheme, if you are thinking of changing jobs, if you are hoping to retire early and so on. You will probably think of plenty of additional points of your own. The questions listed are simply an indication of some of the key information you may require in order to plan sensibly ahead.

Before you join the scheme

● What are the criteria for eligibility to become a member of the scheme? For example, there may be different conditions for different grades of staff. There may be an age ceiling for new entrants. Often too, there is a minimum period of service required before you can join.

● If it is a final pay scheme, what is the exact definition of 'final pay'? This could be very important if the organisation offers phased retirement or the opportunity of a sponsorship in the voluntary sector and, as some employers do, adjusts your remuneration to take account of a shorter

working week or less onerous responsibilities.
- Is anything deducted from the scheme to allow for the State pension?
- What is payable if you die within the next year?
- Is there a widow/widower's pension and does it get contractual increases?

If you want to leave the organisation to change jobs

- Can you have a refund of contributions?
- How much will your deferred pension be worth? Is there a contractual increase for a deferred pension? Or if not, what is the history of increases?
- Can you have a transfer payment to a Section 32 insurance policy?

If you leave for other reasons

- What happens if you become ill – or die – before pension age?
- What are the arrangements if you want to retire early? Most schemes allow you to do this if you are within about ten years of normal retirement age *but* your pension may be reduced accordingly. Many schemes, in fact, operate a sliding scale of benefits with more generous terms offered to those who retire later rather than earlier.

If you stay until normal retirement age

- What will your pension be on your present salary? And what would it be assuming your salary increases by, say, 5 or 10 per cent before you eventually retire?
- What spouse's pension will be paid? Can a pension be paid to other dependants?
- Is there any contractual increase to reduce the effect of inflation? If not, ask what the history of discretionary increases has been (both for members' own pension and for spouses).
- What happens if you continue working with the organisation after retirement age? Normally, any contributions you are making to the scheme will cease to be required and your pension (which will not be paid until you retire) will be increased to compensate for its deferment.
- What are the arrangements if you retire from the organisation as a salaried employee but become a retained consultant or contractor?

What to do before retirement

In addition to understanding your current pension scheme, you may also need to chase up any previous schemes of which you were a member.

The DHSS Records Division may be able to give you the names and details of the scheme administrators. Alternatively, you may be able to get the information from your previous employer(s). This is well worth pursuing as you could be owed money from one or more schemes, which will all add to your pension on retirement day.

Individual pension schemes

These are often known as either personal or self-employed pension schemes. The term 'self-employed' is a bit misleading, because while they apply primarily to those who work on their own account they may equally be used by employees who work for companies which do not have a pension scheme or which have schemes for which they, as individuals, are not eligible.

To use the technical jargon, individual pensions are called Section 226 Policies. They are usually sold by insurance brokers or insurance company salesmen, or sometimes by banks or building societies. In all cases, however, they are insurance policies designed to invest people's money for their retirement.

The maximum amount that you are allowed to invest in an individual pension plan is 17.5 per cent (or more if you are over 52 at the end of 1986) of relevant earnings. To achieve anything like the goal of two-thirds your final salary by the time you retire, you would have needed to make maximum payments from the age of 35. However, even if you are a late starter, there is still plenty you can do to maximise your pension.

Types of investment policy

There are four different types of investment policy: with profits, unit linked, deposit administration and non-profit policies. Brief descriptions of each follow.

With Profits policies. These are one of the safest types of pension investments. They guarantee you a known minimum cash fund and/or pension on your retirement and, while the guaranteed amount is not usually very high, bonuses are added at regular intervals, according to how the investments in the fund perform. Additionally, a terminal (or final) bonus is given when the pension policy matures. An important feature is that once bonuses are given, they cannot later be withdrawn or put at risk due to some speculative investment.

Unit Linked policies. These are less safe than with profits policies but they offer the attraction of potentially higher investment returns. Unit linked policies have performed very well over the last few years and are consequently growing in popularity. However, there is always the risk that they might not continue to perform as well in the future and, if there were a down-turn, the size of your pension could obviously be affected. For this reason, many advisers recommend that their clients swop their unit linked policies to the with profits type about five years before they retire, provided market conditions are favourable at the time.

Deposit Administration policies. These lie somewhere between with profits and unit linked policies in terms of their risk/reward ratio. They operate rather like bank deposit accounts, where the interest rate is credited at regular intervals.

Non Profit policies. These have lost favour in recent years. Although they provide a guaranteed pension payment, the return on investment is usually very low. As a rule, they tend only to be recommended for people starting a plan within five years of their retirement.

Choosing the right policy. This is one area where it really pays to shop around. Great care is needed when choosing the insurance company to invest your pension savings. Once you have committed yourself to a policy, you will not be able to move your money without considerable financial penalty.

As a general rule, it is sensible to select a large, well known insurance company that has been in the market for a long time. Before deciding, you should compare several companies' investment track records. What you should look for is evidence of good, *consistent* results over a period of ten to twenty years.

An important point to be aware of is that insurance companies give future projections of their investment performance: in other words, their own forecast as to how their funds will perform. Projections, however, are not the same as guarantees and if in the event the results are disappointing you are most unlikely to have any claim.

You should aim at very least to talk to two or three insurance brokers and make it clear to all of them that you are doing so. If you need further advice – and particularly if a large sum of money is involved – it could be wise to see an independent pension consultant. For further information about both this and insurance brokers, see Chapter 5.

A lump sum?

Members of company pension schemes and people with individual pension policies are allowed to take a lump sum of money tax free when they retire. The greatest amount normally permitted is $1\frac{1}{2}$ times your average final salary.

Taking a lump sum reduces the pension you receive but, on the other hand, if you invest the money wisely you could end up with a higher income. Alternatively, of course, as many people do, you could use the capital for a worthwhile project such as improving your home; or, if you were planning to give something to your grandchildren, this could be an opportune time to settle it on them. Thanks to the new Inheritance Tax which has replaced Capital Transfer Tax, life time gifts (in contrast to money left in a will) will normally escape the taxman. The first priority, however, is to ensure that you will have enough income for your own needs.

If you take a lump sum, the amount by which your pension will be reduced is mainly determined by your age and sex. The younger you are, the smaller the reduction. Women, the same age as men, also have a smaller reduction because of their longer life expectancy.

Another consideration is your tax status. Since the lump sum is tax free, as a general rule the higher your top rate of tax after retirement, the greater the advantage in opting for a lump sum.

Your life expectancy can also be an important factor. The shorter this is, the more sense it makes to take the lump sum, rather than deny yourself for a longer term pension that you will not be around to enjoy. If you come from a long line of octogenarians, then clearly you will need to work out the sums on the basis of the next twenty years or longer.

Contrary to what some people believe, it is not 'an all or nothing' decision. You have considerable flexibility and can choose between: not taking a lump sum, taking the maximum amount allowed or taking a portion of it only (whatever sum you decide).

Often the deciding factor when choosing whether to take a lump sum is the problem of investing it. If you have never had to think of it before, the prospect of what to do with several thousand pounds can seem a very daunting challenge. It could be prudent to 'invest' some of it getting good financial advice.

Before consulting an expert, it would be helpful to both of you if you could work out – at least in very general terms – what your financial priorities are. The sort of questions your adviser will ask are: whether you are investing for income now or capital growth in the future; whether you need to go for absolute security with every penny you have or whether you can afford slightly more risky investments in the hope of making more money in the long run; what other sources of income you have, or might expect to receive.

As is normal conservative practice, you will probably find that you will be recommended to spread your lump sum across a mixture of investments. Depending on your circumstances, these might be long or short term investments; income or capital producing; or quite likely, a combination of all of them.

An outline of the different types of investment appears in Chapter 4.

Pension rights if you continue to work

When you reach retirement age (65 for men, 60 for women) you will stop making contributions into your company pension scheme, even if you decide to carry on working.

There are then two options:

- You can leave your pension in the fund where it will continue to earn interest until you retire. In most private schemes, you can expect to receive an extra 9% for every year that you delay retirement. If you continue working until you are 70 (65 for women) your pension will then be 45% higher than if you had started taking it at 65 (60). You will also have been earning a salary meanwhile, so you are likely to be considerably better off as a result.
- Alternatively, there could be an advantage in taking your pension when you reach retirement age. The Inland Revenue does not permit anyone in a company pension scheme to contribute to another personal pension scheme. Even though you are no longer contributing to your company scheme, the over 65 (over 60) worker is still deemed to be a member of that scheme and is therefore prohibited from putting any of his/her earnings (from which he/she is making no pension payments) into a separate scheme.

However, if you were to draw your pension, even though you continued to work, you could then put up to 17.5% of your earnings into a different pension scheme. (This is allowed because your earlier contributions are not being rolled up to earn you a higher pay-out on eventual retirement.)

You may well get a better deal from this arrangement as the older you are when you start an annuity scheme, the better value you get.

Equal retirement age

The Government has recently published proposals which would make it illegal for employers to require women to retire at an earlier age than male colleagues. The proposed legislation will give women increased employment rights from about May 1987.

The legislation is unlikely to change the position regarding occupational pension rights. Under both the State and private pension arrangements, men will be able to defer their retirement up to the age of 70 and so let their pension increase over the period. However, women will still only be able to defer their pension up to the age of 65; after that they will not get any more money by waiting longer even if they continue to work until they are 70 plus.

Useful reading

What Will my Pension Be? published by the Consumers' Association, Castlemead, Gascoyne Way, Hertford, SG14 1LH. Price £5.95.

Pensions for women

Women who have worked all their adult lives and paid full Class 1 contributions should get a full basic pension in their own right at the age of 60. The current amount is £38.70 a week. As from 1987, this will be up-rated each year in April (previously November).

Women who have only worked for part of their adult lives may not have enough contributions to get a full basic pension on their own record. Instead, they may receive a reduced pension or one based on their husband's contributions. A wife entitled to a reduced pension in her own right can claim it at 60, regardless of whether her husband has retired.

Married women who have never worked are also entitled to a pension on their husband's contributions. In money terms, the value is about 60 per cent of the full basic pension. There are several important conditions, however.

Firstly, women can only receive a pension based on their husband's contributions if he himself is in receipt of a full basic pension. Additionally, the wife must be over 60 to qualify.

If she is still under 60 when her husband retires and does not work or her earnings do not exceed £30.80 (for this purpose, a wife's occupational pension counts as earnings), *he* should be able to obtain a supplement of around £23 to his pension, on the grounds of having a wife to support. Your local Social Security Office will be able to advise.

In contrast, **if a wife has had her sixtieth birthday but her husband has not yet reached 65** (or has decided to defer his retirement), she must wait until her husband retires to receive her share of the married couple's pension.

If a wife who formerly worked is over 60 and retired but cannot get a basic pension on either her own or her husband's contributions, she should normally be able to qualify for an additional or graduated pension based on her own contributions. These are described below.

But first a word about three other important matters: Reduced Rate Contributions, Abolition of the Half Test and Home Responsibilities Protection.

Reduced rate contribution

Many women retiring today have paid a reduced rate of NI contribution, also known as 'the small stamp'. This option was given to working wives in 1948 and withdrawn in 1978 but women who had already chosen to pay the reduced rate were allowed to continue.

If you have never paid anything but reduced rate contributions, you are not entitled to a basic pension in your own right but instead must rely on your husband's contributions for the married couple's pension.

Abolition of the Half Test

Until recently, married women had to have paid full NI contributions for half the time they were married and working to get anything at all in their own right. This rule, known as the 'half test', has now been abolished.

If you were born before April 6, 1919 and were a married woman when you reached age 60, having paid full NI contributions while working, you should contact your local DHSS office.

Home Responsibilities Protection (HRP)

Women who have been unable to work regularly because they have had to stay at home to care for children and/or a disabled or elderly person may be able to safeguard their pension by claiming Home Responsibilities Protection.

This is a very important benefit, especially for the many single women in their fifties who are sacrificing their career to look after an elderly parent. Married women can of course also claim if they can satisfy the fairly stringent conditions of eligibility.

This measure was introduced in 1978 and protection only applies from this date. The person you are caring for must come into one of the following categories:

- a child under 16 for whom you are getting child benefit
- someone whom you are looking after regularly for at least 35 hours a week, who is in receipt of attendance allowance or constant attendance allowance
- someone – for example, an elderly person – for whom you have been caring at home and in consequence have been getting supplementary benefit
- a combination of the above situations

A married woman or widow cannot get HRP for any tax year in which she was only liable to pay reduced rate national insurance contributions.

HRP can only be given for complete tax years (6 April to 5 April), so if you simply gave up work for a few weeks in order to help out, you would be unlikely to qualify.

Additionally, HRP cannot be used to reduce your total working life to below 20 years.

To obtain a claim form, you should ask your local Social Security Office for leaflet NP 27.

Since 1978, anyone in receipt of child benefit or supplementary benefit who is caring for someone in one of the eligible categories listed above is automatically credited with HRP. All other claimants should obtain Leaflet NP 27 from their local Social Security Office.

Graduated pension

This scheme operated between April 1961 and April 1975. Anyone earning over £9 a week and over age 18 at the time would probably have paid graduated contributions and be due a pension. You can only get a graduated pension based on your own personal contributions.

However, the pension from the graduated scheme is likely to be small. Further, women were penalised because their pension was calculated at a worse rate than for men on account of their longer life expectancy.

Additional pension

Commonly known as SERPS, the additional pension is also likely to be small because the scheme only started in 1978. Contributions are earnings-related, paid by both employer and employees, as are the pension payments. Women in contracted-out pension schemes get a guaranteed minimum pension, which must be at least as much as the pension they would have received from SERPS.

SERPS was designed in part to favour women. Particularly helpful features include: allowing pension rights to be calculated on the best 20 working years (instead of a working lifetime); and giving widows the right to inherit all of their late husband's additional pension, as well as retain their own.

The Government is intending to scale down SERPS. However, anyone retiring before 1998 will not be affected.

Divorced wives

If you have a full basic pension in your own right, this will not be affected by divorce.

However if, as applies to many women, despite having worked for a good number of years you have made insufficient contributions to qualify for a full pension, you should contact your local Social Security Office, quoting your pension number and national insurance number. It is possible that you may be able to obtain the full single person's pension, based on your ex-husband's contributions.

Your right to use your ex-husband's contributions to improve or provide you with a pension depends on your age and/or whether you remarry.

As a general rule, you can use your ex-husband's contributions towards your pension *for the years you were married* (i.e. until the date of the Decree Absolute). After that, you are expected to pay your own contributions unless you are already over 60 or you remarry.

If you are over 60 when you divorce, then whether you remarry or not, you can rely on your ex-husband's contributions. If you remarry before the age of 60, then you cease absolutely being dependent on your former husband and instead, your pension will be based on your new husband's contribution record.

N.B. The same rules apply in reverse. Although it happens far less frequently, a divorced man can rely on his former wife's contribution record during the years they were married to improve his basic pension.

Graduated or additional pensions are of no help to a divorced partner of either sex, as these are earnings-related and, therefore, only benefit the individual who has earned and paid for them.

For further information, ask your local Social Security Office for leaflet NI 95, *Divorced Women: NI Guide*. You should also read leaflet NI 32A *Retirement Pension if you are Divorced or Widowed*.

Separated wives

Even if you have not lived together for 20 years, from a national insurance point of view you are still considered to be married. The normal pension rules apply including of course the fact that, if you have to depend on your husband's contributions, you will not be able to get a pension until he is both 65 and retired.

If you are not entitled to a State pension in your own right, you will still receive only the dependant's rate of benefit of 60 per cent of the full rate. In such a case, you can apply for supplementary benefit.

Once you are 60, you can personally draw the wife's pension of £23.25 a week, without reference to your husband.

If you are close to 60 when your husband retires and you are not earning more than £30.80 a week, you may be able to obtain a special supplement up to the same amount of £23.25. For further information, ask your local Social Security Office for leaflet N195.

If your husband dies, you will be entitled to widow's benefit in the same way as any other wife. If there is a possibility that he may have died but that you have not been informed, you can check by writing to or visiting St.

Catherine's House, where the indexes of registered deaths are filed. The address is: St. Catherine's House, 10 Kingsway, London WC2, T: 01-242 0262.

Widows

There are two important benefits to which widows may be entitled: widow's pension and widow's allowance.

Widow's pension. Widows' pensions are complicated, mainly because they vary according to the widow's age when her husband dies. Leaving aside very young widows, there are four main possibilities:

● Women who become widowed between the ages of 40 and 50 receive an age-related widow's pension. At age 40 this will be £11.61, rising to £35.99 by the age of 50.

● Women who become widowed between the ages of 50 and 60 receive a widow's pension. This is currently £38.70 a week. Widows also normally receive the whole of the additional pension (SERPS) earned by their husbands' contributions, subject to an overall maximum.

● When a widow reaches 60, she can choose between three options:

– she can retire and claim a retirement pension, based on her own or on her husband's contributions (or both)
– she can draw a widow's pension as before
– she can continue working, defer her pension and receive the increased amount when she eventually retires.

● Women who become widowed over the age of 60 can get a retirement pension in the normal way, based on their own or their late husband's contributions or both.

For further information about widows' pensions, ask for leaflet NP 32A at your local Social Security Office.

Separate from the basic pension, a widow may also receive money from her late husband's occupational pension, whether contracted in or out of SERPS. She may also get half of any of his graduated pension.

Widow's allowance. When her husband dies, a widow may be able to get a widow's allowance for the first 26 weeks after his death. The current amount is £54.20.

To qualify, she must be under 60. Additionally, at the time of his death, her late husband must not have been drawing his pension. He must also have paid sufficient contributions to entitle her to claim. There is some discretion about the latter condition and in special circumstances, even if her husband's contribution record was insufficient, a widow may be able to obtain the allowance.

When a widow registers her husband's death, she is given a certificate which she should fill in and return to her local Social Security Office. She will then be sent a claim form BW 1 for the allowance, which she should complete and send back to the Social Security Office together with her marriage and her birth certificate.

3. Tax

Unfortunately, much as we should like to leave this out, the taxman never seems to retire!

Unless you are on a very low income, you will almost certainly be paying income tax and possibly one or two other varieties as well. Paradoxically, however, although over the years you may have been contributing many thousands of pounds to the Inland Revenue, in practice you may have had very little direct contact with the tax system.

As a salaried employee, the accounts department will have automatically deducted – and accounted for – the PAYE on your earnings. So unless you have been self-employed or have had other money, not connected with your job, you may never really have needed to give the question much thought.

Come retirement, although for most people the issues are not particularly complex, a bit of basic knowledge can be invaluable. Firstly, it will help you to calculate how much money (after deduction of tax) you will have available to spend: the equivalent, if you like, of your take-home pay. At a more sophisticated level, understanding the broad principles could help you save money, by not paying more in taxation than you need.

The purpose of this Chapter, however, is not to suggest clever ways of reducing your liability – although in fact almost everyone has a certain amount of scope to do so without in any way cheating the system.

But apart from some general points, listed here (as well as scattered elsewhere in the book where especially relevant, such as Chapter 8, giving tax planning advice is the job for a specialist; and moreover one who is fully conversant with your financial affairs, so that he can advise in the light of your own particular circumstances.

If you are lucky enough to be fairly wealthy or if some of the points mentioned in connection with the 1986 Budget changes, for example the new Inheritance Tax, give you genuine cause to wonder whether you are taking advantage of the concessions available to you, you should talk to an accountant.

The aim here is simply to remind you of the basics and to draw your attention to some of the new provisions that could have a bearing on your immediate or longer term plans.

Income tax

This is calculated on all (or nearly all) your income, after deduction of your personal allowance. The reason for saying 'nearly all' is that some income you may receive is tax free: types of income on which you do not have to pay tax are listed below under 'Tax free income'.

Most income, however, counts and you will be assessed for income tax on: your pension, interest you receive from savings, dividends from investments, any earnings (even if these are only from casual work) plus rental on a property, including regular or occasional money you get from taking in a lodger or paying guest. Many social security benefits are also taxable.

The tax year runs from 6 April to 5 April the following year, so the amount of tax you pay in any one year is calculated on the income you receive (or are deemed to have received) between these two dates.

The current basic rate tax is 29 per cent. Or put another way, for every £100 of your income that counts for income tax purposes, you have to pay £29 to the Exchequer – and are allowed to keep the remaining £71. The basic rate sometimes changes: for example, in the 1986 Budget it was reduced from 30 per cent to the present 29 per cent. The Government has announced its intention to make further reductions, when circumstances allow. Any changes, whether reductions or increases, are invariably announced in the Budget.

Not all income is taxed at the same rate. There are various tax bands and income over £17,201 starts to attract higher rate tax (below under 'Tax bands).

Personal allowances

Income tax is not levied on every last penny of your money. There is a certain amount you are allowed to retain before income tax becomes applicable. This is known as your personal allowance.

Therefore, when calculating how much tax you will have to pay in any one year, you should first deduct from your total income the amount represented by your personal allowance.

If your total income is no higher than your personal allowance, you will not have to pay any income tax.

The sums are slightly complicated by the fact that not everyone receives the same personal allowance. There are differences according to whether you are single or married; whether only one partner, or both husband and wife, works (or has worked); and further possible differences according to your age.

Without going into every variation, the main points are as follows:

- the single person's allowance is £2,335
- the married man's allowance is £3,655
- the wife's earned income allowance which is added to the married man's

allowance if he has a working wife is £2,335 (or less, of course, if her earnings are lower).

N.B. *A wife's earned income allowance does not cease on retirement.*
A married man can claim this on top of his own allowance if:

● his wife is still working
● she is getting a pension from a previous job
● she is getting a state pension based on her own National Insurance contributions
● she is entitled to a state pension of her own but is in fact drawing one on her husband's contributions (because it is higher than her own would be). In this last case, the husband should indicate on his tax form the value of the pension she would be entitled to receive in her own right; the tax allowance is then worked out on the actual value of the wife's unclaimed pension.

Age allowance

People aged 65 and over may be entitled to a more generous personal allowance, by virtue of their age. Eligibility, however, is on a tapering basis and the full amount is only given to people whose income does not exceed £9,400. Providing your income is within these limits:

● the single person's allowance is increased to £2,850
● the married allowance is increased to £4,505 (a couple can qualify if either partner is over the age of 65).

The ceiling limits for any claim to age allowance are an income of £10,173 for a single person; £10,675 for a married couple. If your income is as high as this or more, you will receive the normal personal allowance without any age addition.

N.B. The age allowance is *normally given automatically*. If you are not receiving it but believe you should be doing so, you should write to your local tax office (see under Inland Revenue in the telephone directory), stating your age and, if applicable, that of your partner. If you have been missing out, you may be able to claim the allowance back for up to six years and should receive a tax rebate.

Widow's bereavement allowance

This is an extra allowance, worth £1,320 a year at current rates, specially given to widows to assist them over the first difficult period. The only qualification is that a widow's late husband must have been entitled to the married man's tax allowance at the time of his death. The allowance is given from the date of bereavement to the end of that tax year, plus the year following.

As with other tax allowances, this is not a cash benefit that can be claimed at the post office. It is an offset against income, before calculation of tax. A widow would therefore be entitled to £3,655 (the total of her single person's allowance and widow's bereavement allowance) before her income would start to be assessed for tax. The sum is the exact equivalent of the married man's allowance.

Other tax allowances

Extra tax reliefs can also be claimed in a number of other circumstances.

The most important of these in financial terms is the **single parent's allowance**, which can be claimed by any parent bringing up dependent children on their own. The current value of the allowance is £1,320 a year. N.B. A married man whose wife is totally incapacitated can also claim this allowance, in addition to his married man's allowance, if he has dependent children living at home.

Registered blind people can claim an allowance of £360 a year. If both husband and wife are registered as blind, they can each claim the allowance. It is called the Blind Person's Allowance.

Housekeeper's Allowance. Eligibility is restricted to widows and widowers, who have someone living with them to act as a housekeeper. This could be a relative and the housekeeper could be either male or female. The allowance is worth £100 a year. However, there are certain rules: for example, if you have a man acting as housekeeper, you would not be able to claim if he is in receipt of the married man's allowance.

Child's Service Allowance. The child must be a son or daughter, who is maintained by you, living at home and on whom you depend for assistance. You must be 65 or over; or alternatively, infirm – in which case, age is not a precondition. The allowance is worth £55 a year. A married man, whose wife is under 65 and in good health, would not normally qualify – regardless of his own age or degree of infirmity.

Dependent Relative's Allowance. This £100 allowance (£145 when the claimant is a single woman) is available to those supporting a dependent relative whose only income is the basic retirement pension.

If you think you might be entitled to any of the above, you should write to your local tax office (see under Inland Revenue in the telephone directory) with full relevant details of your situation. As with age allowance, if you were entitled to receive the allowance earlier but for some reason missed out doing so, you may be able to obtain a tax rebate.

Tax relief

Separate from any personal allowances, you can obtain tax relief on the following:

- Interest payments on the first £30,000 of a mortgage
- Covenants, whether for the benefit of your grandchildren, a charity or your own children, if aged over 18 (technically, the tax relief is given to the recipient of any money paid under a covenant).
- Self-employed pension plans
  - if you were born after 1933, you can pay up to $17\frac{1}{2}$ per cent of your earnings into a self-employed pension scheme, tax free
  - if you were born before this date, you can pay up to 20 per cent of your earnings into a pension plan
  - even higher rates are allowed for those aged over 70
- Some maintenance payments, if you are divorced or separated.

Tax free income

Some income you may receive is entirely free of tax. It is not taxed at source. You do not have to deduct it from your income, as in the case of personal allowances. Nor, do you have to go through the formality of claiming relief on it.

If you receive any of the following, you can forget about the tax angle altogether – at least as regards these particular items:

- Mobility Allowance
- Invalidity Pension
- Industrial Injuries Disablement Pension
- Supplementary Pension
- Housing Benefit
- Any extra which may be added to your state pension if you support children under 16
- All pensions paid to war widows (plus any additions for children)
- Pensions paid to victims of Nazism
- Certain disablement pensions from the armed forces, police, fire brigade and merchant navy

- Pensions paid to the holders of certain gallantry awards
- £10 Christmas Bonus (paid to pensioners).

Other tax free money

The following are not income, in the sense that they are more likely to be 'one off' rather than regular payments. However, as with the above list they are tax free:

- Virtually all gifts (in certain circumstances you could have to pay tax if the gift is above £3,000 or if, as may occasionally be the case, the money from the donor has not been previously taxed).
- Redundancy payment, or a golden handshake in lieu of notice, up to the value of £25,000
- Lump sum commuted from a pension
- A Matured Endowment Policy.

Tax bands

The income tax system is progressive, which means that high incomes are taxed on a rising curve. Basic rate tax of 29 per cent applies up to the figure of £17,200. Sums over that amount begin to be taxed at a higher rate. The top rate of income tax is 60 per cent.

The following bands indicate exactly at what points your income could be liable to be taxed at higher rates.

1986/87

Taxable income (£)	Rates
0 – 17,200	29%
17,201 – 20,200	40%
20,201 – 25,400	45%
25,401 – 33,300	50%
33,301 – 41,200	55%
41,201 upwards	60%

Income tax on investments

For most investments on which you are likely to receive interest or dividends, basic rate tax will already have been deducted before the money is paid to you.

If you are a basic rate taxpayer, the money you receive will be yours in its entirety and you will not have to worry about making deductions for tax.

If you pay tax at the higher rate, you will have to pay some additional tax and should allow for this in your budgeting, as its deduction is not automatic. Normally, you will receive a tax demand for the extra tax owing at the end of the year.

Exceptionally, there are one or two types of investment where the money is paid to you gross – without the basic rate tax deducted. These include National Savings income bonds and deposit bonds and also certain specialist types of gilts. As with higher rate taxpayers, you will receive a tax demand for the amount owing.

Reclaiming tax overpaid

Some people overestimate the amount of tax they need to pay. To allow for this, there is a special tax form for retired people to reclaim any tax they have overpaid on investment income.

If you think this might apply to you, you should obtain Tax Claim Form R40 from your local tax office (see under Inland Revenue in the telephone directory). Complete the form and return it to the tax office, together with the tax vouchers concerned.

Mistakes by the Inland Revenue

The Inland Revenue sometimes also makes mistakes. Normally, if they have charged you insufficient tax and later discover the error, they will send you a supplementary demand requesting the balance owing.

However, under a provision known as the 'Official Error Concession', allowances are sometimes made and it is possible that you may not have to pay the full amount. This is more likely if you have a modest income. Extra leniency is sometimes also shown to widows and the retired.

Tax rebates

When you retire, you may be due for a tax rebate. If you are, this would normally be paid automatically, especially if you are getting a pension from your last employer.

The matter could conceivably be overlooked: either if (instead of from your last employer), you are due to get a pension from an earlier employer; or if you will only be receiving a state pension – and not a company pension in addition.

In either case, you should ask your employer for a P45 Form. Then, either send it – care of your earlier employer – to the pension fund trustees; or, in the event of you only receiving a state pension, send it to the tax office together with details of your age and the date you retired. Ask your employer for the address of the tax office to which you should write.

Capital gains tax (CGT)

You may have to pay capital gains tax if you make a large profit on the sale of a capital asset, for example: stocks and shares, jewellery, any property that is not your main home and other items of value.

CGT only applies to the actual profit you make, so if you buy shares to the value of £25,000 and sell them later for £35,000 the taxman will only be interested in the £10,000 profit you have gained.

Not all your profits are taxable. There is an *exemption limit of £6,300 a year*: so if during the year your total profits amount to £10,000, tax would only be levied on £3,700. Additionally, certain items are free altogether of capital gains tax; and others, such as the sale of a family business, get special treatment. Details are given a little further on.

Since 1982, the burden of CGT has been eased by the welcome introduction of *index-linking*. This means that any part of an asset's increased value, from 1982 or its subsequent purchase to its disposal, which is due to inflation is not counted for CGT purposes.

Unlike income tax, capital gains tax is not progressive. There is a flat rate of *30 per cent*, which applies to smaller and larger profits alike.

An important point for married couples to know is that in matters relating to CGT husband and wife are treated as one person. This has the advantage that when an asset is passed from husband to wife – or vice versa – no capital gains tax is payable. The big drawback, however, is that a couple's gains are aggregated (in other words, their profits are added together) and they have only one exemption of £6,300, as opposed to an exemption each.

Free of capital gains tax

The following assets are not subject to capital gains tax and do not count towards the £6,300 profits you are allowed to make:

- Your Main Home (however, see next section)
- Your Car
- Personal Belongings up to the value of £3,000 each
- Proceeds of a Life Assurance Policy (in most circumstances)
- Profits on British Government Stocks
- National Savings Certificates
- SAYE Contracts
- Building Society Savings
- Futures and Options in Gilts and Qualifying Corporate Bonds
- Premium Bond Winnings
- Football Pool and Other Bettings Winnings
- Gifts to Registered Charities
- Personal Equity Plan Scheme
- Small Part Disposals of Land (limited to 5 per cent of the total holding, with a maximum value of £20,000).

Providing both parties agree, capital gains on gifts may be held over until the recipient decides to sell. This means of course that the donor will not have to pay CGT.

Additionally, it was announced in the 1986 Budget that relief would also be given on the first sale of BES holdings.

Your home

Your main home is usually exempt from capital gains tax. However, there are certain 'ifs and buts' which could be important.

If you convert part of your home into an office or into self-contained accommodation on which you charge rent, that part of your home which is deemed to be a 'business' may be separately assessed – and CGT would be payable when you come to sell it. (CGT would not apply, if you simply take in a lodger who is treated as family, in the sense of sharing your kitchen or bathroom).

If you physically vacate your home and let it for profit – perhaps because you have decided to live permanently with a friend – under tax law, the property would be treated as an investment and would be assessed for CGT at such a time as it was sold.

Part of the argument hinges on *owner occupation*. If you are not living in the property (or a part of it which you have let out for rent), then the house – or that section of it – is no longer considered to be your main home.

If you leave your home to someone else who later decides to sell it, then he/she may be liable for CGT when the property is sold. There may also be inheritance tax implications, so if you are thinking of leaving or giving your home to someone, you are strongly advised to consult a solicitor or accountant.

If you own two homes, only one of them is exempt from CGT: namely the one you designate as your 'main residence'. An exception may be allowed if your second home is occupied by a dependent relative, who lives in it rent free.

Selling a family business

If you sell all or part of your business when you retire, you may not have to pay tax on the first £100,000 of capital gain. Relief is on a sliding scale and to get maximum relief, you must be aged at least 60 and when selling shares must have owned 25 per cent as a working director for 10 years. (Lower share ownership is allowed if, together with your immediate family, you collectively own 50 per cent of the business).

If you are forced to retire early through ill health, you may be entitled to more generous relief than would otherwise normally be the case.

There are also certain provisions for what is termed 'semi-retirement', which are hedged around with important rules.

Since this is a very complex field, before either retiring or selling shares, you are strongly recommended to seek professional advice.

Selling shares for gain should not be confused with *giving* part of your family business to the next generation, which has now been made easier under the new Inheritance tax. However, the advice about seeking professional help still applies.

Inheritance tax

Capital transfer tax was abolished in the 1986 Budget and has been replaced by inheritance tax which, for those who can remember it, seems largely modelled on the old estate duty.

The big change is that all tax has now been abolished on most life-time gifts, providing certain important conditions are met.

For exemption to apply, *the gift must have been made at least seven years before the donor's death* and moreover, it must have been *unconditionally given*; or to use the jargon, 'without reservation'. A gift in which the donor retains an interest or some direct control – for example, a house 'given' to his children in which the parent continues to live – does not qualify for exemption.

The seven year period is not totally inflexible, in that there is *taper relief*: in other words, a tapering rate of tax, according to how close to the seven year limit the death of the donor occurred. Gifts made within three years of death do not qualify for any relief and the tax will have to be paid in full. For gifts made more than 3 years before death, the rates are as follows:

- Death between 3 and 4 years of gift   80%
- Death between 4 and 5 years of gift   60%
- Death between 5 and 6 years of gift   40%
- Death between 6 and 7 years of gift   20%

If death occurs within the first three years, the gift will be taxed in a similar fashion to capital transfer tax. The first £71,000 of an individual's estate is tax free. After that, the following rates apply:

Band (£)	Rate	Cumulative tax
		nil
0 – 71,000	nil	7,200
71,001 – 95,000	30%	19,100
95,001 – 129,000	35%	33,100
129,001 – 164,000	40%	52,000
164,001 – 206,000	45%	77,500
206,001 – 257,000	50%	110,500
257,001 – 317,000	55%	
317,001 upwards	60%	

Gifts made prior to the introduction of inheritance tax will not be assessed more harshly than they would under CTT, had it continued. Similarly, the £3,000 annual exemption and the exemption on gifts to spouses will remain unchanged.

An immediate consequence of the announcement of inheritance tax was a collapse in the market for inheritance trusts (sometimes known as capital preservation plans), since these have now been rendered ineffective.

At the same time, it was widely forecast that there would be a revival in the types of term insurance contracts (popular in the days of estate duty), designed to insure against the risk of a hefty tax bill in the event of premature death.

Although the initial reaction to the advent of inheritance tax was that giving has now become simple and, in tax terms, painless, anyone thinking of disposing of their property or planning the long term future in terms of their estate would be strongly recommended to seek professional advice.

Another important consideration that should not be overlooked is the need to make a will. The rules of intestacy are very rigid and neglecting to make a proper will can have serious consequences for those whom you might wish to benefit. For further information, see Chapter 14.

Value added tax (VAT)

Unless you are thinking of starting a business or already run one, you do not require any special information about VAT. You pay it automatically on most goods and services, at the flat rate of 15 per cent. As a general rule, if you purchase a tangible object, it will be included in the price. For most services, including restaurant bills, it is itemised separately.

Small firms that are not registered for VAT naturally do not charge it. However, even for very small enterprises, there maybe definite advantages in registering. If you are planning to become self-employed or start a business after you retire, you should read the VAT section in Chapter 9.

Corporation tax

This is a business tax and unless you are involved in running a company, there is nothing you need to know.

If you are already engaged in running a small business, you will probably hardly need reminding that the small companies rate of corporation tax was reduced for the financial year 1986 from 30 to 29 per cent.

The lower and upper limits for the application of marginal relief are £100,000 and £500,000 respectively.

Useful reading

Which? Tax-Saving Guide, published by the Consumers' Association.
Allied Dunbar Tax Guide.
Your Taxes and Savings in Retirement – 1986 published by Age Concern. £1.50.

The Inland Revenue publishes a number of booklets which could be helpful:
Capital Gains Tax (CGT 8)
Income Tax: Separation and Divorce (IR 30)
Income Tax: Personal Allowances (IR 22)
Income Tax and Married Couples (IR 31)
Tax – Employed or Self-employed (IR 56).

Retiring abroad

The stories are legion of people who retired abroad in the expectation of being able to afford a higher standard of living and who returned home a few years later, thoroughly disillusioned.

As with other important decisions, this is an area where homework really pays!

Holiday memories of dinner for two complete with bottle of wine for the princely sum of a fiver are, alas, no guide to the cost of actually living in a country – especially if the holiday in question took place five years ago or more.

While some services may be cheaper, others may be very much more expensive; and the same goes of course for any goods you buy in the shops. In particular, if you want to purchase British brands, you can expect to pay considerably more than you do at home.

Property prices are crucial to investigate, as is of course the cost of health care. As anyone who has ever needed a doctor or dentist abroad knows, the term 'free health service' does not always mean what it says.

While these and similar points are perhaps obvious, a vital question that is often overlooked are the taxation effects of living overseas.

Taxation abroad

Tax rates vary from one country to another: a prime example being VAT, which in some parts of Europe at the time of writing is over 20 per cent on certain items.

Additionally, many countries levy taxes that happily do not apply to Britain. Wealth tax exists in quite a few parts of the world. Estate duty between husbands and wives is also fairly widespread. There are all sorts of property taxes, different from our own, which – however described – are variously assessable as income or capital. Sometimes a special tax is imposed on foreign residents. Some countries, including Spain, charge income tax on an individual's worldwide income, with none of the (by British standards) normal exemptions allowed.

Even so-called tax havens may fail to live up to their privileged reputation. While admittedly not actual taxation, many impose all sorts of conditions on foreigners, effectively excluding all but the super rich. The terms may vary but could include any, or all, of the following. Only property above a minimum (and pretty exorbitant) price may be purchased. You could have to produce evidence of a sky high annual income. You may be required to invest in a local business. Or, insultingly, you could be requested to deposit a sum with the government to cover you against repatriation costs, should the necessity arise.

The only sensible advice is to investigate the situation thoroughly before you take an irrevocable step, such as selling your home; or worse, investing in a property overseas.

However, if many people blithely ignore the 'nasties' that may await them overseas, an even more common mistake is to misunderstand their UK tax liabilities after their departure.

Your UK tax position if you retire overseas

Many intending emigrants cheerfully imagine that once they have settled themselves in a dream villa overseas, they are safely out of the clutches of the UK taxman. This is not so, however. You first have to acquire *non-resident status*.

If you have severed all your ties, including selling your home, to take up a permanent job overseas, this is normally granted fairly quickly. But for most retirees, acquiring unconditional non-resident status can take up to three years.

The purpose is to check that you are not just having a prolonged holiday but are actually living as a resident abroad. During the check period, the Inland Revenue will allow you *conditional non-resident status*; and if they are satisfied, full status will be granted retrospectively.

Rules
The rules for non-residency are pretty stringent. You are not allowed:

- to spend more than 183 days in the UK in any one tax year
- to spend more than an average of 90 days per year in the UK for four consecutive tax years
- to come to the UK at all, if you continue to own property.

Even if you are granted non-resident status, some of your income may still be liable for British taxation.

Income tax

- All overseas income is exempt from UK tax liability
- Income deriving from a U.K. source is, however, normally liable for U.K. tax. This includes any director's or consultant's fees you may still be receiving, as well as more obvious income.
- An exception is made if the country in which you have taken up residency has a double tax agreement with the United Kingdom (see below). If this is the case, you will be taxed on the income in your new residence – and not in the UK.
- Additionally, interest paid on certain British Government securities is not subject to tax.
- Non-residents can arrange for their interest on a British bank deposit or building society account to be paid without deduction of composite rate tax.
- Some former colonial pensions are also exempted.

Double tax agreement. This is an agreement between the United Kingdom, all EEC and certain other countries, whereby the individual does not pay more tax than would be the highest rate in either the UK or the new country of residence.

Capital gains tax

- This is only charged on British residents, so if you are in the position of being able to realise a gain, it is advisable to wait until you acquire non-resident status.
- An exception to the rule are gains made from the disposal of assets in a UK company. These are subject to normal CGT.

Inheritance tax

- You only escape tax if you are *domiciled* (as opposed to resident) overseas. If you do not have an overseas domicile, you will have to pay the tax at the same rates, as if you lived in Britain.

Domicile. Domicile is distinct from both residence and nationality – although in practice, it often means one or both. The definition is your permanent, long-term home.

If you are resident in a country and intend to spend the rest of your days there, it could be sensible to opt for a change of domicile. If, however, you are resident but there is a chance that you might move, the country where you are living would not qualify as your domicile. This is a complicated area, where professional advice is recommended if you are contemplating a change.

Pensions

- Any queries about your pension should be addressed to the DHSS overseas office at Newcastle Central Office, Longbenton, Newcastle-upon-Tyne NE98 1YX.
- Technically your state pension could be subject to income tax, as it derives from the UK In practice, if this is your only source of UK income, tax would be unlikely to be charged.
- If you have an occupational pension, UK tax will normally be charged on the total of the two amounts.
- Both state and occupational pensions can be paid gross to any country.
- If the country where you are living has a double tax agreement with the UK, as previously explained your income would normally be taxed there – and not in Britain. Countries which have this reciprocal arrangement include: all EEC countries; Austria; Cyprus; Guernsey; Israel; Jamaica; Jersey; Malta; Mauritius; Switzerland; Turkey; the USA; and Yugoslavia.
- If your pension is taxed in the UK, you will be able to claim part of your personal allowance as an offset.

4. Investment

Investment is a subject for everyone. One of your single most important aims must be to make your existing money work for you, so you will be more comfortable in the years ahead.

The younger you start planning the better. If you are already 65 or over, there is still plenty you can do.

Many articles written on the subject of financial planning for retirement concentrate almost exclusively on ways of boosting your immediate income to compensate for your loss of earnings. Frankly, this is very misleading and short-sighted advice. An equally if not even more critical consideration must be to safeguard your long term security, even if this means some minor sacrifice of your current standard of living.

The likelihood is that you will live for 20 years or longer after you retire and your partner may live longer still. Your investment strategy must therefore be aimed not just for your sixties but also for your eighties.

Inflation is another essential factor that must be taken into account. People on fixed incomes are the hardest hit when inflation rises and, as happened in the 1970s, many even quite wealthy people were drastically impoverished as a result of their savings being slashed in value.

Even low inflation, as we have today, takes its toll to an alarming extent. For example, if you have an after tax income of £3,500 a year and inflation averages 4 per cent for the next decade, your spending power will be reduced to £2,336. If it averages 6 per cent, it will have dropped still further to £2,094. And if it averages 10 per cent, which is not inconceivable, you will end up with a miserable £1,327 in purchasing power terms.

Sources of investable funds

You do not need to be in the director league to have money for investment. Possible sources of quite significant capital include:

- *Commuted lump sum* from your pension. The maximum you are allowed to take is $1\frac{1}{2}$ times your final earnings. There is no tax to pay when you receive the money.
- *Insurance policies*, designed to mature around your retirement. These are normally tax free.
- *Profits on your home*, if you sell it and move to smaller, less expensive

accommodation. Providing this is your main home, there is no capital gains tax to pay.

- *Redundancy money, golden handshake* or other farewell gift from your employer. You are allowed £25,000 redundancy money free of tax. The same is usually true of other severance pay up to £25,000 but there can be tax if, however worded, your employment contract indicates that these are deferred earnings.
- *Sale of SAYE and other share option schemes.* The tax rules vary according to the type of scheme and how long the shares have been held before disposal.

General investment strategy

Investments differ in their aims, tax treatment and the amount of risk involved. One or two categories are only suitable for the very rich, who can afford to take more significant risks. Others, such as certain types of National Savings, are only really suitable for those on a very low income.

These two groups apart, the aim for most people should be to acquire a balanced portfolio: in other words, a mix of investments variously designed to provide some income to supplement your pension and also some capital appreciation to maintain your standard of living long term.

Except for annuities and National Savings, which have sections to themselves, the different types of investment are listed by groups, as follows:

- variable interest accounts
- fixed interest securities
- equities
- long term lock-ups

As a general strategy, it is a good idea to aim to choose at least one type of investment from each group.

Annuities

Definition. An annuity is a very simple investment to understand. You pay a capital sum to an insurance company and in return are guaranteed a fixed income for life. The money is paid to you monthly or quarterly and will remain exactly the same year in, year out.

Payments are calculated according to life expectancy tables and for this reason an annuity is not really a suitable investment for anyone under the age of 70.

It would probably give you more immediate income than any other form of investment. But whether you actually get good value depends on how long you live. When you die, your capital will be gone and there will be no more payments. So if you die a short while after signing the contract, it will represent very bad value indeed. On the other hand, if you live a very long time, you may more than recoup your original capital.

As a precaution against early death, it is possible to take out a term annuity: in other words, an annuity that runs for a specified period.

Should you die before the end of the contract, the payments will go to your partner or other beneficiary. The major drawback to this arrangement is that if you outlive the contract, you will not receive any more annuity income and your capital will have gone along with your security.

There are also annuities, known as capital and income plans which pay you a small income, say, for a 10 year period, at the end of which your capital is returned. These are sometimes taken out, as a kind of holding operation, by people who are too young to obtain sufficiently attractive terms on a normal life annuity. You have to assess whether you could get a better return from another fixed interest security.

Tax. Income tax is relatively very low, as part of the income is allowed as a return on capital which is untaxed.

How to obtain. You can buy an annuity either direct from an insurance company or via an insurance broker. But shop' around, as the payments vary considerably. For example: typical annual income for a man aged 70, on a £10,000 annuity purchased in December 1985, ranges from £1,700 to £1,765; for a woman of 75 (same insurance companies, same purchase date), the sums range from £1,716 to £1,799.

To find an insurance broker, contact the **British Insurance Brokers' Association**, BIBA House, 14 Bevis Marks, London EC3A 7NT (see Chapter 5).

Assessment. Safe. Attractive if you live to a ripe old age. But highly vulnerable to inflation. Sacrifice of capital that might otherwise benefit successors.

National Savings

National Savings is one of the biggest savings institutions in the country. It is guaranteed by the government and it is therefore impossible that it could go bankrupt.

It is extremely easy to invest via National Savings, as all you need do is go to the post office. Most types of investments it offers are broadly similar to those provided by banks and other financial bodies. So rather than explain in detail the exact terms and conditions of, say, a National Savings investment account, it is easier to suggest that you pick up the relevant leaflet at the post office counter; or telephone the individual department headquarters to which enquiries should be directed. Telephone numbers are listed a little further down.

However, National Savings have two very special features: one that is likely to be of particular interest to higher rate taxpayers; the other of special benefit to non taxpayers.

National Savings Certificates, of which there are three types – fixed interest, index linked and yearly plan – are free of tax, providing they are retained for the necessary period. Of the three, the least interesting are the index-linked certificates – or 'Granny Bonds' as they used to be known – because their particular appeal was that they are inflation-proofed and today, with relatively low inflation, there are better investments available. However, generally speaking any investment that is tax free is of potential interest to higher rate taxpayers.

The other specially attractive feature of National Savings, which is of real benefit to non taxpayers, is that income receipts are paid gross – without deduction of tax. This means that non taxpayers can retain all their income without any deductions.

The main investments offered by National Savings are:

Ordinary account. Pays a fairly low rate of variable interest. You can invest between £1 and £10,000. The first £70 of interest each year is free of tax. Ask for leaflet DNS 700 or telephone Glasgow (041) 649 4555.

Investment account. Pays a high rate of interest. You must give one month's notice if you wish to withdraw money. You can invest between £5 and £50,000. Interest is taxable. Ask for leaflet DNS 701 or telephone Glasgow (041) 649 4555.

Income bonds. Pay high interest. Three months' notice of withdrawal is necessary. You can invest between £2,000 and £50,000. Ask for leaflet DNS 709 or call Blackpool (0253) 697 333.

Indexed income bonds. Offer an inflation-proofed return for ten years. You can invest from £5,000 to £50,000. Three months' notice of withdrawal is required. Ask for leaflet DNS 714 or telephone Blackpool (0253) 697 333.

Deposit bonds. Pay a high rate of variable interest. You can invest in units from £100 to £50,000. Three months' notice of withdrawal is necessary. Ask for leaflet DNS 702 or call Glasgow (041) 649 4555.

31st (current) issue of National Savings certificates. Offer an attractive rate of fixed interest that is tax free. You can invest from £25 to £5,000. For maximum benefit, you must hold the certificates for five years. Ask for leaflet DNS 703 or call Durham (0385) 64900.

Index linked certificates (3rd issue). You can invest from £25 to £5,000. Interest is 3.45 per cent plus the increase in the Retail Price Index but, to obtain this rate, certificates must be retained for five years. Interest is tax free. Ask for leaflet DNS 704 or call Durham (0385) 64900.

Yearly plan. Produces high tax free income, paid at a fixed rate for five years. You can invest from £20 to £200 per month. Repayment takes about three weeks. Ask for leaflet DNS 705 or call Durham (0385) 64900.

Gilts. Can be bought through the National Savings Stock Register. Ask for leaflet DNS 708 or call Blackpool (0253) 697 333.

Information about all National Savings products is available by telephoning: 01-605 9461.

Variable interest accounts

Definition. These are all deposit accounts of one form or another, arranged with banks, building societies, the National Savings Bank and with some financial institutions that operate such accounts jointly with banks.

They include among others: basic deposit accounts, high interest accounts and fixed term deposit accounts.

Your money collects interest while it is on deposit, which may be automatically credited to your account or for which you may receive a regular cheque.

The rate of interest will vary, up or down, according to the level of national interest rates. While you may get a poor return on your money if interest rates drop, your savings will always be safe as you are not taking any kind of investment risk.

Access. Access to your money depends on the type of account you choose: you can have a cheque book and withdraw your money when you want; you may have to give a week's notice or slightly longer; or if you enter into a term account, you will have to leave your money deposited for the agreed specified period. In general, accounts where a slightly longer period of notice is required earn a better rate of interest.

Sum deposited. It is not usually sensible to consider a deposit account unless you have a minimum of £1100. For certain types of account, the minimum investment could be anything from £500 to about £5,000. The terms tend to vary according to how keen the institutions are, at a given time, to attract small investors.

Tax. In order to encourage savings, banks and building societies have been able to negotiate a lower rate of composite tax on interest bearing accounts (25.25 per cent at present as opposed to the standard rate of 29 per cent), so giving them a definite edge compared with investments where the full rate of tax has to be paid.

With the exception of the National Savings Bank, where interest is paid gross, tax is deducted at source – so you can spend the money without worrying about the tax implications. However, you must enter the interest on your tax return; and if you are a higher rate taxpayer, you will of course have additional liability.

Choosing a deposit account

There are two main areas of choice: the type of deposit account to choose and where to invest your money.

The relative attractions of the different types of account and of the institutions themselves can vary, according to the terms being offered at the time. Generally speaking, however, the basic points are as follows:

Basic deposit account. This attracts a relatively low rate of interest. But it is both easy to set up and very flexible, as you can add small or large savings when you like and can withdraw your money without penalty, usually at about a week's notice. It is a much better option than simply leaving your money in a current account (which earns no interest at all) and is an excellent temporary home for your cash if you are saving short term for, say, a holiday. However, it is not recommended as a long term savings plan.

High interest deposit account. Your money earns a higher rate of interest than it would on an ordinary deposit account. A further advantage is that you may receive a cheque book, which you can use in the normal way and so have instant access to your money. However, to open a high interest account you will need to deposit a minimum sum, which could be of the order of £500 to £1,000. While you can always add to this amount, if your basic deposit drops below the required minimum, your money will immediately stop earning the higher interest rate. If you frequently dip into overdraft, a high interest deposit account is worse than useless.

Fixed term deposit accounts. You deposit your money for an agreed period of time, which can vary from a few months to several years. In return for this commitment, you will be paid a relatively star rate of interest.

As with high interest accounts, there is a minimum investment: roughly £1,500 to £5,000. If you need to withdraw your money before the end of the agreed term, there are usually hefty penalties. Before entering into a term account, you need to be sure that you can afford to leave the money on deposit. Additionally, if the proposed agreement lasts for several years, you will need to take a view about interest rates: if they are generally low, your money may be better invested elsewhere.

A further important point is that you should keep a note of the date when the agreement expires. As a rule, your money will no longer earn preferential rates after the term has come to an end (unless of course you renew the agreement). The bank or other institution may not notify you in advance and may, quite legitimately, simply credit you with the normal interest rates after the contract's expires.

Information

For banks, enquire direct at your local high street branch. There will be leaflets available, describing the different accounts in detail. Or if you have any questions, you can ask to see your bank manager. You can also investigate the other banks to see whether they offer better terms.

For building societies, enquire at any building society branch or, better still, pop into several as the terms and conditions may vary quite widely.

The **Building Societies Association** at 3 Saville Row, London W1X 1AF, offers a free range of helpful booklets, including *Building Societies and House Purchase* which, despite its somewhat misleading title, includes a general guide to the services offered by building societies.

You can also buy *Building Society Choice*, which is a monthly magazine that gives up-to-date details of the terms offered by the various building societies. Price £2.50 (inc. postage) from Riverside House, Rattlesden, Bury St. Edmunds, Suffolk IP30 0SS.

'Safe' accounts

Interest-bearing accounts have been described as safe. The Building Societies Association has urged that we say that there is always some risk, however minute in practice. A reason for their caution is that in 1987, their voluntary scheme is being replaced by a statutory investor protection scheme, the details of which at time of writing have not been finalised.

Other accounts

Led by Save & Prosper a few years ago, some unit trusts and other financial institutions now offer interest bearing accounts that are very similar to those run by banks and building societies. Examples include: Britannia/Cater Allen, Charterhouse Japhet, the Co-op Bank, Henderson/Bank of Scotland, M & G Kleinwort Benson, Save & Prosper/Robert Fleming, Tyndall & Co., Western Trust & Savings.

Fixed interest securities

In contrast to variable interest accounts, fixed interest securities offer a fixed rate of interest which you are paid regardless of what happens to interest rates generally.

If you buy when the fixed rate is high and interest rates fall, you will nevertheless continue to be paid interest at the high rate specified in the contract note. However, if interest rates rise above the level when you bought, you will not benefit from the increase.

As a generalisation, these securities give high income but only modest, if any, capital appreciation.

The list includes: high interest gilts, local authority bonds and stock exchange loan and preference shares.

Stock exchange loan & preference shares

Definition. Companies use fixed interest loan, debenture and preference shares as one of the ways of raising money for expansion. Unlike ordinary shares, these securities pay a fixed guaranteed rate of interest, usually six monthly, but do not entitle the holder to share in the profits or to vote at the annual general meeting.

They are bought and sold on the stock exchange and, similar to gilts, their price rises and falls with the market view of future interest rates.

As with other shares, they are backed by the assets of the company and are therefore secure unless the company actually fails. But while your interest payments are virtually guaranteed, you could make a loss when you sell the shares – but equally, of course, a profit.

In theory, you could buy today and sell tomorrow. However, generally speaking it is inadvisable to purchase these shares other than as a long term holding.

There will be stockbrokers' commission to pay and there is normally a 14 to 21 day delay between selling and receiving the money.

To find a stockbroker, see Chapter 5.

Tax. Income tax on your interest is deducted at source. If you make a profit, there could be liability for capital gains tax.

Assessment. Normally pay better interest than gilts – but a more risky investment. There is a chance of a windfall in the event of a takeover. Only really suitable for experienced investors.

Gilt edged securities

Definition. Usually known as 'Gilts', these are stocks issued by the government who guarantee both the interest payable and the repayment price which is promised on a given date.

The maturity date varies and can be anything from a few months to twenty years or longer. Accordingly, stocks are variously known as: short-dated, medium-dated and long-dated. A further category is undated. Additionally, there are index-linked gilts.

Prices for gilts are quoted per £100 of nominal stock. For example, a stock may be quoted as: 10% Treasury Stock 1992, 99½ – 100¼. In plain English, this means the following:

- 10% represents the interest you will be paid. The rate is fixed and will not vary, whatever happens to interest rates generally. You will receive the interest payment twice yearly, 5% each time.
- You are buying Treasury Stock
- The maturity date is 1992
- To buy the stock, you will have to pay £100.25p (i.e. 100¼).
- If you want to sell the stock, the market price you will get is £99.50p (i.e. 99½).

Gilts are complicated by the fact that you can either retain them until their maturity date, in which case the government will return the nominal value in full (less the commission charged to buy them). Or you can sell them on the stock exchange at market value. This accounts for the different buying and selling prices that may be quoted.

Prices are affected by current interest rates. If interest rates are at 7 per cent, a gilt with a guaranteed interest payment of 10 per cent is a very attractive buy – so the price will rise. Conversely, if interest rates are 15 per cent, a guaranteed interest payment of 10 per cent is a poor proposition, so there will not be many buyers and the price will drop. Because gilts are so closely tied to interest rates, the price can fluctuate daily, often by quite big jumps.

Index-linked gilts, while operating on the same broad principle, are different in effect. They are designed to shield investors against inflation: they pay very low interest but are redeemable at a higher price than the initial purchase price, as their value is geared to the cost of living. They are most valuable when inflation is high but are even more sensitive than other gilts to optimum timing when buying or selling.

Tax. Income tax is normally deducted at source. However, this does not apply if you buy gilts on the National Savings Stock Register from the post office (see below), when instead the interest will be paid to you gross. This does not mean that you avoid paying it, simply that you must allow for a future tax bill before spending the money.

Buying through a post office is of special advantage to non taxpayers, since they will retain that part of their interest that – had they bought the stock anywhere other than through the National Savings system – would have been automatically deducted.

A particular attraction of gilts is that no capital gains tax is charged on any profit you may have made but equally no relief is allowed for losses.

How to obtain. You can buy gilts through banks, a stockbroker, at a post office or from the National Savings Bond and Stock Office direct. In all cases, you will be charged commission.

The prices are published every day in all the quality newspapers under the heading 'British Funds'.

If you purchase through a stockbroker (see Chapter 5 below), you will get fairly immediate action. If you buy through the post office, there will be some delay and in consequence the price may be different from what you had expected. Additionally, although the National Savings system is slightly cheaper, you will not get advice as you would from a stockbroker.

Buying at a post office is, however, extremely easy. All you need do is complete a National Savings Stock Register Form (GS1), available at the counter, and hand it in with your cheque.

If you use a post office to buy, you must also sell through one.

A leaflet *Buying Gilts on the N.S. Stock Register* is available at most post offices. Or if you have any queries, you can contact the **Bonds and Stock Office**, Blackpool, Lancs FY3 9YP, T: 0253 697333.

Assessment. Gilts normally pay reasonably good interest and offer excellent security, in that they are backed by the government. You can sell at very short notice and the stock is accepted by banks as security for loans, if you want to run an overdraft.

However, gilts are not a game for amateurs as, if you buy or sell at the wrong time, you could lose money; and if you hold your stock to redemption, inflation could take its toll on your original investment. Index-linked gilts, which overcome the inflation problem, are generally speaking a better investment for higher rate taxpayers – not least because the interest paid is very low.

Local authority bonds

Definition. One of the ways local authorities raise money is by selling bonds to the public. These come in two forms: Over the Counter or Tap bonds, which can be purchased from local authorities direct; and Yearlings, which are bought and sold on the stock exchange.

In both cases, you receive a fixed rate of interest, which is paid to you automatically every six months. The interest rate offered can vary quite considerably from one council to another.

Tap bonds are similar to term deposit accounts, in that you undertake to keep your money deposited for a specified period of time, which can be anything from one to ten years. Once bought, they are non-negotiable: in other words, you cannot cash them before the end of the agreed term. Tap bonds are usually issued in units of £500 upwards.

Yearlings, as the name implies, are one year bonds. However, because they are traded on the stock exchange, you are not locked into your investment and can sell at any time. The minimum investment is £1,000. Additionally, you will have stockbrokers' commission to pay.

Tax. The 1985 Finance Act brought local authorities along with building societies and banks into the composite rate tax scheme. Tax on Tap bonds is deducted at source so, if you are a basic rate taxpayer you only need enter the interest on your tax return. Non taxpayers will not be able to reclaim the tax. Higher rate taxpayers will have the additional tax to pay. In the case of Yearlings, if you make a profit by selling, there may be a liability for capital gains tax.

How to obtain. Apart from Yearlings for which you have to go to a stockbroker or your bank manager (see Chapter 5 below), you simply contact the local authority whose bonds you wish to buy. You should ask for the Treasurers' Department.

At time of writing, CIPFA supplies a very useful list giving details of all the local authority bonds on offer, together with their various interest rates. It is not certain whether this service will continue or not. To find out, you should write to or telephone CIPFA at 3 Robert Street, London WC2, T: 01-930 3456.

Assessment. Like gilts, local authority investments can offer reasonably high income. Risk is fairly low but all holdings are vulnerable to inflation and long term bond, especially so. Yearlings offer you the possibility of a capital gain.

Equities

These are all stocks and shares, purchased in different ways and involving varying degrees of risk. They are designed both to achieve capital appreciation as well as give you some regular income. Most allow you to get your money out within thirty days or less.

In the past, equities were by and large only considered suitable for a privileged minority. Today, there are an estimated six million shareholders and the number is rapidly increasing. One reason is that, as the flotation of British Telecom demonstrated, equities can be excellent money-spinners. Another is that over the last few years, investment has become very much easier, largely as a result of the growth in the unit trust movement.

Whatever people say, equities are always risky. But for those who believe in caution, the gamble can now be very much reduced. The list includes: ordinary shares, unit trusts and the new Personal Equity Plan.

Unit trusts

Definition. Unit trusts offer an alternative to buying shares on the stock exchange. Your money is put in a fund, run by professional managers, who invest the proceeds in a wide range of shares and other securities.

The advantages are that: it is usually less risky than buying individual shares; it is very simple; you get professional management and there are no day to day decisions to make. Additionally, every trust is required by law to have a trustee to protect investors' interests.

Over the last twenty years, the number and variety of trusts has increased dramatically. Some specialise in producing high income; some in maximising capital gains; others are mixed trusts, aiming to combine both virtues. Some of the newer trusts concentrate on particular sectors, such as: gilts, convertible shares, European, American or other overseas markets.

The minimum investment in some of the more popular trusts is £250; in others, it can be as high as £10,000. Some trusts allow you to purchase units for smaller amounts on a regular monthly plan.

There is a front end fee of around 5 per cent to join the trust and there is also an annual management charge.

Investors' contributions to the trust are divided into units, and proportionate to the amount they have invested, all unit holders receive an income distribution – normally paid every six months.

As with ordinary shares, you can sell all or some of your investment by telling the unit trust managers that you wish to do so. The price you will receive is called 'the bid price'. This is published daily, in respect of all the main unit trusts, in the financial pages of the quality newspapers.

How to obtain. Units are purchased off the management companies, which can be: banks, insurance companies, stockbrokers or specialist unit trust management groups. Some advertise direct in the national newspapers and financial magazines. Some use salesmen, others employ insurance brokers or financial intermediaries. The bigger groups tend to use all these techniques.

You will be asked to complete a form, stating how many units you want in which particular trust, and then send it to the company with your cheque.

For a complete list of unit trusts, you can look in the *Financial Times*. Or alternatively, write to the **Association of Unit Trusts**, Park House, 16 Finsbury Circus, London EC2M 7JP. (Enclose sae 8½" x 4").

Tables comparing the performance of the various unit trusts are published in specialist magazines, such as *Money Management*.

With over 900 trusts from which to choose, it is important to get professional advice. You can ask your bank, an accountant, an insurance broker or a unit trust specialist. However, beware those whose recommendations only cover their own in-house trusts or who stand to get a hefty commission from the unit trust company. For information about insurance brokers and others, see Chapter 5.

Tax. Identical to ordinary shares (see next section).

Assessment. An ideal method for smaller investors to buy stocks and shares: both less risky and easier. Some of the more specialist trusts are also suitable for those with a significant investment portfolio.

Ordinary shares listed on the Stock Exchange

Definition. Public companies issue shares as a method of borrowing money.

When you buy shares and become a shareholder in a company, you own a small part of the business and are entitled to participate in its profits through a dividend which is normally paid six monthly.

Dividends go up and down according to how well the company is doing and it is possible that in a bad year no dividends at all will be paid. However, in good years, dividends can increase very substantially.

The money you invest is unsecured. This means that, quite apart from any dividends, your capital could be slashed in value – or if the company goes bankrupt, you could lose the lot. Against this, if the company performs well you could enormously increase your wealth.

The value of a company's shares is decided by the stock market. Thousands of large and small investors are taking a view on each company's prospects and this creates the market price. The price of a share can fluctuate daily and this will affect both how much you have to pay, if you want to buy; and how much you will make (or lose), if you want to sell.

Only officially listed shares are traded on the stock exchange. To become an investor you can write to the **Stock Exchange**, London EC2N 1HP for a list of brokers who would be willing to deal for you (see Chapter 5 below). Alternatively, you can go to the securities department of your bank who will place the order for you. Either way, you will be charged both commission and stamp duty (reduced to $\frac{1}{2}$ per cent as from the end of October).

When you buy shares, the company issues you with a share certificate which you or your advisor must keep, as you will have to produce it when you wish to sell all or part of your holding.

There are two types of shares both quoted on the stock exchange that are potentially suitable for small investors. These are investment trusts and convertible loan stocks.

Investment Trusts, like unit trusts, invest your money in a variety of companies. They provide a spread of risk with potentially good capital appreciation. However, their yield tends to be on the low side. For further information and a list of brokers who specialise in these trusts, write to: **Association of Investment Trusts**, 16 Finsbury Circus, London EC2M 7JP.

Convertible Loan Stocks give you a fixed guaranteed income for a certain length of time and offer you the opportunity to convert them into ordinary shares. While capital appreciation prospects are lower, the advantage of convertible loans is that they usually provide significantly higher income than ordinary dividends.

Tax. The 29 per cent tax is deducted at source before you receive your dividend. If during the year you make profits by selling shares that in total exceed £6,300, you could be liable for capital gains tax.

Assessment. Although dividend payments generally start low, in good companies they are likely to increase over the years and so provide a first class hedge against inflation. The best equities are an excellent investment. In others, you can lose all your money. Good advice is critical as this is a high risk/high reward market.

Personal Equity Plan

Definition. This is an entirely new scheme, which comes into effect on 1st January 1987. It is designed to encourage more individuals to invest in British quoted shares and is highly tax advantageous.

The scheme works as follows: anyone over the age of 18 can invest £200 a month or a total of £2,400 a year in U.K. shares listed on the stock exchange.

The money will have to be invested through an authorised manager, for example: a stockbroker, bank, or licensed dealer (see FIMBRA, Chapter 5).

As with other equities, regular dividends will be paid and there is also the chance of capital appreciation.

Providing the funds are left in the scheme for a minimum period (this will vary between one and nearly two years, depending on the actual month when you invested your money), the proceeds will normally be entirely free of both income tax and capital gains.

The plan will only apply to UK quoted shares and specifically excludes: preference shares, futures, options and one or two other specialised categories. Plan managers will have all the details and will know which investments qualify under the scheme.

Tax. The normal 29 per cent will be claimed back on your behalf by the Plan manager. There is no liability for higher rates of income tax. Additionally all profits will be free of capital gains tax.

Assessment. This looks like a good investment for almost everyone. Specially advantageous to higher rate taxpayers.

Long term lock ups

Certain types of investment, mostly offered by insurance companies, provide fairly high guaranteed growth in exchange for your undertaking to leave a lump sum with them or to pay regular premiums for a fixed period, probably ten years.

The list includes: life assurance policies, investment bonds and some types of National Savings certificates.

Life assurance policies

Definition. Life assurance can provide you with one of two main benefits: it can either provide your successors with money when you die or it can be used as a savings plan to provide you with a lump sum (or income) on a fixed date.

In the past, it was very much an 'either – or' situation: you chose whichever type of policy suited you and the insurance company paid out accordingly. In recent years, however, both types of scheme have become more flexible and many policies allow you to incorporate features of the other. This can have great advantages from the point of view of enabling you 'to have your cake and eat it'. But the result is that some of the definitions appear a bit contradictory.

There are three basic types of life assurance: whole life policies, term policies and endowment policies.

Whole life policies are designed to pay out on your death. In its most straightforward form, the scheme works as follows: you pay a premium every year and, when you die, your beneficiaries receive the money.

As with an ordinary household policy, the insurance only holds good if you continue the payments. If one year you did not pay and were to die, the policy would be void and your successors would receive nothing.

Term policies involve a definite commitment. As opposed to paying premiums every year, you elect to make regular payments for an agreed period of time: for example, up until such time as your children have completed their education, say ten years.

If you die during this period, your family will be paid the agreed sum in full. If you die after the end of the term (when you have stopped making payments), your family will normally receive nothing.

Certain term policies are more flexible. Instead of getting nothing back if you survive, in exchange for a higher premium you can arrange to have your payments returned to you as a lump sum at the end of the term.

Most policies, whether term or otherwise, pay the money in lump sum form. Under term assurance, it is possible, however, to arrange for the benefit to be paid out as regular income. This is known as *family income benefit*. The income payments will cease at the end of the insured term.

There is a fairly widespread view that term and whole life policies, while eminently sensible for people in their thirties or forties, are not really suitable for older people, since: on the one hand death is at some stage inevitable; while on the other, when children grow up, there is less requirement to provide for their security. Additionally, many people argue that when income is tight, as it often is on retirement, this is one expense that can cheerfully be dropped.

While generally true, the thinking could nevertheless prove short-sighted. A major problem for many widows is that, when their husband dies, part of his pension dies with him – leaving them with a significantly reduced income. A lump sum or regular income plan could make all the difference in helping to bridge the gap.

Alternatively – and for many this is a more attractive option – whole life or term can be converted into an endowment policy.

Endowment policies are essentially a savings plan. You sign a contract to pay regular premiums over a number of years and in exchange receive a lump sum on a specific date.

Most endowment policies are written for periods, varying from ten to twenty-five years. Once you have committed yourself, you have to go on paying every year (as with term assurance). There are heavy penalties if, after having paid for a number of years, you decide that you no longer wish to continue. According to the terms of the policy, you may receive a token lump sum based on the premiums you have paid; or you may receive nothing at all. This is especially likely to apply if you withdraw during the early years.

An important feature of endowment policies is that they are linked in with death cover. If you die before the policy matures, the remaining payments are excused and your successors will be paid a lump sum on your death.

Endowment policies are a very popular way of making extra financial provision for retirement. They combine the advantages of guaranteeing you a lump sum with a built-in life assurance proviso.

Options

Both whole life policies and endowment policies offer two basic options: with profits or without profits. Very briefly the difference is as follows:

Without profits. This is sometimes known as 'guaranteed sum assured'. What it means is that the insurance company guarantees you a specific fixed sum (providing of course you meet the various terms and conditions). You know the amount in advance and this is the sum you – or your successors – will be paid.

With profits. You are paid a guaranteed fixed sum plus an addition, based on the profits that the insurance company has made by investing your annual or monthly payments. The basic premiums are higher and, by definition, the profits element is not known in advance. If the insurance company has invested your money wisely, a 'with profits' policy provides a useful hedge against inflation. If its investment policy is mediocre, you could have paid higher premiums for very little extra return.

Unit linked. This is a refinement of the 'with profits' policy, in that the investment element of the policy is linked in with a unit trust.

Other basics. Premiums can normally be paid monthly or annually, as you prefer.

Size of premium varies enormously, depending on: the type of policy you choose and the amount of cover you want. Also, of course, some insurance companies are more competitive than others. As very general guidance, £20 a month would probably be a normal starting figure. Again as a generalisation, higher premiums tend to give better value as relatively less of your contribution is swallowed up in administrative costs.

As a condition of insuring you, some policies require that you have a medical check. This is more likely to apply if very large sums are involved. More usually, all that is required is that you fill in and sign a declaration of health. It is very important that this should be honestly completed: if you make a claim on your policy and it is subsequently discovered that you gave misleading information, your policy could be declared void and the insurance company could refuse to pay.

Most insurance companies offer a better deal if you are a non-smoker. Some also offer more generous terms if you are teetotal.

How to obtain. Policies are usually available either through banks or insurance companies. The biggest problem for most people is the sheer volume of choice. Another difficulty can be understanding the small print: terms and conditions which sound very similar may obscure important differences which could affect your benefit.

An accountant could advise you in general terms whether you are being offered a good deal or otherwise. However, if it is a question of choosing a specific policy best suited to your requirements, it is usually advisable to consult an insurance broker. For help in contacting a broker in your area, write to: **British Insurance Brokers' Association**, BIBA House, 14 Bevis Marks, London EC3A 7NT, T: 01-623 9043.

The Association of British Insurers (ABI) have a number of useful explanatory leaflets on life assurance. Contact **ABI**, Aldermary House, Queen Street, London EC4N 1TU, T: 01-248 4477.

Tax. Under current legislation, the proceeds of a qualifying policy – whether taken as a lump sum or in regular income payments (as in the case of Family Income Benefit) – are free of all tax.

Assessment. Life assurance is normally a sensible investment, whether the aim is to provide death cover or the benefits of a lump sum to boost your retirement income. It has the merit of being very attractive from a tax angle and, additionally certain policies provide good capital appreciation.

However, you are locked in to a long term commitment; and even more than most areas, choosing the right policy is very important. Shop around, take advice and, above all, do not sign anything unless you are absolutely certain that you understand every last dot and comma.

Investment bonds

Definition. This is the method of investing a lump sum with an insurance company, in the hope of receiving a much larger sum back at a specific date – normally ten years later.

All bonds offer life assurance cover as part of the deal.

A particular feature of some bonds is that the managers have wide discretion to invest your money in almost any type of security. The risk/reward ratio is, therefore, very high. While bonds can achieve significant capital appreciation, you can also lose a high percentage of your investment.

You receive no income on your bond but you have the option to withdraw up to 5 per cent of your initial investment each year, free of tax, for 20 years.

Companies normally charge a front end fee of around 5 per cent plus a small annual management fee, usually not related to performance.

Most financial institutions – banks, unit trusts, and others – offer investment bonds through their insurance subsidiaries. Accordingly, almost any type of financial advisor will have some knowledge of this area. See Chapter 5.

The performance of existing bonds is monitored each month in *Money Management* and other specialist magazines.

Tax. Tax treatment is very complicated, as it is influenced by your marginal income tax rate in the year of encashment. For this reason, it is generally best to buy a bond when you are working and plan to cash it after retirement.

Assessment. This investment is more likely to be attractive to the sophisticated investor, with high earnings in the years before retirement.

Watch out for changes

The financial services market is undergoing a major shake-up. Until now, the different institutions have tended to specialise in their own fields. The growing trend today, however, is for organisations to offer a far greater variety of services. This does not just apply to one or two individual giants. Whole sectors, such as building societies for example, look set to start operating across a much wider spectrum.

At the same time, some of the existing trade bodies (self-regulating organisations) are being combined and, in consequence of this merging, their terms of reference – and the various protection schemes they offer – are liable to be slightly altered.

If you are referred to a body whose name we have not mentioned, or if you are told that one we have no longer exists, this is likely to be the explanation. It is expected, however, that most of the addresses we have given will remain unaltered in terms of functioning as an advisory service.

5. Financial Advisors

If there is one golden rule when it comes to money matters, it must be: when in doubt, ask.

This applies as much if it is a term with which you are unfamiliar, used in connection with your pension; or whether you are wondering how best to invest your savings.

When thinking ahead to retirement planning, it is especially important to get as much advice as possible. Nearly everyone has a certain amount of leeway in budgeting for the future and the difference between an unwise choice and a sensible one could very significantly affect your standard of living.

While a great deal of unnecessary mystique seems to pervade the financial services sector, questions to do with money are often genuinely more complex than they first appear.

There may be important tax angles to consider. Phrases commonly used in conversation may, when written into a formal document, have legal implications of which you are unaware. The jargon is apt to be confusing: for example, the term 'bond' has a variety of different meanings. So too is the volume of propaganda. There are plenty of enticing advertisements seeming to offer the moon which, if you were to take them at face value without being totally sure that you understand the commitment, could prove a sorry mistake.

Moreover, whereas most professional advisors are extremely sound, not everyone who proffers advice is qualified to do so. Before parting with your money, it is essential to ensure that you are dealing with a registered member of a recognised institution.

Checking should become easier. Under the new Financial Services Bill, not only are those claiming to be specialists required to register with their appropriate professional body and obey its code of conduct but, as a further safeguard, the institutions themselves must comply with the regulations of a new government watchdog, the Securities and Investment Board.

Even if you have never done so before, there is no cause to feel hesitant about approaching financial advisors. Nor should you feel that because you have asked for advice, you are morally obliged to use a particular individual's services. Indeed, when it comes to investment decisions, you are strongly recommended to shop around in order to compare the many different options on offer.

As someone who may shortly be retiring, you are seen as a very attractive potential client especially if you are a member of a pension scheme with a sizeable commuted lump sum to invest.

However, before making contact, it is generally a good idea to try to sort out your priorities, for example: whether you are looking for capital growth or whether your main objective is to increase your income. Also, if you have any special plans such as helping your grandchildren or if you need several thousand pounds to improve your home, these too should be thought through in advance as they could affect the advice you receive.

A further reason for doing some advance thinking is that, whereas certain types of advisors – for example, insurance brokers – do not specifically charge you for their time, others such as accountants and solicitors charge fees by the hour. Drinking coffee in their office and musing aloud about the future delights of retirement may be a pleasant way of spending the afternoon but it can also work out to be pretty costly!

Choosing an advisor

When choosing an advisor, there are usually four main considerations: respectability, suitability, price and convenience.

Where your money is concerned, you cannot afford to take unnecessary risks. Merely establishing that an individual is a member of a recognised institution, while a basic safeguard, is insufficient recommendation if you want to be assured of dealing with someone who will personally suit you. The principle applies as much with friends, as with complete strangers.

If you are thinking of using a particular advisor whom you do not already know in a *professional* capacity, you should certainly check on their reputation and, ideally, talk to some of their existing clients. No one who is any good will object to your asking for references. On the contrary, most will be delighted if this means that the relationship will be founded on a basis of greater trust and confidence.

However, quite apart from their general competence, enlisting professional help is very much a question of 'horses for courses'. Just as you would hardly consult a divorce lawyer if you were planning to buy a house, so too in the financial field most practitioners have different areas of expertise. It is, therefore, important to establish that your advisor has the particular capability you require.

This issue is less of a consideration if you choose a sizeable firm, with at least four or five partners, since the likelihood is that between them they will be able to offer a mix of skills. But it can be a problem with the one or two man band who, though outstanding generalists, may lack the specialist knowledge if you require sophisticated advice in, say, tax planning or investment strategy.

Although some people enjoy bobbing up to London to consult their solicitor, or whoever, generally speaking it makes more sense to choose a firm that is reasonably accessible.

If you live in a part of the country where the choice of financial advisors is limited, you can approach one of the organisations listed on the following pages that maintain a register of members – or alternatively, you could ask your bank manager to recommend someone suitable.

Finally, you should be aware that some specialist advisors are in the business of selling; or at least stand to gain some financial advantage from persuading you that the investments they market are best for you.

In some cases, the commissions are publicly known. In others, they tend to be disguised. Also some brokers and dealers are tied agents for certain companies, so naturally will push their products to the exclusion of all else. To know where you stand, you should ask any agent whom he represents and if it is a single company or group, however excellent the prospect sounds, you should aim to investigate at least two or three other propositions before signing on the dotted line.

Accountants

Accountants are, above all, specialists in matters concerning taxation. If there is scope to do so, they can advise on ways of reducing your tax liability and can assess the various tax effects of different types of investment you may be considering.

Likewise, they can help you with covenants, the preparation of tax returns and if you are thinking of becoming self-employed or starting your own business, they will be able to assist you with some of the practicalities – such as registering for VAT and establishing a system of business accounts.

Additionally, they may be able to advise in a general way about pensions and your proposed investment strategy. Most accountants, however, do not claim to be experts in these fields and may refer their clients to stockbrokers and other advisors for these more specialised services.

If you need help in locating a suitable accountant, any of the following should be able to help you:

Institute of Chartered Accountants in England and Wales, PO Box 433, Chartered Accountants' Hall, Moorgate Place, London EC2P 2BJ.

Institute of Chartered Accountants in Scotland, 27 Queen Street, Edinburgh, EH2 1LA.

Institute of Chartered Accountants in Ireland, 87-89 Pembroke Road, Dublin 4, Eire. (This covers accountants in both Ulster and Eire).

Association of Certified Accountants, 29 Lincolns Inn Fields, London WC2.

Complaints. Anyone with a complaint against an accountant can write to the Secretary of the Institute or Association's Investigating Committee who, if the complaint is valid, will refer the matter to the Disciplinary Committee.

Banks

Most people need no introduction to the clearing banks since, if they have a bank account, they have probably been popping in and out of their local branch for years.

Yet despite the fact that the counter is usually well decorated with leaflets – and additionally some are apt to come in the post – many customers do not actually realise what a fully comprehensive service their bank can offer.

In addition to the normal account facilities, all the major high street banks offer (either direct or through one of their specialised subsidiaries) investment, insurance and tax planning services, as well as advice on drawing up a will, together with a host of special arrangements for small businesses.

While some of their services are excellent and moreover approaching your bank manager is a very convenient solution, especially if you are not very well up on stockbrokers and the like, the banks have tended to be criticised in the past for their rather pedestrian investment advice.

Again as a generalisation, most of their specialist services are not particularly cheap and for certain functions, such as the administration of estates, their fees could be higher than a solicitor's. Also, although this is not a criticism, you should be aware that the banks run their own unit trusts and insurance broking divisions and not surprisingly may direct their clients to these.

Brief information follows on the main clearing banks but there are other more specialised banks such as Williams and Glynn, Coutts, Hoares and overseas banks that are all part of the UK clearing system and can offer a very good service.

The addresses given are those of the head office.

Barclays Bank, Juxon House, 94 St. Paul's Churchyard, London EC4M 8EH.

Barclays offers free banking to customers whose current account is in credit or whose average current account is £500 during the during the quarterly charging period, even if at times it is temporarily overdrawn.

A range of investment services is offered by Barclay's Trust Company, both to clients and the public. You can either write to the above address or apply through your local Barclays Bank. There are services to customers in their home, including a charged-for-tax consultancy and a service for drawing up wills and trusts.

Personal investment advice is given by Barclays Unicorn Group at the above address or through your local branch. A team of District Service Managers throughout the country will provide investment counselling to customers and non-customers of the bank free of charge and without obligation.

Lloyds Bank, 71 Lombard Street, London EC3P 3BS.

Lloyds offers free banking to clients with accounts in credit or whose average current account balance during their one month charging period is £500, even if it is temporarily overdrawn.

Lloyds Financial Services and Trust Division chief office is at Capital House, 1/5 Perrymount Road, Haywards Heath, West Sussex RH16 3SP. There is a fee-paying service for customers and non-customers: you can apply for consultation with a specialist advisor through your Lloyds Bank branch. The Trust Division also provides a personal taxation and wills service and fees are calculated on a time basis.

Lloyds Bank Insurance Services (at the Haywards Heath address above) acts as an insurance broker on many kinds of personal insurance, including for example life assurance, pensions and health plans.

Lloyds Bank Unit Trust Managers (see London address) offer 12 unit trusts for investment. There is a minimum investment of £500 per trust and additional sums must not be for less than £100. There is also a regular savings scheme with a minimum of £25.

Lloyds Bank will also offer a full asset management service if you have more than £25,000. The service features a high interest investment account, linked to your current account, so any surplus funds are automatically put into your higher interest investment account – and any shortfall on your current account is covered. You have instant access to your current account up to £300 a day.

Midland Bank, Poultry, London EC2P 2BX.

Midland was the first high street bank to offer its customers free banking if their current account was in credit and also pioneered the idea of providing special services to assist retirement planning.

People aged 55 and over, who are within six months of retiring and have a high interest cheque account with the Midland are offered free personal financial counselling. The service includes reductions on Thomas Cook Holidays and there is also an excellent free booklet, entitled *Guide to Retirement – A New Beginning*.

The Midland Bank Trust Company offers advice and services on investment and portfolio management, tax and tax planning (including setting up deeds of covenant) and also on the preparation of wills and administration of estates.

Additionally, there are both a unit trust division (Midland Bank Unit Trusts) and one specialising in insurance and life assurance (Midland Bank Insurance Services).

Information about all these services is available through local branches of the Midland.

National Westminster Bank, 41 Lothbury, London EC2P 2BP.

National Westminster offers free banking to customers with current accounts in credit during the quarterly charging period.

The National Westminster Trust and Tax Services Section offers services to clients on a fee paying basis. You can apply at any branch of the bank or write to: Freepost, (KE 2355/2), PO Box 106, Bristol BS99 7XY. The services include: advice on drawing up a will and the administration of an estate, an investment management service which will devise an individual investment policy for you; and a personal taxation service. In certain circumstances for the elderly the investment management service can be extended to paying bills and household expenses.

National Westminster Insurance Services offers a 55-plus Bonus Benefit Plan to customers aged between 55 and 80 years. No medical examination is required. Write to: National Westminster Insurance Services Ltd., Freepost (BS 2614) Bristol BS99 7YS.

Investment services are provided by Nat West's County Bank Unit Trusts Ltd., which ofers a choice of 14 unit trusts. Also of interest will be three services linked to these unit trusts: UNITSAVE for people who wish to save as little as £20 per month and receive valuable loyalty bonuses; a monthly income plan which provides a high net income each month with potential for your capital to increase and, most recently introduced, an investment management service, minimum investment £5000. For information, write to: The Manager, County Bank Unit Trust Services, 161 Cheapside, London EC2V 6EU.

Royal Bank of Scotland, 42 St. Andrew Square, Edinburgh EH2 2YE.

The Royal Bank of Scotland offers free banking for customers whose current account is in credit.

The Bank's Executor and Trustee Services offer free advice in making a will, although the usual legal fees are applicable if you proceed. This is available to customers and non-customers and you should write to the Royal Bank of Scotland, Freepost, Edinburgh EH2 0DB. You can also write to this address or approach your local branch manager for a personal tax service. The service, again available to customers and non-customers, is charged according to the complexity of the work involved.

Information on the Royal Bank Investment Services can be obtained from the manager of your local branch or by writing to their investment manager in main centres. The Edinburgh address is: Royal Bank of Scotland, Investment Service, PO Box 40, 31 St. Andrew Square, Edinburgh EH2 2PS. There is a charge for the service but you will have your own individual investment policy tailored for your changing needs.

Complaints

The Banking Ombudsman acts as an independent arbiter, who aims to resolve complaints about the banking practices of the 19 banks that come within his orbit. These include all the main English and Scottish clearing banks and also Standard and Chartered.

Complaints can be handled on any aspect of personal banking, including insurance and trustee services. However, the Ombudsman's services do not extend to taking up disagreements if you are refused an overdraft or loan.

The address to which to write is: **The Banking Ombudsman**, Citadel House, 5-11 Fetter Lane, London EC4A 1BR.

Insurance brokers

The insurance business covers a very wide range from straightforward policies – such as motor or household insurance – to the rather more complex areas, including life assurance and pensions.

Quite apart from the confusion of the enormous choice of policies available and the importance of ensuring that you understand the conditions laid down in the small print, a further difficulty is the number of different categories of people – agents, salesmen, consultants, brokers – who may try to sell you insurance.

Unless you are already dealing with an insurance company whose advice you value, as a general rule you would be advised to consult an insurance broker since both individual brokers and the firms they represent must be registered with the Insurance Brokers' Registration Council, which operates a code of conduct.

An insurance broker should be able to help you choose the policies that are best suited to you, help you determine how much cover you require and explain any technical terms contained in the documents. He can also assist with any claims and advise you when renewals are necessary.

Although a condition of registration is that a broker must normally deal with a minimum of at least ten insurers and therefore be in a position to offer a comprehensive choice of policies, most companies pay insurance brokers on a commission basis; so, despite the code of conduct which emphasises that the customer's interest is paramount, it is possible that you could be offered advice that is not totally unbiased. If you are worried about this, you are perfectly entitled to ask a broker how much commission he is receiving.

Generally speaking, you are safer to use a larger brokerage with an established reputation. Also, before you take out a policy, it is advisable to consult several different brokers in order to get a better feel for the market.

The British Insurance Brokers' Association, which represents over 3,500 insurance broking businesses, can put you in touch with a member broker in your area. If you have a complaint you should contact their consumer relations department, which operates a conciliation service. BIBA also publishes a useful range of free information leaflets. Write to:

British Insurance Brokers' Association, BIBA House, 14 Bevis Marks, London EC3A 7NT, T: 01-623 9043.

Another organisation that you can contact in the event of a complaint against a registered broker is the Insurance Brokers' Registration Council. You should write to the Registrar, at:

Insurance Brokers' Registration Council, 15 St. Helen's Place, London EC3A 6DS.

Also useful to know about is the Association of British Insurers. It represents over 420 companies (as opposed to brokers), providing all types of insurance from life assurance and pensions to household and other general policies. About 90 per cent of the business done by British insurance companies is handled by members of ABI. The Association publishes a wide range of leaflets and booklets and will also intervene on your behalf, if you are in dispute with one of its member companies. There are regional offices in: Belfast, Birmingham, Bristol, Glasgow, Leeds, Liverpool, Manchester, Newcastle-upon-Tyne, Norwich and Southampton. The head office is at:

Association of British Insurers, Aldermary House, Queen Street, London EC4N 1TT, T: 01-248 4477.

Finally, there is the Insurance Ombudsman. The Ombudsman and his Council are paid for by the insurance companies in the scheme – over 170 belong – but maintain complete independence in all negotiations.

As with the ABI, the Ombudsman can only try to settle a dispute if the company in question is within the scheme. You can find this out from your insurance company, insurance broker, from a citizens' advice bureau – or from the Insurance Ombudsman Bureau.

You can only contact the Ombudsman after you have attempted to resolve the difficulty, at the highest level, with the company itself.

The Ombudsman exists to help private policy holders only and cannot take up the cudgels on behalf of commercial organisations, however small. The policy must have been written in the United Kingdom, Isle of Man or Channel Islands. Also, the Ombudsman is powerless to act if legal proceedings have been started.

While he can arbitrate on most issues, some matters are outside his scope. The Ombudsman cannot assist with third party claims and with certain types of dispute concerning life assurance (for example, actuarial decisions).

You must contact the Ombudsman within six months of the insurance company's final decision on the dispute, giving the details as briefly as possible. Currently, there is no charge for the service. You may accept or reject the Ombudsman's decision. If you reject it, your right to take legal action is not affected. If you want help from the Ombudsman, you should contact:

The Insurance Ombudsman Bureau, 31 Southampton Row, London WC1B 5HJ, T: 01-242 8613.

Other pension advisors

To individuals in paid employment

If you are (or have been) in salaried employment and are a member of an occupational pension scheme, the normal person to ask is the personnel manager or pensions adviser – or via them, the pension fund trustees.

Alternatively, if you have a problem with your pension you could approach your union, since this is an area where most unions are particularly active and well informed.

For wider information on how pension schemes work and how they are affected by legislation, you might find it useful to contact the *Company Pensions Information Centre* who publish a series of very good booklets, including: *How to Understand your Pension Scheme, Pensions for Women* and *How Changing Jobs Affects your Pension*. The Information Centre does not deal with individual cases. However, you may be able to pick up some helpful advice by attending one of their public talks which they arrange with Trade Unions, Chambers of Commerce, Citizens' Advice Bureaux and other groups. The address to contact is:

Company Pensions Information Centre, 7 Old Park Lane, London W1Y 3LJ, T: 01-493 4757.

If you are in need of specific help, a source to try could be the Occupational Pensions Advisory Service. This is a registered charity, with a network of over 100 unpaid advisors who can be contacted through Citizens' Advice Bureaux. OPAS mainly confines its help to the elderly and those in need, who cannot afford to consult a solicitor. Last year, the vast majority of enquiries were from early leavers affected by pension penalties.

Occupational Pensions Advisory Service, Room 327, Aviation House, 129 Kingsway, London WC2 6NN, T: 01-405 6922 Ext. 205.

Two other important organisations who, while they do not advise on individual cases, are interested in matters of principle and broader issues affecting the pensions debate. These are:

National Association of Pension Funds, 12-18 Grosvenor Gardens, London SW1W ODH, T: 01-730 0585.

Occupational Pensions Board, Government Buildings, Lynwood Road, Thames Ditton, Surrey KT7 ODP, T: 01-398 4242.

To employers or the self-employed

If you are self-employed and want to make pension arrangements, you would probably approach an insurance broker (see above). However, in certain circumstances you might be better off to pay for the services of a pension consultant.

The two roles are fairly similar. In general, however, pension consultants would normally only be used by employers and by individuals with significant self-employment income.

Another distinction is that, unlike most insurance brokers, pension consultants usually charge their clients fees, as opposed to receiving commission from insurance companies whose policies they sell. Although apparently expensive, the best consultants are independent specialists who can give very valuable advice.

While anyone can call himself a pension consultant, many bona fide consultants are members of the Society of Pension Consultants and must comply with its code of conduct.

If you contact the Society, it can put you in touch with a pension consultant in your area. Additionally, anyone with a complaint about a member consultant can write to the Secretary. For further information, contact:

Society of Pension Consultants, Ludgate House, Ludgate Circus, London EC4A 2AB, T: 01-353 1688.

Solicitors

Solicitors are specialists on subjects to do with the law or on matters that could have legal implications. They can assist with the purchase or rental of property, drawing up a will, preparing a deed of covenant – or if you are charged with some offence, either civil or criminal.

Additionally, their advice can be invaluable in vetting any important document before you sign it, for example: an employment contract, the purchase of a business, a trading arrangement or other form of contract, where either you or the other party is giving an undertaking of some kind.

A solicitor can also help with the legal formalities of setting up a business; trusts; guardianship arrangements or other agreement, where the intention is to make it binding. Likewise, a solicitor would normally be the first person to consult if you were thinking of suing an individual or commercial organisation.

If you do not have a solicitor (or if your solicitor does not have the specialist knowledge to advise on, say, a business matter), often the best way of finding a suitable lawyer is through the recommendation of a friend or of another professional advisor, such as an accountant or maybe your bank manager.

If you need a solicitor specifically about a business or professional matter, organisations such as chambers of commerce, small business associations, your professional institute or trade union may be able to put you in touch with someone in your area who has relevant experience.

Another solution is to consult the *Solicitors' Directory and Diary*, available in public libraries, which lists the names and addresses of solicitors all over the country, together with brief details about the type of work in which they specialise.

If you want fairly basic advice or information about your rights, you could approach a *Law Centre* (sometimes known as Neighbourhood or Community Law Centre). They are mainly to be found in towns and cities but exist in other parts of the country as well.

You can get the address by asking at your town hall or Citizens' Advice Bureau. Or you can write to the Law Centres Federation for the address of your nearest centre. The advice is normally free but if the matter is complex or likely to be protracted, the centre will probably refer you to a solicitor.

Law Centres Federation, Duchess House, 18-19 Warren Street, London W1P 5DB.

Legal aid

If you need a legal aid solicitor (or want to find out if you are eligible for legal aid), the place to go is your Citizens' Advice Bureau.

Ask for leaflet *The Legal Aid Guide and Financial Limits*, which will enable you to work out if you qualify for assistance. The financial limits are more generous than are generally supposed so it could be worth checking, even if you expect to be disappointed. If you *are* entitled to legal aid, your CAB will explain what is involved and will refer you to a legal aid solicitor.

Instead of going through your CAB, if you prefer you can contact the Law Society, care of its Legal Aid Head Office. You should write to the Secretary:

Legal Aid Head Office, Newspaper House, 8-16 Great New Street, London EC4 3BN, T: 01-353 7411.

Complaints

The *Law Society* is the professional body for solicitors and is responsible for ensuring its members observe proper standards of behaviour when dealing with clients.

The Society can investigate such complaints as delay in answering letters or enquiries; delay in dealing with your case; overcharging; dishonesty or deception.

If you have a complaint, you should write to the Professional Purposes Department of the Law Society, giving the name and address of your solicitor, together with details of the problem. Your letter should state that the Society can send a copy of it to your solicitor. On receiving your solicitor's reply (of which you will get a copy), the Law Society will decide what action should be taken.

If your solicitor has blatantly over-charged you, the Law Society can order him to reduce the fee, or if it appears that he has been incompetent, the Society may put you in touch with a new solicitor for a free one hour interview.

Only a court, however, can decide whether a solicitor has been incompetent or negligent and make him/her pay compensation. If you decide to take the matter to court, in the same way as if you were suing anyone else, you will have to pay a solicitor to act for you.

An independent Solicitors' Complaints Board, with rather more teeth than the Law Society, is expected to be set up during 1987 to handle complaints concerning solicitors. In the meantime, the address to which to write is:

The Law Society, Professional Purposes Department, 8 Bream's Buildings, London EC4A 1HP, T: 01-404 4355.

If you are unhappy with the Law Society's handling of your complaint, you may write to The Lay Observer whose opinion may be helpful if you decide to take legal proceedings. You must write within three months of the decision taken by the Law Society and you should quote the reference number on its correspondence to you.

The Lay Observer, Royal Courts of Justice, Strand, London WC2A 2LL.

General queries

For queries of a more general nature, you should approach:

The Law Society, 113 Chancery Lane, London WC2A 1PL, T: 01-242 1222.

Stockbrokers

Stockbrokers buy and sell shares quoted on the Stock Exchange and Unlisted Securities Market (USM) and as from the 'Big Bang' – end of October 1986 –

they also expect to deal in Over the Counter (OTC) shares. All stockbrokers handle gilts, which are government securities. The large firms also deal in overseas markets and maintain offices in the major centres including New York, Tokyo and Frankfurt.

Although London is the dominant UK stock exchange, there are also branches in: Manchester, Birmingham, Liverpool, Bristol, Glasgow and Belfast. Additionally, there is a Provincial exchange operated from London and an affiliated Irish exchange located in Dublin.

As well as buying and selling on their behalf, most clients look to their stockbroker for investment advice and, in some cases, total portfolio management. According to your temperament and expertise, you can give a stockbroker partial or total discretion – or insist that he consults you on every deal.

Stockbrokers do not earn fees but instead make their living by charging commission on every transaction. Whereas there used to be a scale rate, varying from $\frac{1}{2}$ per cent to 2 per cent according to the size of order, today this no longer applies. However, as before, small orders tend to be relatively more costly in commission terms.

Until a short while ago, the accepted wisdom was that it was pointless to go to a stockbroker unless you had at very least £50,000 to invest. However, this is rapidly changing. Some of the smaller firms, particularly in the provinces, are more than happy to deal privately for a client with half, or even less, this amount. Additionally, nearly all the major stockbrokers now run unit trusts and, because through these they are investing collectively for their clients, welcome quite modest investors, with around £2,000.

There are two ways of finding a stockbroker: either through recommendation or by writing to the Stock Exchange for a list of brokers. If you want an out-of-London stockbroker, you could write to one of the regional branches. See addresses below.

Alternatively, if you are more interested in investment trusts, you can write to the **Association of Investment Trust Companies** at 16 Finsbury Circus, London EC2M 7JP, for their booklet listing all stockbrokers who operate in this field.

Complaints. If you have a complaint about your stockbroker, the Stock Exchange advises that you approach the senior partner of the firm, to try to sort out the problem. If this fails, you can write to the Secretary of the Stock Exchange Council, who will investigate the complaint with the firm concerned and, if necessary, disciplinary action will be taken.

Stock Exchange addresses

London: The Stock Exchange, London EC2N 1HP, T: 01-588 2355.

Irish: The Stock Exchange, 28 Anglesea Street, Dublin 2, T: 0001-778808.

Midlands & Western: The Stock Exchange, Margaret Street, Birmingham B3 3JL, T: 021-236 9181. The Stock Exchange, St. Nicolas Street, Bristol BS1 1TH, T: 0272-24541.

Northern: The Stock Exchange, 6 Norfolk Street, Manchester M2 1DS, T: 061-833 0931. The Stock Exchange, Silkhouse Court, Tithebarn Street, Liverpool L2 2LT, T: 051-236 0869.

Northern Ireland: The Stock Exchange, Northern Bank House, 10 High Street, Belfast BT1 2BP, T: 0232-21094

Provincial: 21st Floor, The Stock Exchange, London EC2N 1HP, T: 01-588 2355.

Scottish: The Stock Exchange, Stock Exchange House, PO Box 141, 69 St. George's Place, Glasgow G2 1BU, T: 041-221 7060

Useful reading

An Introduction to Buying and Selling Shares, free from the Stock Exchange.

Other investment advisors

In recent years there has been an explosion of alternative investments to those that can only be purchased on the stock exchange. These include: Business Expansion Scheme (BES) opportunities, OTC shares (some but not all of these will feature on the stock exchange after the 'Big Bang') plus a variety of overseas trusts being marketed, often by direct mail, in this country.

While some of these investments offer attractive possibilities, others are more suspect – as are the individuals trying to sell them.

In order to protect the public, an association called the Financial Intermediaries, Managers and Brokers Regulatory Association (formerly NASDIM) has been formed, which operates a strict code of conduct, has a disciplinary procedure and is one of the bodies recognised by the Securities and Investment Board.

FIMBRA requires its members to meet a number of stringent criteria. These include: sufficient financial resources, annual audits, a proper client contract if there is any discretionary investment and professional indemnity insurance.

While some very respectable dealers may not join FIMBRA, membership has been soaring in anticipation of the Financial Services Act and, unless you have other first class references, generally speaking you would be wise to check whether the individual or company he represents is licensed by FIMBRA. You should contact the Secretary:

Financial Intermediaries, Managers and Brokers Regulatory Association, 22 Great Tower Street, London EC3R 5AQ, T: 01-283 4814.

Budget Planner

Whether you are about to retire tomorrow or not for several years' time, completing the following Budget Planner (even if there are a great many gaps) is well worth the effort.

If retirement is imminent, then hopefully doing the arithmetic in detail will not only reassure you but will enable you to plan your future life with the confidence of really knowing how you stand financially. Moreover, even at this stage, there are probably a variety of options available to you and just examining the figures you have written down will highlight the areas of greatest flexibility.

An imaginative tip, given to us by one of the retirement magazines, is to start living on your retirement income some six months before you retire. Not only will you see if your budget estimates are broadly correct but since most people err on the cautious side when they first retire, you will have the added bonus of all the extra money you will have saved.

If retirement is still some years ahead, there will be both more unknowns and more opportunities. When assessing the figures, you should take account of your future earnings; and perhaps more to the point, since your pension may well be based on it, what your final salary is likely to be. Also, though it may mean stinting a bit now, you should consider whether (if your scheme allows it) you should be paying AVCs and/or making other investments. Imprecise as they will be, the Budget Planner estimates you have made in the various income/expenditure columns should indicate whether, unless you take action now, you could be at risk of having to make serious adjustments in your standard of living.

To be on the safe side, you must assume some increase in inflation. Equally, everyone should budget for a nest egg, to pay for any emergencies or special events – perhaps a family wedding – that may come along.

1. Possible savings when you retire

Item   *Est. monthly savings*

National Insurance contributions ....

Pension payments ....

Travel expenses to work ....

Bought lunches ....

Incidentals at work, e.g. drinks with
    colleagues, collections for presents ....

Special work clothes ....

Concessionary travel ....

Free NHS prescriptions ....

Mature Drivers' Insurance Policy ....

Life Assurance Payments and/or
    possible endowment policy premiums ....

Other ....

TOTAL ....

N.B. You should also take into account reduced rates/running costs, if you move to a smaller home; any expenses for dependent children that may cease; plus other costs, e.g. mortgage payments, that may end around the time you retire. Also the fact that you may be in a lower tax bracket.

2. Possible extra outgoings when you retire

Items   *Est. monthly cost*

Extra heating/lighting bills . . . .

Extra spending on hobbies and other entertainment . . . .

Replacement of company car . . . .

Private health care insurance . . . .

Cost of substituting other perks,
  e.g. expense account lunches . . . .

Out-of-pocket expenses for voluntary
  work activity . . . .

Other . . . .

TOTAL . . . . , , ...

N.B. Looking ahead, you will need to make provision for any extra home comforts you might want; and also, at some point, of having to pay other people to do some of the jobs that you normally manage yourself. If you intend to take out a covenant for your grandchildren or a charity, this too should be included on the list. The same applies to any new private pension or savings plan, that you might want to invest in to boost your long term retirement income.

Note on Table 3

The British tax system is a complicated one and you should certainly take professional advice if you are in any doubt at all. However, if you fill in the following table carefully, it should give you a pretty good idea of your income after retirement and enable you to make at least provisional plans.

Remember too that you may have one or two *capital sums* to invest, such as:

- the commuted lump sum from your pension

- money from an endowment policy

- gains from the sale of company shares (SAYE or other share option scheme)

- profits from the sale of your home or other asset.

3. Expected sources of income on retirement

A. *Income Received Before Tax*

State Basic Pension . . . .

Graduated Pension . . . .

SERPS . . . .

Occupational Pension(s) . . . .

State Benefits . . . .

Other earnings . . . .

Total . . . .

Less Personal Tax Allowance . . . .

Basic Rate Tax . . . .

TOTAL A . . . .

B. *Income Received After Tax*

Dividends (Gilts, Unit Trusts,
Shares, etc.) . . . .

Bank Deposit Account . . . .

Building Society Interest . . . .

Annuity Income . . . .

Other . . . .

TOTAL B . . . .

TOTAL A & TOTAL B . . . .

Less Higher Rate Tax (if any) . . . .

Plus Other Tax-free Receipts . . . .

Investment Bond Withdrawals . . . .

National Savings Interest . . . .

Other . . . .

TOTAL NET INCOME . . . .

4. Unavoidable outgoings

Items   *Est. monthly cost*

Food . . . .

Rent or mortgage repayments . . . .

Rates . . . .

Repair and maintenance costs . . . .

Heating . . . .

Lighting and other energy . . . .

Telephone . . . .

TV licence/rental . . . .

Household insurance . . . .

Clothes . . . .

Laundry, cleaners bills, shoe repair . . . .

Domestic cleaning products . . . .

Misc. services, e.g. plumber, window cleaner . . . .

Car (incl. licence, petrol etc.) . . . .

Other transport . . . .

Regular savings/life assurance . . . .

HP/other loan repayments . . . .

Outgoings on health . . . .

Other . . . .

TOTAL . . . .

N.B. Before adding up the total, you should look at the 'Normal additional expenditure' list, as you may well want to juggle some of the items between the two.

5. Normal additional expenditure

Items	*Est. monthly cost*
Gifts	
Holidays	
Newspapers/books	
Drink	
Cigarettes/tobacco	
Hairdressing	
Toiletries/cosmetics	
Entertainment (hobbies, outings, home entertaining etc.)	
Misc. subscriptions/membership fees	
Charitable donations	
Covenants	
Expenditure on pets	
Other	
TOTAL	

N.B. For some items, such as holidays and gifts, you may tend to think in annual expenditure terms. However, for the purpose of comparing monthly income versus outgoings, it is probably easier if you itemise all the expenditure in the same fashion. Moreover, if you need to save for a special event such as your holiday, it helps if you get into the habit of putting so much aside every month (or even weekly).

6. Your Home

One of the most important decisions to be taken as you approach retirement is where you will live.

To many people, one of the biggest attractions is the pleasure of moving home. No longer tied to an area within easy commuting distance of work, they can indulge their cherished dreams of a wisteria-covered cottage in the Cotswolds or a white-washed villa in some remote Spanish resort.

While this could turn out to be everything they hoped for, and more, a problem is that we are so conditioned to the idea that retirement means moving to a cosy little place, preferably miles from civilisation, that many people rush full steam ahead without any real assessment of the pros and cons.

It is normally sensible at least to examine the other options, even if you end up rejecting them. An obvious possibility is to stay where you are and perhaps adapt your present home to make it more suitable for your requirements. You might move in to live with family or friends. Or looking further ahead, you could consider buying or renting some form of 'sheltered' accommodation.

Before you come to any definite decision, first ask yourself a few down-to-earth questions.

What are your main priorities? To be closer to your family? To have a smaller, more manageable home that will be easier to run – and less expensive? To realise some capital in order to provide you with extra money for your retirement? To live in a specific town or village, which you know you like and where you have plenty of friends? Or to enjoy the security of being in accommodation that offers some of the facilities you may want as you become older, such as a resident caretaker and the option of having some of your meals catered?

Whatever choice you make is bound to have its advantages and drawbacks, but, if you weigh these up, you will be far less likely to take a decision which – while attractive in the short term – you may later regret.

Staying put

While there may be plenty of arguments for moving there are probably just as many for staying where you are. Moving house can be a traumatic experience at the best of times and even more so as you become older, when emotional ties are harder to break and precious possessions more painful to part with, as is usually the necessity especially when moving somewhere smaller.

Although ideally you may want to remain where you are, you may feel that your home is really too large or inconvenient for you to manage in the future. However, before you heave your last sigh of regret and put it on the market, it is worth considering whether there are ways of adapting it to provide what you want.

If your house is too big, you might think about re-using the space in a better way. Would it be possible, for example, to turn a bedroom into a small upstairs study? Or perhaps you could convert a spare room into a separate workroom for hobbies and get rid of the clutter from the main living area? Equally, have you thought about letting one or two rooms? As well as solving the problem of wasted space, it would also bring in some extra income.

A few judicious home improvements invested in now could make the world of difference in terms of comfort and practicality. Many of us carry on for years with totally inefficient heating systems that could be improved relatively easily and cheaply. Stairs need not necessarily be a problem, even when you are very much older, thanks to the various types of stair lifts now on the market. Even so, a few basic facilities installed on the ground floor could save your legs in years to come. Similarly, gardens can be endlessly replanned to suit changing requirements: for example, extending the areas of lawn or paving could spare you hours of exhausting weeding.

Moving to a new home

If you do decide to move, the sooner you start looking for your new home the better. There is no point in delaying the search until you retire and then rushing round expecting to find your dream house in a matter of weeks. With time to spare, you will have a far greater choice of properties and are less likely to indulge in any panic buying.

While a smaller house will almost certainly be easier and cheaper to run, make sure that it is not so small that you are going to feel cramped. Remember that when you are both at home, you may need more room to avoid getting on top of each other. Also if your family lives in another part of the country, you may wish to have them and your grandchildren to stay. Conversely, beware of taking on commitments such as a huge garden. While this might be a great source of enjoyment when you are in your sixties, it could prove a burden as you become older.

Moving house can be an expensive exercise. It is estimated that the cost is between five and ten per cent of the value of a new home, once you have totted up such extras as removal charges, insurance, stamp duty, legal fees and estate agents' commission. If you plan any repairs, alterations or decorations, the figure will be considerably higher. On the other hand, if you move to smaller or cheaper accommodation you will be able to release money for other uses.

If you are thinking of moving out of the neighbourhood, there are other factors to be taken into account such as: access to shops and social activities, proximity to friends and relatives, availability of public transport and even health and social support services. While these may not seem particularly important now, they could become so in the future. Couples who retire to a seemingly 'idyllic' spot often return quite quickly. New friends are not always easy to make. So-called 'retirement areas' can mean that you are cut off from a normal cross-section of society and health services are likely to be over-taxed.

After a hard week's wheeling and dealing it is tempting to wax lyrical about exchanging the rat race for a life of rustic solitude. While retiring to the country can be glorious, city dwellers should, however, bear in mind some of the less attractive sides of rural living. Noise, for example low flying aircraft and church bells, can be an unexpected irritant. If you are not used to it, living near a silage pit or farm can also be an unpleasant experience.

Prices in village shops are often higher than in city supermarkets and bus services tend to be more infrequent. Finally, would a small village offer sufficient scope to pursue your interests once the initial flurry of activity is over?

Even if you think you know an area well, check it out properly before coming to a final decision. If possible take a self-catering let for a couple of months, preferably out of season when rents are low and the weather is bad. A good idea is to limit your daily spending to your likely retirement income rather than splurge as most of us do on holiday.

This is even more pertinent if you are thinking of moving abroad, where additional difficulties can include learning the language, lower standards of health care and the danger of losing contact with your friends. Another problem for ex-patriates could be a change in the political climate, resulting perhaps on the one hand in your not being so welcome in your adopted country and on the other, in a drop in the purchasing power of your pension. For more information on the tax and other financial implications of moving abroad, see Chapter 3.

Removals

Transporting your worldly goods from A to B is an exhausting business. Professional help can remove many of the headaches if carried out by a reputable firm. Not only will they heave all the heavy furniture around for you, but they will also wrap your china and knick-knacks safely in packing cases which they provide as part of the service. A useful organisation to contact is:

British Association of Removers, 277 Gray's Inn Road, London WC1X 8SY, T:01-837 3088.

They will send you a free leaflet advising you on what to do when you move house and a list of approved removal firms.

Moving in with family or friends

This may be accommodation such as a self-contained flat or actually living together as part of the family. It may be possible to get a home improvement grant from your local council to help with any conversion costs. Ask about the availability of such grants *before* any work is started.

There are many advantages to such an arrangement. While you are active, you can contribute to the household. Should you become frail or ill, help will be at hand.

Living together can also be fraught with problems, however. You only need to think back to any bachelor flat-sharing days to be reminded of the countless petty arguments – over washing up, noise or bills – that can develop if you are not careful.

As a general precaution, try to work out in advance any potential problems or you may have a month of honeymoon and years of regret. Questions worth considering include: whether you will share any meals, social life or transport; whether you will contribute in any practical ways, like baby-sitting, shopping, cleaning or looking after the house during the family's holidays; also, whether you can keep a pet and have friends to stay.

Money is also a common source of dispute. Decide whether you will have your own telephone or whether you will share one. If you will be paying rent, make it a formal arrangement exactly as if you were a normal tenant. You must agree a set figure: what it will cover, how it will be assessed in future and how it will be paid, i.e. weekly, monthly, cash or standing order. If you make a contribution towards the cost of any conversion work, work out beforehand how you would be reimbursed should the arrangement have to be terminated for one reason or another.

Living with family or friends is generally an informal arrangement. However, it is worth having a word with your solicitor or local housing advice centre about how it might affect your rights and obligations as either landlord or tenant. In particular, you should take advice before embarking on any construction work, such as a self-contained 'granny flat', which might affect the property's exemption from Capital Gains Tax in the future.

Sharing with friends

Yet another possibility is to share your own home with one or two friends.

For some this can be a perfect solution, but the same pitfalls as living with your family apply, so work out the arrangements carefully beforehand. Legal advice is an absolute 'must' in these circumstances. Your solicitor or housing advice centre will be able to explain any important points that could affect you, as will your building society or bank should you be considering actually buying a property together.

Sheltered accommodation

The term 'sheltered accommodation' covers a wide variety of housing but generally means property with a warden and some communal facilities such as living rooms, garden, laundry and optional meals. Designed to bridge the gap between the family house and residential care, such housing offers continued independence for the fit and active within a secure environment. Much of it is owned and run by local authorities, housing associations and charities. There are also an increasing number of private developments and so-called 'retirement homes' now on the market, for sale or rent, at prices to suit all pockets.

Many of the more attractive developments – and the most expensive – are in converted country houses of architectural or historic merit.

As a general rule, you have to be under 70 when you apply. While you may not wish to move into this type of accommodation just now, if the idea interests you in the long term it is worth planning ahead as there are often very long waiting lists.

Full details on the various types of sheltered accommodation, together with a price guide and some addresses, are given in Chapter 13.

Other options

Boarding houses

At least 30,000 people live in privately-run premises such as boarding houses, guest houses, hotels or hostels at which they have accommodation, meals and some services, but not nursing care.

If you are attracted to this idea, make sure you are dealing with a reputable establishment. Following evidence that many retired people were being 'ripped off' by their landlords, anyone offering this type of accommodation to four or more people must now register with the local social services department. For those who qualify for supplementary benefit, it may also be possible to get help with board and lodging costs.

Caravan or mobile home

Many retired people consider living in a caravan or mobile home which they keep either in a relative's garden or on an established site, possibly at the seaside or in the country. You may already own one as a holiday home which you are considering turning into more permanent accommodation.

If you want to live in a caravan on your own or other private land, you will require planning permission and a site licence from your local council. Contact your local Housing Development Officer. If on the other hand you want to keep it on an established site, make absolutely sure that the site owner has all the necessary permissions. Stories abound of people who have been taken for a ride by unscrupulous operators. Find out what conditions the proprietor attaches to any letting agreement as well as your rights regarding security of tenure and resale. Legal advice is strongly advisable.

That said, it should also be noted that caravans are not really very suitable as long-term accommodation for the over 60s. They tend to be damp as well as cramped and what may have been an enjoyable adventure on holiday may soon pall when it is your only option. However, if you do decide to go ahead with the plan, it is a good idea to subscribe to the magazine *Mobile Home*, available through your local newsagent.

Making your home more practical

Unless you are determined to sell, it is sensible to set about any home improvement plans earlier rather than later. For one thing, these are often easier to afford when you are still earning a regular salary. For another, any building work is tiresome and most people find it easier to put up with the mess when they are not living among it 24 hours a day. Thirdly, if you start early, you will enjoy the benefit that much sooner.

A perhaps unnecessary point to mention is that when embarking on changes a specific aim should be to make your home as economic, labour-saving and convenient as possible. A reason for saying this is that many couples become so involved with the decorative aspects that they forget to think about some of the longer term practicalities which, at next to no extra cost, could have been incorporated along with the other work.

Heating and insulation

When you retire, you may be at home more during the day so are likely to be using your heating more intensively. One of the best ways of reducing the bills is to get your house properly insulated.

Heat escapes from a building in four main ways: through the roof, walls, floor and through loose-fitting doors and windows. Insulation can not only cut the heat loss dramatically but will usually more than pay for itself within four or five years.

Loft insulation

As much as 25 per cent of heat in a house escapes through the loft. The answer is to lay a layer of glass fibre insulating material, at least 100mm (4 inches) thick, between or over the roof joists. You can lay this yourself quite easily and the materials are readily available from builders merchants. If you need assistance, contact the **National Association of Loft Insulation Contractors**, P.O. Box 12, Haslemere, Surrey GU27 3AN (T:0428 54011) who will be able to advise on a good local builder. Alternatively, your local Age Concern group or volunteer bureau may be able to help.

Loft insulation grants. If you have less than 30mm of loft insulation, you can get a grant for 66 per cent of the cost up to a maximum of £69. If you are disabled or over retirement age and receive supplementary pension or housing benefit, you can get a 90 per cent grant up to a maximum of £95. A condition of receiving the grant is that the hot and cold water tanks and pipes in the loft are also lagged, where this has not already been done.

Contact your local council for an application form but do not start work until the council has given its approval. The Department of Environment has a free leaflet *Save Money on Loft Insulation*, which explains what to do and how to get help. This is obtainable from any local authority housing department.

Doors and windows

A further 25 per cent of heat escapes through single-glazed windows, half of which could be saved through double-glazing. There are two main types: sealed units .

Compared with other forms of insulation, double glazing is expensive; however, there are now a number of DIY systems on the market. If using a contractor, make sure that the company you deal with is a member of the **Glass and Glazing Federation**, 6 Mount Row, London W1. (T:01-629 8334).

Effective draught-proofing saves heat loss as well as keeping out cold blasts of air. It is also relatively cheap and easy to install. For gaps around windows and doors, use compression seals that can be taped or tacked onto the frames. For very loose fitting frames, gap fillers that can be squeezed from a tube provide a more efficient seal between frame and surround. For advice about contractors, contact: the **Draught Proofing Advisory Association**, P.O. Box 12, Haslemere, Surrey GU27 3AN, T:0428-54011.

Heat loss can also be considerably reduced through heavy hanging curtains (both lined and interlined) over windows and doors. Make sure all curtains cover the window sill or rest on the floor. It is better to have them too long than too short.

Grants. Recipients of supplementary benefit may qualify for a single payment, on the basis of 'exceptional need' to help with the cost of buying materials for draught proofing. Contact your local social security office for details.

Cavity wall insulation

More heat is lost through the walls than perhaps anywhere else in the house: it can be as much as 35 per cent. Cavity wall insulation involves pumping a foam or similar type of insulating material into the cavity through holes drilled in the outside wall.

It is work for a specialist and consequently is one of the most expensive forms of insulation, costing from around £150 for a terraced house up to £600 to £900 for a fully detached house. Against this, it is estimated that you could save up to 25 per cent on your annual heating bill.

Solid wall insulation can be considerably more expensive, as can walls with tile hanging or weather boarding.

For addresses of contractors, contact:

External Wall Insulation Association, P.O. Box 12, Haslemere, Surrey G27 3AN, T:0428-54011.

Cavity Foam Bureau, P.O. Box 79, Oldbury, Warley, West Midlands B69 4BW, T:021-544 4949.

Insulating the floor

Up to 15 per cent of heat loss can be saved through filling the cracks or gaps in the floorboards and skirting. If you can take up your floorboards, a glass fibre blanket can be extremely effective when fixed underneath the joists. Filling spaces with papier mache or plastic wood will also help especially if a good felt or rubber underlay is then laid under the carpet.

Hot water cylinder insulation

An insulating jacket around your hot water cylinder will cut wastage by three-quarters. Most hot water tanks now come ready supplied with insulation. If not, the jacket should be at least 80mm thick and will cost around £10.

Jackets come in various sizes, so measure your cylinder before buying. Only purchase one that carries BSI's kitemark no. 5615. If you have difficulty in finding a suitable jacket locally, contact the **Insulating Jacket Manufacturers Federation**, Little Burton West, Derby Street, Burton-on-Trent, Staffs DE14 1PP, T:0283-63815.

Methods of heating

It may be possible to save money by using different fuels or by heating parts of your house off different systems. This could apply especially if some rooms are only occasionally used.

Your local high street gas and electricity showrooms can advise on heating systems, running costs and energy conservation, as well as heating and hot water appliances. Your local office of the **Solid Fuel Advisory Council** (see telephone directory) will also give free advice and information on all aspects of solid fuel heating, including appliances and installation.

The oil industry does not have an advisory council as such but the **Heating and Ventilating Contractors' Association**, ESCA House, 34 Palace Court, London W2 4HY, T:01-229 2488, has a home heating enquiry line (T:01-229 5543) and can advise on all types of oil central heating.

If you are in London, a visit to the **Building Centre**, 26 Store Street, London WC1E 7BT, T:01-637 1022, could save you a lot of leg work. It has a very wide range of appliances on display with experts on hand to advise you.

The environmental lobby group **Friends of the Earth**, 377 City Road, London EC1B 1NA, T:01-837 0731, will provide unbiased advice on heating and insulation. Enclose sae when writing to them.

Shopping note. Many people get rushed into expensive purchases on the promise of cheaper energy bills. A point to remember when comparing, say, gas with electricity is that fuel prices are volatile and relative cost advantages are not always maintained. If you have an otherwise adequate system, it could be false economy to exchange it for the sake of a small saving in current heating costs.

Buying and installing heating equipment

When buying equipment, check that it has been approved by the appropriate standards approvals board.

For electrical equipment, the letters to look for are BEAB (British Electrotechnicals Approvals Board) or CCA (Cenelec Certification Agreement), which is the European Community equivalent.

For gas appliances, look for the BSI kitemark, which denotes performance, reliability and safety. The same applies for domestic solid fuel appliances, which should be approved by the Solid Fuel Appliances Approval Scheme (see sales literature)

When looking for contractors to install your equipment, check that he/she is a member of the relevant trade association.

Electricians should either be approved by the **National Inspection Council for Electrical Installation Contracting**, 237 Kennington Lane, London SE11 5Q1, T:01-582 7746, or be members of the **Electrical Contractors Association**, 34 Palace Court, London W2 4HY, T:01-229 1266. Local electricity showrooms maintain a list of approved contractors.

Gas appliances can either be installed by British Gas or by a member of the **Confederation for the Registration of Gas Installers (CORGI)**.

The relevant associations for solid fuel and oil central heating installers are respectively the **Solid Fuel Advisory Service** (see local telephone directory) and the **Heating and Ventilating Contractors' Association**, ESCA House, 34 Palace Court, London W2 4HY, T:01-229 2488.

Tips for reducing your heating bills

Energy can be saved in lots of small ways. Taken together, they could amount to quite a large cut in your heating bills. You may find some of the following ideas worth considering:

● Set your central heating timer and thermostat to suit the weather. A saving of half an hour or one degree can be substantial.

● A separate thermostat on your hot water cylinder set at around 140 degrees Fahrenheit will enable you to keep hot water for taps at a lower temperature than for the heating system.

● If you run your hot water off an immersion heater, have a time switch fitted attached to an Economy 7 meter so that the water is heated at the cheap rate overnight. An override switch will enable you to top up the heat during the day if necessary.

● Showers are more economical than baths as well as being easier to use in your eighties when you become older.

● Reflective foil sheets put behind your radiators help to reduce heat loss through the walls.

● Switch off or reduce the heating in rooms not being used.

● If you have an open fire, a vast amount of heat tends to be lost up the chimney. A wood burning stove can help reduce heat loss as well as maximising the amount of heat you get from your wood or solid fuel in other ways. If you dislike the idea of losing the look of an open fire, there are now a number of appliances on the market that are open fronted and fit flush with the fireplace opening. Contact your local Solid Fuel Advisory Service for further information.

● Finally, it is a good idea to get in the habit of reading your electricity and gas meters regularly. This will help you keep track of likely bills.

Other useful addresses

Electricity Consumers' Council, Brook House, 2-16 Torrington Place, London WC1E 7LL, T:01-636 5703.

This is a statutory body representing electricity consumers' interests in England and Wales at national level.

Alternatively, if you have a problem about electricity which you cannot resolve with the Area Board, approach your local **Electricity Consultative Council** *which is independent of the Electricity Supply Industry and deals with complaints and enquiries from consumers. Addresses are as follows:*

Eastern Area: 8 Arcade Street, Ipswich, Suffolk IPI IEJ, T:0473-59355.

East Midlands: Caythorpe Road, Lowdham, Nottingham NG14 7EA, T:0602-663208/663748.

London: Newspaper House, 8-16 Great New Street, London EC4A 3BN, T:01-353 6738.

Merseyside and North Wales: First Floor, Barratt House, North John Street, Liverpool L2 6RR, T:051-236 8681.

Midlands: Shawton House, 794 Hagley Road West, Oldbury, Warley, West Midlands B68 OPJ, T:021-422 8087.

North Eastern: Room 103, Centro House, Cloth Market, Newcastle-upon-Tyne NE1 1UA, T:0632-322780.

North Western: Longridge House, Longridge Place, Corporation Street, Manchester M4 3AJ, T:061-834 4362.

Southern: 8a St. Mary's Butts, Reading, Berks RG1 2LN, T:0734-599657.

South Eastern: 50 St. John's Road, Tunbridge Wells, Kent TN4 9NY, T:0892-20947/8.

South Wales: Caradog House, St. Andrew's Place, Cardiff CF1 3UF, T:0222-24585/8.

South Western: Northernhay House, Northernhay Place, Exeter, Devon EX4 3RL, T:0392-58968.

Yorkshire: Wetherby Road, Scarcroft, Leeds LS14 3HS, T:0532-892038.

Gas Consumers' Council, 4th Floor, 162 Regent Street, London W1R 5TB, T:01-439 0012.

This is the statutory body representing consumers' interests in England, Wales and Scotland. It is likely to be changing its address towards the end of 1986 but, at time of writing, has not yet found suitable accommodation. The telephone number given above will, however, continue to be manned until well into 1987.

If you have a query or problem about gas which you cannot resolve with your area gas board, you can approach your **Regional Gas Consumers' Council**. Addresses are as follows:

Scotland: 86 George Street, Edinburgh EH2 3BU, T:031-226 6523.

Northern: Plummer House, Market Street, Newcastle-upon-Tyne NE1 6NR, T:0632-619561.

North Western: Boulton House, Chorlton Street, Manchester M1 3HY, T:061-236 1926.

North Eastern: 3rd Floor, National Deposit House, 1 Eastgate, Leeds LS2 7RL, T:0532-439961.

East Midlands: Pennine House, 31-33 Millstone Lane, Leicester LE1 5JN, T:0533-536633.

West Midlands: Broadway House, Calthorpe Road, Birmingham B15 1TH, T:021-454 5510 and 021-455 0285.

Wales: Caradog House, St. Andrew's Place, Cardiff CF1 3BE, T:0222-26547.

Eastern: 51 Station Road, Letchworth, Herts SG6 3BQ, T:0462-685399

North Thames: 18 Gt. Marlborough Street, London W1V 1AF, T:01-437 7422.

South Eastern: Helena House, 348 High Street, Sutton, Surrey SM1 1QA, T:01-642 1127.

Southern: 2nd Floor, Hill House, 189 Old Christchurch Road, Bournemouth BH1 1JX, T:0202-26654.

South Western: Third Floor, Prudential Building, 115 Armada Way, Plymouth PL1 1HP, T:0752-667707.

Domestic Coal Consumers' Council, Gavrelle House, 2 Bunhill Row, London EC1Y 8LL, T:01-638 8914.

You should contact the Council if you need help in resolving a dispute with your coal merchant.

Paraffin Heating Advisory Council, 121 Gloucester Place, London W1H 3PJ, T:01-935 8180.

Advises on all aspects of paraffin heating.

Useful reading

The Government **Energy Efficiency Office**, Room 1312 Thames House South, London SW1 4AJ, publishes a number of useful guides (free) on insulating and heating your home:

> *Make the Most of Your Heating*
> *Handy Hints to Help You at Home*
> *Help with Your Winter Heating*
> *How to Get Help with Insulation*
> *Cutting Home Energy Costs – a step-by-step monergy guide (Gas, Electricity, Solid Fuel, Oil and Liquid Petroleum Gas editions)*

The **Energy Projects Office**, 2-4 Bigg Market, Newcastle-upon-Tyne NE1 1UW (T:0632-615677) can supply a series of 'Briefing Sheets' on key aspects of energy conservation in the home.

Age Concern and the **Health Education Council** produce a free leaflet *Warmth in Winter*, available from Citizens Advice Bureaux or from Age Concern. Age Concern also publishes a free fact sheet *Help with Heating*.

Improvement and repair

Building work is notoriously expensive and can be a major deterrent to doing some of the alterations to your home that may be necessary. Before abandoning the idea, it is worth investigating whether you could take advantage of some of the various grants or tax relief available.

A bank loan may be the simplest way of raising funds for most repairs and improvements. Tax relief is available on the interest paid on loans up to £30,000 for home improvements in the same way as for a mortgage. 'Improvements' in this sense cover all permanent alterations to a building or land, such as: extensions, double-glazing, a damp course, central heating, insulation, loft conversion, building a garage, converting a house into flats or landscaping a garden.

Because tax relief at 29 per cent is given through a reduction in the interest charged on your improvement loan, you enjoy the benefit whether or not you pay basic rate tax.

Other work like rewiring or retiling a roof is likely to be classified as 'repairs' and would not be tax allowable. If you plan a major job, check this in advance.

Improvements and repair grants

Major improvements and structural repairs, especially to older houses, often qualify for grants from the local council as does conversion work such as creating a granny flat. Most grants are discretionary and are more likely to be given either if the council has a policy of encouraging improvements or if a member of the household is disabled. There are four types of grant as follows:

Improvement Grant. Designed to improve homes to a good standard or to provide additional housing through conversions. Grants are not normally available to enlarge a house or for the installation of central heating unless it forms part of a major improvement scheme.

Intermediate Grant. Designed for putting in missing standard amenities such as: bath, inside lavatory, and running hot water. These grants are mandatory and are yours *by right*, providing you meet the normal eligibility conditions (see 'Eligibility' below).

Repairs Grant. Designed for major structural repairs – such as to roofs, floors, walls or foundations – to houses or flats built before 1919. Routine maintenance work, like rewiring or the replacement of worn fixtures, does not qualify.

Special Grant. This is only available to the owner of a multi-occupied property, where tenants share facilities. Similar to intermediate grant, it is intended to provide standard amenities including a fire escape.

Eligibility

You may qualify for a grant as a home owner, landlord or tenant, providing the property is your main residence (or let on a residential basis) and was built or converted before 1961.

Eligibility may also depend on rateable value which must not exceed £400 in Greater London or £225 elsewhere. Higher rateable limits apply for conversion work: £600 in Greater London, £350 in other areas. Rateable limits are waived for intermediate grants and also in housing action areas or for work to help a disabled person.

Amount of grant

This will depend on your local council and on the amount of work involved. The maximum will be: 75 per cent of eligible expenses in priority cases (e.g. houses in particularly bad repair; improvements for a disabled person or homes in housing action areas); 65 per cent in general improvement areas; 50 per cent in other cases. In very exceptional cases of hardship, a slightly higher grant may be given.

   Eligibility expense limits are relatively generous; for example:

Improvement Grants	*Greater London* £	*Elsewhere* £
Repairs, replacements and conversions of houses of less than 3 storeys:		
priority cases:	13,800	
non-priority cases:	9,000	6,600
Conversions of 3-storeys plus:		
priority cases:	16,000	11,800
non-priority cases:	10,400	7,700

Conversion limits are per dwelling

Intermediate Grants		
Fixed bath, shower or sink:	450	340
Water Closet	680	515
Hot/Cold Water at bath/shower:	570	430
sink:	380	290
General Repairs	4,200	3,000

Repairs Grants		
Major structural repairs	6,600	4,800

Special Grants		
Repairs:	6,600	3,000
Fire Escapes:	10,800	8,100

For more details, see Department of the Environment Housing Booklet No.14, *Home Improvement Grants*, available from Citizens Advice Bureaux, Town Halls and Housing Aid Centres.

To apply for a grant, contact the Home Improvement section of your local council for an application form. **Do not start work until approval has been given to your plans.**

Grants for the sick and disabled

As mentioned above, improvement and repair grants are generally more readily available if you are sick or disabled, and many of the normal criteria for eligibility are often waived.

Your local authority may also be able to help with the provision of certain special facilities such as a stair lift, telephone installations or a ramp to replace steps.

Apply to your local Social Services department and, if you encounter any difficulties, ask for further help either from your local Age Concern Group or from RADAR (Royal Association for Disability and Rehabilitation), 25 Mortimer Street, London W1N 8AB, T:01-637 5400.

Useful addresses

The Building Centre, 26 Store Street, London WC1E 7BT, T:01-637 1022.

The Centre has displays of building products, heating appliances, kitchen layouts and other exhibits and can advise about building problems including energy conservation. It has manufacturers' lists and other free literature you can take away and there is also a well stocked bookshop.

The Centre can also put you in touch with building experts in your local area.

Building Employers Confederation, 82 New Cavendish Street, London W1M 8AD, T:01-580 5588

Keeps a register of members, classified by area and also operates a guarantee scheme where, for a fee of 1 per cent of the contract value, the BEC will underwrite satisfactory completion of the work.

Federation of Master Builders (FMB), 33 John Street, London WC1N 2BB, T:01-242 7583.

Lists of members are available from regional offices. Warranty Scheme giving two-year guarantees available from some of its members.

Institute of Plumbing, 64 Station Lane, North Street, Hornchurch, Essex RM12 6NB, T:04024-72791.

Can provide list of registered plumbers; sae appreciated.

Royal Institute of Chartered Surveyors, 12 Great George Street, Parliament Square, London SW1P 3AD, T:01-222 7000.

The RICS will nominate a few qualified surveyors in your area. They also publish a number of useful leaflets, including: *What is a Structural Survey?* and *Surveys and Valuations*.

Royal Institute of British Architects, 66 Portland Place, London W1N 4AB, T:01-580 5533.

The RIBA has a Clients' Advisory Service which will recommend two or three suitable architects.

Care and repair projects

Local Care and Repair or Staying Put projects exist in some areas to help house owners aged 50 plus repair and adapt their homes. They will help to assess your needs, get a builder, supervise the work, raise the finance and check the estimate and the work done.

There are local authority Care and Repair projects in Merseyside, Portsmouth, Middlesborough, Newcastle, Omagh, Liverpool and in some London boroughs. Schemes run by private sector organisations include:

The Abbeyfield Society, 186-192 Darkes Lane, Potters Bar, Herts EN6 1AB, T:0707-44845. The Society operates schemes in Belfast, York, Mid-Glamorgan, Bradford, Newcastle, Birmingham, Brighton, Nottingham and some London boroughs. If your town is not on the list it is worth contacting Abbeyfield to see if they are introducing a scheme in your area.

The Anchor Housing Association, Oxenford House, 13-15 Magdalen Street, Oxford OX1 38P, T:0865-722261, runs Staying Put schemes in Southport, Bradford, Newcastle, Brixton, Hackney, Lambeth, Brighton and Birmingham.

Age Concern. A directory of care and repair schemes is available from Age Concern England, giving details of the projects and their contact addresses.

Some building societies also offer special schemes for older people wishing to improve their homes. These include:

Halifax Building Society, Head Office, P.O.Box 60, Trinity Road, Halifax, West Yorkshire, T:0422-65777.

The Halifax promotes a range of services for older people who are purchasing a retirement home or adapting their existing home.

Nationwide Building Society, Head Office. New Oxford House, High Holborn, London WC1V 6PW, T:01-242 8822.

The Nationwide offers schemes (linked with Housing Associations) in some areas to help retired people and those approaching retirement to improve their homes. The schemes involve local authority improvement grants plus interest-only mortgages from the building society, which, for those on supplementary benefit, may be partly paid by the DHSS. Ask your Branch Manager for details.

Safety in the home

Nearly 7,000 people die from accidents in the home every year. Seventy per cent of these victims are over retirement age and nearly eighty per cent of deaths are caused by falls. A further 3 million people need medical treatment.

The vast majority of accidents are caused by carelessness or by obvious danger spots in the home that for the most part could very easily be made safer. Tragically, it is all too often the very little things that we keep meaning to attend to but never quite get round to doing that prove fatal.

Steps and stairs are a case in point. These should be well lit with light switches at both the top and bottom. Frayed carpet is notoriously easy to trip on and, on staircases especially, should be repaired or replaced as soon as possible.

All stairs should have a hand rail along the wall to provide extra support – and on both sides, if the stairs are very steep. It is also a good idea to have a white line painted on the edge of steps that are difficult to see – for instance in the garden or leading up to the front door.

It is perhaps stating the obvious to say that climbing on chairs and tables is dangerous – except we all do this. You should keep proper steps, preferably with a hand rail, to do high jobs in the house such as hanging curtains or reaching cupboards.

Floors can be another danger zone. Rugs and mats can slip on polished floors and should always be laid on some form of non-slip backing material. Stockinged feet are slippery on all but carpeted floors and new shoes should always have the soles scratched before you wear them. Remember also that spilt water or talcum powder on tiled or linoleum floors is a number one cause of accidents.

The bathroom is particularly hazardous for falls. Sensible precautionary measures include using a suction-type bath mat and putting handrails on the bath or alongside the shower.

For older people who have difficulty in getting in and out of the bath, a bath seat can be helpful. Soap on a rope is safer in a shower, as it is less likely to slither out of your hands and make the floor slippery.

Regardless of age, you should make sure that all medicines are clearly labelled and throw away any prescribed drugs left over from a previous illness.

Fires can all too easily start in the home. If you have an open fire, you should always use a fireguard and sparkguard at night. The chimney should be regularly swept at least once a year and maybe more if you have a wood burning stove. Never place a clothes horse near an open fire or heater and be careful of inflammable objects that could fall from the mantlepiece.

Portable heaters should be kept away from furniture and curtains and positioned where you cannot trip over them. Paraffin heaters should be handled particularly carefully and should *never* be filled while alight. Avoid leaving paraffin where it will be exposed to heat, including sunlight. If possible, it should be kept in a metal container outside the house.

Gas appliances should be regularly serviced by an approved British Gas or CORGI contractor. You should also ensure that there is adequate ventilation when using heaters. Never block up air vents: carbon monoxide fumes can kill.

British Gas publishes a free booklet *Help Yourself to Gas Safety* which describes how to deal with a gas leak as well as how to use your gas appliances safely and effectively.

A free safety check on gas appliances is available to anyone over the age of 65 or any disabled person living alone. If additional work needs to be done, you will receive an estimate and may be able to get help with the cost. These checks can be arranged through your local gas showroom or gas service centre (look under Gas in your local telephone directory).

More than one in three fires in the home are due to accidents with *cookers*. Chip pans are a particular hazard: only fill the pan one third full with oil and always dry the chips before putting them in the fat. Or better still, use oven-ready chips which you just pop into the oven to cook.

Pan handles should be turned away from the heat and positioned so you cannot knock them off the stove. If called to the door or telephone, always take the pan off the ring and turn off the heat before you leave the kitchen.

Cigarettes left smouldering in an ashtray could be dangerous if the ashtray is full. Smoking in bed is a potential killer!

Faulty *electric wiring* is another frequent cause of fires, as are overloaded power points. The wiring in your home should be checked every five years and you should avoid using too many appliances off a single plug. Ask an electrician's advice what is the maximum safe number.

Only use plugs that conform to the British Standard 1365 and it is a good idea to get into the habit of pulling the plug out of the wall socket when you have finished using an appliance, whether TV or toaster. All electrical equipment should be regularly checked for wear and tear and frayed or damaged flexes immediately replaced.

In particular, *electric blankets* should be routinely overhauled and checked in accordance with the manufacturer's instructions. It is generally advisable not to use both a hot water bottle and electric blanket – and never use an underblanket as an overblanket.

Electrical appliances are an increasing feature of labour-saving *gardening* but can be dangerous unless treated with respect. They should never be used when it is raining. Moreover, gardeners should always wear rubber soled shoes or boots and avoid floppy clothing that could get caught in the equipment. For other good advice, see leaflet *Safety in Your Garden*, available from your electricity showroom.

As a general precaution, keep *fire extinguishers* handy and make sure they are maintained in working order. Small hand-held portable extinguishers are now available and easier to use but are only suitable for very small fires. All fire extinguishers should conform to the British Standard BS5423 or BS5306 part 3.

Useful reading

The Royal Society for the Prevention of Accidents, Cannon House, The Priory, Queensway, Birmingham B4 6BS, T:021-233 2461, publish various leaflets: *Safety in Retirement* (75p inc. p&p); *Home and Leisure Safety Catalogue* (free); *The Home Safety Book* (75p inc. p&p); *DIY Safety* (75p inc. p&p).

The British Insurance Association, Aldermary House, Queen Street, London EC4N ITU, T:01-248 4477, has produced a 22-minute colour video, *Nobody Told Me*, to alert people to the everyday risks they run at home. It can be borrowed free of charge from the Association by writing to the above address.

Safety Measures in Your Home (free) from the **Halifax Building Society**, P.O.Box 60, Trinity Road, Halifax, West Yorkshire HX1 2RG.

Living in Safety (25p plus p&p) from **Pre-Retirement Association**, 19 Undine Street, London SW17 8PP.

How to Avoid Falls (free) from **Age Concern** (send s.a.e.).

Keep Living (free) from **County Road Safety Officers' Association**, County Hall, Spetchley Road, Worcester WR5 2NP.

Security

Many people, particularly city dwellers, are concerned about home security. The Crime Prevention Officer attached to your local police station will come and check your security arrangements, advise you how to improve them and also tell you whether there is a Neighbourhood Watch Scheme and how you join it. This is a free service which the police are happy to provide.

Additionally, you might consider fitting secure bolts, a burglar chain and a spyhole to your front door. Slightly more elaborate precautions could include outside lights to illuminate night-time visitors and an ansaphone system requiring a caller to identify himself before you open the door.

Windows offer another point of entry. Best advice is to fit locks to secure them when partially open. Install proper bolts on french windows and draw your curtains at night, so potential intruders cannot see in. Both double glazing and venetian blinds act as a further deterrent. If you are particularly worried, you could also have bars fitted to the windows.

An obvious point is to ensure that the house is securely locked whenever you go out, even for five minutes. Insist that official callers such as meter men show their identity cards before you allow them inside. Finally, consider a time switch (cost between £7 and £15) which will turn the lights on and off when you are away and can be used to switch on the heating before your return.

Burglar alarms and safes

A burglar alarm is one of the best means of deterring a casual thief. Many insurance companies now insist that an alarm – and sometimes other electronic equipment – be installed and will recommend suitable contractors.

Alternatively, you can write to the **National Supervisory Council for Intruder Alarms**, St. Ives House, St. Ives Road, Maidenhead SL6 1QS, T:0628-37512. It operates a code of practice and maintains a nationwide list of about 220 approved installers, who will provide equipment to British Standard 4737. The Council also runs a complaints service.

If you keep valuables or money in the house, you should think about buying a concealed wall or floor safe.

A dog can also be an excellent burglar alarm: small dogs are often best as they tend to be the loudest barkers.

If you are going away, it is a good idea to inform your neighbours so that if your alarm goes off they will know something is wrong. Burglar alarms have an unfortunate habit of going off for no reason (a mouse can trigger the mechanism) and many people ignore them as a result. It is advisable to give your neighbours a key so that they can turn off and reset the alarm should the occasion arise.

Personal safety

Older people who live on their own can be particularly at risk. A number of personal alarms are now available which are highly effective and can generally ease your peace of mind.

A sensible precaution is to carry a 'screamer alarm', sometimes known as a 'personal attack button'. These are readily available in department stores, electrical shops and alarm companies.

A firm called Aid-Call provides a service which enables anyone living alone to call for help simply by pressing a button. The subscriber wears a small radio transmitter the size of a wristwatch from which a message can be sent, via the telephone, to a 24 hour monitoring centre. The centre alerts a list of nominated relatives and friends that something is wrong. There is both an installation (£200 to £375) and on-going (£65 to £150) charge for the service. For a brochure, contact: **Aid-Call**, 15 Radnor Walk, London SW3 4BP, T:352-2822.

A telephone can also increase your sense of security. Some families come to an arrangement whereby they ring their older relatives at regular times to check that all is well.

Insurance

As you near retirement, it is sensible to reassess your building and home contents policy. If the insurance was originally arranged through your building society it may cease when your mortgage is paid off, in which case it will be essential for you to arrange new cover direct.

Over the last forty years the value of your home may have doubled or more and the chances are that the cost of replacing the fabric of your house, were it to burn down, would be significantly greater than the amount for which it is currently insured.

The same applies to the contents of your home. Insurance that simply covers the purchase price is normally grossly insufficient. Instead, you should assess their replacement cost and make sure you have a 'new for old' or 'replacement as new' policy.

Most insurance companies offer an automatic inflation proofing option for both building and contents policies. While it is obviously prudent to take advantage of this, many people unthinkingly sign on the dotted line quite forgetting to cancel items such as furniture or jewellery which they may have given away or sold and so lumber themselves with higher charges than necessary. Equally, many forget to add new valuables they have bought or received as presents.

In particular, do check that you are adequately covered for any home improvements you may have added such as an American style kitchen, new garage, conservatory, extra bathroom, swimming pool or other luxury.

Your policy should also provide money to meet architects' or surveyors' fees as well as alternative accommodation for you and your family if your house were completely destroyed.

If you are in doubt about the cost of replacing your home the **Royal**

Institute of Chartered Surveyors, 12 Great George Street, London SW1P 3AD, T:01-222 7000, publishes a *Guide to House Rebuilding Costs for Insurance Valuations*.

The **Association of British Insurers**, Aldermary House, Queen Street, London EC4N 1TT, T:01-248 4477, will send you free leaflets on *Building Insurance for Home Owners* and a *Guide to Home Contents Insurance* which describe what policies you need and indicate the correct amount of cover. The ABI can also send you a list of insurance brokers in your area.

If you are planning to move into accommodation which has been converted from one large house into several flats or maisonettes, check very carefully that the insurance on the structure of the total building is adequate. All too many people have found themselves homeless because each tenant only insured their own flat and the collective policies were not sufficient to replace the common parts.

Some insurance companies now offer Retired Householders Insurance Policies at substantially reduced rates. The rationale behind such schemes is that older people are less likely to leave their homes empty on a regular basis (i.e. 9 to 5) and are therefore less liable to be burgled. In some cases also, policies are geared to the fact that many retired people have either sold or given away many of their more valuable possessions and therefore only need to insure their homes up to a relatively low sum.

Two such policies are arranged through **Age Concern** and **Hill House Hammond Ltd.**, Retired Householders Insurance Department, Freepost (BS1162), Lewins Mead, Bristol BS1 2BR.

Raising money on your home

One of the sadnesses for many retired people is the need to sell their home and move somewhere smaller in order to provide extra income. There are, however, several ways of raising money on your home while you continue to live in it. These include: mortgage annuity schemes, home reversion plans and 60 plus mortgages.

Mortgage annuity schemes

These work as follows: you take out a mortgage on your home and use the money raised to buy an annuity. Part of the income from the annuity goes to pay the interest on the loan (which is tax deductible up to £30,000), while you receive the balance as spending money every year.

You still own the house and any increase in the value of the property remains with the family. No capital is repayable until the death of the borrower, or surviving partner, when it will come out of the estate. Alternatively, if you decide to sell the property, the annuity will continue.

Normally these schemes are only available to people over 70 and the older you are the better the annuity payments. If you are married, your combined ages should ideally be at least 150.

As with other annuities, the longer you live the greater the benefit. As a safeguard against early death, some schemes offer a 'capital protection' policy, which can be taken in return for lower payments. Typically, these provide that should you die after only one year, only a quarter of the original loan would have to be repaid. This rises to half after two years; and to three-quarters after three years. Thereafter, the loan would normally be repayable in full from the estate.

While one of the particular attractions of mortgage annuity schemes is the tax relief which is given on the borrower's top rate of tax, those on low incomes should watch for two possible pitfalls. In consequence of receiving extra money from the annuity payments, they could suddenly find themselves liable to pay tax and at the same time might cease to be eligible for some of the benefits they were previously receiving.

Further information about mortgage annuity schemes can be obtained from the **Association of British Insurers**, at: Aldermary House, Queen Street, London EC4, T:01-248 4477.

Building Societies and Insurance Companies offering annuity-based home income plans include:

Abbey National Building Society, Abbey House, Baker Street, London NW1 6XL, T:01-486 5555 or local branches.

Allied Dunbar Provident plc, 9/15 Sackville Street, London W1X 1DE, T:01-434 3211.

Chatham Reliance Building Society, Reliance House, Manor Road, Chatham, Kent ME4 6AF, T:0634-48944.

Halifax Building Society, Head Office, P.O. Box 60, Trinity Road, Halifax HX1 2RG, T:0422-65777.

National and Provincial Building Society, Provincial House, Bradford BD1 1NL, T:0274 733444.

Newcastle Building Society, Hood Street, Newcastle-upon-Tyne, NE1 6JP, T:091-232 6676.

Home reversion plans

With these schemes, you *sell* all or part of your home – generally at a substantial discount – but retain the right to live in the house for the remainder of your life at a peppercorn rent.

You are only likely to receive about 50 per cent of the market value of your property, as the price will be based on a 'sitting tenant' valuation according to your life expectancy.

The proceeds from the sales are received as a lump sum or can be invested in an annuity. You would continue to be responsible for keeping the property in good repair.

While such plans provide a higher income than mortgage annuity schemes, they have the double disadvantage that you lose the benefit of all future increases on the value of the property and you cannot leave the house to your beneficiaries, since you no longer own it. Furthermore, your options are reduced should you wish to move in the future.

Before committing yourself you are strongly advised to consult a solicitor, especially with a view to guaranteeing your security of tenure.

Home reversion plans are offered by:

Abbey National Building Society, Abbey House, Baker Street, London NW1 6XL, T01-486 5555.

Allied Dunbar Provident plc, 9-15 Sackville Street, London W1X 1DE, T:01-434 3211.

Home Reversions Ltd., 30 Windsor Place, Cardiff CF1 3UR, T:0222-371726.

Inishowen Ltd., 235 High Street, Aldershot, Hants GU11 1TJ, T:0252-319463.

Investment Property Reversions Ltd., 108 Stafford Road, Wallington, Surrey SM6 9AP, T:01-669 9444.

Premium Life Assurance Co. Ltd., Eastchester House, Harlands Road, Haywards heath, West Sussex RH16 1LW, T:0444-458721.

Property Consultants, 4 Purkess Close, Chandler's Ford, Eastleigh, Hants SO5 2ED, T:04215-65415.

Residential Home Reversions Ltd., Gorse Lane House, High Salvington, Worthing, Sussex BN13 38X, T:0903-692080.

Royal Life, P.O. Box 30, New Hall Place, Liverpool L69 3HS, T:051-227 4422.

Stalwart Assurance, Tuition House, St. George's Road, Wimbledon, London SW19 4XE, T:01-879 1299.

Other mortgages

A possible scheme of interest to older home owners is the 60 Plus Mortgage run by the **Building Trust**, 25-26 Albemarle Street, London W1X 4AD, T:01-493 9899. The Trust lends up to 50 per cent of the value of the property on a 25 year repayment mortgage, at a substantially reduced interest rate.

When the loan is paid off however, the borrower is liable to pay a supplementary interest element geared to the rise in the house price index over the intervening period.

Letting rooms in your home

Rather than move, many people whose home has become too large are tempted by the idea of taking in tenants. For some, it is an ideal plan; for others, a disaster. At best, it could provide you with extra income and the possibility of pleasant company. At worst, you could be involved in a lengthy legal battle to regain possession of your property.

Before either rushing off to put a card in the newsagent's window or rejecting the idea out of hand, it is helpful to understand the different options together with your various rights and responsibilities.

There are three broad choices: taking in paying guests or lodgers; letting part of your home as self-contained accommodation, or renting the whole house for a specified period of time.

In all cases for your own protection it is essential to have a written agreement and to take up bank references, unless the let is a strictly temporary one where the money is paid in advance.

From a tax point of view, any money you receive will be treated as income and if this exceeds £75 a week, your state pension could be reduced (see Chapter 2).

Finally, if you have a mortgage or are a tenant yourself (even with a very long lease), check with your building society or landlord that you are entitled to sublet.

Paying guests or lodgers

This is the most informal arrangement and will normally be either a casual holiday type bed and breakfast let or a living-in lodger who might be with you for a couple of years.

In either case, the visitor would be sharing part of your home, the accommodation would be fully furnished and you would be providing at least one full meal a day and possibly also basic cleaning services.

There are no legal formalities involved in these types of lettings and rent is entirely a matter for friendly agreement.

As a resident owner you are also in a very strong position if you want your lodger to leave. Normally you can expect him to go at the end of the week/month or other agreed period. Should you be unfortunate enough to have a lodger who refuses to go, you can apply to the county court for a possession order.

Holiday lets. It is a good idea to register with your Tourist Information Centre and to contact the Environmental Health Office at your local council for any help and advice.

Letting part of your home

You could convert a basement or part of your house as a self-contained flat and let this either furnished or unfurnished. Alternatively, you could let a room or rooms as bed-sitters with no meals provided.

In general terms, providing you continue to live in the house yourself you will be in much the same position as if you had a lodger or paying guest.

However, even though you agree a rent, either party can apply to a rent tribunal at any time for a *reasonable rent* to be registered. To find out what this might be, you can examine the register of rents at your local rent assessment panel office. You might also find it useful to see Housing Booklet No.7, *Regulated Tenancies*, published by the Department of the Environment (DoE), available from your local Citizens Advice Bureau or Housing Department.

As a resident landlord, you have a guaranteed right to re-possession of your property. If the letting was for a fixed term (i.e. 6 months or a year), the tenancy will automatically cease at the end of the fixed period. If the arrangement was on a more ad hoc basis with no specified leaving date, you will have to give at least four weeks' notice in writing.

Should you encounter any difficulties, you can apply to the county court for a possession order. It is usually possible to get an early hearing within about three weeks. The court can postpone the date when the order comes into effect by up to three months but no longer.

Tax Note. If you subsequently sell your home, you may not be able to claim exemption from Capital Gains Tax on the increase in value of a flat if it is entirely self-contained. It is therefore a good idea to retain some means of access to the main house or flat, but take legal advice as to what will qualify.

Renting your home on a temporary basis

If you are thinking of spending the winter in the sun or are considering buying a retirement home which you will not occupy for a year or two, you might be tempted by the idea of letting the whole house.

In spite of changes in the law, there are plenty of true horror stories of owners who cannot regain possession of their own property, when they wish to return.

To avoid many of the problems, you should write the lease under the shorthold tenancy rules, which are designed to protect a landlord's rights. See DoE Booklet No.8, *Shorthold Tenancies*. It is essential to ask a solicitor to help you draw up the agreement.

Although this provides for greater protection, you could still have a great deal of hassle if your tenants refuse to leave.

In most circumstances, by far the safest solution is to let your property to a company rather than to private individuals. You must take legal advice. You might also find the DoE Housing Booklet No.5, *Letting Your Home or Retirement Home* useful reading.

Other recommended reading

Housing Booklet No.4, *Letting Rooms in Your Home*, Housing Booklet No.11, *Notice to Quit*, both available from Citizens Advice Bureaux and local authority Housing Departments.

The *Which? Guide to Renting and Letting (England and Wales)*. Price £5.95. Available from Consumers' Association, Castlemead, Gascoyne Way, Hertford, SG14 1LH.

Housing Benefit

Many people can get help with their rent and rates from their local council. You may qualify for Housing Benefit whether you are a council or private tenant or a home owner. The amount you get depends on your income, the number of people in your household, and how much rent or rates you pay. Even if you have a relatively high income (and lots of savings) it is still possible you could be eligible, especially if you live in an area with particularly high rates.

Housing Benefit is unbelievably complicated and has been known to flummox a number of local authorities and DHSS offices let alone benefit claimants. The following outline is only intended as a very general guide. For more detailed advice about your own particular circumstances, contact your local Citizens Advice Bureau.

The amount of benefit you get depends on three factors: your eligible rent and rates; your eligible income; and your needs allowance. These are defined as follows:

Needs allowance. Everyone is deemed to have a statutory 'needs allowance', which is up-rated annually in April. There are different rates according to whether you are single (£48.10), married (£70.85), over pension age (£48.95 single; £71.70 married), disabled (extra £5.55) or have a dependent child (extra £14.60).

Eligible rent/rates. This includes service charges but excludes any part of your rent that goes towards: hot water, lighting, heating or cooking. It also excludes water rates and sewerage charges and any contributions towards rent and rates from a sub-tenant.

Eligible Income. Some of your income will be ignored for housing benefit purposes including: roughly £17 of any earnings, attendance or mobility allowances, rent or rates paid by a sub-tenant or any payments you get from someone living with you.

If your weekly income is *equal* to your needs allowance, housing benefit would be calculated as 60 per cent of your eligible rent and rates.

If your income is *less* than your needs allowance, you will receive more. If it is *higher* than your needs allowance, you may still receive something. Couples where both are over pension age are assessed according to a more generous scale.

If you have a low income but are not on supplementary benefit you could be eligible for Housing Benefit Supplement.

How to claim

An application form is contained in leaflet RR1, *Who Pays Less Rent and Rates?*, available from any social security office.

Your local council will work out whether you are entitled to housing benefit and should let you know within 14 days of receiving your completed application.

Special accommodation

If you live in a mobile home or houseboat, you can claim housing benefit for site fees or mooring charges.

If you live in boarding accommodation and do not get any supplementary benefit, housing benefit could be available to help with the charges.

Useful organisations

The following should be able to provide general advice about housing and help with housing problems.

- Local Authority Housing Departments
- Housing Advice or Housing Aid Centres
- Citizens Advice Bureaux
- Local Authority Social Service Departments if your problem is linked to a disability
- Welfare Rights Centres if your problem, for example, concerns a landlord who does not keep the property maintained
- Local Councillors and MPs

Other organisations that provide a useful service are as follows.

Catholic Housing Aid Society, 189a Old Brompton Road, London SW5 OAR, T:01-373 4961.

The Society serves anyone in housing need regardless of race or religion. It provides an advice and, where necessary, an advocacy service for people with housing problems through its central office and 20 local CHAS groups. CHAS local groups work to make use of rented accommodation in the private sector, nominate clients to housing associations and give advice to elderly home owners on maintenance and repairs and on how to meet fuel bills.

Federation of Private Residents' Associations, 11 Dartmouth Street, London SW1H 9BL, T:01-222 0037.

The Federation is an organisation for long leaseholders and tenants in private blocks of flats. It advises on setting up residents' associations and provides legal and other advice to its member associations. It publishes a quarterly newsletter, information sheets and a pack on how to start a tenants/residents' association (£5).

Shelter, 157 Waterloo Road, London SE1 8XF, T:01-633 9377, or 65 Cockburn Street, Edinburgh EH1 1BU, T:031-226 6347, or 23a University Road, Belfast BT7 1NA, T:0232-47752.

Shelter has more than 30 housing aid centres throughout England and Wales plus additional ones in Scotland and Northern Ireland. These centres will help anyone who has a housing problem whether it is social or financial.

Shac, 189a Old Brompton Road, London SW3 OAR, T:01-373 7276.

This is an independent housing advice centre which provides information and help with housing problems in the Greater London area. It also publishes *Moving Home in Retirement*, price 85p (inc.p&p).

Useful reading

The Housing Year Book. This is published annually in the Longmans Community Information Guide series and will be found in most library reference sections. It lists, among others: all national and local government offices responsible for housing, all national advisory bodies, major house builders, housing associations, professional bodies and trade associations involved with house building. This is an invaluable book for anyone considering the options for retirement housing.

Your Retirement Home. Discusses: grants for home improvement and repair, choosing contractors, home finance, Housing Benefit, how and where to move, tied housing, and a variety of schemes available to older people. (Available from the Greater London Pre-Retirement Association, Room 203, 19 Old Jewry, London EC2 8EU, T:01-601 4484. Price 95p incl. p&p.

Householder's Action Guide. Price £5.95. Covers such information as rates, local government services, planning permission, getting grants, house maintenance, employing a builder, insurance, problems with neighbours.

The Which? Encyclopedia of the Home. Price £16.95. Covers a wide variety of household matters: legal, financial, medical and others relating to security.

Which? Way to Buy, Sell and Move House. Price £8.95. Describes how to move house painlessly and cheaply, including buying and selling.

Which? Book of Home Improvements and Extensions. Price £14.95.

The last three are all available from Consumers' Association, Castlemead, Gascoyne Way, Hertford SG14 1LH.

7. Leisure

Whether you are looking forward to devoting more time to an existing interest, resuming an old hobby, studying for a degree or trying your hand at an entirely new pastime, the choice is enormous.

You can do anything from basket-weaving to bridge, archery to amateur dramatics. You can join a music-making group, a scrabble club, a photographic society or become a beekeeper. There are any number of historic homes and beautiful gardens to visit, as well as museums, art galleries, abbeys and castles.

Almost every locality now has excellent sports facilities and thanks to the Sports Council's 50 Plus campaign, there is scope for complete novices to take up bowls, golf, badminton and many others. Similarly, there are dancing and keep fit classes, railway enthusiasts' clubs and groups devoted to researching their local history.

Many of the organisations offer special concessionary rates to people of retirement age, as do a number of theatres and other places of entertainment.

This chapter should be read in conjunction with Chapter 12, as many of the organisations listed there – such as the Field Studies Council – could apply equally well here. However, to avoid repetition, most are only described once. Those that appear in Chapter 12 tend in the main either to offer residential courses or would probably involve most people in spending a few days away from home to take advantage of the facilities.

While every effort has been made to ensure that prices are correct, these cannot be guaranteed and those quoted should, therefore, only be taken as a guide rather than gospel. The reason is that most organisations alter their charges from time to time and since there is no set date when this happens, it is impossible to keep track.

In addition to the suggestions contained in this chapter, your library, local authority recreation department and adult education institute will be able to signpost you to other activities in your area.

Given the immense variety of tantalising options on offer, it is perhaps no wonder that many retired people find that they have never been as busy in their lives.

Animals

If you are an animal lover, you will already know about such events as sheep dog trials, gymkhanas and the many wild life sanctuaries around the country.

Our list is effectively limited to 'the birds and the bees' with just a couple of extra suggestions for fun.

British Beekeepers' Association, National Agricultural Centre, Stoneleigh, Coventry, Warwickshire CV8 2LZ, T: 0203-552 404.

The Association will put you in touch with one of 700 local organisations. It runs correspondence courses and practical demonstrations and also publishes a monthly magazine.

Royal Society for the Protection of Birds, The Lodge, Sandy, Bedfordshire, T: 0767-80551.

The Society encourages conservation of wild birds and manages over 100 reserves to which members have access. It organises local groups and also publishes a quarterly journal. Membership costs £9; £4.50 for Senior Citizens.

Royal Zoological Society, London Zoo, Regent's Park, London NW1 4RY, T: 01-722 3333, and Whipsnade Park Zoo, Dunstable, Bedfordshire LU6 2LF, T: 0582-872171.

You can become a Friend of the Zoo, which gives you free admission to both Whipsnade and the London Zoo, as well as regular mailings and entrance to the many special events for Friends. These include occasional animal 'open houses', lunchtime talks and evening receptions. Individual membership: £12 a year; family membership, £30.

Our Dogs, 5 Oxford Road Station Approach, Manchester M60 1SX, T: 061-236 2660.

If you would enjoy showing a dog, the weekly newspaper *Our Dogs* gives details of local shows, rule and registration changes and also news and addresses of canine and breed societies all over the country. There is an *Our Dogs* diary, which contains feeding and other hints, advice about the Kennel Club and much other useful information.

Adult education

Ever longed to take a degree, learn about computing, study philosophy or do a course in archaeology? Opportunities for education abound with these and scores of other subjects easily available to everyone, regardless of age or previous qualifications.

Adult education institutes

There is an Adult Education Institute in most areas of the country. Classes normally start in September and run through the academic year. Many AEIs allow concessionary fees for students over 60.

Choice of subjects is enormous and at one institute alone we counted over fifty options, ranging from Indian history, video production and creative writing to self defence, calligraphy, dressmaking and drama.

Ask at your local library for details. Or in London, buy booklet *Floodlight*, available from most bookstalls or from the ILEA direct at County Hall, London SE1 7PB, T:01-633 5000.

For information about educational opportunities in Scotland, contact:

Scottish Institute of Adult Education, 30 Rutland Square, Edinburgh EHI 2BW, T:031-229 0331 or ask in your local library for their *Handbook of Adult Education in Scotland*.

Council for the Accreditation of Correspondence Colleges, 27 Marylebone Road, London NW1 5JS, T: 01-935 5391.

If you want to study at home by correspondence, the Council will give you a list of colleges which teach your chosen subject. Prices vary and some colleges have special rates for retired people.

National Adult School Organisation, Norfolk House, Smallbrook, Queensway, Birmingham B5 4LJ, T: 021-643 9297.

National Adult Schools 'Friendship through Study' groups meet in members' homes or in halls, weekly or fortnightly. They follow either a national study syllabus or a course of their own choice. Some groups organise social activities and weekend conferences and there is also a national summer school each year. For information about your local group, write to the above address, enclosing sae.

National Extension College, 18 Brooklands Avenue, Cambridge CB2 2HN, T: 0223-316644.

The NEC is a non-profit-making body established to provide high quality home study courses for adults. It runs about 95 courses, listed in their *Home Learning Catalogue* (send A5 sae). A student adviser will help you choose an appropriate course. You can have a 6-week trial period, with cash refunded if you decide not to continue. The choice includes among many others: GCE 'O'and 'A' level studies, City and Guilds courses, modern languages, bird watching, gardening and 'Making the Most of your Memory'. Cost is from £25 upwards depending on subject.

Network Scotland Ltd., 74 Victoria Crescent Road, Glasgow G12 9JQ, T: 041-357 1774.

Network Scotland is the Scottish Broadcasting Support and Educational Information Agency. It can help you find out about courses of all descriptions, whether part-time, full-time or correspondence. The range includes both proper academic studies and leisure learning. Network Scotland will also advise on facilities for the disabled and for those who are housebound. The service is free and enquiries are welcomed.

Open University, Student Enquiries Office, P.O.Box 71, Milton Keynes MK7 6AG, T: 0908-74066.

Why not take a degree or a short course through the Open University? Students are all ages – the oldest OU graduate was 91 – no academic qualifications are required and there is a vast range of subjects from which to choose. Courses normally involve a mix of: correspondence work, radio and TV programmes, cassettes, contact with local tutors and, in some cases, also a week's summer school. You can study entirely at your own speed: many people take up to 6 or 8 years to acquire a degree. However, there is no long term commitment and it is quite possible to sign on for a year at a time. Fees are from £10 to £300 or upwards, depending on the course you choose. Some local authorities will give financial assistance. In addition to its degree studies, the Open University offers a 'Continuing Education' programme, consisting of short vocational and general interest courses. There are also 'Community Education' programmes designed for groups on such subjects as planning for retirement and caring for older people.

Televison and radio

Both the BBC and Channel 4 are very active on the learning front.

Education Broadcasting (30/BC), BBC, London W1A 1AA, T: 01-580 4468.

Will supply details of forthcoming educational programmes. Many have back-up material in the form of books, records or cassettes.

Channel Four, Years Ahead, P.O. Box 4000, London W36 XJ (England and Wales); P.O. Box 4000, Belfast BT2 7FE (Northern Ireland); P.O. Box 4000, Glasgow G12 9JQ (Scotland).

Some of the programmes in the 'Years Ahead' series have linked booklets covering such topics as money, health and leisure. For a catalogue and order form, write to Channel 4 'Years Ahead' at one of the above addresses, enclosing sae.

University extra mural departments

Many universities have a Department of Extra Mural Studies which arranges courses for adults, sometimes in the evening or during the vacation periods. For example, the University of London runs over 800 part-time courses through its Extra Mural Studies Department, including such subjects as: astronomy, music, philosophy, social studies and history. Classes meet about once weekly and students are encouraged to do reading and written work. Fees vary according to the length of the course. For information about the University of London, write to:

Department of Extra Mural Studies, University of London, 26 Russell Square, London WC1B 5DQ, T: 01-636 8000.

For other universities, enquire locally.

University of the Third Age, Parkside Gardens, London SW19 5EY, T: 01-660 5431, for groups outside London. For London, **University of the Third Age in London**, Langton Close, Wren Street, London WC1X 0HD, T:01-833 4747.

U3A operates through a national network of branches which each determine, according to their members' interests, choice of courses and a social activities programme. Participants are essentially in the retirement age group but studies are by no means confined to cosy topics and include such challenging subjects as computer studies, mathematics and languages as well as gardening, dressmaking and others. You can obtain a brochure and list of local groups from the above addresses. Please enclose sae.

Workers' Educational Association, Temple House, 9 Upper Berkeley Street, London W1H 8BY, T 01-402 5608.

There are WEA branches in all parts of the country, offering a wide range of adult education courses covering both academic and leisure orientated subjects. There is normally a choice of part-time, evening or full time classes. Your library or education authority should be able to put you in touch with your local branch. Alternatively, contact the above address.

Arts

Enjoyment of the arts is certainly no longer confined to London. Whether you are interested in active participation or just appreciating the performance of others, there is an exhilarating choice of events including theatre, music, exhibitions, film-making and so on. Many entertainments offer concessionary prices to retired people.

Regional Arts Associations and Councils

For first-hand information about what is going on in your area, contact your regional arts association; or in the case of those living in Scotland, Wales and Northern Ireland, the Arts Council. Most areas arrange an immensely varied programme with musical events, drama, arts and craft exhibitions and sometimes more unusual functions, offering something of interest to just about everyone. Most of the Associations actively welcome members who can often make a real contribution in terms of fostering artistic events within their community.

There is a regular newsletter and cost of membership which varies is roughly in the region of £5.

Eastern Arts Association, 8-9 Bridge Street, Cambridge CB2 1UA, T:0223 357596/7/8/9.

For Bedfordshire, Cambridgeshire, Essex, Hertfordshire, Norfolk and Suffolk.

East Midland Arts, Mountfields House, Forest Road, Loughborough, Leicestershire LE11 3HU, T: 0509-218292.

For Derbyshire (excluding High Peak District), Leicestershire, Northamptonshire, Nottinghamshire and Buckinghamshire.

Greater London Arts Association, 25/31 Tavistock Place, London WC1H 9SF, T:01-388 2211.

For the 32 London Boroughs and the City of London.

Lincolnshire and Humberside Arts, St. Hugh's, Newport, Lincoln LN1 3DN, T: 0522-33555.

For Lincolnshire and Humberside.

Merseyside Arts, Bluecoat Chambers, School Lane, Liverpool L1 3BX, T: 051-709 0671/2/3.

For Metropolitan County of Merseyside, District of West Lancashire, Ellesmere Port and Halton Districts of Cheshire.

Northern Arts, 10 Osborne Terrace, Newcastle-upon-Tyne NEZ 1NZ, T: 0632-816334.

For Cleveland, Cumbria, Durham, Northumberland, Metropolitan County of Tyne and Wear.

North West Arts, 12 Harter Street, Manchester M1 6HY, T: 061-228 3062.

For Greater Manchester, High Peak District of Derbyshire, Lancashire (except District of West Lancashire), Cheshire (except Ellesmere Port and Halton Districts).

North West Arts Information Centre, Town Hall Extension, Manchester M60 2LA, T: 061-236 7076.

Southern Arts Association, 19 Southgate Street, Winchester SO23 7EB, T: 0962-55099.
For Berkshire, Hampshire, Isle of Wight, Oxfordshire, West Sussex, Wiltshire, Districts of Bournemouth, Christchurch, Poole.

South East Arts, 9/10 Crescent Road, Tunbridge Wells, Kent TN1 2LU, T: 0892-41666.
For Kent, Surrey and East Sussex.

South West Arts, Bradninch Place, Gandy Street, Exeter EX4 3LS, T: 0392-218188.
For Avon, Cornwall, Devon, Dorset (except Districts of Bournemouth, Christchurch and Poole), Gloucestershire, Somerset.

West Midlands Arts, Brunswick Terrace, Stafford ST16 1BZ, T: 0785-59231.
For County of Hereford and Worcester, Metropolitan County of West Midlands, Shropshire, Staffordshire, Warwickshire. Press & Information Office: 10 Needless Alley, Birmingham B2 5AE, T: 021-643 6479 (Press) 021-643 6281 (Region Marketing Officer).

Yorkshire Arts Association, Glyde House, Glydegate, Bradford, Yorkshire BD5 OBQ, T: 0274-723051.
For North Yorkshire, South Yorkshire, West Yorkshire.

North Wales Association for the Arts, 10 Wellfield House, Bangor, Gwynedd LL57 1ER, T: 0248-532 48.
For Clwyd, Gwynedd and District of Montgomery in the County of Powys.

South East Wales Arts Association, Victoria Street, Cwmbran, Gwent NP4 3JP, T: 063-33 67530.
For South Glamorgan, Mid-Glamorgan, Gwent, Districts of Radnor and Brecknock in the County of Powys and the City of Cardiff.

West Wales Association for the Arts, Dark Gate, Red Street, Carmarthen, Dyfed, T: 0267-4248.
For Dyfed, West Glamorgan.

Regional Arts Councils

Scottish Arts Council, 19 Charlotte Square, Edinburgh EH2 4DF, T: 031-226 6051

The Scottish Arts Council is technically a committee of the Arts Council of Great Britain, but with a very considerable degree of autonomy.

Welsh Arts Council, Holst House, Museum Place, Cardiff CF1 3NX, T: 0222-394711.
Same as above but for Wales.

Arts Council of Northern Ireland, 181 Stranmillis Road, Belfast BT9 5DU, T: 0232 663591.
The Arts Council of Northern Ireland is not connected with the Arts Council of Great Britain.

Films & film making

The cinema continues to flourish as an art form with film societies, opportunities for movie-making, as well as chances to view some of the great performances.

British Federation of Film Societies, 81 Dean Street, London W1, T: 01-437 4355.
The British Film Institute's *Film and TV Yearbook* lists all film societies in the country and should be available from your local library. Many societies offer reduced rates for senior citizens.

Institute of Amateur Cinematographers, 63 Woodfield Lane, Ashstead, Surrey KT21 2BT, T: 03722-76385.
Members can ask for advice on all matters from scripting to animation. There is a library of some of the world's greatest amateur films and also a tape library with illustrated lectures, available to all members and groups. The Institute runs an amateur film festival while regional councils organise local competitions, workshops and meetings. Members receive a bi-monthly magazine *Amateur Film Maker*. Cost of joining is £10 a year, with a discount for members over 65.

National Film Theatre, South Bank, London SE1 8XT, T: 01-928 3232.
Membership of the NFT is available from the theatre or from the British Film Institute, 81 Dean Street, London W1, T: 01-437 4355. There are a variety of membership rates, offering different facilities including the possibility of taking guests to perfomances.

Music and ballet

Scope ranges from becoming a friend and supporting one of the famous

'Houses' such as Covent Garden to music-making in your own right.

If you live close enough to take advantage of the 'perks', subscribing as a Friend allows you a number of very attractive advantages including in all cases priority for bookings.

Friends of Covent Garden, Royal Opera House, Covent Garden, London WC2, T: 01-240 1066.

Friends receive regular bulletins, opportunities to attend lectures and an invitation to a Christmas party. They may also attend rehearsals and are offered reductions on some ballet or opera performances. Membership is £21 a year. Without becoming a Friend, you can obtain advance booking lists for £1 a year. If tickets are available, senior citizens can buy reduced tickets one hour before the start of performances.

Friends of the English National Opera, London Coliseum, St. Martin's Lane, London WC2N 4ES, T: 01-836 0111.

As a Friend of the ENO, you can attend dress rehearsals, tour backstage, go to lectures, enjoy a Christmas party and obtain reduced tickets for many of the productions. Membership is about £12 a year (£18 for husband and wife) with cheaper rates for those of retirement age.

Friends of Sadler's Wells Theatre, Rosebery Avenue, London EC1R 4TN, T: 01-278 8916.

Sadler's Wells has an ever-changing programme, mainly of ballet and light opera. Friends are invited to open rehearsals, lectures, films and social events with the resident and visiting companies. They can also tour backstage and receive a regular newsletter. Subscription is £10 a year (£15 joint); and roughly half for senior members. Contact the Friends' Secretary on 01-278 6563 or write to the above address. Older people can obtain reduced tickets for some performances.

Music making

Just about every style of music is catered for, from bell-ringing to recorder playing. There is even an orchestra for retired people. Information about local societies and other groups contained in the *British Music Federation Yearbook* and the *British Music Yearbook*, both of which should be in the reference section of your library.

Amateur Music Association, 43 Renshaw Street, Liverpool L1 2SF, T:051-709 6862.

The Association is involved with all forms of music, although there is a classical bias. It can put you in touch with your local music society and advise you as to which of the many groups are most likely to meet your requirements.

Galpin Society, 38 Eastfield Road, Western Park, Leicester LE3 6FE.

The Galpin Society encourages the study of musical instruments, their history, construction and use. It publishes a learned journal of original research and also organises meetings.

Handbell Ringers of Great Britain, 2 Holt Park Approach, Holt Park, Leeds LS16 7PW, T: 0532-677711.

The Society exists to promote the art of handbell tune ringing. It arranges rallies, concerts, workshops and lectures. To contact your local group, write to the above adress, enclosing sae.

National Association of Choirs, 13 Stafford Close, Bulkington, Nuneaton, Warwickshire CU12 9QX.

The Association will put you in contact with an amateur choir in your area.

Society of Recorder Players, 469 Merton Road, London SW18 5LD, T: 01-874 2237.

The Society has groups in many areas where members play together regularly. The branches welcome players of all standards and ages but do not provide tuition for beginners. Write to the Society, enclosing sae, for a list of addresses.

Poetry

There seems to be rather a dearth of organised facilities for poetry lovers who live out of London. Some pubs, however, run the occasional poetry evening and, from all accounts, these are becoming more popular.

The Poetry Society, 21 Earl's Court Square, London SW5 9DE, T: 01-373 7861.

Membership of the Society is open to anyone who enjoys reading, listening to or writing poetry. Typical activities (which are mainly in London) include lecture series, poetry readings and linked social functions. Each year the Society organises a National Poetry Competition. Additionally, members receive poetry journals. Annual subscription is £14 for addresses in London, £11 elsewhere and £10 for Senior Citizens.

Television and radio audiences

If you would like to be part of the invited studio audience for a radio or television programme, you can apply to the BBC and Independent

Broadcasting Authority headquarters, through one of their regional centres or to the programme which particularly interests you direct. The addresses are:

BBC TV Centre, Shepherd's Bush, London W12.

BBC Radio, Portland Place, London W1.

IBA, 70 Brompton Road, London SW3.

Theatre

Details of current and forthcoming productions, as well as theatre reviews, are contained in the newspapers. As general wisdom, preview performances are invariably cheaper and there are often concessionary tickets for matinees.

Listed here are one or two theatres and organisations that offer special facilities of interest, including priority booking and reduced price tickets. Also included are two associations for enthusiasts of amateur dramatics.

Barbican Centre, Silk Street, London EC2Y 8DS, T: 01-638 8891.

The Barbican Centre combines theatre, art gallery, cinema and concert hall. There are free musical events in the foyer at mid-day and early evenings, including both modern jazz and classical. Reduced tickets for senior citizens are available for many of the performances. For £4 a year you can join the Barbican mailing list which gives you the monthly programme with priority booking arrangements.

British Theatre Association, 9 Fitzroy Square, London W1P 6AE, T: 01-387 2666.

The BTA offers many services to members: access to its library; a loan scheme of play sets; an information service; advice on setting up an amateur theatre group; playwriting critiques; training courses for professi3onals and amateurs; a newsletter; regular visits to plays in and around London; discounts on records, tapes and theatrical supplies. Full membership is £20 a year, half price to people over retirement age.

Friends of the Lyric, Lyric Theatre, King Street, Hammersmith, London W6, T: 01-741 0824.

As a Friend, you receive a Newsletter with: details of theatre programmes; invitations to Sunday guest evenings to meet actors and authors; coach trips to other theatres; studio suppers with the cast after a show and press night viewings. Most productions offer special reductions for Friends who also help the theatre voluntarily with clerical work and audience surveys. Membership costs £6 a year for residents of Hammersmith and Fulham, £7.50 for others.

Additionally, the Lyric runs a Senior Citizens' Club which meets every Thursday from 2.30–5. There is tea and biscuits (25p), a guest speaker and Bingo. Open to all, free.

National Theatre, South Bank, London SE1, T: 01-928 2252 (Box Office: 01-928 2033).

The National Theatre offers tours of the building, live foyer music before performances, free exhibitions and restaurant facilities as well of course as its three theatres. There are group price reductions for some performances and pensioners can buy any seat for matinees at special concessionary prices. The National Theatre has a Mailing List Membership (£4.50 a year) which supplies: advance information, priority booking, a regular newsletter, reduced prices for some performances and the opportunity to go to NT Literary Lunches.

Society of West End Theatre, Bedford Chambers, The Piazza, Covent Garden, London WC2E 8HQ, T: 01-836 0971.

The Society offers a scheme under which Senior Citizens can get substantial reductions for matinee performances at many West End theatres. To join, you fill in an application form and send it with £1 and proof that you are 60-plus. Cost of a subscription to *Theatre Guide* is £5. The Society presents Laurence Olivier Awards (formerly SWET Awards) annually. Members of the general public serve on the judging panels. If you would like to be considered for the Theatre, Opera or Dance panel write for an application form. Members of the panels receive 2 complimentary tickets for all productions during the judging period. You can buy West End theatre gift tokens in £1 and £5 units.

Scottish Community Drama Association, Saltire House, 13 Atholl Crescent, Edinburgh EH3 8HA, T: 031-229 7838.

The Association is the umbrella organisation for amateur dramatic societies in Scotland, and offers them advice, encouragement and practical help. Membership (£5.50 a year) gives you access to the Association's libraries, training courses and summer schools. The Association also runs playwriting competitions and can put you in touch with local amateur dramatic societies. Members receive the quarterly magazine *Scene*.

Leicester Square Ticket Booth

The booth sells tickets to most West End Theatres at half price (plus a small service charge) on the day of performance. It is open to personal callers only Monday – Saturday at 12 noon for matinees, 2.30 – 6.30 for evening performances. (Payment in cash only).

Theatre and Concert Rail Club, P.O. Box 1, St. Albans, Herts AL1 4DP, T: 0727-34475.

The Club arranges package bookings for theatre (or concert), rail travel and hotel. Most visits are to London, but there is a nationwide booking service. Membership is £8 a year which entitles you to discount travel and also a monthly newsletter.

Late Night Trains

British Rail runs late night trains for theatregoers. Ask at Travel Centres or your local station for details.

Visual Arts

If you enjoy attending exhibitions and lectures, membership of some of the arts societies offers you a number of delightful privileges.

Contemporary Arts Society, 20 John Islip Street, London SW1P 4LL, T: 01-821 5323.

The aim of the Society is to promote the development of contemporary art and to acquire works by living artists for gift or loan to public collections. Members can take part in an extensive programme of events including: visits to artists' studios and private collections, previews and parties at special exhibitions, day or weekend trips throughout Britain and abroad, lectures and films. Members have half-price entry to exhibitions at the Tate Gallery and some provincial galleries. The annual subscription is £10 for individuals, £15 for two people at the same address.

National Art-Collections Fund, 20 John Islip Street, London SW1P 4LL, T: 01-821 0404.

The Fund, whose aim is to retain works of art in this country, has branches all over the country. Membership gives you: reduced or free admission to most galleries and exhibitions; private evening views of every major art exhibition in London and elsewhere; visits to houses not normally open to the public (including some Royal Palaces); a programme of social events and concerts; a magazine three times a year, and art tours at home and abroad led by experts. Local groups in the regions also arrange their own events. The subscription is £10 for individuals (£15 for couples) and £7 for senior citizens over 60 (£10 for couples).

National Association of Decorative & Fine Arts Societies, 36 Ebury Street, London SW1W OLU, T: 01-730 3041.

Member Societies of NADFAS have programmes of monthly lectures, museum and gallery visits. These are usually held in the daytime and some societies may be able to help with transport. Many societies have voluntary Conservation Corps groups and also work on Church Recording, studying the history and detail of church furnishing. A list of member societies is available from NADFAS. Membership of a local society is about £10 a year. It gives you reduced price entry to the Courtauld Gallery, antiques fairs, the Royal Academy, some historic houses and others.

Royal Academy of Arts, Piccadilly, London W1V 0DS, T: 01-734 9052.

Senior citizens enjoy reduced entrance charges to all exhibitions, including the big annual Summer Exhibition. Alternatively you can become a Friend of the Royal Academy, which gives you free admission with a companion, saves you from queuing and entitles you to reduced price catalogues. Members may also use the Friends' Room to meet for coffee, are invited to private views, have access to the Library and Archives and may attend lectures, concerts and go on tours. Subscriptions: Friends – £22.50 a year; Pensioners – £15; Museum staff and teachers – £17.50; Country Friends (over 75 miles from London) – £15.

Tate Gallery and Turner Gallery, Millbank, London SW1, T: 01-821 1313.

The gallery contains the National Collection of Modern Art. There are free lectures and guided tours each week and special tours for disabled people. Friends of the Tate enjoy free admission to all exhibitions and can also bring two guests at times when the Gallery is closed to the public. Additionally, they are invited to private views and have opportunities to attend lectures at other galleries. There is a Members' room and a library. Membership is £12.

The Tate in the North, a new gallery of modern art in Liverpool, will open in the summer of 1988 and facilities for Friends will also apply.

Painting as a hobby

If you are interested in improving your own painting technique, rather than simply viewing the works of great masters, contact your local Adult Education Institute for details of courses in your area. Your library may have information about local painting groups, clubs and societies.

Crafts

The vast majority of suggestions are contained in Chapter 12, variously under 'Arts and Crafts' and 'Special Interest Holidays', the reason being most of the organisations concerned make a feature of arranging residential courses or of organising, for example, painting holidays. However, if you are interested in a particular form of craft work and want information or advice, many of the societies and others listed in Chapter 13 should be able to help you. Herewith one or two additional possibilities.

The Basketmakers' Association, Martins, Lee Common, Great Missenden, Bucks HP16 9GP, T: 024-020 492.

The Association promotes better standards of design and technique in the art of basketry, chair seating and allied crafts. It arranges day schools, residential courses, demonstrations and exhibitions and also keeps a register of basketry classes at Adult Education Colleges. There is a quarterly newsletter. Membership costs £7 (£10 joint membership).

Crafts Council, 12 Waterloo Place, London SW1, T: 01-930 4811.

As well as arranging exhibitions, the Crafts Council also runs an information centre which can give advice on almost everything you could possibly want to know: different craft courses throughout the country, suppliers of materials, addresses of craft guilds and societies, fact sheets on business practices for craftsmen as well as details of craft fairs and markets, exhibitions, galleries, shops and other outlets for work. Additionally, the Council has a slide and film library, publishes a variety of leaflets and maintains a national register of craftsmen.

The Embroiderers' Guild, Apartment 41a, Hampton Court Palace, East Molesey, Surrey KT8 9AU, T: 01-943 1229.

The Guild exists to promote the craft to the highest possible standards. Membership is open to all, beginners and experts, with an interest in embroidery and related crafts. Members receive a newsletter twice a year giving information about embroidery activities throughout the country. They can use the Guild's facilities at Hampton Court: visit the collection of embroideries and lace, borrow study folios and attend classes and lectures. As well as being an individual member, they can join one of the Guild's 100 local branches which organise lectures, workshops and other activities. Individual membership is £12.50; £7.50 for those over 60. Branches have their own subscription rates.

Studio 1 D (China Restorers), Kensington Church Walk, London W8, T: 01-937 7583.

This china restoration studio runs 2-week courses for beginners, which teach all the basic skills including use of tools and materials to enable you to restore china on your own. Cost is about £300 for two weeks (10 – 5 Monday to Friday). After doing a course, you can spend single days in the Studio to use its facilities, with supervision and advice from the resident china restorers (about £12 a day including materials).

Dance/Keep fit

Clubs, classes and groups exist in all parts of the country, variously offering: ballroom, Old Tyme, Scottish, folk, ballet, disco dancing and others. Additionally, there are music and relaxation classes, aerobics and more gentle keep fit sessions. Many of the relaxation and keep fit classes in particular cater for all standards and some are specially designed for older people to tone up muscles, improve circulation and to make friends in an agreeable atmosphere. Best advice is to contact your adult education or sports centre, or alternatively the library, to find out what is available in your area. Listed here are some of the national organisations that can advise you and put you in touch with local groups. There are also some extra names in Chapter 11.

The Central Council of Physical Recreation, (Movement and Dance Division), Franers House, Franers Street, London SW1P 1DE, T: 01-828 3163.

The Council will send you a list of organisations that offer keep fit and relaxation to music classes.

English Folk Dance and Song Society, Cecil Sharp House, 2 Regent's Park Road, London NW1 7AY, T: 01-485 2206.

There are some 56 groups around the country which organise both regular and special events. In addition to ordinary folk dancing, programmes may include: morris dancing, 'knees up', clog workshops, musician band sessions, sea shanties, lectures and carol concerts. Membership, which includes journals and other information, costs about £12 (£18 for husband and wife); and about half price for those of retirement age. Contact the Society for details of your nearest branch.

Imperial Society of Teachers of Dancing, Euston Hall, Birkenhead Street, London WC1H 8BE.

Throughout the UK there are some 7,000 teachers offering instruction in virtually all forms of dancing. Many organise classes and events particularly for older people. The Society has lists of teachers in each geographic area. There is no standard charge but dance classes and social dancing tend to be an inexpensive activity.

Keep Fit Association, 16 Upper Woburn Place, London WC1H 0QP, T: 01-387 4349, and **Scottish Keep Fit Association**, 18 Ainslie Place, Edinburgh EH3 6AU, T: 031-226 4401.

The Keep Fit Association has a responsible attitude and emphatically does not believe in 70 year olds trying to ape Olympic gymnasts. For advice, information and local classes, contact either of the above addresses.

Royal Scottish Country Dance Society, 12 Coates Crescent, Edinburgh EH3 7AF, T: 031-225 3854.

The Society has members from 16 to 80-plus in its many branches and groups all over the world. It publishes books, records and tapes and holds an annual summer school at St. Andrew's University. The branches offer instruction at all levels and members join in dance events with their group. Information about your local group can be obtained from the RSCDS Secretary.

For the disabled

Happily there are increasingly fewer activities from which handicapped people are debarred through lack of suitable facilities, as will be evident from many of the suggestions listed earlier in the chapter. This section therefore only deals with one topic not covered elsewhere, namely enjoyment of books which for many blind or partially sighted people can be a special problem.

British Wireless for the Blind, 226 Great Portland Street, London W1N 6AA, T: 01-388 1266.

The Fund provides radio-cassette recorders on free permanent loan to all registered blind people in Britain who need a radio. You can apply through your blind welfare officer or direct to the above address.

Calibre, Wendover, Aylesbury, Buckinghamshire, T:0296-32339 and 0296-81211.

Calibre is a lending library of 2000 recorded books on standard cassettes. These are available to anyone who cannot read printed works because of their sight or physical difficulty in holding a book. A doctor's certificate is required describing why the service is needed. The range includes both fiction and non-fiction across a wide variety of classifications. Borrowers are allowed 2 books at a time, which they may keep for a month. Members of Calibre must supply their own machines. The library is free and depends on donations.

National Library for the Blind, Cromwell Road, Bredbury, Stockport, Cheshire SK6 2SG, T: 061-494 0217.

The Library lends books in Braille and Moon free to any blind reader who registers with them. It also provides enlarged music scores for people who are partially sighted. You should make a written application to the Library.

RNIB'S Talking Book Service, Mount Pleasant, Wembley, Middlesex, T: 01-903 6666.

This is a loan service for registered blind or partially sighted people (the latter require the signature of a consultant ophthamologist on their application form). The annual subscription is £15.70 but local authorities or local blind associations may assist with the cost.

Talking Books for the Handicapped, (National Listening Library), 12 Lant Street, London SE1 1QR, T:01-407 9417.

Membership is open to all people who are unable to read printed books but who do not qualify on grounds of less severe incapacity for the RNIB Talking Book Service. Membership costs £15 and for this, a Talking Book reproducer is loaned and cassettes are supplied, post free, both ways. In cases of need your social services department may help towards the cost. Members are sent a catalogue of titles and may borrow up to two books at a time.

Games

Many local areas have their own bridge, chess, whist, dominoes, scrabble and other groups who meet together regularly, either in a club, hall, pub or other social venue to enjoy friendly games. Competitions are organised and certainly in the case of bridge and chess, district and county teams are usually taken very seriously. Your library should know about any clubs or regular group meetings. Alternatively, you can contact the national organisations listed below.

British Chess Federation, 9a Grand Parade, St. Leonards on Sea, East Sussex TN33 0DD, T: 0424 442500.

English Bridge Union, 15b High Street, Thame, Oxfordshire OX9 2BH, T: 08442-2221.

Scrabble Club Co-ordinator, 42 Elthiron Road, London SW6 4BW, T: 01-731 2633.
There are about 150 Scrabble Clubs up and down the country. Some have their own premises and are highly competitive. Others meet in halls or members' houses for a friendly game. A number have a social caring content, with members visiting housebound people to play. A great many competitions are organised, including an Annual Scrabble Championship and a big tournament for clubs. A special tournament for over-60s is under consideration. For details of your nearest Scrabble Club, write to the co-ordinator above.

Gardens and gardening

Courses, gardens to visit, special help for the disabled, how to run a gardening association – these and other interests are all catered for by the organisations listed.

The English Gardening School, at the Chelsea Physic Garden, 66 Royal Hospital Road, London SW3 4HS, T: 01-351 4347.
The School teaches all aspects of gardening. Courses held in the historic lecture room of the Chelsea Physic Garden, the centre for the study of horticulture for over 300 years. Some courses last 6 days, some just a day.

Topics include among others: Scented Plants, Roses, the Mixed Border, Planting for Summer Colour and Botanical Drawing. Cost is £40 per day. There is also a 6 week course, 'The Cultivated Gardener', structured towards potential writers and designers with visits to famous gardens. The cost is about £2900 including overnight stays and meals when out of London. The School will advise on accommodation in London.

Gardens for the Disabled Trust & Garden Club, Little Dane, Biddenden, Ashford, Kent, T: 0580-291214.

The Trust provides practical and financial help to disabled people who want to garden actively. Their Garden Club publishes a quarterly newsletter, gives answers to horticultural questions and encourages disabled gardeners to meet. The annual subscription is £1 (£2 for groups). Life membership is £15. The Trust also sells its own specially designed garden aids.

Horticultural Therapy, 51 Catherine Street, Frome, Somerset BA11 1BA, T: 0373-64782.

Horticultural Therapy helps elderly or disabled people to garden. It runs an advisory service by post, telephone or if necessary a counsellor will visit. Members receive a quarterly magazine and there are also demonstrations, workshops and meetings. The centre can also advise on special tools and where these can be obtained. Membership is £10; £7.50 for older people and those in receipt of benefit.

National Gardens Scheme, 57 Lower Belgrave Street, London SW1W 0LR, T: 01-730 0359, for England and Wales, and **Scotland's Garden Scheme**, 31 Castle Terrace, Edinburgh EH1 2EL, T: 031-229 1870.

The Scheme covers 2,000 private gardens which are open to the public, perhaps one day a year, to raise funds mainly for nursing associations and retired gardeners. Tea is normally served and entries are listed in the Scheme's handbooks (£1 from booksellers or £1.50 incl. p&p. direct from the Scheme's London address, above, for England and Wales; Edinburgh address for Scotland). The organisation is always looking for new gardens. Should you wish to offer yours, however small, apply to the county organiser whose address is in one of the handbooks. Sometimes two or more gardens share a group opening.

National Society of Allotment and Leisure Gardeners, Ltd., Hunters Road, Corby, Northants NN17 1JE, T: 0536-66576.

The Society promotes all forms of horticultural education and encourages local gardening associations. It also acts as a national voice for gardeners. Life membership costs £10; annual membership, £4. This gives you access to free help and advice, the right to attend the annual meeting plus receipt of the

Society's bulletin. There is also a Seeds Scheme, offering special prices. Leaflets are available on how to form and run a gardening association.

Royal Horticultural Society, Vincent Square, London SW1P 2PE, T: 01-834 4333.

Members receive free tickets to shows, including the Chelsea Flower Show, and can also attend lectures and practical demonstrations in London, Wisley and various other parts of the country. There is a monthly magazine and a lending library. Additionally, one of the Society's experts will visit your garden and give advice: this is a service for which you have to pay. There is an enrolment fee of £5 and individual membership costs £14 a year (or joint membership, £24).

Useful reading

Gardening in Retirement by Isobel Pays (£1.95) from **Age Concern**, Bernard Sunley House, Pitcairn Road, Mitcham, Surrey CR4 3LL, T: 01-640 5431.

Directory of Scented Gardens and Gardens for the Blind/Disabled; and *Trails for Blind People*. Both free from: **Royal National Institute for the Blind**, 224 Great Portland Street, London W1N 6AA, T: 01-388 1266.

Hobbies

Whether your special enthusiasm is stamp collecting or model flying, most of the organisations listed organise events, answer queries and can put you in contact with kindred spirits.

The British Association of Numismatic Societies, Department of Numismatics, Manchester Museum, The University, Oxford Road, Manchester.

BANS is an umbrella organisation that helps to co-ordinate the activities of some 60 local societies throughout England, Wales and Scotland. It organises two conferences a year, maintains a slide library and will be able to put you in touch with your nearest group.

British Jigsaw Puzzle Library, Old Homend, Stretton Grandison, Ledbury, Hereford HR8 2TW, T: 053-183 462.

This is a lending library with puzzles exchanged by post. The puzzles are wooden and have no guide pictures. They vary in difficulty, style and size and the library tries to suit each member. Subscriptions range from about £20 for three months to £46 for a year. Postal charges are extra.

Miniature Armoured Fighting Vehicle Association, 15 Berwick Avenue,

Heaton Mersey, Stockport, Cheshire SK4 3AA, T:061-432 7574.

The MAFVA provides advice, information, issues a bi-monthly magazine and can put you in touch with a local branch. There are meetings, displays and competitions. Membership is £4.50 a year.

National Association of Flower Arranging Societies of Great Britain, 21a Denbigh Street, London SW1, T: 01-828 5145.

The Association can put you in touch with local groups and classes.

National Philatelic Society, Room 28, 27 King Street, London WC2 8JD, T: 01-240 7349.

The Society holds monthly afternoon meetings near Marble Arch which normally consist of an auction and display with questions to its collector. There is an annual competition and visits are arranged to philatelic collections. Members receive a free quarterly journal and may use the Society's library. An Advisory Service can help with queries. Membership costs £10 a year.

Radio Society of Great Britain, Alma House, Cranbourne Road, Potters Bar, Herts EN6 3J10, T: 77-59015.

The Society provides advice on how to join the many thousands of amateur radio operators around the world.

Railway Correspondence & Travel Society, 20 Baker Street, York YO3 7AX, T: 0904-642155.

The Society is among the leading railway enthusiast groups, with nearly 6,000 members all over the country. Members receive the monthly magazine, *The Railway Observer*, which includes the Society's fixtures. There are regular meetings at about 30 centres and the RC&TS also organises visits, rail trips and overseas tours to see railways in other countries. The Society has a library with postal loan facility. Membership costs £7.50 a year, including the magazine. *Railway World* is a magazine for railway enthusiasts. It lists railway preservation events and gives information about local railway societies – including how to contact them. £1.10 monthly.

Royal Photographic Society of Great Britain, The Octagon, Milsom Street, Bath, Avon, T: 0225-62841.

The Society promotes photography through meetings, lectures, conferences and exhibitions. There are regional and specialist groups, for example: aerial photography, film and video, visual journalism. The Society arranges an attractive programme, including: workshops, field days and social events. Membership is open to anyone interested in photography. There is an enrolment fee of £5. Individual membership is £17; £11 for over 65s.

Society of Model Aeronautical Engineers 20 Links Road, West Wickham, Kent BR4 0QW, T: 01-777-5533.

The SMAE concerns itself with everything of interest to enthusiasts of model flying. It organises competitions, provides guidelines for flying and can put you in touch with a local group. Many older members make a special hobby of indoor and radio controlled flying.

Wine Mine Club, Vinter House, River Way, Harlow, Essex CM20 2EA, T:0279-416 291.

Joining a wine club is an excellent way of increasing your knowledge of wine and of buying good vintages. The Wine Mine Club, run by Peter Dominic, organises tastings and wine festivals in many parts of the country. Membership is £5 a year and in return you receive a £5 wine voucher redeemable for wine purchased at any Peter Dominic branch or ordered through the Club.

History

People with an interest in the past have a truly glorious choice of activities to sample. You can visit historic monuments, including ancient castles and stately homes, in all parts of the country; explore the City of London; study genealogy, research the history of your local area, attend lectures and receptions.

Architectural Heritage Society of Scotland, 43b Manor Place, Edinburgh EH3 7EB, T: 031-225 9724.

The Society promotes knowledge of Scottish architecture and seeks to conserve good buildings. Members have a year round programme of talks and visits and those with the relevant skills can volunteer to assist the Society in its work. There are groups in Dumphries and Galloway, Forth and Borders, Highland, North-East, Strathclyde, Tayside and NE Fife. Membership is £6; £9 for a family.

British Association for Local History, The Mill Manager's House, Cromford Mill, Cromford, Matlock, Derbyshire DE4 3RQ, T: 062-982 3768.

The Association exists to study and promote local history. It will put you in touch with your local group, give advice and invite you to seminars and courses. Typical topics include introductory days at the Public Records Office, computers in local history and writing about your local area. There are some competitions and membership entitles you to special rates for the *Local Historian*. Membership is £5 a year.

City of London Information Bureau, P.O. Box 270, Guildhall, London EC2, T: 01-606 3030.

The City of London offers enough interest to occupy you for a year or longer. The Information Bureau acts as a tourist office for the area, giving advice and guidance. Among the many attractions all of which are open to the public at varying times are: St. Paul's Cathedral, the Guildhall (open Monday – Saturday, 10am to 5pm, through most of the year, free), Dr. Johnson's House, the Monument, Prince Henry's Room, the Royal Exchange, the Tower of London, the Barbican, the Central Criminal Court and several museums. There are livery halls, food markets and, of course, the Stock Exchange (viewing gallery open Monday – Friday, 10am to 3pm). Many of the 43 churches give organ recitals and in the summer, you can enjoy open air concerts. Useful reading is *Visitor's Guide*, price 50p.

English Heritage, (Membership Office), P.O. Box 43, Ruislip, Middlesex HA4 OXW, T: 01-845 7788.

The Historic Buildings and Monuments Commission of England – popularly known as English Heritage – manages over 350 historic sites in England. Members may enter the sites free and join special guided tours and guest lectures both there and at some of the Royal Palaces, such as Hampton Court. Cost is £8 a year; £4 for senior citizens. The English Heritage Guide shows which sites have access for the disabled.

Friends of the Scottish Monuments, P.O. Box 1577, Edinburgh EH3 7QD, T: 031-226 2570.

Membership gives you free access to 330 of Scotland's historic buildings and ancient monuments and also a directory of the sites, many of which are open all year round. Cost is £7 a year; £3.50 for senior citizens.

Northern Ireland Monuments, Department of the Environment, 66 Balmoral Avenue, Belfast BT9 6NY.

Membership gives you free entry to 30 sites where you would normally pay, including castles, abbeys and Roman remains. There are organised lectures and you also receive a twice-yearly newspaper and map, showing all sites and monuments in the guardianship of Heritage. £5 a year; £4 for senior citizens.

Heritage in Wales, Welsh Historic Monuments, Brunel House, 2 Fitzalan Road, Cardiff CF2 1UU.

About 100 of the best ancient monuments in Wales are maintained by the Welsh Office. Most are open summer and winter. Season or single entry tickets can be purchased on site.

Garden History Society, P.O. Box 27, Haslemere, Surrey GU27 3DR.

The Society is concerned with the importance of historic gardens. It organises visits and lectures for members. An annual summer conference and a foreign tour are also arranged. There is a newsletter three times a year and a journal, *Garden History*. Subscriptions are £12 single, £15 joint.

Georgian Group, 37 Spital Square, London, E1, T: 01-377 1722.

The Group exists to preserve Georgian buildings and to stimulate public knowledge and appreciation of Georgian architecture and town planning. Activities include day visits, long weekends to buildings and gardens, private views of exhibitions and a programme of evening lectures in London. There are groups in Gloucester, Avon, South Yorkshire and in the Midlands. Membership: £10 a year, £15 for a couple.

Historical Association, 59a Kennington Park Road, London, SE11 4JH, T: 01-735 3901.

The Association brings people together to share their interest in history and to support such causes as the protection of our national heritage and the preservation of historical records. Members receive *The Historian* quarterly and may join in a wide variety of activities such as lectures, outings and conferences organised by local branches and at a national level. New members automatically receive the programme of their local branch. Overseas tours with expert lecturers are also arranged. Membership costs £13.50 a year.

Historic Houses Association, 38 Ebury Street, London, SW1W 0LU, T: 01-730 9419.

Friends of the HHA enjoy free entrance during normal opening hours to 260 HHA houses and gardens throughout the country, get the quarterly magazine *Historic House* and receive invitations to lectures, concerts, receptions and other events. Members act as volunteer helpers in many of the houses. Membership (HHA, P.O. Box 21, Spirella House, Bridge Road, Letchworth, Herts. T: 04626-79356): Individual £12.50, Double £20.

London Appreciation Society, 17 Manson Mews, London SW7 5AF, T: 01-370 1100.

The Society arranges frequent guided visits to galleries, museums, cathedrals and other places of interest. There is an imaginative activities programme, which recently included, for example, visits to: a brewery, a recycling centre, the Independent Broadcasting Authority, the annual church service for clowns, dinner at a Dutch restaurant (£9.45) and a coach tour to the site of the Battle of Naseby (£15.60). Details of forthcoming events are listed in the *Blue Book*, published twice yearly. Membership of the Society costs £5.

Monumental Brass Society, c/o Society of Antiquaries of London, Burlington House, Piccadilly, London W1V 0HS.

The Society encourages the preservation and appreciation of monumental brasses. Members attend three General Meetings with lectures and discussions and receive a portfolio of plates, bulletin and an invitation to the annual excursion. The annual subscription is £8.

There are many brass rubbing centres around the country where facilities are provided for the craft. Westminster Abbey for example is open Monday to Saturday, 9am – 5.30pm, where, for about £2 including materials you can make a rubbing from the replicas which come from all over England.

National Trust, 36 Queen Anne's Gate, London SW1, T: 01-222 9251.

The National Trust exists to protect historic buildings and areas of great natural beauty. Membership gives you free entry to the Trust's many properties. You also receive magazines and details of activities in your own region. Hundreds of special events are arranged each year, including guided tours, fairs and outdoor entertainments. The Trust also publishes a leaflet on facilities for the disabled. Individual membership is £14.50 and includes copy of the annual handbook.

National Trust for Scotland, 5 Charlotte Square, Edinburgh EH2 4DU, T:031-226 5922.

The National Trust for Scotland cares for 97 properties and 100,000 acres of countryside. Members also enjoy free admission to any of the properties in England, Wales and Northern Ireland. Individual membership is £12 a year; for a family, £20. Senior citizens: single membership is £6 a year; £10 for couple.

Oral History Society, Department of Sociology, University of Essex, Wivenhoe Park, Colchester CO4 3SQ.

The Society co-ordinates groups around the country who research and record the history of their area, as recounted by local people. It publishes twice yearly journals. Write to the secretary for the address of your nearest group.

Society of Genealogists, 14 Charterhouse Buildings, London EC1M 7BA, T:01-251 8799.

The Society promotes the study of genealogy and heraldry. Lectures are arranged in the winter and there are also a variety of annual courses, including day and weekend seminars. Members have access to the library and also receive a quarterly newsletter and magazine. There is a joining fee of £7.50. Annual membership is £20; £14 for country members.

Streets of London, 32 Grovelands Road, London N13 4RH, T: 01-882 3414.

Organises a range of 12 guided walking tours around London, each lasting 1½ to 2 hours, winter and summer. Each walk is linked to a theme, for example: 'In the Footsteps of Charles Dickens', 'Lawyers' London', 'Government and

Parliament'. You join the walk of your choice at the local underground station and pay £2 ·o go along. Alternatively, you can buy block tickets in advance: cost is £8 for ·· walks. You can write or phone for the programme; there is also a recorded message service, giving full details of the day's events.

Victorian Society, 1 Priory Gardens, Bedford Park, London W4 1TT, T:01-994 1019.

The Victorian Society campaigns to preserve fine Victorian and Edwardian buildings. It organises walks, tours, lectures and conferences through its national office and many regional groups. Typical events include: a walk in Victorian Windsor, private view of a Punch cartoon exhibition and a conference of Victorian churches. Advice is given on restoration and repairs. Individual membership: £10; senior citizens, £6.

Museums

Most museums organise free lectures, guided tours, and sometimes slide shows, on aspects of their collection or special exhibitions. As with art galleries and theatres, an increasing trend is to form a group of 'Friends' who pay a membership subscription to support the museum and in return enjoy certain advantages, such as: access to private views, visits to places of interest, receptions and other social activities.

British Association of Friends of Museums, 18 Garland Way, Northfield, Birmingham B31 2BT.

There are now well over 100 groups of Friends, supporting museums across the country including Wales, Scotland and Northern Ireland. The Association aims to help all these groups exchange ideas and present a united front. Additionally, it publishes a Yearbook (£1.50), listing all the groups in the Association. Only a handful of the major museums are given here. If you like the idea, enquire locally or contact the Association to discover what scope exists in your area.

British Museum Society, c/o The British Museum, London WC1 3DG, T: 01-637 9983.

Members receive a magazine three times a year and can enjoy regular lectures at the Museum, private views of special exhibitions, 'behind the scenes' visits and expeditions at home and abroad. There is a comfortable Members' Room. The subscription is £10 a year, plus £2 for each member at the same address.

Friends of Fashion, Museum of London, London Wall, London EC2Y 5HN, T: 01-600 3699 Ext. 248 280.

The Friends' group was founded to support the work of the Costume Department of the Museum which includes fashion, theatre, ceremonial and historical. Members fund-raise and in return are invited to special talks, private views and social occasions. Annual subscription is £7; or £10.50 for two people from the same household.

Friends of the National Maritime Museum, Park Row, London SE10 9NF, T:01-858 4422.

The Museum, housed in Greenwich Park, is the largest maritime museum in the world. Friends enjoy free entry to all exhibitions, private views, the opportunity to attend lectures designed for the museum staff, use of the library and visits to exhibitions of interest both in Britain and abroad. The subscription is £10 a year or £15 for husband and wife; £5 for pensioners and disabled people.

National Museum of Wales, Cathays Park, Cardiff. T:0222-397951 Ext. 69.

The Museum of Wales encompasses some 10 different museums, including the National Museum in Cardiff and Turner House in Penarth. Friends receive a monthly programme listing forthcoming lectures, films, concerts and other events including certain private social functions to which they are invited. Membership is £2 a year; £3 for couples.

Friends of Royal Scottish Museum, Chambers Street, Edinburgh EH1 1JF, T:031-552 5346.

Members are invited to private views, lectures, collectors' nights and discussion groups and 'behind the scenes' visits. The subscription is £3 a year, or £30 for life membership.

Friends of the V & A, The Victoria and Albert Museum, London SW7 2RL, T: 01-589 4040.

Friends enjoy free admission to: the V & A, Apsley House, Ham House, Osterley Park House and the Bethnal Green Museum. Membership also entitles you to private evening views of special exhibitions, a quarterly mailing of events, lunches at the Museum with speakers, free use of the library and slide library plus a small discount in the book and craft shops. Membership (which admits the member and one guest) is £15, £10 for pensioners.

Welsh Folk Museum, St. Fagan's, Cardiff, T: 0222-569441.

Friends support the museum which among other attractions features craftsmen demonstrating their work throughout the year. Typical crafts include: coopering, wood and metal restoration, sheepdog working, basket weaving, plaiting and farmhouse baking. A programme is available from the Department of Public Services at the Museum.

Nature and conservation

Many of the conservation organisations are very keen to recruit volunteers and are, therefore, listed in Chapter 10 rather than here. By the same token many of those concerned with field studies arrange courses and other special activity interests which, because there is usually a residential content, seem more appropriate in Chapter 12. The potential list is enormous. To give you a flavour, herewith a short 'mixed bag', highlighting a range from canals to molluscs.

Amenity organisations

If you are interested in conservation and the environment, you might like to join your local amenity society. You should be able to contact it through your public library.

The Civic Trust, 17 Carlton House Terrace, London SW1Y 5AW, T: 01-930 0914.

Publishes both an Environmental Directory (£3 post paid) listing 300 organisations including voluntary societies; and a bi-monthly journal, *Heritage Outlook*, with articles on planning architecture, transport, pollution and landscaping (Annual subscription £7).

British Ecological Society, Burlington House, Piccadilly, London W1V OLQ, T: 01-434 2641.

Membership is open to all who are interested in 'the scientific study of the pattern of relationships between living organisms and their environment'. The Society holds general and special interest group meetings and supports various ecological projects. Membership costs about £6, more if you wish to receive journals.

The Conchological Society of Great Britain and Ireland, 24 Park Hill Court, Addiscombe Road, Croydon, Surrey CRO 5PG.

The Society promotes the study of molluscs in the widest sense, including fossil molluscs and land and freshwater molluscs throughout the world. It organises lectures and field meetings, encourages the publication of papers and produces a newsletter.

The Conservation Foundation, 11a West Halkin Street, London SW1X 8JL, T:01-235 1743.

For those interested in wild life, nature conservation and protecting the environment, both rural and urban, the Conservation Foundation is a good starting point. Founded 5 years ago, its aims are to co-ordinate and publicise conservation work. The *Conservation Review*, published by the Foundation, lists over 500 groups and societies – everything from your local County Naturalist Trust to the International Federation of Organic Agricultural Movements. It costs £4.95 inc. p&p from the above address.

Epping Forest Conservation Centre, High Beach, Loughton, Essex 1G1O 4AF, T:01-508 7714.

This Field Studies Council Day Centre is easily accessible from London and East Anglia. It runs evening classes, weekend and other field study courses.

Forestry Commission, 231 Corstophine Road, Edinburgh EH12 7AT, T:031-334 0303.

The Commission publishes a number of useful books, including: *Forest Parks* (HMSO, 40p), describing its forest parks, arboreta and facilities for visitors; and a regional series (free) *See Your Forests* describing forest walks, picnic places and special activities such as canoeing, horseriding, birdwatching, hill climbing and fishing, clay pigeon shooting, field archery, stalking and wild fowling. Visitors' Centres have exhibitions explaining the role of the forest in the locality.

Royal Society for Nature Conservation, The Green, Nettleham, Lincoln LN2 2NR, T:0522-752326.

The Society is the national association of the 46 Nature Conservation Trusts throughout the United Kingdom, which manage over 1500 nature reserves. By joining your local society, you can visit the reserves and help in their wardening and management. Local groups run their own activities, surveys, newsletters, field meetings, lectures and film shows. The RSNC will send you a list of addresses. Membership fees vary from one Trust to another, ranging from £4 to £12.

Scottish Inland Waterways Association, 11 Arden Street, Edinburgh EH9 1BR, T:031-229 7149.

The Association co-ordinates the activities of local canal preservation societies and will put you in touch with your nearest group.

Pen-friends

Despite the telephone, pen-friendship is flourishing. It is an ideal activity for those who have difficulty in getting out and about and many life-long friendships develop this way. Among the organisations that promote pen-friend schemes are:

Friends by Post, 6 Bollin Court, Macclesfield Road, Wilmslow, Cheshire SK9 2AP.

Please enclose sae.

Letter-Link, 31 Chanters Hill, Barnstaple, Devon EX32 8DN.
Please enclose sae.

Saga Magazine Club, P.O. Box 65, Sandgate, Folkstone, Kent.
Membership of the club is £3.70, £3.80 for couples.

International Friendship League, 4 Wilton Close, Taunton, Somerset TA1 4E2.
The League aims to promote friendship among people of the world by social contact, travel and correspondence. Pen-friends abroad are organised through the IFL Pen-Friend Service, Saltash, Cornwall; pen-friends in Britain, through the IFL Pen-Friend Service UK, P.O. Box 117, Leicester. In both cases, please enclose sae. Additionally, there are some 20 local groups in Britain which organise activities such as dances, talks, rambles and service to the community. Members can be put in contact with IFL members abroad when they travel and may also use IFL's accommodation in London and Gloucester. Membership costs £4 a year; £5.50 for couples; £3 for senior citizens.

Scottish focus

Just about every section in this chapter includes events and activities in Scotland, as elsewhere in the country. In contrast, the two organisations listed here cater exclusively for those with a special interest in Scottish traditions and the Scots language.

The Saltire Society, Saltire House, Atholl Crescent, Edinburgh EH3 8HA, T:031-228 6621.
The Society champions all things Scottish, past and present. Typical activities include: musical evenings with bagpipes, Scottish dancing, dinners, excursions, lectures on architecture and history plus many others. The Society has branches in Aberdeen, Edinburgh and Helensburgh. Annual membership is £8; £5 for senior citizens.

Scots Language Society, c/o 26 Balgreen Road, Edinburgh EH12, T:031-337 3938.
The Society exists to promote the Scots Language, in both its urban and rural dialects. Members receive a twice-yearly journal and may attend the annual conference addresses by eminent writers, scholars and educationalists. The Society runs a competition to encourage writing in the Scots language. Membership £3.50 a year, £5 for families.

Sport

Retirement is no excuse for giving up sport. On the contrary, it is an ideal time to get into trim. Facilities abound and, unlike people with a 9 to 5 job, you enjoy the great advantage of being able to book out of peak hours.

The Sports Council is running a campaign called '50-plus All to Play For' throughout the 1980s, aimed at encouraging people over 50 to become involved in sport and physical recreation. An inherent feature of the promotion is that those who are out of condition, or beginners, are welcomed at Sports Council Centres and are advised as to suitable sports they might enjoy. To find out about opportunities in your area, contact your local authority recreational department, or your sports/leisure centre. Both should have the 50-plus leaflets together with information about coaching and medical advice for older people. If you have any difficulties contact the regional office of the Sports Council, address from:

Sports Council, 16 Upper Woburn Place, London WC1H 0QP, T:01-388 1277.

Angling

National Anglers Council, 11 Cowgate, Peterborough, Cambridgeshire PE1 1L2, T:0733-54084.

If you want to join an angling club, ask your local Water Authority for a list of addresses. You will require a licence from them to fish in all rivers. Alternatively, write to the NAC. Among other information, it can advise on fishing venues with access and facilities for disabled anglers.

Archery

Grand National Archery Society, Seventh Street, The National Agricultural Centre, Stoneleigh, Kenilworth, Warwickshire LV8 2LG, T:0203-23907.

The Society is the governing body for archery, including field archery. It will put you in touch with a local group who will advise you on equipment and help you to develop your skills. There are often prizes or classes for 'veterans' in tournaments organised by the GNAS. The Society also holds week-end events.

Badminton

Badminton Association of England, National Badminton Centre, Bradwell Road, Laughton Lodge, Milton Keynes, Bucks MK8 90A, T:0908-568822.

Most sports and leisure centres have badminton courts and give instruction, as do many adult education institutes. If you need advice, contact the

Association. As well as offering information, it runs a number of short residential courses in several parts of the country.

Billiards and snooker

The Billiards and Snooker Control Council, Coronet House, Queen Street, Leeds LS1 2TN, T:0532-440586.

The Council is the governing body of the sport. It is responsible for the rules and organises national competitions for non-professional players. It can give you a list of clubs and advise about events including holiday-linked activities.

Bowling

There are many clubs all over the country and a number of local authorities may also provide facilities. Alternatively contact:

English Bowling Association, 2a Iddesleigh Road, Bournemouth, Dorset BH3 7JR, T: 0202-22233.

Women's Bowling Association, 2 Inghalls Cottages, Ditteridge, Box, Corsham. Wilts SN14 9PP, T: 0225-742 852.

Indoor Bowling Association, 290a Barking Road, London E6 3BA, T:01-470 1237.

There are qualified coaches for beginners in over 2,000 local clubs, and some clubs have reduced rates for senior citizens. A National Saga Competition for 60-plus singles and pairs is organised through clubs each year. If you decide to take up bowls, you are advised not to buy your equipment without advice from the club coach.

Clay pigeon shooting

Clay Pigeon Shooting Association, 107 Epping New Road, Buckhurst Hill, Essex 1G9 5TQ, T:01-505 6221.

The CPSA is an association of individual shooters and a federation of clubs. As a member you have public liability insurance, your scores are recorded in the national averages and you can compete in national events. The CPSA can supply you with a list of clubs and various publications including *Buying a Shotgun*, with advice on how to obtain a shot gun certificate. Membership is £10 a year.

Cricket

National Cricket Association, Lord's Cricket Ground, London NW8 8QN, T: 01-289 6098.

If you want to play, watch or help at cricket matches, contact your local club, or send a stamped addressed envelope to the above address. The NCA can put you in touch with your county cricket association. It also organises the Dunlop 50-plus County Cricket Championship.

Croquet

The Croquet Association, Hurlingham Club, Ranelagh Gardens, London SW6 3PR, T:01-736 3148

A growing number of local authorities as well as clubs now offer facilities for croquet enthusiasts. The Croquet Association runs coaching courses and can advise you about club membership, events and similar.

Cycling

Cyclists' Touring Club, Cotterell House, 69 Meadrow, Godalming, Surrey GU7 3HS, T:04868-7217.

The CTC is the largest national cycling organisation. It offers members cycle insurance, a club magazine and handbook, organised cycling holidays and introductions to 200 local cycling groups. Membership costs £13 a year.

Golf

English Golf Union, 1-3 Upper King Street, Leicester LE1 6XF, T:0533-553042.
Scottish Golf Union, Bank of Scotland Building, 54 Shandwich Place, Edinburgh EH2 4RT, T:031-226 6711.
Golfing Union of Ireland, Glencar House, 81 Eglinton Road, Donnybrook, Dublin 4. T:0001-69 41 11
Welsh Golfing Union, 2 Isfryn, Burry Port, Dyfed SA16 0BY.

The National Golf Unions can provide information about municipal courses and private clubs, of which there are some 1,400 in England alone. Additionally many adult education institutes and sports centres run classes for beginners.

Rambling

Ramblers' Association, 1-5 Wandsworth Road, London SW8 2LJ, T:01-582 6878.

Rambling can be anything from a gentle stroll to an action-packed weekend trek with stout boots and a rucksack. The Ramblers' Association has over 200 local groups throughout the country, many of whom survey and warden footpaths in their area. Additionally the Association has scores of activities including overseas rambling holidays. Membership is £8 a year; £4 for the retired.

Rifle shooting

National Rifle Association and **National Small Bore Rifle Association**, Lord Roberts House, Bisley Camp, Brookwood, Woking, Surrey GU24 ONP, T:048-676969.
The Association can put you in touch with a local club. It also arranges competitions and publishes a journal called *Rifleman*. Annual Membership is around £15, less for those over 65.

Swimming

Amateur Swimming Association, Harold Fern House, Derby Square, Loughborough, Leics LE11 0AL, T:0509-230431.
Over the past decade, there has been a huge increase in the number of excellent pools in municipal sports and leisure centres. Coaching is usually available and many reserve the pool at various times of the week for older people who prefer to swim without schoolchildren splashing around and shouting. The Association runs an award scheme to encourage greater proficiency in swimming.

Tennis

Lawn Tennis Association, Barons Court, West Kensington, London W14 9EG, T:01-385 2366.
As with swimming, facilities have been greatly improving and your local authority Recreation Department should be able to advise you. The LTA will be able to put you in touch with your County Association.

Veteran rowing

The Amateur Rowing Association, 6 Lower Mall, London W6 9DJ, T:01-748 3652.
Veteran rowing as a sport is fast growing in popularity. Enthusiasts range in age from 27 to well past 80. For those who enjoy a competitive edge, there are special races and regattas with types of craft including eights, fours, pairs as well as single and double sculling. Touring rowing is also on the increase and

additionally there is plenty of scope for those who simply want the exercise and a pleasant afternoon afloat. Nearly all clubs welcome novice veterans, both male and female, and usually the only qualification required is the ability to swim. Coaching is provided and membership is normally in the range of £50 to £80 a year. For information about clubs in your locality, contact the ARA at the above address.

Yachting

Royal Yachting Association, Victoria Way, Woking, Surrey GU21 1EQ, T:048-62 5020.

There are 1,400 sailing clubs affiliated to the RYA and more than 1000 recognised teaching establishments. Membership costs £8.50 a year.

Sciences

If astronomy fascinates you or you would like to understand more about meteorology (who wouldn't, given our uncertain climate!), there are several societies and associations who would welcome you as a member.

British Astronomical Association, Burlington House, Piccadilly, London W1V ONL, T:01-734 4145.

The Association is open to all people interested in astronomy. Members' work is co-ordinated in such sections as: Moon, Terrestrial Planets, Meteors, Artificial Satellites, Historical, Observing Techniques, and so on. The Association holds meetings both in London and elsewhere and loans instruments to members who may also use the library. Membership costs £20 a year, or £14.70 for those over 65.

Geologists' Association, Burlington House, London W1V 0JU, T:01-734 2356.

The Association organises lectures, field excursions and monthly meetings at Burlington House, as well as introductory talks for those new to geology. There are varying levels of subscriptions, ranging from about £6 to £12. Local groups organise their own programmes. These exist in Brent, Essex, Midlands, Lancashire, Staffordshire, South Wales and Avon.

Royal Geographical Society, 1 Kensington Gore, London SW7 2AR, T:01-589 5466.

The Society is a national source of geographical information and a focal point for exploration activity. Fellows need no special qualifications but must be proposed and seconded by existing Fellows. Once elected, you can attend lectures, meetings and frequent social events and can also enjoy the facilities of the library and map room. Fellows: Election fee £15, annual subscription £25.

Royal Meteorological Society, James Glaisher House, Grenville Place, Bracknell, Berkshire, T:0344-22957.

The Society, which includes among its membership both amateurs and professionals, exists to advance meteorological science. Members may attend scientific meetings and field courses and receive the monthly magazine *Weather*. Membership costs £20 a year.

Women's organisations

Although today women can participate in almost any activity on equal terms with men, women's clubs and organisations continue to enjoy enormous popularity. Among the best known are Women's Institutes, the Mothers' Union and Townswomen's Guilds.

Co-operative Women's Guild, 342 Hoe Street, London E17 9PX, T:01-520 4902.

The Guild's objects are to encourage women to play a full part in the co-operative movement and in local, national and international affairs. Branches throughout England and Wales organise their own programme, partly linked to a national theme, which is usually a major topical concern, such as Famine in Africa. Branches also raise funds for a nationally agreed charity. Membership is £4.20 a year; 35p a month.

Mothers' Union, 24 Tufton Street, London SW1P 3RB, T:01-222 5533.

The Mothers' Union is a world-wide society which aims to foster Christian values in the sphere of marriage and family life. It is open to all those who have been baptised and who declare their support for the Union's aims. Members of the Mothers' Union are involved in social and practical activities such as, for example, neighbourhood schemes. Indoor members who are housebound are linked through prayer circles. There is a quarterly magazine and the Mothers' Union runs an 'Adopt a Granny' scheme and provides holidays for families under stress.

National Association of Women's Clubs, 5 Vernon Rise, King's Cross Road, London WC1X 9EP, T:01-837 1434.

There are 620 Women's Clubs with a membership of 40,000. They are open to women of all ages and interests. Each club is self-governing, choosing its own meeting times and programme. Typical activities include: crafts, home-making, beauty and health care, music, dancing, drama and keep fit. There are outings to theatres and exhibitions and visits to places of interest and many clubs arrange holiday groups in Great Britain and abroad. Some do voluntary service in their communities for the sick, elderly and handicapped. A number run co-operative shopping ventures and mutual self-help projects. From January 1987 there will be an individual membership fee of £2 per member.

National Federation of Women's Institutes, 39 Eccleston Street, London SW1W 9NT, T:01-730 7212.

The Women's Institute has over 9,000 branches in England and Wales with some 350,000 members. Though once essentially a countrywomen's organisation, today this is no longer the case and flourishing branches exist all over the country. Local WI's run courses, social events and arrange many leisure activities including: crafts, gardening, sport, music, art, drama and current affairs. Members may participate in both county and national functions and also attend the WI residential college for a short special interest course. Additionally, there are around 500 weekly market stalls for which volunteers – both to sell and to supply produce – are always in demand. Membership is £5. There is a national magazine *Home and Country* (£4.25 for 12 issues, via your local WI, £6 by post).

Scottish Women's Rural Institutes, 42 Herlot Row, Edinburgh EH3 6ES, T:031-0225 1724.

This is the Scottish counterpart of the Women's Institute movement. There are 46,500 members of all ages who enjoy social, recreational and educational activities. There are talks and demonstrations, classes in arts and crafts and discussions on matters of public interest. You can be put in touch with your local group through your County Federation or the headquarters office.

If you live in Northern Ireland, contact the **Federation of Women's Institutes of Northern Ireland**, 209-211 Upper Lisburn Road, Belfast BT10 0LL, T:0232-665506.

National Housewives Register, 245 Warwick Road, Solihull, West Midlands B92 7AH, T:021-706 1101.

The NHR is a nationwide organisation of women who meet to discuss literally anything from poetry to politics as well as engage in activities such as learning to play bridge, undertaking research or forming a book reading club. It has about 24,000 members in some 1,200 local groups who meet, usually in members' houses, to talk and get to know each other. Inter-group conferences are arranged and there is also a newsletter. The annual subscription is £2.50.

Townswomen's Guilds, 75 Harborne Road, Birmingham B15 3DA, T:021-455 6216.

The Guilds' purpose is to provide a meeting ground for women of all ages and social backgrounds to 'widen their knowledge of life and living'. They help members to develop new interests and make new friends. There are over 2,350 Guilds that meet variously in the morning, afternoon or evening to suit participants. Programmes may include: drama, music and singing, craft demonstrations, lectures, teach-ins on money, health and beauty days, family residential weekend courses, sports and many other opportunities for informal education. Annual subscription is £5. A monthly journal is available at 30p a copy.

Women's Gas Federation, Orchard House, 14 Great Smith Street, London SW1P 3BU, T: 01-222 3677.

The Federation is a non-commercial voluntary organisation which provides a link between home-makers and the gas industry. There are branches throughout the country and meetings are normally held once a month in the evening or afternoon. Programmes include one gas cookery and gas use presentation a year as well as speakers and demonstrations on a wide variety of subjects. Additionally members organise many social activities, such as: dramatic performances, cheese and wine parties, coffee mornings for charity, barn dances and carol services. There are regional offices in: Rochdale, Edinburgh, Newark, Reading and Stourbridge, West Midlands. Membership is £4.50 a year.

Other information

Pensioners Link, 19 Balfe Street, London N1 9EB, T:01-278 5501.

Formerly known as Task Force, Pensioners Link is a pressure group with around 15 centres in London that believes in the right of pensioners to live full, healthy, active and independent lives. It works in partnership with pensioners by providing resources, information and support to enable them to be self-reliant and to instigate their own initiatives. There are social clubs offering a wide range of activities including dancing, handicrafts and films. Some groups run health courses to discuss subjects facing the elderly, together with practical sessions on diet, yoga and exercise. Others run 'Reminiscence Projects', building up a picture of their joint pasts by focussing for example on the Second World War. Additionally, Pension Action Groups campaign on such issues as fuel, benefits and transport facilities. There is also an Advisory Service which assists pensioners with pension and benefits queries. Individual membership is £3; 50p for pensioners.

Public transport

One of the big gains of reaching retirement age is the availability of cheap travel. Most local authorities offer concessionary fares to senior citizens during the off-peak periods and it is widely anticipated that many of the new bus services will follow suit. Coaches too very often have special rates for older people and as everyone knows British Rail Senior Citizens' Cards, available to men and women over 60, offer wonderful savings. Details of these are given in Chapter 12.

Useful reading

The Time of Your Life – A Handbook for Retirement. £4.50 incl. postage from Help the Aged Education Department, St. James Walk, London EC1R OBE, (T:01-253 0253).

8. Starting Your Own Business

Running a small business can be one of the most satisfying retirement occupations. There are hundreds of success stories of those who took the plunge at 55-plus to build a company that provided involvement, fun and income plus a legacy for their children. However, a word of warning. For every success story there is a failure and your money will disappear fast if you set up in big company style. Small business is all about cutting costs, doing it yourself and driving second hand cars until you are making profits with a positive cash flow. Your partner's attitude is probably crucial. Even if he or she is not directly involved they will have to accept the loss of a sitting room as an office, the out-of-hours phone calls and the suddenly cancelled social engagement. If you have a skill to offer, the drive to sell it and the health to support your ambition, this chapter will give you the information you need to set up or buy into a small concern and join the ranks of other successful entrepreneurs.

Legal structure

If you are thinking of starting a business, you have three main choices as to the legal form it can take. You can operate as: a sole trader, a partnership, or a limited company.

Sole trader

This is the simplest form of trading, with virtually no start-up expenses and minimal bureaucracy involved. If you trade under your own name then, apart from informing the Inland Revenue and the Department of Health and Social Security, there are no legal formalities. If you use another name, you must indicate on documents such as letterheads that you are the owner (see below, under Business Names).

Even if you employ others, you will be treated as self-employed for both tax and National Insurance purposes and will be liable to pay personal income tax on your profits, after deducting allowable expenses. You will also be required to pay National Insurance contributions on your earnings.

The main disadvantage of operating as a sole trader – and it is a major one – is that it carries unlimited liability so you would be personally liable for all business debts. Should the business fail, your own assets as well as your business ones would be at the disposal of your creditors – and if the worst came to the worst, you could be made personally bankrupt.

Partnership

A partnership is a business with two or more proprietors. Similar to operating as a sole trader, a partnership can be formed without any legal formalities or documentation other than informing the Inland Revenue and DHSS.

To avoid any possible future misunderstanding however, it is advisable to have a formal Partnership Agreement drawn up at the outset, covering such points as: distribution of profits (equal or unequal shares), voting rights, control of the bank account and arrangements for admitting new partners. While it is a simple matter to form a partership, it can be very irksome to settle the affairs of one that has gone wrong. A few legal expenses at the beginning could prove a worthwhile investment.

As with sole traders, partners are treated as self-employed for both tax and National Insurance purposes. Profits are divided and taxed as the personal income of individual partners. However, if one partner fails to pay his/her share the other partners will be called upon to meet the shortfall. Similarly each partner carries unlimited liability for all the debts of the business.

An exception to this rule – although rare today – is that of a *limited partnership*. This has to be registered at Companies House and at least one partner has to incur unlimited liability. The limited partners (sometimes known as sleeping partners) cannot take part in the running of the business in any way and their liability is limited to their share of the partnership capital.

Accounts need to be prepared at least once a year, but they do not need to be published.

Limited company

A limited company is a legal entity in its own right. As its name implies, liability for the company's debts in the event of insolvency is limited to the amount invested in the business by each shareholder. As a director of a limited company, you will be treated for tax and National Insurance purposes as an employee of the business, paying income tax under the PAYE system. Corporation Tax will also be payable on the profits of the company.

The main disadvantage of a limited company is the bureaucracy. The Government is reducing the red tape for small firms but for the time being, there are a number of legal requirements that must be fulfilled, both before and after trading starts. A limited company must be registered by the Registrar of Companies for England and Wales (or, in Scotland, by the Registrar of Companies for Scotland): this involves the filing of both a Memorandum of

Association and the Articles of Association (see below). The company's accounts have to be audited once a year by a firm of qualified accountants and a set showing, among other details, a profit and loss account must be filed annually with the Registrar of Companies together with basic information about the company and its directors, all of which are open to public inspection.

Registering a limited company

You may register a limited company yourself and the Companies Registration Office will advise on the procedures to be followed. Alternatively, you can get a professional accountant, solicitor or Company Registration Agent to do it for you. Charges vary considerably, but are likely to start from around £120 upwards.

To register a limited company, you need to fill in: Form 10, *Notification of First Directors and Secretary and Location of Registered Office*; Form 12, *Declaration of Compliance*; and PUC I, giving details of share capital. These must be sent to the Registrar of Companies together with the *Memorandum of Association* (stating the company's name, share capital and nature and scope of the business arrangements, including the extent of liability) and the *Articles of Association* (stating the internal rules of the company).

All the necessary forms can be got either from law stationers or from the Companies Registration Office. Specimen memoranda and articles can only be obtained from law stationers.

Fees. It costs £50 to register (plus an additional £20 per year, payable when the annual accounts are sent in for public display). Minimal stamp duty must also be paid to the Inland Revenue.

'Off the shelf'

The whole process of registering a new company will take several weeks. However, if you are not too fussy about the company name it is possible to buy a previously registered company 'off the shelf' from a Company Registration Agent. This will cost, on average, about £120 for all the documentation, including the company books and seal. There will be a further charge of around £75 should you decide to change the name and a charge of around £25 to change the articles of association. For more information, contact:

The Registrar of Companies for England and Wales, Companies House, Crown Way, Maindy, Cardiff C84 3UZ, T: 0222 388588; or **The Registrar of Companies for Scotland**, Companies Registration Office, Exchequer Chambers, 102 George Street, Edinburgh EH2 3DJ, T: 031-225 5774.

Workers' co-operative

This is another possible form of business structure. Co-operatives are basically run and owned by the workers according to general principles of co-operation – for instance, all members have equal voting rights irrespective of financial involvement and profits are distributed according to the number of hours worked rather than the amount of money invested in the business.

Legally, they can be structured as a partnership or as a limited company and are taxed and regulated as such. Most co-operatives register as a limited company, either through incorporation under the Companies Acts in the normal way, in which case a minimum of two sponsors is required; or through registration under the Industrial and Provident Societies Acts (minimum of seven sponsors).

Registration under the Industrial and Provident Societies Acts costs £140 plus a Co-operative Development Agency negotiation fee of £25; registration under the Companies Acts costs £150. If, as opposed to using CDA model rules, you write your own, registration can cost up to £300. For more information, contact:

The Co-operative Development Agency, Broadmead House, 21 Panton Street, London SW1Y 4DR, T: 01-839 2988 or **Industrial Common Ownership Movement (ICOM)**, Head Office: 7 Corn Exchange, Leeds LS1 7BP, T: 0532 461737/8, and 7 Bradbury Street, London N16, T: 01-249 2837.

ICOM provides advice on setting up a co-operative and publishes a number of useful books, including *Workers' Co-operative Handbook* (£3.75).

Business names

It is no longer necessary to register a business name. However, where a sole trader uses a business name that is different from his real name, or where a partnership trades under a name that differs from those of *all* the partners, or a limited company trades other than under its full corporate name, then certain legal requirements have to be met:

All business stationery – including letterheads, order forms, invoices and receipts – must contain the real name(s) of the sole trader, partner or company, together with the official address of the business. These details must also be prominently displayed on all business premises. Failure to do so is a criminal offence, punishable with a fine of up to £200.

There are also certain regulations governing the words that may be used in a business or company name *without justification*. Prohibited words include: those considered offensive or those that imply connection with the Crown, the Government or a local authority, e.g. British, National, European.

Other prohibited categories are titles like Society or Institute which suggest a representative status or words which imply a specific function such as insurance or banking. In all such cases, approval must be sought from the appropriate Government Department or governing body that the use of such words is justified.

The Registrar of Companies will also refuse to register a company name that is identical or 'too like' one already on the register, even if it is your own name.

For more information see *Notes for Guidance on Company Names* and Notes for Guidance on Business Names and *Notes on Sensitive Words and Expressions* from the Companies Registration Office.

Alternative ways of starting

Rather than start a business from scratch, you could buy into one that is already established or instead, consider franchising.

Buying a business

Buying an established business can be an attractive route to becoming your own boss, as it eliminates many of the problems of start-up. The enterprise is likely to come equipped with: stock, suppliers, an order book, premises and possibly employees. It may also have debts.

Take professional advice before buying any business, even one off friends. In particular, you should consider *why* the business is being sold. It may be for perfectly respectable reasons – for instance, a change of circumstances such as retirement. But equally, it may be that the market is saturated, that the rent is about to go sky high or that major competition has opened up nearby.

The value of the company's assets will be reflected in its purchase price, as will the 'good will' (or reputation) that it has established.

Before parting with your money, make sure that the assets are actually owned by the business and get the stock professionally valued. You should also ensure that the debts are collectible and that the same credit terms will apply from existing suppliers. Get an accountant to look at the figures for the last three years and have a chartered surveyor check the premises. It is also advisable to ask a solicitor to vet any legal documents, including staff contracts: you will automatically inherit any existing employees. See Department of Employment leaflet No.10 *Employment Rights on the Transfer of an Undertaking*.

Franchising

Franchising has become an increasingly popular form of distribution, with attractions for both franchisor and franchisee. The franchisor gains in that it enables an ambitious group to expand very quickly. The advantage to the franchisee is that there are normally fewer risks than starting a business from scratch.

A franchisee buys into an established business and builds up his own enterprise under its wing. In return for his investment plus regular royalty payments, he acquires the right to sell its products or services within a specified geographic area and enjoys the benefits of the organisation's reputation, buying power and marketing expertise. Examples of well known franchises include Wimpy Bar, Budget Rent-a-Car, Servicemaster and Benetton.

As a franchisee you are effectively your own boss. You finance the business, employ the staff, and retain the profits after the franchisor has had his cut. You are usually expected to maintain certain standards and conform to the broad corporate approach of the organisation. In return, however, the franchisor should train you in the business, provide management support and give you access to a wide range of back-up services.

Cost
The amount of capital needed to buy a franchise varies enormously according to the type of business and can be anywhere between £2,000 and £250,000. The franchisee is normally liable to pay:

- **a deposit**, covering the period during which he undergoes training and raises the necessary finance. The deposit is usually partially refundable if no franchise agreement is concluded;
- **an initial fee**, covering both the entry cost and the initial support services provided by the franchisor, such as advice about location, market research and so on. The British Franchise Association estimates that on average this represents roughly 5 to 10 per cent of total setting up costs. Advice should be taken as to whether the fee will be partially or wholly allowable for tax purposes;
- **recurring fees or royalties**, which are usually based on a percentage of gross sales (typically 11 per cent), exclusive of VAT. Sometimes, where the franchisor supplies his own exclusive products, he may derive his income from the usual mark-up on the sale of products to you.

Length of agreement
The length of the agreement will depend both on the type of business involved and the front end fee. Agreements can run from one to fifteen years, with five years being average. Many franchisors include an option to renew the agreement, which should be treated as a valuable asset.

Raising the finance
Franchising has now built up a good track record with a relatively low rate of business failures, so raising the money for a franchising venture is rarely a major

difficulty. Most of the leading High Street banks operate specialist franchise loan sections. Another useful source of funds is **Franchise Investors Ltd (FIL)**, Davidson House, Green Man Lane, Hatton Cross, Feltham, Middlesex TW14 OPZ, T: 01-890 9896, which includes among its backers a number of leading City institutions.

Franchisors may also be able to help in raising the money and can sometimes arrange more advantageous terms through their connections with financial institutions. For more information, contact:

The British Franchise Association, 75a Bell Street, Henley on Thames, Oxon RG9 2BD, T: 0491-578049.

The British Franchise Association (BFA) represents 'the responsible face' of franchising and its members have to conform to a stringent code of practice. The BFA publishes a Franchise Information Pack (£6.00) which provides comprehensive advice on buying a franchise together with a list of BFA members and those on the pre-qualification register.

It is well worth visiting the annual National Franchise Exhibition, usually held at the beginning of October where you can see and compare the various franchise options on offer.

A good franchisor will provide a great deal of invaluable help. However, some franchisors are very casual in their approach, lacking in competence, or even downright unethical. Points to look out for include overpricing of exclusive stock and lack of back-up services. Make careful enquiries before committing any money and check first with the BFA what they know about the business. Talk to some of the other franchisees to find out what their experience has been.

Taxation

Taxation arrangements vary considerably according to whether you are operating as a sole trader, partnership or limited company. As you will know, tax rates, bands and allowances are revised annually and take effect at the beginning of the financial year in April. Figures quoted in this section apply to the 1986/87 financial year.

Sole trader or partnership

As soon as you start work on your own account, you should inform your local Inspector of Taxes. To do so, you should obtain Form 41G from your local Inland Revenue office (see telephone directory for address) and return it, when completed, together with your Form P45 which your employer will have given you when you left.

As a sole trader or member of a partnership, you are treated as self-employed for tax purposes. Profits are aggregated with any other personal income and are taxed at the normal rates of income tax. The basic rate of 29 per cent extends to the first £17,200 of taxable income rising to a maximum of 60 per cent on taxable income in excess of £41,200.

Not all your income is taxable. In common with everyone else, you get a *personal tax allowance* (the single person's and wife's earned income allowance is £2,335; the married man's allowance, £3,655). Additionally, as a self-employed person (Schedule D), you are allowed certain other reliefs. As a general guideline, the following expenses and allowances are tax deductible:

Business expenses: these must be incurred 'wholly and exclusively' for the purposes of the trade. Professional publications would probably qualify; however, your 'wages', national insurance contributions and any business entertaining (other than for overseas customers) would not. Bad debts are usually allowable. Certain expenses incurred in advance of getting the business started are also allowable. For example: necessary travelling, printing costs and telephoning.

Partially allowable expenses: these mainly apply if you are working from home. They include such items as that part of your rent, rates, heating, lighting and telephone usage that you devote to business purposes; also possibly, some of the running expenses on your car.

Spouse's wages: if you employ your partner in the business, his/her pay (providing this is reasonable) qualifies as a legitimate expense, in the same way as any other employee's, but must of course be accounted for through the PAYE system.

Pension contributions: you are allowed to invest up to 17.5 per cent of your earnings in a pension plan, free of tax.

Capital allowances: a percentage of the cost of some items is 'allowed' for tax relief, for example, an annual allowance of 25 per cent (on the reducing balance) of the cost of plant and machinery, including office furniture and cars. For further information, see Inland Revenue leaflet CA 1 *Capital Allowances on Machinery and Plant*.

Interest on loans: tax relief is given on money borrowed to invest in a small firm, in most normal circumstances.

Some other advantages include:

Basis of assessment: the first year's trading results will normally be used as the basis for tax assessments for up to three years. This can be an advantage if low profits are earned in the first twelve months.

Tax losses: any tax losses in the first four years may enable you to recover PAYE from your last three years in employment. A tax loss made by the business can also be set against any other income the proprietor may have.

Because of these reliefs, being a sole trader or partner can offer substantial tax advantages. As a result, the Inland Revenue has become increasingly strict about the definition of self-employed. If you work as a consultant or freelancer and most of your income derives from one employer, your Inspector of Taxes may argue that you are an employee of that firm – and not a self-employed person.

Capital gains tax. Capital gains tax is payable at 30 per cent by sole traders or partners if they sell the company or any of its assets. Each individual is exempted from tax on the first £6,300 of gain. However, no tax will be payable if the proceeds are reinvested within three years in another business (or business assets). Assets bought the previous year might also qualify. This is normally referred to as roll-over relief.

If the owners want to give part of their business (or its assets) to their family, capital gains tax need not be payable until a sale to a third party occurs. This is called hold-over relief.

Trading losses cannot be set off against capital gains tax. For further information, see Inland Revenue leaflet CGT 11 *Capital Gains Tax and the Small Businessman*. You should also speak to an accountant about the implications of inheritance tax.

Preparation of accounts. Accounts must be submitted annually to the Inland Revenue. These are normally in two parts: the Trading Account and Profit and Loss Account, which provide a summary of the year's trading transactions; and the Balance Sheet, which shows the 'assets' and 'liabilities' of the business at the end of the year.

The accounts of a sole trader or partnership do not have to be audited by an independent qualified accountant. However, whether you draw up the accounts yourself or engage professional help, full and accurate records must be kept from the start. While not essential, there is a very strong argument for having a qualified accountant to help you, since his/her advice is likely to prove invaluable in a whole range of matters. For assistance in finding a local accountant, contact: **The Institute of Chartered Accountants**, 1 Moorgate Place, Chartered Accountants Hall, P.O.Box 433, London EC2P 2BJ, T: 01-628 7060.

Making a tax return. As an employee, you will have had income tax deducted from your gross pay automatically under the PAYE system. When you become self-employed, you become responsible for the payment of tax and are required by law to make a true return of your income each year. Tax is usually payable in two equal instalments: on January 1 and July 1 on the preceding year's profits. You should therefore remember to make provision, so you can pay when the tax demand comes.

The Inspector of Taxes will send you annual tax return forms and formal notices of assessment to tax. If you have an accountant, arrangements can be made for these to be sent to him direct. Normally, no assessments will be made until you have completed twelve months' trading. If you disagree with the amount of taxable profits given in the notice of assessment, you have 30 days in which to appeal.

Useful reading. For more information about the tax position of sole traders and partnerships, see Inland Revenue booklet, IR 28, *Starting in Business* (obtainable from any tax office).

Limited company

The Inland Revenue will be automatically notified when a limited company is formed and will contact the directors in due course.

Corporation tax. A company pays corporation tax on its profits at the rate of 35 per cent. There is, however, a *special small companies' rate* of 29 per cent, which applies where profits do not exceed £100,000 per annum. Tax is normally payable nine months after the date to which the accounts are made up.

As a director of a limited company, the business will pay your salary which will be subject to PAYE. *Allowable expenses*, similar to those for sole traders and partnerships, are deductible before corporation tax is charged. Directors' expenses may however be disallowed, in whole or in part, if the Inland Revenue takes the view that these benefited directors personally – as opposed to being a legitimate business expense. Such expenses may be taxed as a personal benefit.

The Inland Revenue does not allow unlimited payments into *pension schemes*, particularly those designed to benefit directors. The limits depend, among other factors, on the age of the individuals concerned: it is advisable to discuss this with the company's accountants.

Relief for losses. If your company makes a loss, the directors cannot offset this against their personal taxable income. The losses can, however, be offset against both future and past profits made by the company.

Preparation of accounts: limited companies are required to file annual accounts, which have been audited by an independent qualified accountant, within twelve months of their year end. These accounts will normally form the basis of the Revenue's tax assessment.

Capital gains tax. When a company sells an asset at a profit, such as a building, it will pay capital gains tax at 30 per cent. If the company itself is subsequently sold, there would be further capital gains tax to pay on the profit realised from the shares.

Hold-over and roll-over relief (see above) are available in certain circumstances. If you are planning to sell a major asset, you should consult your accountant to avoid the possibility of a double tax payment.

Unlike sole traders and partnerships, where an exemption of £6,300 is allowed, there is no exemption on capital gains tax when a limited company sells its assets.

CGT offset: If your company makes a trading loss, this can be used as an offset against profits made on the sale of assets, provided the sale takes place in the same or previous year.

Value added tax (VAT)

VAT is imposed on most business transactions. The legal structure of the enterprise does not affect the issue.

Registration. Consult your local Customs & Excise Office (see telephone directory) about registration for VAT. Registration is required if your 'taxable turnover' exceeds £20,500 (for financial year 1986/87). 'Taxable turnover' applies to the gross turnover of goods or services which are made or supplied by the business.

Charging and paying VAT. You collect VAT from your customers by including it in, or adding it to, the price you charge (Output Tax). Similarly, you will be charged VAT by your suppliers on the goods and services you buy (Input Tax). When you receive a VAT return your input tax is subtracted from your output tax and the difference is paid to Customs & Excise. If the input tax is greater than the output tax, you can claim a refund on the difference.

Taxable supplies and exempt supplies. Most transactions are liable to VAT at either the *standard rate* (currently 15 per cent) or the *zero-rate* (nil).

Zero-rated supplies include: most food (but not catering), books and newspapers, sales of new buildings, construction of most new buildings (but not renovations), young children's clothing and footwear, export of goods, dispensing of prescriptions and the supply of many aids for handicapped persons, mobile homes and houseboats. Zero-rated suppliers have to complete and return a VAT form, even though they are not liable to pay this tax.

Exempt supplies include: lettings and property leases (but not garage lettings, parking charges, hotel/guest house bedrooms or service flats used by tourists as an alternative to hotel accommodation), insurance, betting, gaming and lotteries, provisions of credit, certain education and training, services of doctors and other medical specialists, certain supplies by undertakers. Such suppliers do not have to complete regular VAT returns but must complete form VAT 1 when they apply for exemption. If you are granted exemption, you will not be able to reclaim the VAT you pay on goods and services for your business.

Below the VAT registration limit. If you are not registered for VAT, any expenditure which you incur which includes a charge for VAT should be entered in your records, inclusive of VAT. Even if you do not have to register at present, you may have to do so in the future if your taxable turnover increases. There could be an argument for early registration, as you would be able to offset the VAT the business has to pay to its suppliers. Another advantage is that VAT usually helps in establishing well kept accounts. For more information, see C & E booklet *Should I be Registered for VAT*, obtainable from any C & E office.

How to register. Fill in Form VAT 1 (or the Welsh equivalent Form VAT 20)E. If the business to be registered is a partnership you will also need Form VAT 2.

If you have acquired a business as a going concern you may be able to have the registration number of the previous owner reallocated to you. See VAT Leaflet *Selling or Transferring a Business as a Going Concern*.

N.B. Don't delay. If you do not notify promptly once you are liable to be registered, you may have to account for tax which you have not collected.

You should start keeping VAT records and charging VAT to your customers as soon as you know you are required to be registered. You will have to account for VAT from this date whether or not you have included VAT in prices.

National insurance

As with tax, your liability for National Insurance contributions will depend on whether you are self-employed (sole trader or partner) or whether you are a director of a limited company.

Self-employed

If you are self-employed, you will have to pay flat rate *Class 2* contributions – currently £3.75 a week – unless:

● you are over 65 for men; 60 for women
● you are entitled to married women's or widow's reduced rate contributions
● you have been granted 'a certificate of exemption' because your earnings are likely to be less than £2,075 a year (see Leaflet NI 27A, available from Social Security Offices).

If your annual profits or profit share is above £4,450, you will also have to play *Class 4* contributions of 6.3 per cent on profits between £4.450 and £14,820 unless you are in one of the following categories:

● partner not resident for income tax purposes in the UK
● trustee, executor or administrator of wills and settlements
● sleeping partner, taking a profit but not active in the business

N.B. There is no additional NI liability on profits that exceed £14,820.

How to pay. Class 2 contributions can be paid by purchasing NI stamps at the Post Office to stick on an annual Insurance card, available from your local Social Security Office; or by direct debit from your bank, see leaflet NI 255.

Class 4 contributions are normally assessed and collected by the Inland Revenue, together with PAYE or Schedule D income tax. As they will be paid retrospectively, remember to keep the necessary cash ready and not spend it as part of your monthly salary. See NI 41, *National Insurance Guide for the Self-employed*.

Husband and wife. If you are assessed separately for income tax purposes, you will also be assessed separately for your Class 4 contributions. In other cases, the husband pays a separate Class 4 contribution on his wife's income. Where a husband and wife are in partnership a separate Class 4 contribution is assessed on the wife's share of profits or gains.

Further information about Schedule D tax assessments and related Class 4 national insurance contributions can be obtained from your local Inspector of Taxes. For help on exception, deferment or refund of Class 4 contributions, contact:

Department of Health and Social Security, Class 4 Group, Newcastle-upon-Tyne NE98 1YX.

Double income. If you are self-employed but also receive a salary you may have to pay NI contributions on both incomes. However, there is an overall limit of £1,361 above which contributions are not payable. If too much has been deducted in total you can reclaim the excess or ask for a reduction of Class 2 and/or Class 4 contributions. See Leaflet NP.28 *More than One Job*, available at social security offices.

Limited company

If you trade as a limited company, the company will pay employer's *Class 1* contributions and you will suffer the same deductions from your salary as any other employee. If you control the company, you will in effect be paying both the employer and the employee's share of NI contributions on your own account. If you are a director of several companies, you may be liable for multiple NI contributions: see Leaflet N1 35 *National Insurance for Company Directors*, available from social security offices.

National insurance benefits

Different classes of contributions qualify you for different types of benefit.

Class 2 and Class 4 Contributions count for:

- basic sickness benefit (Leaflet NI16)
- basic invalidity benefit (Leaflet NI16A)
- basic retirement pension (Leaflet NP32)
- basic widow's benefit (Leaflets NP35 and NP36)
- basic maternity allowance (Leaflet NI17A)
- child's special allowance (Leaflet NI93)
- death grant (Leaflet NI49)

Class 1 Contributions entitle you to all the above and additionally to unemployment and redundancy pay, should the need ever arise.

Class 3 Contributions. These may be paid voluntarily to help you qualify for benefits, if your contribution record is insufficient. A flat rate of £3.65 a week is payable. See Leaflet NI 42, available from your local social security office.

Pensions

Sole traders and partners are self-employed for pension as well as tax purposes and must make their own arrangements. Directors of limited companies are treated as employees and may be included in their company's pension scheme or may run their own self-administered pension schemes.

Self-employed pensions

The self-employed can invest up to 17.5 per cent of their earnings in self-employed retirement annuities (SERA's) arranged through a life assurance company and can claim tax relief on the contributions at their top rate of tax. For those over the age of 50, higher percentages can be invested.

If the full 17.5 per cent relief is not used in any one tax year, it can be carried forward for up to six years. Similarly, it may be possible to offset the premium against the previous year's earnings if there are no taxable profits in the current year.

Loan-back facilities

Almost all self-employment pension plans carry loan-back facilities which can provide a useful and tax efficient line of credit for small businesses. Such loans can take one of two forms: either the self-employed can borrow up to the accumulated value of the pension fund, or the loan can be calculated as a multiple of the annual premiums paid.

In both cases, suitable security is required as collateral. You can usually delay the repayment of the loan (but not the interest) until you receive your tax free lump sum on retirement. There are no restrictions on the purposes for which the loans can be used.

Directors

Company pension schemes have limits on the maximum level of benefits they can provide: for instance, the maximum pension is limited to two-thirds of an employee's final salary. However, unlimited contributions can be pumped into the fund by the company and written off against corporation tax so long as these maximum benefits are not exceeded. The employee (i.e. director) can make additional voluntary contributions up to a total of 15 per cent of his salary and offset the premiums against his top rate of tax.

Company pension schemes can either be effected through an insurance company in much the same way as for self-employed schemes; or set up as a self-administered scheme, run mainly by its members and one independent 'pensioner trustee'. The investment of the funds is almost entirely a matter for the trustees, subject to certain limitations imposed by the Inland Revenue to prevent abuse.

Investments may include the company's own property, loans to the company and the company's own shares.

Company loan-back facilities

Loans by a company pension scheme to its members are not normally allowed; loans to director controlled companies are the exception, where a direct loan-back of up to 50 per cent of the fund is permitted.

Such funds can therefore provide useful working capital in a tax efficient way. Cash can be transferred into a tax exempt fund and written off against corporation tax. The company can then borrow back up to 50 per cent, claiming tax relief on the interest payments while the tax exempt fund receives the interest payments gross. The loans can be used to finance property developments as well as other forms of capital investment. The loans must be on a commercial basis and have the approval of the independent pensioner trustee.

Your responsibilities as an employer

Many people starting a business wisely limit recruitment to the minimum in the early days, until they are sure that they can afford the cost of having permanent staff. Once you become an employer, you take on responsibilities. As well as paying the salaries, you will have to account for PAYE, keep National Insurance records and conform with the multiple requirements of employment legislation. While this may sound rather daunting – and information is given for those who want to do it themselves – the good news is that your bank and possibly your accountant are likely to offer a full payroll service which will cost you money but will take the worry off your shoulders.

PAYE

If you employ someone in your business (including your wife/husband) you are responsible for deducting income tax under the PAYE arrangements and accounting for it to the Collector of Taxes.

Contact your local Inland Revenue office for a copy of booklet *Employer's Guide to Paye* (P7). You will also be provided with Tax Tables and Working Sheets.

The Tax Office will then notify you of the various PAYE tax codes in respect of your employees and explain how to use the Tax Table to work out the deductions.

If an employee does not have an existing P45, you should ask him/her to complete a Starting Certificate Form P46, obtainable from the tax office.

An individual is liable for tax after deduction of their personal allowance and various reliefs. As a rough guide, for someone in receipt of the single person's allowance (£2,335), this would be on earnings of £45 pw; for someone in receipt of the married man's allowance (£3,655), £70 pw.

Even if an employee's pay is less than the threshold, there could still be PAYE implications, as he/she may have other earnings.

National Insurance for employees

The National Insurance threshold is £38 a week. With one or two exceptions, in particular persons over state retirement age, anyone earning this amount or over will be liable for National Insurance.

You are responsible for the payment of both the employer's and employee's contributions but are entitled to deduct the employee's share from his/her earnings.

National Insurance is payable on a graduated scale for both employers and employees: starting at 5 per cent on earnings of £38 pw, with upper limits of 9 per cent for employees on earnings of £140 to £285; 10.45 per cent for employers on all earnings in excess of £140 pw.

Contact your local social security office for booklet NP15 *Employer's Guide to National Insurance Contributions*. The staff will explain to you how the system works and answer any queries.

You will be sent a payslip booklet by the Collector of Taxes, together with official Deductions Working Sheets P.11 and P.14. Payments must be made within 14 days of the end of each income tax month.

Statutory Sick Pay

Employers are responsible for paying Statutory Sick Pay to their employees for up to 28 weeks of sickness absence.

The rates and earnings bands are subject to annual uprating. The 1986/87 SSP rate is £31.60 on average weekly earnings, with an upper limit of £46.75 on earnings over £74.50 a week. SSP is subject to deduction of income tax and NI contributions in the same way as ordinary pay.

The gross amount of any SSP paid to an employee is recoverable by the employer, by holding it back from the NI contributions you pay each month. You can also deduct an extra amount to compensate for the employer's NI contributions paid on SSP, calculated as 9 per cent of the total paid to employees.

Full details are contained in the *Employers' Guide to Statutory Sick Pay* NI 227, available from social security offices. See also form NI 208 for details of current rates.

Personnel records

Many businesses find it useful to keep personnel records, covering such information as national insurance numbers, tax codes, merit appraisal reports and so on. If using any of the computerised systems on offer, you may need to register with the Data Protection Registrar. For advice and information, contact: **Data Protection Registrar**, Springfield House, Water Lane, Wilmslow, Cheshire SK9 5AX.

Employment legislation

As an employer, you have certain legal obligations in respect of your staff. The most important cover such issues as: health and safety at work, terms and conditions of employment and the provision of employee rights including, for example, maternity leave, trade union activity and protection against unfair dismissal.

Very small firms are exempted from some of the more onerous requirements and the Government is taking steps to reduce more of the red tape. However, it is important that you understand in general terms what legislation could affect you.

Health and Safety at Work. The Health and Safety at Work Act applies to everyone in a business whether employer, employee or the self-employed. It also protects your neighbours and the general public who may be affected by your business activity.

The **Health and Safety Commission** publishes a number of useful pamphlets, such as *Some Legal Aspects and how they will Affect You*. The address to write to is: 256-269 Marylebone Road, London NW1 5RR, T: 01-229 3456.

Discrimination. An employer may not discriminate on the grounds of sex, race or marriage. Firms employing fewer than five people are currently exempt from sex discrimination legislation. However, a recent European ruling could bring small firms into its orbit in the future. If you have more than 20 employees, you are required to employ a small quota of disabled people.

Pay. In a few industries, statutory minimum rates of pay are laid down by Wages Councils. If you think you might be affected, contact the **Wages Inspectorate**, Department of Employment, Steel House, 11 Tothill Street, London SW1H 9NF, T: 01-213 3881.

Contract of employment. A contract of employment exists as soon as an applicant accepts a job, whether or not the offer and acceptance are made in writing. Within 13 weeks of the job starting, the employer must give the employee either a written contract or, in bigger firms, a written statement highlighting the contract's main terms. This does not apply to employees who work less than 16 hours a week until they have been with you for 5 years.

There is a useful guide prepared by the Department of Employment, *Written Statements of Terms and Conditions of Employment*. Your solicitor or accountant may also be able to advise you.

Main sources of advice

The Department of Employment can provide advice on all aspects of employment legislation and also supplies several free booklets available. The most handy place to obtain these is your local *jobcentre* and, while picking them up, you could take the opportunity of introducing yourself to the manager and discussing any recruitment needs. Alternatively, you can write to the **Department of Employment**, Caxton House, Tothill Street, London SW1H 9NF, T:01-213 5551, who will be able to put you in contact with your local Small Firms Centre.

Disputes

If you find yourself with a potential dispute on your hands, it is sensible to approach the Advisory, Conciliation and Arbitration Service (ACAS), which operates an effective and little known advisory service for employers on employment legislation and industrial relations. Contact: ACAS, 11/12 St. James' Square, London SW1Y 4LA, T:01-210 3600, or one of its regional offices:

- Northern Region: Westgate House, Westgate Road, Newcastle upon Tyne NE1 1TJ, T:0632-612191
- Yorkshire and Humberside: Commerce House, St.Albans Place, Leeds LS2 8HH, T:0532-431371
- London Region: Clifton House, 83-117 Euston Road, London NW1 2RB, T:01-388 5100
- South East: Clifton House, 83-117 Euston Road, London NW1 2RB, T:01-388 5100 (as London Region)
- Midlands: Alpha Tower, Suffolk Street, Queensway, Birmingham Bn1 1TZ, T:021-643 9911
- Notts: 66-72 Houndsgate, Nottingham NG1 6BA, T:0602-415450
- North West: Boulton House, 17-21 Chorlton Street, Manchester MI 3HY, T:061-228 3222
- Merseyside: Cressington House, 249 St.Mary's Road, Garston, Liverpool LI9 ONF, T:051-427 8881
- Scotland: Franborough House, 123-157 Bothwell Street, Glasgow G2 7JR, T:041-204 2677
- Wales: Phase 1, Ty Glas Road, Llanishen, Cardiff CF4 5PH, T: 0222-762636.

Trading regulations

Trading regulations laying down your obligations to your customers are contained in various Acts of Parliament, such as the Trade Descriptions Act and the Sale of Goods Act. For advice, contact: **Office of Fair Trading**, Field House, Breams Building, London EC4A 1PR, T:01-242 2858. Solicitors are also qualified to advise on such matters.

Licences

Certain types of business require a licence or permit to trade, including: pubs, off licences, employment agencies, nursing agencies, pet shops, kennels, mini cabs or buses, driving instructors, betting shops, auction sale rooms, cinemas, hairdressers, street traders and, in some cases, travel agents and tour operators. You will also require a licence to import certain goods.

Your Local Authority Planning Office will advise you as to whether you require a licence and in many cases your council will be the licensing authority. Other useful addresses include:

Department of Employment, Agency Licensing Office, City House, New Station Street, Leeds LS1 5JH, T:0532-438232.

Department of Trade Import Licensing, Charles House, 375 Kensington High Street, London W8. T:01-603 4644.

The Consumer Credit Act 1974 also imposes a licensing requirement on various types of businesses that offer credit and hire facilities. The Act is administered by the Office of Fair Trading (see above), which publishes a booklet *Licensing*, containing the necessary application forms.

Finding suitable premises

A few years ago, finding premises was often a real problem for small firms. Today, however, thanks to the relaxation of many planning regulations together with an increase in small workshops, it has become very much easier. The sources to tap when you start looking include:

Newspapers. There are property pages in publications such as *Dalton's Weekly*, *Exchange & Mart* and the *Estates Gazette*. Evening and local newspapers also carry advertisements for industrial, commercial and retail property.

Estate agents. Ask for the department dealing with commercial premises. You will have to pay commission, which may be structured in various ways. Check carefully on the terms and conditions.

Local authorities. Councils often maintain a list of vacant property including a register of small units. Many authorities own and manage workshop developments. Contact the Industrial Development Officer.

Chambers of commerce. These are often an excellent source of information about vacant premises, as they have wide contacts with local businesses and others.

Enterprise agencies. Again, a first class contact point. An increasing number of agencies run managed workshops. Their premises often provide shared facilities such as typing, telex and photocopying. An example is the London Enterprise Agency (LEntA) which, through its subsidiary LEntA Properties, develops small units for let as managed work-space for start-up businesses. It keeps a list of other London property suitable for small firms and also produces a useful leaflet for those interested in running a market stall. Contact: **LEntA**, 4 Snow Hill, London EC1A 2DL, T:01-236 3000.

Assisted areas

A wide range of industrial and commercial property is available for rent or sale in the Assisted Areas. Premises can often be built or converted to suit your specific requirements. Many of the leases are very flexible, with short in-out options, to allow for the changing needs of expanding firms. Rent-free periods are sometimes available.

In England, contact: **English Estates**, St. George's House, Kingsway, Team Valley, Gateshead, Tyne & Wear, T:0632-878941.

For Wales, Scotland and Northern Ireland contact, as appropriate: **Welsh Development Agency, Scottish Development Agency, Highlands & Islands Development Board** and **Local Economic Development Unit (LEDU)**. See below for addresses.

New Town development corporations

There are 13 New Towns in England, 5 in Scotland and 2 in Wales, all of which have large industrial estates. Contact: **Commission for the New Towns**, Glen House, Stag Place, London SW1E 5AF, T:01-212 7158, or the Industry Sections of the local development corporations.

CoSIRA

The Council for Small Industries in Rural Areas is an agency of the Development Commission. It provides wide-ranging assistance, including practical help with premises, for those planning to start, or expand, a business in country areas of England not exceeding 10,000 in population. It also has a network of organisers in virtually every county, who will advise on such matters as conversions and planning permission.

Additionally, CoSIRA has limited funds to help finance or improve premises and to purchase necessary equipment. Loans can be up to 30 per cent of project costs, to a maximum of £75,000, with repayment between 2 and 20 years. In more remote areas, outright grants can sometimes be arranged.

CoSIRA can also advise on the various Development Commission grants for building small advance factories and workshops, both in and outside Rural Development Areas. For further information, contact: **CoSIRA**, 141 Castle Street, Salisbury, Wiltshire, T:0722-336 255.

Enterprise zones

Enterprise Zones have been set up in various parts of the country, with the intention of attracting business to these areas. The major attraction is that EZs are exempt from industrial and commercial rates and are also largely free of planning controls, although the normal health and safety regulations apply. The rates holiday only lasts for 10 years from an EZ's designation date, so in a majority of cases only a few years remain.

EZs are located in the following places: Invergordon, Tayside, Clydebank, Tyneside, Hartlepool, Workington, Middlesbrough, Salford/Trafford, Wakefield, Glanford, Scunthorpe, North East Lancashire, Speke, Rotherham, Delyn, Telford, Dudley, Corby, Wellingborough, Isle of Dogs, North West Kent, Milford Haven, Lower Swansea Valley, Londonderry and Belfast.

Contact the relevant local authority or the **Department of the Environment**, 2 Marsham Street, London SW1P 3EB, T:01-212 7158, for further information.

British Rail property

Vacant railway arches and other commercial property are available to rent from British Rail. Contact **British Rail Property Board**, 274 Bishopsgate, London EC2, T:01-247 5444. In Scotland, the address to write to is: Buchan House, 58 Port Dundas Road, Glasgow, T:041-332 9811.

Scotland

Scottish Development Agency, Letting Section, Franborough House, 120 Bothwell Street, Glasgow, T:041-248 2700.

The SDA is the largest provider of factory space in Scotland. It can advise and assist on commercial and industrial property, ranging from large complexes built to a company's own specification to nest units of under 1,000 sq. ft. for start-up businesses.

Highlands and Islands Development Board, Bridge House, 27 Bank Street, Inverness IV1 1QR, T:0463-234171.

The HIDB builds advance factories and workshops for sale or lease. Rents are generally lower than in other parts of the country and in some circumstances, premises can be made available on a rent free basis for a period of up to two years.

Clyde Workshops Ltd., Tollcross Industrial Village, Fullarton Road, Glasgow, T:041-641 4972.

On behalf of British Steel Corporation (Industry) Ltd., Clyde Workshops have pioneered developments of small premises on short term rentals.

Wales

Welsh Development Agency, P.O.Box 100, Greyfriars Road, Cardiff CF1 1WF, T:0222-32955.

The WDA is one of the largest developers of industrial property in the UK and has a comprehensive range of business premises, ranging in size from 50,000 sq.ft. to small workshops and mini units of 280 sq.ft. Limited rent free periods may sometimes be arranged.

In the county of Powys and districts of Meirionnydd (Gwynedd) and Ceredigion (Dyfed), industrial sites are provided by the Mid Wales Development Board, based at Newton Powys.

Northern Ireland

Local Economic Development Unit, LEDU House, Upper Galwally, Belfast BT8 4TB, T:0232 691031.

LEDU offers much the same service as the development agencies: it can provide practical help and advice and maintains a register of both public and privately owned vacant property. Very generous grants are available to businesses locating in Northern Ireland.

Get expert advice

However impeccable the organisation offering you property for lease or sale, you should always consult a solicitor before you sign a contract. If you are thinking of buying either a long lease or freehold, you are strongly advised to get a surveyor's report. Though you will have to pay for the service, it could save you a fortune if you later discovered dry rot, rising damp or worse.

Planning permission

If you intend to build or convert property, use a mobile shop or change the use of existing business premises, from say an office to a workshop, you will need to get planning permission from your local authority. This often used to take months and months but the procedure has now been greatly speeded up, especially where small businesses are concerned.

Tempting as it is to take a chance or to install workmen before you have officially heard, this is very unwise because in the event of permission not being granted, you could be ordered to restore the property to its original condition, which could be hugely expensive if you have knocked down the odd wall.

In rural areas, CoSIRA can often be of assistance when preparing a planning application. As general advice, it recommends that before an application goes to a planning committee, every effort should be made to sound out local opinion, explain what the intention is and allay any fears. The blessing of the Parish Council can often tip opinion in your favour.

The department to contact is your *district council planning office*.

Other authorities

Depending on the nature of your business, other permissions may also need to be obtained, including those of the police, the environmental health department, licensing authorities and the fire prevention officer. In particular, there are special requirements concerning the sale of food and safety measures for hotels and guest houses. Your local authority will advise you what is necessary.

Working from home

Many people quietly 'set up shop' from home and there are no questions asked. There could, however, be trouble if in consequence of your business, there was an increase in traffic on your street, noise, smells or other inconvenience caused to your neighbours.

Even more likely, unless you own the freehold of your home, you could have problems with your landlord if the tenancy agreement states that the accommodation is for domestic use only. If you simply use your home as a telephone base, this will probably not be an issue but if you have a stream of callers and a van parked outside, you could be accused of violating the lease.

You could also be liable to pay commercial rates on that part of your home you use as business premises.

Advice

The Department of the Environment has recently published a booklet, *Planning Permission for Small Businesses: A Step by Step Guide*, explaining the planning system, and giving clear guidance on working from home. Copies can be obtained from your local authority or ordered from: **Department of the**

Environment, Distribution Section, Building 3, Victoria Road, South Ruislip, Middlesex HA4 0ONZ.

Insurance

Insurance is more than just a wise precaution. It is essential if you employ staff, have business premises or use your car regularly for commercial purposes. Many insurance companies now offer 'package insurance' for small businesses that cover most of the main contingencies in a single policy. This usually works out more cheaply than buying a collection of individual policies. If you buy a package, check that it contains whichever of the following are relevant to your needs.

Employers' liability

This is compulsory if you employ staff. It provides indemnity against liability for death or bodily injury to employees and sub-contractors, arising in connection with the business.

Product and public liability

Insures the business and its products against claims by customers or the public. It could also cover legal expenses and the cost of complying with enforcements or judgements.

Material damage risk

Covers against fire or other risk to the property, damage to equipment and theft. You can also be insured against loss of money or goods in transit.

Loss of profits or business interruption risk

Insures the business against loss of profits in the event of your having to cease or curtail trading for a time, due to material damage. The two policies are normally linked. It should also cover the risk of break-down of a key item of machinery.

Motor risks

Compulsory for all motor vehicles.

Life assurance

Essential should you wish to provide for your own or key employees' families or to ensure that funds are available to pay off any debts or to enable the business to continue in the event of your death. Likewise, your business partners or fellow directors may require funds to buy your shares in the company.

Permanent health insurance against your long-term disability should also be considered.

Insurance when working from home

If you are self-employed, you may need to extend your existing private policies to cover your commercial activities. A fire at home could destroy business products as well as your domestic possessions. Likewise your motor insurance may not be sufficient for business purposes, if the loss of your car could cause serious interruption to your trading. You should discuss these points with your insurance company or a broker.

Insurance brokers

To find an insurance broker, contact: **British Insurance Brokers' Association, BIBA House, 14 Bevis Marks, London EC3A 7NT, T:01-623 9043.**

Marketing

Unless you were employed in sales or marketing, you may suspect that this is likely to be a weak point in your business plan.

The essence of good marketing is very simple. Find out what the customer wants and then try to supply it rather than design a product or service and hope that buyers will come flocking to your door. You have to sell the sizzle as well as the sausage.

The points you need to consider are:

- what kinds of individuals (or companies) are likely to be your customers, including their age group and sex
- whether you are competing with existing suppliers or are offering a genuinely new concept (including for example, a delivery service which other local shopkeepers do not supply)
- whether the market is expanding or contracting with particular emphasis on how many potential customers live close by
- finally, how you can inform the potential market that your new product or service is available

This sort of preliminary thinking is essential. The following organisations may be able to help you formulate a realistic marketing plan:

Your local library will probably have trade directories and yellow pages from which you can see how many other organisations already offer a similar local service. It may also have copies of trade magazines relevant to the industry you plan to enter.

Your local council will have information on the population and demographic profile of the area and will be able to give you details of any development plans that could affect customer potential.

Your chamber of commerce should be able to offer practical advice and training in marketing techniques and may also be able to assist with useful contacts.

Your local enterprise agency exists to help small businesses and should be able to offer valuable marketing advice.

National organisations that may be useful include:

Institute of Marketing, Moor Hall, Cookham, Berks, T:06285 24992.

Runs courses for non-members who need general marketing advice and maintains a panel of consultants who can be retained to help you for an appropriate fee. Charges vary enormously but most consultants will assist a new business for less than their normal rate.

Business Statistics Office, Cardiff Road, Newport, Gwent NP9 1XG, T:0633 56111.

Holds information on all aspects of the economy, showing sales and other data for all types of retail outlets.

British Institute of Management, Management House, Parker Street, London WC2B 5PT, T:01-405 3456

Runs an extensive library which non-members can visit with the agreement of the Institute. It also maintains a panel of consultants on marketing and other business specialities.

Market Research Society, 175 Oxford Street, London W1R 1TA, T:01-439 2585.

The MRS can put you in touch with a research company or could mount a research exercise on your behalf. Cost could range from a couple of hundred pounds to several thousand.

Design Council, 28 Haymarket, London SW1Y 4SU, T:839 8000.

As its name implies, this organisation can help you if your product needs first class industrial design to increase its commercial potential.

British Standards Institute, 2 Park Street, London W1 2BS, T:01-629 9000.

Will provide technical help to ensure that products comply with standards laid down by the UK and EEC governments.

Promotion

Once you have assessed where your market lies, you have to decide how to promote yourself. Methods of advertising your product (service) might include:

- direct mail shots and leaflet drops
- advertising in specialist publications or local newspapers with a potentially high readership among your target market
- exhibitions and local displays at functions such as school prize givings, agricultural shows or local sporting events
- telephone sales, perhaps with the help of a small team
- editorial coverage in the press or on local radio programmes

You are likely to succeed better with any of these techniques if you discuss your plans with a professional consultancy. The names of local practitioners should be available from:

Advertising Association, Abford House, 15 Wilton Road, London SW1V 1NJ, T:01-828 2771.

Institute of Public Relations, Gate House, 1, St. John's Square, London EC1M 4BH, T:01-253 5151.

Institute of Marketing, Moor Hall, Cookham, Berks, T:06285-24992.

Competitors

It is useful to know who your competitors are and what they are doing. One way is to get copies of their annual reports, by writing to the companies concerned who will usually be glad to supply them free of charge; alternatively, these are available for a small fee from the **Registrar of Companies**, Companies House, Crown Way, Maindy, Cardiff C84 3UZ, T:0222-388588.

It is also sensible to attend trade shows of the industries within which you are planning to compete. Your local library will probably hold a directory listing what shows are held each year.

Exports

Although we are members of the EEC, exporting is still much more difficult than trading at home. Your local Chamber of Commerce should have first-class information on some of the problems you will encounter. If you are considering an export business, it is advisable to contact:

British Overseas Trade Board, 1 Victoria Street, London SW1H 0ET, T:01-215 7877
     The BOTB can advise you on the peculiarities of each export market and mobilise local embassies to assist if this would be helpful. The BOTB will also help you find overseas agents and will investigate local markets for which they may charge a fee.

Overseas Publicity Service, Central Office of Information, Hercules Road, London SE1 7DU, T:01-928 2345.
     OPS can help you advertise and promote your products overseas.

Institute of Export, 64 Clifton Street, London EC2, T:01-247 9812.
     The IOE maintains a register of experts with marketing and sales experience overseas and can help you with the necessary documentation.

Your bank will also have up-to-date information on the market conditions in most overseas countries, which it will supply free of charge.

Raising finance

Before you approach anyone for money, you must have a proper Business Plan. This means that you are bound to spend some time researching your business ideas and producing a realistic projection of cash flow needs.
     Your Business Plan should be brief and to the point but must contain the following items:

- a clear statement of what product or service you plan to offer
- sales and marketing projections, based if possible on some research or knowledge of the market
- your initial investment plus on-going cash flow requirements
- basic information concerning premises, staff, equipment and development plans
- profit and loss projections, showing when you expect the business to start making money.

It is a good idea to ask an accountant to vet your business plan. Some High Street banks offer the same service for a low fixed fee.
     The different types of finance now available to small businesses through traditional sources such as banks and other institutions are more extensive than

ever before. They fall into four broad categories: overdrafts, commercial and bank loans, equity finance and government loans and grants.

Overdrafts

You will be familiar with overdrafts from your private banking arrangements. The bank allows you to borrow money up to a predetermined limit but only charges you interest on the amount outstanding.

If you trade as a limited company the bank will almost certainly require a personal guarantee, which will make you liable for the overdraft if the company fails.

Although overdrafts are theoretically repayable at a day's notice, in practice the banks will normally review the arrangement with you once a year.

Interest on overdrafts fluctuates in line with bank base rate and you will usually have to pay a premium of 2 per cent to 5 per cent over this level.

Loans

There are various types of loans including: bank loans for a fixed period; leasing and hire purchase arrangements; credit factoring and invoice discounting; stock financing; and the loan guarantee scheme.

In each case, your loan will be for a specific period but interest will normally fluctuate as it does with overdrafts.

Most loans are made against the security of a specific asset, such as vans, office equipment, your debtors, or stock. Lenders will generally ask for a personal guarantee, which you should resist unless there is clearly no other way of obtaining the money.

Bank loans

Unlike an overdraft, the bank undertakes to lend you money for a fixed period, say, five years. You will be required to repay a percentage of the loan each year and before lending the bank will want to check your business plan to see that the agreed repayments are realistic. The bank may ask for a debenture which gives it security over all the assets of your business but does not involve you in pledging personal possessions such as your house.

Leasing and hire purchase

These are both methods of using equipment or vehicles and paying for them by instalments. Leasing is normally slightly cheaper, as the supplier owns the asset and benefits from the relevant tax allowances.

As an alternative to negotiating an agreement with the supplier, it may be cheaper to ask your bank or other lender to arrange the necessary finance for you.

Interest is usually fixed at the start and will remain at the same level throughout. This has the advantage that you know what your commitment is. However, such agreements tend to be expensive.

Credit factoring and invoice discounting

Credit factoring is a continuous financial arrangement whereby the trade debts of a business are sold to a factoring company as they arise. In return, you immediately receive about 80 per cent of the debt, less the factoring company's charges, and the balance of the money when your customer pays.

A potentially useful aspect of factoring is the provision by the finance company of a full sales ledger, credit control, cash collection and bad debts service. Although this service sounds marvellous, it can be extremely complicated if your customers are not well known companies with good credit rating.

Invoice discounting is somewhat similar but is only useful if you deal with prestigious companies whose credit is good. You sell selected invoices for about 75 per cent of their face value for immediate cash. You retain full responsibility for collecting the money and in the event of your customer defaulting have to repay the sum involved. In effect, you are paying a high premium for cash up front.

Both factoring and invoice discounting are offered by specialist companies within the major banking groups.

Stock financing

This is a new approach for helping small manufacturing businesses finance their stock of raw materials and finished products.

The finance company purchases and sells back to the manufacturer, say, £10,000 of stock. The financier pays the manufacturer an immediate cheque, less his charges, and takes out a 90 day bill of exchange.

This is quite an expensive method of financing working capital but can be useful if your High Street bank will not lend you money against the security of your stock.

At the moment, the best known of the companies offering this service is **Arrows Ltd**, Arrows House, Kingsway, Manchester M19 1BA, T:061-224 8800.

Loan guarantee scheme

Exists to help supply loan finance for businesses which would not normally be able to raise a loan because they cannot offer adequate security or do not have a proven track record.

The Government provides a guarantee of 70 per cent of the money borrowed, up to a maximum of £75,000. The scheme is run through the High Street banks who charge an arrangement fee plus a small premium over their normal lending rate. Additionally, there is a government premium of $2\frac{1}{2}$ per cent on the guaranteed portion of the loan. Although theoretically personal security is not required, the banks like to see some backing for the 30 per cent not covered by the government guarantee and will always require the business assets to be pledged.

Loans are available to both start up and established firms, excluding certain types of businesses, such as: agriculture, financial services and property development.

The most usual way of arranging loan guarantee finance is through your normal clearing bank. Certain merchant banks will sometimes also offer this facility, for example: Brown Shipley, County Bank, Hill Samuel and Standard Chartered.

Equity finance

With equity finance, as opposed to simply borrowing money, you are taking in a financial partner who will own part of your business.

For this reason most small businessmen have traditionally been reluctant to accept equity investment. However, this is changing as the value of the Business Expansion Scheme (BES) and venture capital are increasingly becoming appreciated.

Unlike loans, equity investment is permanent capital. If a shareholder wishes to sell out, the company is not bound to buy back his shares but sometimes has an option to do so.

Most investors will fall into one of the following categories: friends or family; BES funding; and venture capital specialists.

Friends and family

You may know people who would like to back you when you are starting a business. It is important that both sides should understand the risks and commitments involved and be aware that these may affect your normal relationship. However close you are, it is sensible to ask an accountant or solicitor to advise you on a formal agreement.

There are specific percentages of shareholdings, such as 25 per cent, that normally carry legal rights; it is important to understand what these are and to decide whether you wish them to apply.

If an investor owns more than 10 per cent of your company, he/she would usually expect to be a director.

Business Expansion Scheme

Many individuals are now interested in direct equity investment as a result of BES, which provides them with tax relief at their highest personal rate of tax on investments up to £40,000 a year. The investment has to be a minority stake in an unquoted private company and must be held for five years to gain full tax relief.

BES is designed to stimulate the growth of manufacturing and service businesses. Certain activities are excluded, in particular: financial services, leasing and hiring, property and the holding of fine wines and antiques.

Under the rules of the Business Expansion Scheme, the following are not allowed to invest in a company controlled by you: spouse, parents, grandparents, children or grandchildren.

Investors cannot be a director, employee or partner of the company and are not allowed to receive any financial benefit from the business for five years. Accountants can sometimes help with introductions.

BES funds

Venture capital and some other financial organisations organise groups of BES investors who collectively take stakes in a spread of companies. The institution will probably want to appoint a director to sit on your Board and will certainly charge you fees.

For a list of BES funds, contact **FIMBRA (Financial Intermediaries, Managers and Brokers Regulatory Association)**, 22 Great Tower Street, London EC3 5AQ, T:01-283 4814. Used to be known as NASDIM.

Formalities

If you want to raise BES money from any source, you will have to secure clearance from your local Inspector of Taxes that your company qualifies for funding under the rules and you can then issue certificates that will allow investors to claim the tax relief. Your accountant should be able to advise you how to do this.

Venture capital

There are now well over 100 specialist venture capital companies in the UK that are willing to consider risk investment in new businesses in the hope of achieving significant capital gains.

These investors will normally look for a company with high growth potential, giving them a minority stake and management fees in return for active support in helping the business to develop as fast as possible.

Sources of venture capital

Your accountant should be able to give you a list of venture capital companies.

Alternatively, contact: **British Venture Capital Association**, c/o Arthur Andersen & Co., 1 Surrey Street, London WC2R 2PS, T:01-836 5702.

The publishers **Venture Economics Ltd.**, 37 Thames Road, London W4 3PF, produce an annual guide to European venture capital sources, which will probably be in your local reference library. They also keep an up-to-date list of venture capital companies.

Among the relatively few venture capital funds prepared to consider investments of under £25,000 are the following:

Under £25,000	Telephone
Baring Brothers Hambrecht & Quist	01-626 5133
British Technology Group	01-403 6666
Capital Partners International	01-351 5511
Centaur Communications	01-439 1305
Commonwealth Development Finance Corpn	01-407 9711
First Welsh General Investment Trust	0222-396131
Hafren Investment Finance	0222-32955
ICFC	01-928 7822
Industrial Development Board for Northern Ireland	0232-223 3239
LEDU Small Business Agency Northern Ireland	0232-691031
Leopold Joseph & Sons	01-588 2323
Midland Bank Equity Group	01-638 8861
Quester Capital Management	01-600 4177
Schroder Wagg (J.Henry) & Co.	01-382 6000
Scottish Development Agency	041-248-2700
Seedcorn Capital	0272-272250
South Glamorgan Investments	0222-396131
Thompson Clive & Partners	01-491 4809
Welsh Development Agency	0222-32955
West Yorkshire Enterprise Board	0924-371205
Under £10,000	
Aberdeen Fund Manager	0224-631999
Energy Finance Trust	01-606 2167
Sapling (NW) £15,000	0772-264382
St.Helens BES Syndicate	0744-692578

Other useful organisations

The **London Enterprise Agency** (**LEntA**) runs a business introduction service, designed to put small businesses who wish to find capital and/or management assistance in touch with suitable people. It publishes a monthly bulletin listing businesses seeking investment – and vice versa. There is also an investors' club, where entrepreneurs seeking finance can present their plans direct to potential investors. The annual membership fee is £30. For further information, contact: **LEntA**, 4 Snow Hill, London EC1A 2DL, T:01-236 3000.

Venture Capital Report publishes a monthly bulletin in which companies describe exactly why they need additional investment. VCR vets the companies to make sure that their claims and plans are realistic. Potential investors subscribe to the report and contact companies of interest to them direct. Companies use VCR to raise sums from £5,000 to £500,000. It costs £100 to be included in the VCR report plus a small percentage fee geared to the amount of equity raised. For further information, contact them at: 20 Baldwin Street, Bristol BS1 1SE, T:0272-737 222.

Government grants and loans

There is a vast range of public sector financial assistance available from local authorities, government sources and the EEC. Small firms could benefit from loans, grants or possibly the Enterprise Allowance Scheme.

Most major firms of accountants and also the banks produce comprehensive publications listing all such resources currently available. A typical example is *Official Sources of Finance and Aid For Industry in the UK* published by the National Westminster Bank (price £5.50).

Those listed below are among the most potentially useful to smaller firms.

Enterprise allowance

This is a national scheme administered by the Manpower Services Commission to help unemployed or redundant individuals start their own business. It offers a flat rate of £40 per week, for 52 weeks. This income could be liable for income tax.

You are only eligible if:

● you have been out of work or under notice of redundancy for 8 weeks
● you are under the state retirement age
● you have £1,000 in cash available for investment in the business, which must be a genuinely new undertaking and not a subsidiary or financially supported by any other company
● you must be prepared to work full time in the business, which must be accepted as a viable proposition and cannot be an agent or labour only sub-contractor.

To apply, contact your local jobcentre or small firms centre (see telephone directory), who will put you in touch with the MSC. The MSC will then send you an invitation to an information and counselling session, which is likely to last for a couple of hours and is usually attended by about 25 people.

If the MSC thinks that your plan is viable and you can prove that you have £1,000 available to invest in the business, you will be signed on for the scheme. The MSC will expect to see you after three months for a progress meeting.

At the time of writing, the **Midland Bank** was offering free banking services for 52 weeks for all those on the scheme. For further information, contact your local branch or telephone 01-606 9911.

Local authority assistance.

Local authorities are now playing a much fuller role in co-ordinating the advice and financial resources available to small companies in their area. Many have developed their own loan and grant schemes. In particular, councils can offer generous mortgages to buy or improve land or buildings. With government agreement, they can sell land below market value and will provide improvement grants, build advance factories and give employment subsidies.

Contact your *local authority planning department* or alternatively, where appropriate, the *industrial development department*.

Grants for assisted areas

A regional development grant is available towards the purchase of assets or the creation of jobs in the Development Areas listed below:

In England:
Bishop Auckland, Corby, Falmouth, Hartlepool, Helston, Liverpool, Middlesborough, Newcastle-upon-Tyne, Newquay, Penzance and St. Ives, Redruth and Camborne, Rotherham and Mexborough, Scunthorpe, South Tyneside, Stockton-on-Tees, Sunderland, Whitby, Widnes and Runcorn, Wigan and St. Helens, Wirral and Chester, Workington and the Isles of Scilly.

In Scotland:
Arbroath, Bathgate, Cumnock and Sanquhar, Dumbarton, Dundee, Glasgow, Greenock, Irvine, Kilmarnock, Lanarkshire.

In Wales:
Aberdare, Cardigan, Ebbw Vale and Abergavenny, Flint and Rhyl, Holyhead, Lampeter and Aberaeron, Merthyr and Rhymney, Neath and Port Talbot, Pontypridd and Rhondda, South Pembrokeshire, Wrexham.

Grants are usually limited to manufacturing companies or those providing certain manufacturing support services. Generally speaking, you need to be considering significant investment for these grants to be worth pursuing. Selective regional assistance may also be available to manufacturing and some service projects in the wider Assisted Areas which include so-called Intermediate Areas as well as Development Areas. If you plan to operate in one of the Assisted Areas, full information is available from:

Department of Trade and Industry, Regional Policy Division, 66-74 Victoria Street, London SW1E 6SJ, T: 01-212 3466; or alternatively, your nearest regional office.

Industry Department for Scotland, Alhambra House, 45 Waterloo Street, Glasgow G2 7BT, T:041-221 9833.

Industry Department for Wales, 24-26 Newport Road, Cardiff CF1 3NQ, T:0222-492 611.

Regional development agencies

If you are planning to start a business in Scotland, Wales or Northern Ireland, these agencies offer financial facilities that may be of assistance to you. To be eligible, your business would almost certainly either have to increase job opportunities, offer export potential, reduce the need for imports or hold promise of significant expansion. You are more likely to get finance – which could be a grant, loan or subsidy – if you are willing to locate in an area of high unemployment, such as one affected by coal or steel closures.

Depending on the area, priority may be given to enterprises involved in: tourism, manufacturing, craft development, new technology and in the Highlands and Islands, fisheries. In the main, agriculture, horticulture and retailing are unlikely to receive assistance.

The sums available vary enormously, from £1,000 to £50,000 and more. For further information, contact the appropriate agency:

Scottish Development Agency, Rosebery House, Haymarket Terrace, Edinburgh EH2 5EZ, T:031-337 9595 or 123 Bothwell Street, Glasgow G2 7PJ, T:041-248 2700.

Highlands & Islands Development Board, 27 Bank Street, Inverness IV1 1QR, T:0463-234 131.

Welsh Development Agency, P.O.Box 100, Greyfriars Road, Cardiff CF1 1W, T:0222-32955.

Local Economic Development Unit (LEDU), Upper Galwally, Belfast BT8 4TB, T:0232-691 031.

Grants for new technology

The Department of Trade and Industry offers a variety of selective grants to help businesses developing products in the hi-tech, electronics, biotechnology, computer and advanced production technology areas. These grants can cover up to half the cost of consultancy and implementation studies; up to 20 per cent of the investment then required; and in special cases, 25 per cent of money spent to bring quality up to the relevant British Standard. For further information, contact:

Department of Trade and Industry, 123 Victoria Street, London SW1E 6RB, T:01-212 7676.

Investment from the European Community

Both the European Investment Bank and the European Regional Development Fund have money available to invest in projects which create new employment or to help small businesses that need 5 to 10 year loans, from £15,000 to £250,000.

These loans are usually limited to industrial projects, tourism or hi-tech service industries. RDF funds (loans and grants) are restricted to companies operating in the Assisted Areas and regions affected by closures in the steel, shipbuilding, textile and clothing industries. A particularly useful grant provided by the Development Fund enables companies to offset half the cost of translating their marketing and technical literature into other European languages. It will also contribute around half the cost of conducting marketing research, cost control and financial planning studies.

For further information, contact:

European Investment Bank, 68 Pall Mall, London SW1Y 5ES, T:01-839 3351.

Department of Trade and Industry, 123 Victoria Street, London SW1E 6RB, T:01-212 7676 or your nearest regional office.

Scotland – Industry Department for Scotland, Alhambra House, 45 Waterloo Street, Glasgow G2 6AJ, T:041 248 2855.

Wales – Welsh Office Industry Department, Government Buildings, Cathays Park, Cardiff CF1 3NQ, T:0222-825111.

Northern Ireland – Industrial Development Board for Northern Ireland, IDB House, 64 Chichester Street, Belfast BT1 4JX, T:0232 233233.

Advice and training

Never has small business been so well served when it comes to general business help and training. A number of agencies offer free advice and low cost consultancy as well as a variety of training schemes ranging from general information on setting up and developing a small business to more specialised courses on such subjects as marketing.

Department of Employment: Small Firms Service

The Small Firms Service provides an information and a counselling service on any aspect of general business administration, from drawing up a business plan to rejigging your production.

The *information service* is completely free. The Small Firms Centres will be able to answer most queries on the spot. If not, they will put you in touch with someone who can.

The *counselling service* is free for up to three sessions. Thereafter, there is a charge of £30 per session. Counsellors (who are businessmen) can give practical, impartial and confidential advice on business matters. Counsellors can also be used to give a second opinion.

An appointment is necessary for all counselling and is made by ringing the nearest Small Firms Centre.

The Small Firms Service also holds Small Business Advice Days at jobcentres monthly. They are free and no appointment is necessary.

The Small Firms Service operates through a nationwide network of Small Firms Centres backed up by over 100 Area Counselling Offices which can be found in most major towns. Your nearest Small Firms Centre can be contacted by dialling 100 and asking for Freefone Enterprise or by writing to: **Small Firms and Tourism Division, Department of Employment**, Steel House, Tothill Street, London SW1H 9NF, T:01-213 3000.

In Scotland and Wales, the Small Firms Service is provided by the **Scottish Development Agency** and the **Welsh Development Agency**. In Northern Ireland, an information service is provided by the **Department of Economic Development**.

Manpower Services Commission

The MSC is a government agency that sponsors a number of training and enterprise courses, designed for the self-employed and those running, or planning to start, small businesses. Courses are normally held at local education institutes, colleges and polytechnics but are staffed and paid for by the MSC. The three most appropriate are:

Self Employment Course. This is for those planning to start a business from their home. It is offered on either a full-time basis (3 weeks) or through evening and weekend classes and covers the following important areas: how to assess and price your product or service; how much money you will need to get started; how to prepare a business plan; cash flow forecasts; preparation of an action plan.

Small Business Course. This is designed for those who are likely to be employing more than three staff after the first year. In addition to the subjects covered on the self employment course, it gives more information on: how to manage your business and employ staff; the necessity for market research which is considered so important that the MSC will actually give you a £500 grant to conduct research during the course; individual review sessions on a one-to-one basis with a supervisor to help you assess the right business decisions for your particular enterprise during the critical early weeks. The course runs for 6 to 10 weeks, on a full and part-time basis.

New Enterprise Programme. This is designed for people starting businesses with high growth potential. It runs for 16 weeks full time including a research period, and is offered in conjunction with the following business schools: London, Manchester, Durham, Warwick and Glasgow. The course entails intensive training in all business techniques, especially market research where you have access to a £1,250 budget. At the end of the course, you continue to have review sessions with a panel of experts.

Eligibility and cost. Eligibility is normally limited to those who are, or are about to be, unemployed. The MSC pays all course fees, any accommodation costs and, in certain circumstances, an allowance to support you while you are training.

How to apply. Telephone the MSC local area office, listed in the telephone directory, or apply to your local jobcentre for an application form.

For information about the New Enterprise Programme, apply to: Room W450, **MSC Special Training Section**, Moorfoot, Sheffield S1 4PQ, T: 0742-703 531.

Adult education centres

Short courses in specific business skills are run by business schools, polytechnics and colleges of higher and further education. Many of these are funded by the **Manpower Services Commission**. Various trade and professional associations also run courses. Enquire through your local education authority (see telephone directory).

Council for Small Industries in Rural Areas (CoSIRA)

CoSIRA is an agency of the Development Commission, set up to promote new industry and jobs in rural areas. Although better known for its work in converting redundant farm buildings into small industrial workshops, it also runs a variety of advisory and training services for small businesses in villages and towns with less than 10,000 inhabitants.

A day's advice on setting up or developing a business is provided free. Should you need further help a very modest fee of about £30 a day is normally charged.

CoSIRA also offers technical training courses for craftsmen covering such skills as: welding, vehicle repairs, pottery, furniture restoration, forge work, saddlery and thatching. These range from one day to one week and are held either at CoSIRA's headquarters, a suitable local venue or on your own premises. Fees are around £150 a week, per person, excluding any residential costs. Unsubsidised fees can also be paid by those generally ineligible for CoSIRA services.

CoSIRA runs very popular weekend courses on such subjects as: micro-computers for the small firm, industrial legislation and its effect on the small firm and buying a country shop. These are all designed for proprietors or potential proprietors and cost between £30 and £150.

Eligibility for all CoSIRA services is normally limited to small manufacturing and service businesses, employing not more than 20 skilled people. The service does not extend to horticulture, agriculture, the professions or firms connected with tourism unless these are located in a rural development area.

For further information, contact: **CoSIRA**, 141 Castle Street, Salisbury, Wilts SP1 3TP, T:0722-336 255 or your nearest regional office. These are located at: Darlington, York, Barnsley, Morpeth, Howden, Penrith, Preston, Bingham, Northampton, Sleaford, Cambridge, Norwich, Ipswich, Wallingford, Bedford, Braintree, Maidstone, Guildford, Lewes, Winchester, Newport (IoW), Exeter, Taunton, Truro, Bristol, Dorchester, Telford, Wirksworth, Malvern and Warwick.

Regional development agencies

These organisations are designed to assist the development of industrial activity in their areas and all have small business divisions that will be only too glad to offer any assistance they can.

Scottish Development Agency

The SDA has a small business division whose services are available to anyone employing (or planning to employ) up to 100 people. It incorporates the

Scottish section of the DTI's Small Firms Information Service and offers the following:

- a business counselling service, to anyone considering setting up a business in Scotland. The first three sessions are free. To use the service, dial 100 and ask for Freefone Enterprise.
- subsidised use of the Better Business Service. The scheme makes available a wide variety of professional and business consultants, with the SDA paying 55 per cent, or £550, whichever is the lesser, of consulting fees.
- evening courses at Scottish colleges on 'starting your own business', which involve 8 evening sessions and one weekend day. There is a modest charge. One-day sales and marketing courses are run by experienced training consultants who offer follow-up meetings as part of the deal. Cost, about £50 including lunch.

The SDA's small business marketing section runs a number of one-day sales training courses for a small fee (approximately £49 including VAT and lunch) and offers highly subsidised market research and marketing consultation. Their consultants can be engaged on a fee basis to implement your marketing plans.

The SDA also offers small firms the chance to join their trade promotion visits to overseas markets and exposure in the Scottish Trade Development Centre in London.

Their Technical Services Unit can help overcome manufacturing problems and improve production efficiency. A modest charge of around £30 a day is made for these services.

Particular help is given to craftworkers directed towards the making, marketing and promotion of craftwork, including some discretionary grants.

For further information, contact:

Scottish Development Agency, Small Firms Information Service, 123 Bothwell Street, Glasgow G2 7JP, T:041-248 2700, or Small Business Division, Rosebery House, Haymarket Terrace, Edinburgh EH2 5ES, T:031-337 9595.

Highland & Islands Development Board

The HIDB covers the Northern and Western parts of Scotland, as well as the Scottish Islands. It offers a free counselling service to small firms and to those considering setting up in these areas. This includes advice on recruitment, rates of pay, labour availability and other employment issues.

The Board runs formal 10-week courses for people who wish to start their own business, during which participants can prepare a full business plan.

Financial assistance may be given to meet training expenses but this does not normally exceed 50 per cent of the cost. The HIDB runs specific training courses on: tourism, fish farming, forestry and agriculture.

For further information, contact:

Highlands & Islands Development Board, 27 Bank Street, Inverness IVI 1QR, T:0463-234 171.

Welsh Development Agency

The WDA runs a business development unit that provides experienced counsellors for those thinking of starting a business in Wales. It also offers an executive secondment service, set up in conjunction with the CBI, that allows small businesses to benefit from the advice of experienced managers, at a fraction of the normal cost.

Additionally, the Agency runs practical 'Getting Into Business' courses, for people starting their own enterprise. These normally consist of 10 to 12 sessions and are completely free of charge.

Another useful service 'Women Into Business' is specifically designed for budding female entrepreneurs. Courses are geared to individual needs and are usually spread over a 3-month period.

For further information, contact:

Welsh Development Agency, P.O. Box 100, Greyfriars Road, Cardiff CF1 1WF, T:0222-32955.

Mid Wales Development Board, Ladywell House, Newtown, Powys SY16 1JB, T:0686-26965.

Local Economic Development Unit (Northern Ireland)

LEDU offers an extensive range of advisory and financial services. If you are planning to start a business, it offers 3 full days' free consultancy sessions. Further consultations only cost £15 a day, with a limit of 10 days at this rate.

A technical enquiry service and a design advisory service are both available free of charge, for up to 4 enquiries which do not in total use more than 5 consultant days.

There is a new enterprise workshop, which allows those with a technical product or process idea to try it out at virtually no cost. The workshop also includes advice on setting up and running a business.

For expanding businesses, the 'Better Business Service' runs courses on accounting, employment, commercial and planning issues.

If you need to use accountants or management consultants, LEDU may meet up to 55 per cent of the costs, with a maximum payment of £1,000.

For further information, contact:

LEDU, Upper Galwally, Belfast BT8 4TB, T:0232-6910 31.

DTI subsidised technical advice

The DTI offers free technical advice – such as which material to use or equipment to buy – to small and medium-sized manufacturing companies. Information can be given over the telephone or provided in up to five days' consultancy. It also offers a range of specialised advisory services in conjunction with research and design associations.

Product and Process Consultancy. Grants of 75 per cent of the cost, up to 15 days' consultancy, is available to help firms improve the quality and design of their products or their manufacturing techniques. The maximum grant is £2,500.

New Technology Feasibility Studies. Exactly the same subsidy is available to small companies who wish to assess the feasibility of their moving into biotechnology, micro-electronics, advanced manufacturing technology, CAD-CAM, robotics and the use of integrated circuits.

Consultants usually come from: The Production Engineering Research Association, Salford University Industrial Centre, The Design Council, Laboratory of the Government Chemist, Warren Spring Laboratory, National Computing Centre and National Engineering Laboratory.

Apply to **Department of Trade and Industry**, Technical Enquiry Service, 123 Victoria Street, London SW1E 6RB, T:01-212 7676 or your nearest DTI Regional Office.

Hotels, catering and tourism

Many retired people plan to run a hotel, restaurant or special tourist attraction. There are two public sector organisations you could find useful. These are: the Hotel and Catering Industry Training Board and the various Tourist Boards.

Hotel and Catering Industry Training Board

The HCITB's Small Business Services provide help both to people considering starting a business in the hotel and catering industry and to those already operating. The service covers a wide range: hotels, restaurants, pubs, cafes, snackbars, guest-houses, wine bars, tea shops, franchise operations, self-catering and other leisure activities. The following services are available:

Information service: advice on training courses, where to seek help and so on. It provides a number of information sheets on different subjects including wine bars, franchising, mobile catering and licensing. Contact: Telephone 01-902 5316. For enquiries concerning Scotland, Telephone 031-337 2339.

Courses before you buy
Stage One: one- or two-day conferences at various venues throughout the country covering 'Is this the right business?'

Stage Two: a three-day course on how to acquire the right business

Stage Three: a longer course (eight weeks sponsored by MSC) for selected candidates who have completed the previous stages.

Cost: Fees start at £40 per person per day.

Courses when you are in business, covering various management skills including marketing. At the Micro Systems Centre at Ramsey House, the HCITB displays representative computer software for Hotel and Restaurant Management Systems and provides training in choosing and using such systems. Sessions are normally held twice a month. Contact: Mark Jones at Ramsay House. T:01-902 8865, Ext.212. Cost: courses are £71 a day including lunch, or £25 to £50 for advice. MSC support grants may be available.

Advice on individual needs: an individual consultancy service can assist with such issues as help in designing premises, advice on legislation, arranging industrial placements for prospective proprietors to give them practice in useful skills or other matters according to the individual requirements of the business. Fees: £35 per hour or £250 per day. To make an appointment, telephone 01-902 8865, Ext.211.

Books and training aids: in addition to a very useful Small Business Information Pack, the HCITB publishes a number of other books and training aids, including: *Starting up your own Business, Small Business Training Aid, Training for Health and Safety in the Hotel and Catering Industry, Marketing for Publicans, Employing People in the Licensed Trade* and *Marketing for Independent Hoteliers*.

For further information, contact: **Hotel and Catering Industry Training Board**, P.O. Box 18, Ramsay House, Central Square, Wembley, Middlesex HA9 7AP, T:01-902 5316.

The regional offices are at the following addresses:

- Ansvar House, 31 St. Leonard's Road, Eastbourne BN21 3UU, T:0323-20579
- West Wing, Prudential Building, Wine Street, Bristol BS1 2PH, T:0272-24074
- The Graftons, Stamford New Road, Altrincham WA14 IDQ, T:061-928 2761

- Stonebow House, The Stonebow, York YO1 2NP, T:0904-26134
- 10 Magdala Crescent, Edinburgh EH12 5BE, T:031-337 2339.

Tourist boards

Advice about the development and marketing of tourist attractions and amenities is available from the regional tourist boards, as follows:

English Tourist Board, Thames Tower, Black's Road, London W6 9EL, T:01-846 9000

Welsh Tourist Board, Brunel House, 2 Fitzalan Road, Cardiff CF2 IUY, T:0222 499909

Scottish Tourist Board, 23 Ravelston Terrace, Edinburgh EH4 3EU, T:031-332 2433

Northern Ireland Tourist Board, River House, 48 High Street, Belfast BT1 1DS, T:0232-31221.

If you are interested in running a pub, see Chapter 9.

Non-Government sources of advice and training

Many Enterprise Agencies, Chambers of Commerce, Business Institutes and Small Business Clubs, scattered around the country, provide counselling services, together with, in some cases, more formal training.

Enterprise agencies

These are partnerships between local businesses, the professions, chambers of commerce, local authorities and others, designed to stimulate the start up and expansion of small businesses with a view to job creation.

There are around 300 EAs now operating in the UK, offering varying facilities which often include: free business advice, provision and management of small business workshops, enterprise training and the facilities of a small business club.

Enterprise Agencies operate under the umbrella of Business in the Community who can put you in direct contact with your nearest EA. For further information, contact:

Business in the Community, 227a City Road, London EC1B 1JU, T:01-253 3716.

Scottish Business in the Community, Eagle Star House, 25 St. Andrew's Square, Edinburgh EH2 1AF, T:031-556 9761.

Alternatively, you can ring your nearest regional office:

North Region: 0632-611142/3
North West Region: 0625-535999
Yorkshire and Humberside Region: 0724-84311 Ext. 2365
West Midlands Region: 021-558 3131 Ext. 4208/9
East Midlands Region: 0604-830236
Eastern Region: 01-253 3716
South East Region: 01-253 3716
South Region: 08765-78697
South West Region: 0761-62836 and 0884-255629
London Central: 01-253 3716
Northern Ireland: 01-253 3716
Wales: 0443-692233.

London Enterprise Agency (LEntA)

An example of a fully comprehensive service is provided by LEntA. This Enterprise Agency offers:

- help in developing a business plan for presentation to banks; this includes advice on which banks might sensibly be approached and what to do if your proposal is rejected
- general advice on market research, marketing strategy and techniques such as direct mail
- a patenting and licensing technical service
- financial help for innovation through a grant system jointly funded through the National Westminster Bank
- a 'marriage bureau' service for introducing investors to companies seeking funds
- promotions designed to introduce small firms to large company buyers who can explain their purchasing policy
- courses in starting up and developing a business, held during the evenings and at weekends.

For further advice, contact:

LEntA, 4 Snow Hill, London EC2A 2DL, T:01-236 3000.

Chambers of commerce

Chambers specialise in providing on-going help, general business advice and training. Examples of regular courses, offered by many, include: telephone sales and data preparation for computers. Costs vary but average £30 a day for non-member companies.

Chambers provide informal networks of contacts with other businessmen who may well need the products/services you plan to offer.

Addresses are listed in the local telephone directory. Alternatively, contact:

Association of British Chambers of Commerce, 212 Shaftesbury Avenue, London WC2, T:01-240 5831.

Institute of Directors Members' Information and Advisory Service (MIAS).

Staffed part-time by four senior businessmen, MIAS gives information, advice and counselling on the more complicated problems of business life from whether a redundancy settlement is fair to advice on raising finance, export marketing or operating a group of companies. General information on such things as the Retail Prices Index can also be supplied, often over the telephone.

Each of the advisors specialises in certain areas, including: finance, tax and small businesses; personnel management, retirement, redeployment and conditions of service; exports and marketing; and company secretarial practice and company commercial and employment law. The service is free to members.

Contact **MIAS**, Institute of Directors, 116 Pall Mall, London W1, T:01-839 1233 for an appointment or to discuss your problem over the telephone with an advisor.

Women in Enterprise

WE is a new national organisation aimed at encouraging women entrepreneurs to set up their own businesses. In addition to providing practical information, a number of training courses are also planned. WE is particularly concerned with helping women establish business credibility and overcome prejudice from unhelpful suppliers or financiers. It can also advise on problems relevant to women who are trying to balance their business life with family commitments. Membership costs £12.50 a year. For more information, contact:

Women in Enterprise, 4 Co-operative Street, Horbury, Wakefield WF4 6DR, T:0924-277267.

British Steel Corporation (Industry) Ltd.

Established to help create jobs in steel closure areas, BSC Industry can offer a package of premises, cash and advice for any business willing to set up in one of the 18 locations that come within its orbit. For further information, contact:

BSC (Industry) Ltd., NLA Tower, 12 Addiscombe Road, Croydon CR9 3JH, T:01-686 0366.

NCB (Enterprises) Ltd.

This provides a similar service to BSC Industry in areas where the Coal Board is closing pits. Heavily subsidised loans are available in addition to free retraining facilities. For further information, contact:

NCB (Enterprise) Ltd., Hobart House, Grosvenor Place, London SW1X 7AE, T:01-235 2020.

Ismailia Business Information Centre

Funded by the Aga Khan, IBIC was founded ten years ago (1976) as a non profit making organisation to aid the thousands of Ismaili Asian refugees from Idi Amin's Uganda. Since then, it has helped some 650 new businesses, initially creating more than 2,000 jobs. IBIC provides individual advice and group seminars for new and expanding small businesses. Though IBIC is primarily for Ismailis, some places are kept at seminars for non-community members. A greater role in training and in encouraging joint ventures is under consideration.

IBIC runs its own version of the Government's Loan Guarantee Scheme in conjunction with Lloyds Bank: the Aga Khan guarantees a third of bank loans for business projects approved by a committee of community members and businessmen.

Applicants must put up 20 per cent of the project costs which cannot exceed £150,000 in total. Unlike the Loan Guarantee Scheme, borrowers are not charged a premium on these loans. So far, some 855 loans, worth £19 million have been guaranteed with a top limit on the guaranteed portion of £25,000. Failure rate runs at less than 1 per cent by value of these loans. For further information, contact:

Ismailia Business Information Centre, 1 Cromwell Gardens, London SW7, T:01-581 2071.

The Ethnic Minority Business Development Unit

Run by the City of London Polytechnic, the development unit aims to increase the number of black people in management and self-employment. Various training courses cover the practical aspects of setting up and expanding a business, with particular reference to the problems often encountered by members of the ethnic communities. The programme runs for eight sessions, held on two evenings a week. The course is free to people living in the Inner London Education Authority area. Contact:

The Ethnic Minority Business Development Unit, Room 125, 110 The Minories, Tower Hill, London EC3 1JY, T:01-283 1030, ext.456.

Urbed

This is a non profit making company which specialises in programmes for private and public sector staff. It runs two courses devoted to those starting their own business. 'Improving Your Prospects' is an evening course on eight consecutive Mondays costing £66. 'Getting Along' is a 10 week programme of part time courses for people about to launch their own business; it is jointly sponsored by the MSC and is free to participants.

If you are not certain whether you are ready to start a business, Urbed holds open evenings at which you can discuss your ideas. It also offers 'New Venture Programmes', designed specifically for managers in large companies who are considering alternative forms of employment. For further information, contact:

Urbed Ltd., 99 Southwark Street, London SE1 OFJ, T:01-928 8515.

Trade associations

Virtually all industries have a trade association that provides advice and other services to members. If you are considering purchasing or starting a business in a particular trade sector, ask at your local library for the name and address of the relevant trade body. Examples are: National Federation of Retail Newsagents, British Institute of Interior Design, the Institute of Employment Consultants and the Booksellers' Association.

Other useful organisations

The following are the key organisations representing small business interests. Some act as pressure groups, conduct research and also provide a service to their members:

Alliance of Small Firms and Self-employed People Ltd., 279 Church Road, London SE19 2QQ, T:01-653 7288.

Association of Independent Businesses, Trowbray House, 108 Weston Street, London SE1 3QB, T:01-403 4066.

Confederation of British Industry, Small Firms Division, Centre Point, 103 New Oxford Street, London WC1A 1DU, T:01-379 7400.

Forum of Independent Businesses, Ruskin Chambers, Drury Lane, Knutsford, Cheshire WA16 6HA, T:0565-4467.

Institute of Directors, 116 Pall Mall, London SW1, T:01-839 1233.

National Federation for the Self-employed and Small Businesses Ltd., 45 Russell Square, London WC1, T:01-636 3828.

9. Looking for Paid Work

Far from thinking of putting up your feet when you retire from your present job, perhaps like many other people today one of your ambitions is to continue working in some form of paid employment.

However, before dashing off a shoal of application letters, it helps to think through some of the practicalities. Start by asking yourself a few basic questions.

Firstly, what is your main motive in wanting to work? The wish to supplement your income? The companionship? Fear of boredom? The desire for mental stimulation? The need to have a sense of purpose? Or the lurking suspicion that without a job, friends and social acquaintances will be less interested in hearing your views?

The answer may well be a combination of factors but you should at least try to pinpoint your priorities, to avoid drifting into a job that does not satisfy your main aims. The stories are legion of people whose prime reason for seeking work was to get out of the house to make new friends and who then plumped for a solitary occupation working from home. Likewise, one frequently hears of those whose real purpose was financial but who somehow signed on instead for unpaid voluntary work.

Another fundamental consideration is how many hours you are thinking of putting in a week. A full Monday to Friday? Or just a couple of half days? And while on the subject of time, is working a long-term goal or simply a pleasant occupation to fill in the next year or so?

What about distance? Would you be prepared to commute or are you aiming for a job that is strictly local? Was there anything, for example the travel, that you particularly disliked about your previous employment and that you are determined to avoid in your future job?

Also very much to the point, are you planning to seek an opening in a similar field, where your experience and contacts would come in useful? Or do you want to do something entirely different? And if so, were this to help, would you be willing to do a training course?

Moreover, have you considered the important economic questions? It may sound stupid when you have been working most of your life but factors such as your age, your total weekly earnings, your pension and other income, as well of course as any out-of-pocket expenses you incur, could mean that at the end of the day the sums look rather different from what you had supposed.

Financial considerations

One of the big flies in the ointment is a provision known as the *Earnings Rule*. It affects men between the ages of 65 and 70 and women between the ages of 60 and 65. Put very briefly, if you come within these age brackets and earn more than an average £75 a week (after deduction of allowable work-related expenses), your state pension will be reduced. For further information, see leaflet NI 196, obtainable from any Social Security office.

If you are working close to a full-time week and/or have enough money to live on, you normally have everything to gain by asking the DHSS to *defer your state pension*. This will both extricate you from the Earnings Rule and entitle you to a bigger pension when you receive it.

National Insurance is another consideration. Unless you are over state retirement age or earning less than £38 a week (1986/87 rates), in which case you can largely forget about NI contributions, you will be liable for the normal Class 1 contributions. If however, as many early retirers do, you work for *2 or more different employers*, you will have to pay Class 1 in respect of each. The maximum you would have to contribute is £1,359.45p (1986/87). To avoid being billed for more, fill in the form attached to leaflet NP 28, available from Social Security offices.

If you obtain work *through an agency* (e.g. catering, nursing, exhibition work), you are usually regarded as an employee of the agency for national insurance purposes and the agency is responsible for the payment of Class 1 contributions on your behalf. However, this does not apply if: you do the work from home; are not subject to anyone's direct supervision; or are in the entertainment business. See leaflet NI 192.

If you are *over retirement age* and have a job, the only requirement is that you obtain an exemption card to give to your employer. See Form CF 384 (Certificate of Exception), also from any Social Security office.

If you do *freelance* or other assignment work (unless virtually all your earnings come from one employer, in which case the Inland Revenue would argue that you are an employee of the organisation), you are officially considered to be self-employed for both national insurance and taxation purposes. (See Chapter 8.).

Assessing your abilities

Some people know exactly what they want to do. They have planned their action campaign for months, done their research, prepared a CV, followed up selective openings and are just waiting for their present employment to come to an end before embarking on a new career. But for most of us, it is not like that. Having merrily announced our intention to find a job, there comes a moment of truth when the big question is *what?*

Knowing what you have to offer is an essential first step. Make a list of everything you have done, both in your formal career and ordinary life, including your outside interests such as: local politics, Rotary, hobbies, voluntary work and even jobs around the home – decorating, gardening, carpentry or cooking. In particular, consider any practical or other skills, knowledge or contacts that you have acquired through these activities which may now prove useful, for example: public speaking, fundraising, committee work, conference organisation, use of mini-computers, production know-how or fluency in a foreign language.

As a result of writing everything down, most people find that they have far more to offer than they originally realised.

Add too your personal attributes and any special assets you can offer an employer. The list might include: health, organising ability, a good telephone manner, communication skills, the ability to work well with other people, use of a car and willingess to do flexible hours.

Maturity can also be a positive asset. Many employers prefer older people as being more reliable and less likely to be preoccupied with family and social demands. Also, in many small firms in particular, a senior person's accumulated experience is often especially valuable.

By dint of looking at yourself afresh in this fashion, you may get a clearer idea of the sort of job that would suit you. Although there is an argument for keeping a fairly open mind and not limiting your applications too narrowly, the worst mistake you can make is to answer scores of advertisements indiscriminately – and inevitably end up with a sackload of rejections.

Of course, offers do sometimes turn up out of the blue; and in some cases in a field where it would never have occurred to you to look. But as a general rule when job-hunting, it helps to know at least in broad terms what you are seeking before you start.

Many people find this extraordinarily difficult. After years of working in one occupation, it takes quite a leap in imagination to picture yourself in another role – even if it is in the same or a related area. If you intend to do something completely different, it will be harder still as your knowledge of what the job entails will probably be second-hand.

Also quite apart from deciding what you would enjoy, in many parts of the country the issue may be more a matter of what is available.

Talking to other people helps. Friends, family, work colleagues or business acquaintances may have useful information and moreover will quite likely be able to appraise your abilities more objectively than you can yourself.

It could also be sensible to consult outside experts, who specialise in adult career counselling and whose advice may be more realistic than that of friends in the context of current employment opportunities.

Job counselling

This is usually a mixture of helping you to identify your talents in a vocational sense combined with practical advice on successful job-hunting techniques. Counsellors can assist with such essentials as writing a Curriculum Vitae, preparing for an interview and locating job vacancies. They can also advise you as to the qualifications you need and point you in the direction of suitable training courses. Counselling is offered both by government agencies and private firms.

Government services

There are two services that could be helpful to adult jobseekers.

Career Change Programme. Commonly known as the 'Bridge Programme', it is designed to advise and give practical help to managers and professional people facing the challenge of finding fresh employment. The Programme is operated through 45 colleges and centres throughout the country and offers individual counselling as well as assistance with interview technique and CV writing. The service includes the facilities of a job search base, often providing secretarial help, telephone and photocopying equipment. This is usually free, although some centres may ask for a small contribution of around £10 towards the cost of the facilities. For further information and the address of your nearest centre, contact your local Professional and Executive Recruitment office (PER), jobcentre or employment office.

Jobcentres. Although not a formal counselling service, jobcentres are often a good starting point, as the staff will know about local vacancies and what training provision exists in the area. An increasing number of jobcentres provide careers libraries with books, articles and leaflets on a whole range of occupations. It is often a good idea to ring beforehand and make an appointment to see the Employment Officer.

Private counselling

Job counselling has become a growth industry in the private sector. Some people find it extremely helpful; others, an expensive waste of time. Best advice is to obtain brochures from a variety of agencies and study the literature carefully to see exactly what you are being offered. You could ask for a list of former clients and then speak to one or two of them direct, to find out whether they found the service useful. Some of the better known organisations include:

Career Analysts, Career House, 90 Gloucester Place, London W1, T:01-935 5452.

Their 'Career Review' service caters specifically for those in the 35-54 age group, who need to consider carefully what they plan to do for the remainder of their working lives. In-depth counselling and practical guidance are offered; and there is a follow-up session after two years. Price is £160 plus VAT.

Career Counselling Services, 46 Ferry Road, London SW13 9PW, T:01-741 0335.

The counselling is staged over a number of sessions, lasting around ten hours in all. The service includes a number of tests and questionnaires to be completed at home, which are used as a basis for discussion. A follow-up session is arranged after a year to assess progress. Price is £200 plus VAT.

Career Guidance Ltd., 20 Bloomsbury Square, London WC1, T:01-631 1209.

Offers a combination of tests with a detailed follow-up interview and a written report. Price is £110, incl. VAT.

Centre for Professional Employment Counselling (CEPEC), 67 Jermyn Street, London SW1Y 6NZ, T:01-930 0322.

CEPEC provides a very comprehensive and personalised service for those in the upper and middle management bracket. Price is very high: 15 per cent of existing (or final) salary plus VAT, but CEPEC continues to support clients until they actually find a job. The service includes counselling, career development guidance, interview training, assistance with CV writing plus introductions to potential employers. Part of the Sundridge Park Management Centre, there are also branches in Kent, Altrincham, York and Bristol.

The National Advisory Centre on Careers for Women, Drayton House, 30 Gordon Street, London WC1H OAX, T:01-380 0117.

This is a registered charity. As a follow-up to an advisory interview, relevant information on careers and training is supplied. Cost is about £25. Those living out of London should look in the 'Yellow Pages' under the words 'Career' or 'Vocational'.

Training opportunities

Knowing what you want to do is one thing. But before starting in a new job, you may want to brush up existing skills or possibly acquire new ones. Most professional bodies have a full programme of training events, ranging from one-day conferences to proper courses lasting a week or longer. Additionally, the **Manpower Services Commission** offers a number of schemes which may be of interest.

Information Technology Training. A new scheme, designed to help beginners gain a grounding in the basics of IT. Anyone under state retirement age is eligible and training is available in the evenings or at weekends. Enquire at your local jobcentre.

'Open Tech' Programme. Rather like the 'Open University', the 'Open Tech' programme allows you to learn at your own pace, as and when it suits you. The course is designed for those who have already reached technician or supervisory level. For further information, obtain leaflet *Open Learning: The Role of the Open Tech Programme* from your local jobcentre or MSC Training Division Area Office. Ask also at your library for the 'Open Tech Directory', which gives a list of all OT projects.

Job Training Scheme. This is a successor to TOPS. It offers a wide range of courses including technology subjects, clerical skills, management training and others, depending on local employment needs. Courses are usually full-time and may last anything from four weeks to a year. All candidates are interviewed and there is usually an aptitude test before acceptance on the scheme. Grants are sometimes given at the discretion of the MSC. Trainees must be out of work on the day the course starts. For further information, obtain leaflet *Thinking About Training* from your local jobcentre.

Wider Opportunities Training. The programme offers a range of modular full and part-time courses at various levels, closely matched to local employment needs. Courses vary according to area but typically include craft, clerical, commercial and new technology. Eligibility is limited to the unemployed or those on a Community Programme. Most courses begin by helping individuals decide what they want to do. Among others, the programme is particularly aimed at women returners and managers seeking new employment. Contact your local jobcentre.

Help with finding a job

The ideal is to find a job for your retirement while you are still at work. Quite apart from it being more difficult to summon the energy to start looking around after a period of being idle, employers tend to give preference to those they see as being busy and involved, rather than those whom they suspect as having got out of the habit of the normal disciplines of work.

However, whether you leave it a while or start hunting well in advance, this will not affect the approach you probably adopt. The only extra tip if you have been retired for some time is to consider doing some voluntary work, or a short course, so you have a convincing answer to the inevitable question: what have you been doing?

There are three basic ways of finding a job: through contacts; by following up advertisements; or by applying to an agency for suitable introductions. As general wisdom, the more irons you have in the fire, the better.

Make sure all your friends and acquaintances know that you are in the market for work – and include on the list your present employer. Some firms actually encourage consultancy links with former executives, or at least are prepared to respond to a good idea. A greater number are more than happy to take on previous employees over a rush period or during the holiday season.

Another obvious move, if you are a member of a professional institute, is to inform them of your availability. Many institutes keep a register of members seeking work, and the encouraging part is that they receive a fair number of enquiries from firms seeking qualified people for projects, part-time or temporary work, or sometimes even for permanent employment.

A further source of very useful contacts is the local Chamber of Commerce, CBI or Institute of Directors. Likewise, if you are a member of a Rotary Club, it can only be useful to spread the word; and the same applies to, say, a golf club, political association where you are active, any committee you sit on or other group with which you are involved. Often the most unlikely person turns out to be the one who helps you most.

If you intend to follow up advertisements, selectivity is the name of the game. Rather than write around to all and sundry, limit your applications to those that sound genuinely promising.

You will save yourself a lot of stationery, not to mention disappointment when another 'sorry' letter arrives – or you fail to hear anything at all. As well as national and local newspapers, remember that the trade press often offers the best bet. Some local radio programmes broadcast a regular weekly 'job spot': it could be useful to check when this is scheduled.

Agencies invariably have more applicants than vacancies, except where skill shortages exist. However, most clearly place a fair number of people (or they would be out of business) and, as with most endeavours, keenness counts. People who simply register their name and then sit back and wait, tend to be forgotten. The moral is, telephone frequently to enquire what opportunities have arrived; or if you live close by, pop into the office from time to time. Like possession, being on the spot at the right time is nine-tenths of success. A selection of agencies that specialise in appointments for people aged 50 plus is listed at the end of the chapter.

Regardless of whether you use contacts, advertisements or agencies – or preferably all three – a prime requirement will be to have a well presented CV.

CV writing

This is your personal sales document. It should contain:

- your name

- address
- telephone number
- age (optional)
- brief details of your education
- a summary of your work experience including: dates, employers, job titles and outline of responsibilities
- other achievements
- key outside interests

Ideally, it should not be longer than two pages of A4 and *it must be typed*.

There are a number of firms that specialise in providing assistance with the writing of CVs, who advertise their services regularly in *The Times* and other serious newspapers. While some are highly professional, a common fault tends to be the production of over-lengthy CVs, which can be definitely counter-productive. If you are thinking of using a specialist service, check the price first as charges can be on the hefty side. As with other purchases, you should do a bit of price comparison before making a decision. The price will normally include a batch of immaculately typed copies of your CV, ready for you to distribute.

A far cheaper option is to take advantage of the government Career Change Programme, available through PER offices (see above under Job counselling).

Another possible source of help are **Jobclubs**, which are run by Jobcentre staff to assist those who have been out of work for six months or more. To attend, you have to be serious about looking for work. Intensive counselling is given to improve job-hunting techniques, including CV preparation, and free facilities are provided including telephone, typewriter and photocopying equipment. Contact your Jobcentre for details.

The Job Change Project, run by the charity Birmingham Settlement, offers a fairly similar service: advice with letters of application; secretarial assistance for the preparation of CVs; plus access to telephones and photocopying. It also advises those planning to start their own business. Further information from:

Job Change Project, Birmingham Settlement, 318 Summer Lane, Newtown, Birmingham B19 3RL, T:021 359 3562.

Interview technique

If you have worked for the same employer for a number of years, your interview skills are liable to be a little rusty. It is a good idea to list all the questions you expect to be asked (including those you hope won't be brought up) and then get a good friend to rehearse you in your answers.

In addition to questions about your previous job, be prepared for some or all of the following: what you have done since leaving employment; why, if you are now seeking a job, you retired earlier than you might have done; whether your health is good – this may take the form of a polite enquiry as to whether you would not find the hours or travelling too much of a strain; why you are particularly interested in working for them; and given the job requirements, what you think you have of special value to offer. You may also be asked what you know about the organisation. If the answer is likely to be 'very little', it could pay you to do a bit of research – such as obtaining a copy of the annual report.

Obvious mistakes to avoid are: claiming skills/knowledge that you do not possess; giving the impression that you have a series of stock answers to problems; criticising your former employer; or by contrast, drawing comparisons which could be interpreted as being faintly disparaging of the organisation where you are attending for interview.

Possibly the most difficult subject of all to come up may be the question, how much money would you expect? As a sad generalisation, most jobs for retired people – including early retirers – pay less well than their previous employment, so you may have to strike a balance between what you want and the risk of pricing yourself out of the market.

Another reason why the pay may appear low is that the work is part-time. For some people, of course, this is the ideal arrangement. Others may regard it as very second best. However, do not sniff at part-time work if the opportunity comes along.

Firstly, it is a way back into the market. Additionally, many part-time or temporary assignments develop into full-time jobs in due course. This is especially true in small firms, who may of necessity be cautious about recruitment while the business is in the early development stage.

Part-time or freelance work can to all intents and purposes become a full-time occupation in its own right. Ask any retired businessman who has taken on half a dozen such appointments and the likelihood is that he will tell you that he is working harder than he has ever done in his life.

The only real note of caution is that many employment rights do not apply to part-timers and those working less than 16 hours a week are particularly vulnerable, for example with regard to redundancy.

Employment ideas

Going the established routes – agencies and so forth – while obviously recommended, may not suffice. Many of the best jobs are never advertised, either because people obtain them through personal recommendation or because – and this is becoming more frequent – individuals have been partially instrumental in creating their own opportunities.

One clear-cut way of doing so is to use a bit of initiative when spreading the word of your availability, by actually suggesting work you could usefully perform. Consultancy is very much a case in point.

Consultancy

Many retired executives make a tidy income by hiring themselves back to their former employer in a consultancy guise. As opposed to being paid a regular salary and working full-time, they undertake specific projects for which they are paid a fee. This may be structured as a lump sum, for example £5,000 for devising and helping to implement a merit appraisal scheme; or as many consultants do, they may negotiate a day-rate.

Consultancy, by definition, is not limited to a single client. By using your contacts judiciously plus a bit of marketing nous, it is quite possible to build up a steady list of assignments on the basis of your particular expertise.

Marketing skills are always in demand, as is computer knowledge, experience in pensions and personnel-related subjects and, increasingly today, public relations know-how.

Small firms are often a good bet for consultants, as they cannot afford to employ specialists full-time, so normally buy in expertise as and when it is required. Any contacts with the Chamber of Commerce or similar could prove fruitful avenues for promoting your services.

Many established consultancies retain a list of associates – a sort of freelance register – whom they call on, on a 'horses for courses' basis, to handle suitable assignments. The Institute of Management Consultants publishes a register of all its members, with brief details of individual firms' specialisations. This should provide you with a number of leads to contact, with a view to becoming an associate. The Institute also publishes a number of useful booklets on management consultancy. For further information, contact:

Institute of Management Consultants, 23 Cromwell Place, London SW7 2LG, T:01-584 7285.

Also worth knowing about is the Temporary Executive Service, launched recently by the CBI in association with Inbucon. It places senior executives with companies on a temporary basis, essentially to bridge management gaps or to provide a specialised service. Projects normally last anything from two to three months up to two years. Applicants inevitably exceed the number of vacancies. Contact:

Temporary Executive Service, Manpower Department, CBI, Centre Point, New Oxford Street, London WC1, T:01-379 7400.

Executives in Scotland should write to:

The Assistant Director, CBI Scotland, Batesford House, 5 Claremont Terrace, Glasgow G3 7XT, T:041 332 8661.

A broadly similar service is provided by the Institute of Directors which runs a Part-Time Executive Appointments Service. Assignments are essentially regular part-time or specific project work, such as export promotions. Most executives on the register are in the age bracket 40 to 65. Client companies tend to be smaller or medium sized businesses. Contact:

Part-time Executive Appointments Service, Institute of Directors, 116 Pall Mall, London SW1Y 5EE, T:01-839 1233.

Another useful organisation is Intex Executives Ltd. Openings tend to be in medium and smaller companies and typically are in general management or marketing, with assignments both at home and overseas. Further details from:

Intex Executives (UK) Ltd., Chancery House, 53/64 Chancery Lane, London WC2A 1QU, T:01-831 6925, and Chancery House, 1 Effingham Street, Ramsgate, Kent CT11 9AT, T:0843 56873.

Another possible source of work is the Department of Employment's **Small Firms Advisory Service**, which retains teams of consultants and advisors all over the country to assist small firms with any problems. Applicants must be experienced business people, who have either worked in small firms themselves or who are used to dealing with smaller companies/subsidiaries. Pay is £30 a day plus expenses and counsellors normally work about 100 days a year.

Contact your regional small firms centre, by dialling the operator and asking for Freefone Enterprise.

Similar openings are sometimes available in rural areas through:

CoSIRA, 141 Castle Street, Salisbury, Wiltshire SP1 3TP, T:0722 336 255.

Openings via a company or other reference

Just as your company could turn out to be your best customer for consultancy services, it could also open other doors. If you are still a couple of years off retirement, you could approach your employer about seconding you to an enterprise agency or charity, where you would be helping small businesses or a worthwhile voluntary organisation in your local community.

Normally only larger employers are willing to consider the idea since, as a rule, the company will continue to pay your salary and other benefits during the period of secondment. However, the concept has been gaining increasing popularity and more and more companies are giving the idea sympathetic consideration, especially since the Inland Revenue now allows companies to offset any secondee's employment costs against tax.

The two major organisations that specialise in co-ordinating secondments are: Business in the Community, which is the umbrella organisation for enterprise agencies; and Action Resource Centre, which acts as a clearing house for inner city projects catering, for example, for groups such as ethnic minorities and the disabled. Addresses are:

Business in the Community, 227a City Road, London EC1B 1JU, T:01-253 3716.

Action Resource Centre, CAP House, Third Floor, 9-12 Long Lane, London EC1A 9HD, T:01-726 8987.

A rather different suggestion, where again your employer could help, is in the field of *public appointments*. The list of 'the great and the good' is an utter mystery to most people but every year thousands of individuals – including many early retirees – are appointed to serve on public bodies, such as district health councils, industrial tribunals, commissions and consumer consultative councils. While many of the appointments are voluntary, chairmen and those serving on key national Quangos receive fees – ranging from token payments to quite handsome salaries. Although individuals are encouraged to put themselves forward, many people suspect that it carries more weight if they are recommended.

You could ask your employer to forward your CV, plus recommendation, to the appropriate government department and/or to the **Public Appointments Unit**, Management and Personnel Office, Whitehall, London SW1.

Additionally, both the TUC and CBI are consulted on some appointments. If you are active on either, there is nothing to lose by letting it be known that you could be interested in a public appointment.

Non-executive directorships

Many retiring executives see this as the ideal. The problem, whichever way you look at it, is: either that more executives want appointments than there are directorships available; or that not enough companies have yet recognised the merits of having outside directors on their board. The two key organisations to which you could apply are:

Promotion of Non-Executive Directors (PRONED), 10 Gough Square, London EC4A 3LR, T:01-583 8033.

Sponsored by the Bank of England, the British Institute of Management and the CBI among others, PRONED maintains a register of candidates for non-executive directorships in companies ranging from the very large to small family businesses. The main requirements for inclusion on the register are: that you should have served on the board of a public limited company (plc) and be under the age of 62/63.

Institute of Directors, 116 Pall Mall, London SW1Y 5EE, T:01-839 1233.

Membership of the IOD is not a necessary requirement, however, though only 'high calibre candidates' would be accepted on the list.

Market research

In addition to the normal consultancy openings in marketing, there is also scope for those with knowledge of market research techniques. The work covers a very broad spectrum; from street or telephone interviewing to data processing, designing questionnaires, statistical analysis and sample group selection.

Many of the specialist market research agencies employ researchers and analysts on a freelance basis. However, as with other fields, supply exceeds demand so there is a certain amount of luck involved, as well of course as ability, in finding regular work.

The Market Research Society, 175 Oxford Street, London W1R 1TA, T:01-439 2585, can supply you with a list of market research organisations that employ freelancers.

Sales

If you are a whizz salesman, you will hardly be reading this chapter. You will have already used your contacts and flair to talk yourself into a dozen jobs, with the only problem being which one to choose. Almost every commercial firm in the country is crying out for people with that particular brand of authority, charm and persuasiveness to win extra orders.

Many people who have never actually thought of sales could be excellent in the job, because of their specialist knowledge in a particular field combined with their enthusiasm for the subject. Educational and children's book publishers for example are often keen to recruit ex-teachers to sell their books to schools and libraries.

There is an almost insatiable demand for insurance salesmen and, having pondered the question of how to invest your pension lump sum, you will probably have some knowledge of the options as well as first hand experience of being on the receiving end of a professional sales pitch.

Selling today is not just standing in a shop or trudging the rounds of sceptical customers. Over the past few years, telephone selling has caught on in a big way and, like mail order, is used by a vast array of very different companies; so if you have a good telephone voice, this could be for you.

Additionally, many firms employ demonstrators in shops or at exhibitions for special promotions. The work is usually temporary or freelance by definition; and while pay is normally good, the big drawback is that you could be standing on your feet for long periods of the day.

The big 'beware' are firms that pay on a commission only basis. Far from merely earning a pittance, you could end up distinctly out of pocket.

If the idea of selling appeals, either study the newspaper advertisements or, better still, approach firms direct that you reckon could make genuine use of your special knowledge. If the idea makes you quail, the likelihood is that selling is not for you. If it fires you with enthusiasm, you could actually find yourself making more money in your retirement than ever before.

Tourist guide

An extrovert personality is also needed for tourist guide work. You will be ferrying coachloads of visitors around London and other places of interest. The work requires tireless energy, enthusiasm and a real liking for people. Qualifications are needed. Courses are run by the British Travel Association but to become a London 'Blue Badge' guide, it is necessary to sit the London Visitor and Convention Bureau exam which is extremely tough – but fascinating for those with a love of history, architecture and the arts. Preference is given to multi-lingual applicants who are under 55 years. Work is freelance and largely seasonal (Easter to October). Pay is in the region of £55 a day. Further information from:

British Travel Association and **London Visitor and Convention Bureau** both at: 26 Grosvenor Gardens, London SW1W 0DU, T:01-730 3450

Other tourist work

If you live in a popular tourist area, there is a whole variety of seasonal work, including: jobs in hotels, restaurants, shops and local places of interest. Depending on the locality, the list might also include: deckchair attendants, play leaders for children, caravan site staff, extra coach drivers and many others. There is also scope for taking in bed and breakfast visitors although, unless you want to make a regular business of it, it is advisable to limit the number of guests to a maximum of five otherwise you will be subject to stringent fire regulation precautions requiring special doors and other expensive paraphernalia. To be on the safe side, contact the local Environmental Health Officer (see telephone directory or enquire at the town hall) who will advise you of anything necessary you should do.

Teaching and training skills

If you have been a teacher at any stage of your career, there are a number of part-time possibilities:

Coaching

With examinations becoming more competitive, demand has been increasing for ex-teachers with knowledge of the public examination system to coach youngsters in preparation for 'A' level and common entrance. Contact local schools or the specialist educational agencies:

Gabbitas Thring, 6 Sackville Street, London W1, T:01-734 0161.

Truman & Knightly Educational Trust, 78 Notting Hill Gate, London W11 3LJ, T:01-727 1242.

It is also worth looking in the Yellow Pages.

Specialist subjects

Teachers are still in short supply in subjects such as mathematics, physical science, computer studies, craft design and technology, business studies and home economics. People with relevant work experience are in demand to give tuition in these subjects, although some formal teaching qualification is now often required. The **Department of Education and Science**, Elizabeth House, 39 York Road, London SE1 7PM, T:01-928 9222, publishes a useful booklet *Training and Retraining to Teach Priority Subjects*.

English as a foreign language

There has been a mini-explosion of new schools teaching English to foreign students. They tend to be concentrated in London and the major academic cities such as Oxford, Bath and York. No formal teaching qualifications are required but a recommended certificate is that of the Royal Society of Arts which can be taken either part-time or through a four-week crash course. A list of colleges offering the course can be obtained from:

Royal Society of Arts Examination Board, Murray Road, Orpington, Kent, T:0689-32421.

Other

Adult Education Institutes and Colleges of Further Education may sometimes have part-time vacancies. Those interested in teaching handicapped children might like to apply for the booklet of this name, available from the Department of Education and Science.

Publishing

Publishers are increasingly using freelance staff with appropriate experience for: proof-reading, copy-editing, design, typography, indexing and similar work. For a list of firms that could be interested, contact:

The Publisher's Association, 19 Bedford Square, London WC1, T:01-580 6321.

Freelance journalism

This is a highly competitive field with very limited scope and other than for professionals, should really be included in the hobbies section. Best bet if you remain undaunted is to approach specialist magazines direct, where you have a real knowledge of the subject. It is normally a waste of time sending articles 'on spec'. Instead, telephone the editor with a list of suggestions – and find out exactly what the magazine wants, including number of words and so on.

Caring for others

There are a number of opportunities for paid work, caring for other people. Mature women or couples are often preferred.

Fostering elderly people

An increasing number of local authorities run fostering schemes, whereby an elderly person lives with a family as an ordinary member of the household, receiving whatever care and special assistance is necessary. As with child fostering, enormous trouble is taken by social workers in matching families with their foster guest. Pay varies from one area to another but averages around £80 a week for every elderly person fostered, up to a legal maximum of three per home. Ask at your Social Services Department whether there is a fostering or 'boarding out' scheme to which you could contribute.

Home helps

Local authorities sometimes have vacancies for home helps, to assist the disabled or elderly in their own home by giving a hand with the cleaning, light cooking and other chores. Ask at your social services department. See also the 'Yellow Pages' for private domestic agencies who place temporary or permanent companions, housekeepers and emergency mothers.

Childminding

If you already look after a grandchild during the day, you might consider caring for an additional couple of youngsters. You will need to be registered with the local social services department who will explain all the requirements.

Nursing

Qualified nurses may be able to find work at their local hospital or alternatively through one of the many nursing agencies. See Yellow Pages. Family Planning clinics could also be worth approaching.

Cashing in on home interests

Cooking, gardening, home decorating, dress-making and DIY skills can all be turned into modest money-spinners.

Cooking

Scope includes: catering other people's dinner parties, selling home-made goodies such as cakes and pâtés to local shops and cooking for directors' lunches. Other than top class culinary skills, requirements are: a large deep-freeze, a car (you will normally be required to do all the necessary shopping) and plenty of stamina. Notify your friends, advertise your services through the Chamber of Commerce or local businessmen's club or, if you are really serious about it, enrol with one of the specialist catering agencies, see Yellow Pages.

Gardening

Small shopkeepers and florists sometimes purchase flowers or plants direct from local gardeners, in preference to going to the market. Alternatively, you might consider dried flower arrangements or herbs for which there has been a sudden increase in demand. However, before spending any money, check around to find out what the sales possibilities are. If you are willing to tend someone else's garden, the likelihood is that you will be inundated with enquiries. Spread the word among friends, acquaintances and in the pub. For information about herb growing techniques, contact:

The Herb Society, 77 Great Peter Street, London SW1, T:01-222 3634.

Dressmaking and home decorating

If you are happy to do alterations, the chances are that you could be kept busy from dawn to dusk. Many shops are desperate for seamstresses. Likewise, many individuals and families would love to know of someone who could alter clothes, as well as dressmake properly. Perhaps to a slightly lesser extent, the same goes for curtains, chair covers and other soft furnishings. Often a good move is to approach firms selling materials for the home who may be only too glad to put work out to you. Alternatively, put up a card in newsagents' shops or run a small advertisement in the local paper.

DIY

Competition is more intense, as many small builders offer this service. However, elderly people often require small jobs, as do women who do not have a handy-man around the house. Advice for getting your services known is the same as for gardening.

Running a pub

Many people dream of running a pub in their retirement – and many people live to regret it. It is more a way of life than a job and one that requires a great deal of stamina. You are on your feet for most of the day, the hours are long and when you are not pulling pints or preparing bar snacks, you will be dealing with the paperwork plus all the other day-to-day requirements.

You can either buy your own 'free' house or become the tenant of one of the big brewery companies. Prices vary according to the length of lease, location and so on but, as a rough guide, you would need a minimum of £10,000 in order to get started.

Although a condition of the tenancy will be that you buy all alcohol from the brewery company, to all intents and purposes you will be running your own business with financial, as well as practical, responsibility for the repairs and decorations, hiring of staff, compliance with fire precautions and so on.

For more information, contact:

The Brewers' Society, 42 Portman Square, London W1, T:01-486 4831.

Useful reading: *Running Your Own Pub*, Kogan Page, £4.95.

Agencies and useful organisations

Job hunting through agencies is very much a question of luck. People can be on their books for months and months and not be sent to a single interview. Someone else can walk through the door and within 48 hours be fixed up with an ideal job. Applicants normally greatly exceed vacancies and the majority of jobs, especially for the over 60s, tend to be on the modest side: clerical, security work, gardening, domestic services and similar. However, more challenging opportunities are sometimes registered and one or two of the organisations listed specialise in executive appointments. Retired accountants in particular are always in demand, as are people with fund-raising skills.

Government agencies

It is easy to forget the obvious. Both jobcentres and the PER service are available to help you.

Jobcentres. These have changed their image considerably over the last few years and now carry a wide range of vacancies for all levels of ability. In particular, many small firms use them for recruitment in preference to the more expensive private employment agencies. There are around 1,000 jobcentres throughout Great Britain which, between them, handle about 2 million vacancies a year. They also act as a gateway to many of the training courses and advisory services. See local telephone directory for address.

Professional and Executive Recruitment. PER provides a recruitment service for those seeking professional, scientific, technical and managerial employment. When you enrol you receive a copy of their *Job Hunting Handbook* and free weekly newspaper *Executive Post*, which will be mailed to your home regularly. *Executive Post* carries several hundred vacancies each week across the range of professional occupations and also contains information on training courses and advisory services. Anyone who enrols with PER is invited to a half day job-hunting seminar, which is run locally and provides information on the employment market, self presentation and job-hunting strategies. For further information about PER, see telephone directory or enquire at your local jobcentre.

Other organisations

Age Concern, 60 Pitcairn Road, Mitcham, Surrey CR4 3LL, T:01-640 5431.
   Age Concern runs employment bureaux for people over 60 in a number of areas around the country. They deal mainly in fairly unskilled part-time work, such as: shop and office cleaning, messengers, clerks, home help for elderly people and manual jobs. Contact your local Age Concern group (see telephone directory).

Charity Appointments, 3 Spital Yard, Bishopsgate, London E1 6AQ, T:01-247 4502.

Charity Appointments maintains a central register of candidates, interested in working in the voluntary sector. It specialises in senior appointments, such as: managers, directors, governors, trustees and professional fund-raisers. Some positions carry a salary; others are voluntary. Charity Appointments offers a counselling service for those requiring advice and career guidance.

Additionally there are a number of interesting opportunities for work overseas, on an expenses paid basis, listed in Chapter 10.

Corps of Commissionaires, 3 Crane Court, Fleet Street, London EC4A 2EJ, T:01-353 2125.

Offers full or part-time work to ex-servicemen or women, police and prison officers, firemen, coastguards and merchant seamen. Jobs cover a fairly broad range, from managerial and administrative posts to others that require the wearing of the Corps uniform, for example: commissionaires, security staff, ushers at sporting or official events. Maximum age is 65 for permanent jobs; 70 for temporary work. The Corps is not an employment agency as such, but operates as a club with annual membership £7. All applicants are invited to an interview and are required to provide references. The Corps has branches in: Belfast, Birmingham, Bristol, Edinburgh, Glasgow, Leeds, Liverpool, Manchester and Newcastle.

Country Cousins Employment Bureau, 10a Market Square, Horsham, West Sussex RH12 1EU, T:0403-61960/65188.

Country Cousins specialises in supplying temporary help in the home, with many of the jobs particularly suitable for retired people or couples. Typical openings include: emergency mothers; cooks; caretakers; and caring for an elderly person. Pay is in the broad range of £60 to £90 a week, although may be higher for those with nursing qualifications.

Executive Standby Ltd., Office 51, The London Wool and Fruit Exchange, Brushfield Street, London E1 6EU, T:01-247 5693.

Executive Standby has sister agencies in Cheshire, Bristol and Worcestershire. Though independently run, all specialise in placing executives of proven competence in management or similar posts in industry, commerce and in voluntary organisations. Most jobs are temporary though sometimes permanent positions do occur, as well as occasional openings abroad.

Addresses of out-of-London offices are: **Executive Standby Ltd.**, 310 Chester Road, Hartford, Northwich, Cheshire, T:0606-883 849; **Executive Standby (West) Ltd.**, Somercourt, Holmfield Road, Saltford, Bristol, T:022 17 3118; **Executive Standby (Midlands) Ltd.**, 91 High Street, Evesham, Worcs. WR11 4DT, T:0386 48703.

HERA – Housing Employment Register and Advice for Women, Basement Office, 120/122 Cromwell Road, London SW7 4HA, T:01-370 2545.

HERA is the employment advisory service of the Over 40 Association for Women Workers. It covers London and the Home Counties. Job seekers receive a fortnightly bulletin of vacancies at all levels in the field of housing, from management to secretarial.

Manpower Ltd., Manpower House, 270-272 High Street, Slough, Berks SL1 1LJ, T:0753 73111.

Manpower is the largest supplier of temporary work in the UK with 120 offices nationwide. Permanent employment is sometimes also available. Jobs cover a wide range from technical and skilled work to assembly, packing and similar services, as well as secretarial and other office work. Additionally, its associate company Overdrive operates a placement service for qualified HGV drivers.

Mid Wales Development, Skills Register, Ladywell House, Newtown, Powys SY16 1JB, T:0686-26965.

Part of the Development Board for Rural Wales, the agency operates a Skills Register with the aim of attracting to Wales skilled people in both production and management fields, to fill vacancies in some of the many new companies that have moved into the area. Write to the above address for a registration form.

The Officers Association, 48 Pall Mall, London SW1Y 5JY, T:01-930 0125.

The Association is part of the Regular Forces Resettlement Service. Eligibility is restricted to those who have held a commission in the armed services (or their families), who must be under 60 and currently unemployed. There are regional offices in Scotland and Eire.

Part-time Careers Ltd., 10 Golden Square, London W1R 3AF, T:01-437 3103.

Specialises in part-time secretarial jobs as well as accountancy, book-keeping and similar.

Pre-retirement Association, 19 Undine Street, Tooting, London SW17 8PP. T:01-767 3225.

Publishes a free pamphlet *Work in Retirement* that lists agencies and other organisations that can assist in finding employment for older people.

Royal British Legion Attendants Co. Ltd., 2 Southend Crescent, London SE9 2SB. T:01-859 5621.

Offers full or part-time work for ex-servicemen and women. Uniform is usually required to be worn and typical jobs are for car park attendants and commissionaires. The RBLAC has regional offices in Preston, Leeds, Cardiff and Poole.

Success after Sixty, 40/41 Old Bond Street, London W1X 3AF, T:01-629 0672, and **Success after Sixty (Croydon)**, 33 George Street, Croydon CRO 1LB, T:01-680 0858.

Despite its name, Success after Sixty also caters for younger people, from age 50. Both full and part-time openings are available. Jobs are essentially secretarial and clerical but openings sometimes exist for accountants and those with other professional skills. Also messenger jobs, hall-portering and similar. Work is mainly in the Central London and Croydon areas.

10. Voluntary Work

There are probably as many different kinds of voluntary work that need to be done, as there are organisations that need your help. The range of tasks and the variety of groups are both enormous. Perhaps this is one reason why some people simply steer clear of the whole area, fearing that the commitment may get out of control and that they may find themselves involved to a greater extent than they wish.

Though this may be true in some few cases there are probably thousands more who, starting in the smallest way, find themselves genuinely caught up in the enthusiasm for their particular cause and immensely rewarded by the contribution that they feel able to make and the new friends that it has brought them.

Very broadly, the voluntary help that is needed falls into four main categories:

Clerical. Any active group is likely to need basic administrative help from typing to telephone answering, stuffing envelopes to organising committees. This may involve a day or so a week or very occasional helping out at peak times.

Fund-raising. Every voluntary organisation needs more money and their ingenuity in raising it seems boundless. Jumble sales, coffee mornings and flag days are probably still the most common, but sponsored events of all kinds need a lot of organisation (you don't actually have to participate in the free-fall parachute drop) and negotiations for contributions from local or national businesses may test anyone's diplomatic skill.

Committee work. This can cover anything from the most occasional of help to virtually full-time commitment as branch treasurer or secretary. People with business skills or financial or legal backgrounds are obviously likely to be especially valuable in this area.

Direct work with the public. Driving, delivering 'meals on wheels', helping the handicapped, visiting the elderly, working in a charity shop, helping with a playgroup, giving the mother of a disabled or sick child a chance to get out of the house for an hour or so ... the list is endless and the value of the work incalculable.

It will be clear from the above that while some skills and experience have particular value in some circumstances — financial, legal, nursing, social work — there are a multitude of interesting and useful jobs for those with either no special training or relatively ordinary abilities like driving or typing.

In the same way, the time commitment can be varied to suit the helper and the organisation: Nearly always it is reliability that counts rather than the total time given.

What is absolutely certain is that, as with a paid job, you should be completely clear about all the terms and conditions before you take it on.

- What sort of work is involved?
- Who will be working with you?
- How much time is involved?
- When will you be needed?
- Are expenses paid? What for? How much?

If you straighten all this out at the beginning there will be less chance of any misunderstandings and you will find that voluntary work can be immensely satisfying and rewarding personally as well as a real contribution to the whole community.

Choosing the right voluntary work

It is one thing to decide that you would like to do some kind of voluntary work, but it may be quite another to find out what is available in your area and what will suit you personally. For this reason we have included a list of organisations, arranged in broad categories of interest, with an indication of the kinds of activities for which they are seeking volunteers. But no such list can be complete — there are literally thousands of voluntary groups, national and local, which need help in some way or other. For further information on needs and opportunities in this sector there are three other major sources to which you can turn:

REACH, Victoria House, Southampton Row, London WC1 4DA, T: 01-404 0940

The Retired Executives Action Clearing House was set up specifically to place retired executives with professional skills in voluntary organisations, charities and community groups. It does not find paid jobs, although expenses will be reimbursed. REACH is itself a charity so no fees are charged to either the applicant or the organisation.

Volunteer Bureaux (or Council of Voluntary Service)

Listed in the telephone book under 'V'. Most towns have a body of this kind which will hold lists of organisations looking for help locally.

Citizens Advice Bureaux

Your local CAB will also have information on local needs and groups to contact.

General

The scope of the work of the Red Cross, the WRVS and the Citizens Advice Bureaux is so broad that they justify a category to themselves.

British Red Cross Society, 9 Grosvenor Crescent, London SW1X 7EJ, T: 01-235 5454

The Red Cross is the world's largest humanitarian organisation. It needs volunteer help from men and women for first aid, nursing and welfare duties. Training is given where needed. It also requires fund-raisers, publicity officers, drivers for escort work and people with teaching, clerical, administrative and management skills. Expenses and, in a few cases, modest salaries are paid. Volunteers may give as little or as much time as they choose. Contact the local branch (under 'British' or 'Red Cross' in the telephone book) or write to the London headquarters.

Women's Royal Voluntary Service, 17 Old Park Lane, London W1, T: 01-499 6040

(See telephone book for your local branch)

The WRVS works with the Local Authority Social Services to cover almost the complete range of needs in the community. It particularly welcomes offers of help from people with time during the working day. Activities are too numerous to list but include 'meals on wheels', visiting and shopping for the elderly, helping in play groups, running canteens in prisons and courts, providing transport in rural areas, assisting with catering and welfare services in emergencies and helping in hospital shops. No special qualifications are required although people with medical training, financial experience or cooking skills are especially valuable.

Citizens Advice Bureaux (See telephone book for your local branch)

Apart from being an excellent source of information on other voluntary organisations needing help, the CAB itself has over 14,000 volunteer helpers working in its 1,000 or so branches throughout the country.

The work involves interviewing, counselling and advising clients on a wide range of questions from welfare benefits to local events and from community schemes to legal rights. No formal qualifications are required but it is essential that the applicant is able to master and explain a considerable amount of complicated and detailed information. Training is given (usually two days a week for six weeks) and volunteers are then expected to work about two days a week in their Bureau. Contact the Organiser at your nearest CAB for further details.

Children and young people

Church of England Children's Society also known as 'The Children's Society', Edward Rudolf House, Margery Street, London WC1X 0JC, T: 01-837 4299

The Children's Society offers a comprehensive child care service to children and families in need. The Society runs approximately 100 homes and projects include family and community centres, teenage units and hostels and special holiday projects for the handicapped. Virtually every parish in the country has an honorary local secretary who is mainly concerned with fund-raising. There are also 80 charity shops, run entirely by volunteers. Apart from this there are opportunities for counselling work via a local home or project. Contact may be made either through the London office or through the local organisation which may be listed in the telephone book.

Dr Barnardo's, Barkingside, Essex IG6 1QG, T: 01-550 8822

Dr Barnardo's provides residential and non-residential care for children and young people in need. Projects include day-care centres, hostels, community projects, play groups, play buses and holiday schemes. Two major areas require help:

Fund-raising. 25,000 people currently work as fund-raisers for Dr Barnardo's. It may include helping in a charity shop or with local flag-days and events. Write to Nicholas Lowe, Appeals Director who will pass on your application to your local branch.

Child care programme. Most often this involves looking after a handicapped child or young person for a few hours or longer to allow the mother a moment off (or just time to do the shopping) or for the rest of the family to have the opportunity of an outing together. Write to Barry Benson, Child Care Administration Officer at the above address.

National Association of Youth Clubs, Keswick House, 30 Peacock Lane, Leicester LE1 5NY, T: 0533-29514

The NAYC provides leisure activities for young people through a network of 45 local associations, mostly at county level. It supports youth clubs, youth employment schemes and business enterprise schemes for young people. The local association needs help with administration and with fund-raising. They may also be aware of particular clubs who can use assistance which may range from help with the accounts to maintenance work on the building. No particular time commitment is required. Expenses may be paid. The address of the nearest association can be found in the telephone book or write to the London office at the above address.

Save the Children Fund, Mary Datchelor House, 17 Grove Lane, London SE5 8RD, T: 01-703 5400

The objective of the fund is to promote the welfare of children, especially the deprived or handicapped, in Britain and abroad. Apart from fund-raising via a flag-day, the national Save the Children Week, charity shops, and the many events organised by local groups, there is also need for practical help with play groups and in youth clubs. Check the local telephone directory for the nearest branch or contact the head office.

Scout Association, Baden Powell House, Queensgate, London SW7 5JS, T: 01-584 7030

The Scout Association encourages the physical, mental and spiritual development of boys through guidance by adult leadership. There are a multitude of opportunities for voluntary help either directly as a Leader or a Commissioner (given some previous experience as a Scout) or through the District Scout Fellowships. These may help to organise events, contribute to training (e.g. vehicle maintenance, map reading, first aid), maintain camp-sites, raise funds, work in a Scout shop, or edit a District Newsletter.

Sea Cadet Corps, Broadway House, Wimbledon, London SW19 1RL, T: 01-540 8222

The Sea Cadet Corps gives sea training to boys and girls aged 12-18 and assists juniors wishing to go to sea in the Royal Navy, Royal Marines or Merchant Navy. It gives instruction in sailing, outdoor pursuits, sports, recreation and naval and merchant vessel training. Branches exist in cities all over the country, not just on the coast, and welcome volunteer help either in the administration or as sailing instructors. Check the telephone directory for your local branch or contact the London headquarters above.

National Association for the Welfare of Children in Hospital, Argyle House, 29 Euston Road, London NW1 2SO, T: 01-833 2041

Supports sick children and their families and advocates proper health service planning for them. Local branches give practical help to parents and professionals in the hospitals. Work is organised through local branches who can be contacted through the London headquarters. Although different branches may operate slightly different schemes, all will welcome voluntary help. Typical activities would be:

Help with transport. Either driving, where a mileage charge is payable, or accompanying mothers with young children.

Help with play. Acting like a 'Granny', visiting and playing with children to relieve overstretched mothers.

Hospital visiting. Visiting children in hospital whose parents cannot do so for some reason.

Conservation and heritage

British Trust for Conservation Volunteers, 36 St Mary's Street, Wallingford, Oxfordshire OX10 0EU, T: 0491-39766

The Trust promotes practical conservation by volunteers and education in nature conservation in rural and urban areas. Regional groups organise working holidays and 400 local groups run weekend projects. Membership, which is open to anyone from 16-70, costs £8 and local newsletters and a national magazine give details of events. Typical projects include planting trees, cleaning ponds, dry-stone walling, scrub clearance and woodland management. Not all of them involve heavy work but a reasonable degree of fitness is required.

Council for British Archaeology, 112 Kennington Road, London SE11 6RE, T: 01-582 0494

Various archaeological excavations take place throughout the UK, mainly from March to September. The work will probably involve lifting, stooping and wheeling barrows so is not suitable for people with bad backs, but no training is necessary. A two-week stay is the average. Accommodation will vary according to the site but may be pretty basic. Information on the various digs is available in 'British Archaeological News' (£6.50 annual subscription, from the above address). The Council will also supply the address of the nearest local Archaeological Society (enclose sae).

Council for the Protection of Rural England, 4 Hobart Place, London SW1W 0HY, T: 01-235 9481

As its name suggests the CPRE's aim is to protect the English rural landscape and to prevent it being despoiled in any way. Voluntary helpers act as local watchdogs, reporting threats to the environment and sometimes representing the Council at local authority planning meetings. There is also a need for help with fund-raising which is carried out by local groups.

Friends of the Earth, 377 City Road, London EC1V 1NA, T: 01-837 0731

Friends of the Earth is one of the leading environmental pressure organisations in the UK, aiming to conserve and protect the resources of the planet. Over 200 groups run local campaigns and fund-raising projects. These can be contacted through the London office which can also use help with the administration and with running the mail-order catalogue business. Travelling expenses and a lunch allowance are paid. Most volunteers work between one and three days a week. People with scientific training may also be able to help on specific research projects.

Greenpeace, 36 Graham Street, London N1 8LL, T: 01-251 3022/3020

A direct-action environmental protection group which campaigns against nuclear and other pollution and in favour of wild-life preservation. Volunteers are needed to help in the London office on an occasional basis and also for fund-raising by 80 local groups across the country.

The National Trust, Queen Anne's Gate, London SW1H 9AS, T: 01-222 9251, Contact: Leslie McCracken

The National Trust uses volunteers in many aspects of the work of conservation in the great houses open to the public and on 500,000 acres of coast and countryside properties. Inevitably the needs will vary and the location of the major sites means that there are relatively few opportunities in London and some of the other big cities. However, last year, nearly 20,000 volunteers worked in support of the professional staff in the 16 regions. If you are interested you can either write to the address above or contact the Volunteer Organiser or Regional Information Officer directly – the address will be in the local telephone book.

Ramblers' Association, 1-5 Wandsworth Road, London SW8 2XX, T: 01-582 6878

The aims of the Ramblers' Association are to keep footpaths open and to protect the countryside. Each of its 40 area offices needs help with the administration and with walking over and checking the condition of the local footpaths. The time involved can be as much or as little as is available. Expenses are paid.

Royal Society for the Prevention of Cruelty to Animals, The Causeway, Horsham, Sussex RH12 1HG, T: 0403-64181

The RSPCA works to promote kindness and to suppress cruelty to animals. It operates through school education, paid inspectors, professional treatment of sick animals and the dissemination of information on animal welfare. It also works for the cause of animal welfare abroad. Volunteers are needed to help with fund-raising at local level. Contact Head Office for the address of your nearest branch.

Scottish Preservation Projects, 70 Maine Street, Doune, Perth FK16 6BW, T: 0786-841479. Contact: Jean McCaffer.

The SPP offers opportunities to train for work as a conservation volunteer, when and where you want, for as much or little time as you can spare. There are residential projects and area offices run weekend and single day events. As a member of a local group you receive the SPP magazine, information about training and have access to residential projects and courses elsewhere in the UK. Annual subscription – £8 or £5 for pensioners or people who are unemployed.

Society for the Protection of Ancient Buildings, 37 Spital Square, London E1 6DY, T: 01-377 1644

The SPAB promotes the preservation and conservation of ancient buildings. It organises courses, scholarships, seminars and lectures and also gives advice on the repair and reconditioning of ancient buildings. There is a need for a small number of volunteers to help on a part-time basis in the London office and also for people with specialist qualifications as architects, surveyors and engineers to work on particular projects.

Victorian Society, 1 Priory Gardens, Bedford Park, London W4 1TT, T: 01-994 1019

There are three areas of opportunity:

(a) At head office, helping with the administration. Expenses and some small remuneration are paid for work done.

(b) At the Linley Sambourne Museum at 18 Stafford Terrace, London W8. Helpers are needed on Wednesdays and Sundays as guides/attendants in this beautifully preserved Victorian house. Basic expenses are paid.

(c) 12 regional offices throughout the country need help with organising tours, visits and recruiting new members. Basic expenses are paid.

In all cases contact should be through the London office.

The elderly

Abbeyfield Society, 186-192 Darkes Lane, Potters Bar, Herts EN6 1AB, T: 0707-44845

Local voluntary workers aim to acquire houses to provide bedsitting rooms for small numbers of residents who are elderly and alone. The aim is to achieve a family setting but preserve the privacy of each resident. There are also household schemes for elderly people who can no longer look after themselves. Voluntary help needed may vary from shopping for a resident, gardening, typing or organising a fun-run to giving specialist financial and legal advice when they buy a new house.

Age Concern England, 60 Pitcairn Road, Mitcham, Surrey CR4 3LL, T: 01-640 5431; **Age Concern Scotland**, 33 Castle Street, Edinburgh EH2 3DN, T: 031-225 5000; **Age Concern Wales**, 1 Park Grove, Cardiff, South Glamorgan CF1 3BJ, T: 0222-371 566; **Age Concern Northern Ireland**, 128 Great Victoria Street, Belfast 2, T: 0232-45729

The aim of Age Concern is to promote the welfare of the aged. It does this by campaigning on behalf of elderly people and by organising services to meet their needs. Local groups, using over 12,000 volunteer helpers, operate all over the country and services include: day care, lunch clubs, home visiting, over 60's clubs and, in some areas, specialist services for physically and mentally frail elderly people. fund-raising activities in all their variety are also organised by the local groups which may be contacted through the central offices listed above.

Contact, 15 Henrietta Street, Covent Garden, London WC2E 8QH, T: 01-240 0630

Contact tries to bring companionship into the lives of old people living alone. Groups of volunteers and elderly house-bound people meet monthly on Sunday afternoons for tea. Help is needed with driving (one Sunday a month) and/or hosting a tea-party for about 10 elderly people once or twice a year. No expenses are paid. There are about 200 Contact groups, nationwide. The name and address of the nearest local organiser can be had from the above address.

Help the Aged, 1 St James's Walk, London EC1R 0BE, T: 01-253 0253

Help the Aged aims to improve conditions of life for the elderly here and overseas. In the UK, it funds day centres and day hospitals, mini-buses, rehabilitation units and sheltered housing. Overseas, it advises on social policy for the elderly and runs projects in urban destitution and health. Help the Aged is essentially a fund-raising charity. Volunteer help is needed to staff charity shops and to assist local organisers in their work. Contact the Office Manager at the above address for details of your nearest local branch.

National Council for Carers and their Elderly Dependants, 29 Chilworth Mews, London W2 3RG, T: 01-724 7776

This organisation helps those who care for elderly or infirm dependants. With some 40 branches in the UK, it provides a postal advisory service, campaigns for better social security benefits and domiciliary services, supports holiday and sitter-in help for carers and organises conferences. Volunteers, who require special training, are needed to give occasional respite to carers – anything from an hour or so to a day. Help is also needed to organise carers' groups, to enable them to meet occasionally to discuss mutual problems. Contact Jill Pitkeathley at the above address for your local branch.

Pensioners' Link, 17 Balfe Street, London N1 9EB, T: 01-278 5501/4

A London charity with 12 branches which works to improve the lot of the elderly through volunteers visiting and helping lonely and house-bound people. It develops neighbourhood care schemes, works with school groups, helps establish and support pensioners' groups and organises courses on health and welfare rights for pensioners. The work needed is essentially practical: shopping, decorating, odd jobs, driving and visiting. There is also a fund-raising campaign at Christmas. Expenses are paid.

The family

Catholic Marriage Advisory Council, Clitherow House, 15 Lansdowne Road, London W11 3AJ, T: 01-727 0141

The Council aims to provide education for marriage and family life through a national network of trained marriage guidance counsellors. Help is required in running and administering the 80 local centres.

Family Service Units, 207 Old Marylebone Road, London NW1 5QP, T: 01-402 5175

23 local units work to prevent the breakdown of family and community life by running services for disadvantaged communities, deprived families and children. They carry out welfare counselling, community work and social work with families and children. The units, which are professionally staffed, are managed by voluntary committees and help is needed on these as well as with administration and fund-raising.

National Marriage Guidance Council, Herbert Gray College, Little Church Street, Rugby, Warwickshire CV21 3AP, T: 0788-73241

The Council works to support marriage and family life. It selects and trains counsellors and runs 160 local marriage guidance councils. Work is undertaken in schools and youth clubs, with engaged couples and married people. All counsellors are volunteers who give up at least one day a week of their time. The work is most likely to appeal to people who have been previously involved with social or community activity of some kind.

Soldiers', Sailors' and Airmen's Families' Association, 16-18 Old Queen Street, London SW1H 9HP, T: 01-222 9221

SSAFA provides a welfare and advisory service for the families of service and ex-servicemen and women. They are helped by 4,000 volunteers in over 1,000 branches throughout the UK and wherever service families are stationed. Case workers deal with every kind of problem – domestic, financial, legal and compassionate. Training is given and although there is no minimum time commitment it is obviously critical to see a case through to the end. Help is particularly needed in inner cities. There is also a need for assistance in the branches as Chairman, Treasurer or administrative helper. A service background may be helpful but is not necessary.

Health and the handicapped

Back Pain Association, 31-33 Park Road, Teddington, Middlesex TW11 0AB, T: 01-977 5474

The objectives of this registered charity are to encourage and support research into the causes and treatment of back pain and educate people to use their bodies sensibly. There are 36 local branches where help is required with fund-raising and with the organisation of the programme of talks, exercise sessions, group therapy, demonstrations and other events which they run. Write to the Chief Executive at the above address for your nearest branch.

British Heart Foundation, 102 Gloucester Place, London W1H 4DH, T: 01-935 0185

The aim of the Foundation is to raise money for research into diseases of the heart and circulation. It also runs public and post-graduate educational campaigns for the improvement of cardiac care and the promotion of healthy living. 500 local voluntary committees are responsible for fund-raising by whatever means they feel appropriate and effective and any additional help will be greatly welcome. The London office will supply the address of the nearest existing committee or indicate the need to set up a new one in your own area.

Cancer Research Campaign, 2 Carlton House Terrace, London SW1Y 5AR, T: 01-930 8972

The CRC attempts to control and if possible prevent cancer. It raises funds which are then distributed in the form of grants for cancer research throughout the country. Voluntary help is needed with fund-raising which is handled by local committees. London office will put you in touch with the one nearest to you.

Horticultural Therapy, Goulds Ground, Vallis Way, Frome, Somerset BA11 3DW, T: 0373-64782

Horticultural Therapy offers help and advice on setting up and running gardening clubs for handicapped and disadvantaged people. The clubs are run by Voluntary Gardening Advisers who should be people with practical gardening knowledge and skills but no special training or qualifications are required. Clubs will vary according to circumstances but they may arrange talks, demonstrate new tools suitable for the handicapped, visit gardens or actually join in gardening work.

Imperial Cancer Research Fund, Lincolns Inn Fields, P.O. Box 123, London WC2A 3PX, T: 01-242 0200

The Fund finances research into the prevention and treatment of cancer. Money is raised by a network of local branches which may be contacted through regional offices listed in the Yellow Pages. A wide variety of activities are involved and any help will be welcomed.

Leonard Cheshire Foundation, Leonard Cheshire House, 26-29 Maunsel Street, London SW1P 2QN, T: 01-828 1822

The Cheshire Foundation aims to encourage severely physically disabled people to live as useful and independent a life as possible. It runs over 75 residential homes in the UK and organises help to handicapped people in their own homes. There are also 147 homes in 45 overseas countries. If there is a Cheshire Home in your area they would be grateful for all kinds of practical help. This might include driving, gardening, painting and decorating or doing shopping or writing letters for patients. They also need help with local fund-raising: jumble sales, bring-and-buy sales and similar events. The London office will give you the address of the nearest home.

Mental Health Foundation, 8 Hallam Street, London W1N 6DH, T: 01-580 0145/6

The Foundation promotes and finances research into mental illness and encourages the care of mentally ill people. Two professional committees, who give their services voluntarily, allocate funding for research across the range of mental handicap and mental illness. County committees, which are mostly situated in the South and South-East, organise fund-raising and local flag-days. Contact them through the London office.

Mind (National Association for Mental Health), 22 Harley Street, London W1N 2ED, T: 01-637 0741

Mind promotes mental health and works to help the mentally disordered. It also acts as a pressure group and promotes research. There are seven regional offices and approximately 200 local mental health associations throughout the UK. Mind runs an information, legal and welfare rights service and also organises courses for professional workers. The local associations, which can be contacted through the London office, vary in size and in the scope of their work. While all will be involved in fund-raising, some will also run clubs, day centres and an advice and information service as well as offering support and help to individuals.

National Association of Leagues of Hospital Friends, 38 Ebury Street, London SW1W 0LU, T: 01-730 0103

This acts as a national resource and advisory service for the 1374 Leagues of Hospital Friends which operate on behalf of hospitals all over the country. Each Hospital League functions autonomously and opportunities for voluntary work will therefore vary. All however are concerned with fund-raising and many run hospital shops and tea bars as well as directly helping patients by visiting and other support work. The National Association will provide names and addresses of local Leagues to contact.

Riding for the Disabled Association, Avenue R, National Agricultural Centre, Kenilworth, Warwickshire CV8 2LY, T: 0203-56107

The Association aims to help provide opportunities for riding for disabled children and adults. You do not have to be horsey to help with the administration in one of the 600 local groups or with raising funds for it. Legal and financial knowledge is particularly valuable in connection with the opening of new centres and keeping the accounts. For those with experience of horses (which may be supplemented by training courses) the main jobs are leading or walking beside the ponies while they are being ridden and accompanying parties on riding holidays. Write to the head office above for the address of your nearest group.

Royal National Institute for the Blind, 224 Great Portland Street, London W1N 6AA, T: 01-388 1266

The RNIB aims to help all blind people to lead full and independent lives. It provides schools for blind children, gives grants and special equipment to students, trains and finds employment for blind adults. It provides a 'Talking Book' library and develops numerous devices to make life safer, easier and more enjoyable for the visually handicapped. Help is mostly required with fundraising by lending a hand on flag-days, arranging sponsorships or placing and emptying RNIB collecting tins. London office will put you in touch with your nearest local group.

St John Ambulance, 1 Grosvenor Crescent, London SW1X 7EF, T:01-235 5231

St John Ambulance provides education and practice in first-aid to the benefit of the community. Volunteers in the UK and abroad give their time freely to the relief of suffering and injury. They invariably assist where crowds gather and also provide help in hospitals and with community social services Volunteers can, if they wish, be trained in first aid and nursing and can then serve as uniformed helpers but assistance is also required with fund-raising, catering, secretarial and general administrative work.

Spastics Society, 12 Park Crescent, London W1N 4EQ, T:01-636 5020

The object of the Society is to alleviate cerebral palsy and try to maximise the independence of people suffering from it. It runs a large research programme and has established more than 160 schools, education centres and industrial units which are supported by local groups. Helpers are needed particularly with transport – either driving or assisting with wheel-chairs – with running open days and events put on by local groups and with fund-raising.

The needy

Christian Aid, P.O. Box No 1, London SW9 8BH, T: 01-733 5500

Christian Aid channels the gifts of Christians and others to areas abroad where human needs are great. It runs community development projects, land reclamation, medical and social services and helps in the UK with the integration of immigrants. Volunteers are needed to assist in fund-raising. Work is organised on a regional basis and can range from helping with coffee-mornings, jumble sales and similar local events to supporting national appeals by selling flags or door-to-door calling. Expenses are paid. Regional organisers may be contacted through the London headquarters.

Distressed Gentlefolks Aid Association, Vicarage Gate House, Vicarage Gate, Kensington, London W8 4AQ, T: 01-229 9341

The DGAA assists people with professional or similar backgrounds either financially or with nursing and care in a number of residential homes. There is a network of county committees as well as committees based on each Home. Work involves general fund-raising and also visiting patients and helping to organise outings and entertainments for them.

The Ockenden Venture, Guildford Road, Woking, Surrey GU22 7UU, T:048-62 72012

Ockenden works to provide houses for international refugees (e.g. Boat People) and handicapped children. Help is needed on an occasional basis in the office and in the homes where work can be domestic, gardening, maintenance, or helping with children. The minimum stay is 6 months and board, lodging and pocket money are provided. The Venture is now importing craft work from Thailand and from Afghan refugees in Pakistan. Help in marketing and selling these artifacts is also required.

OXFAM, Oxfam House, 274 Banbury Road, Oxford OX2 7DZ, T: 0865-56777

Oxfam aims to provide long-term and short-term relief for poverty, starvation, illness and physical calamity in any part of the world. It supplies food, medication, clothing, housing, training and education. There are about 20,000 volunteers working in all parts of the country mainly on fund-raising and administration. The Oxfam 2000 group is also a lobbying organisation, writing articles and targetting specific campaigns at opinion leaders and the general public. There are some opportunites as well for technical consultants, especially for people with medical experience in the field and anyone with knowledge of water engineering. Contact the local branch listed in the telephone book.

Quaker Workcamps, Friends House, Euston Road, London NW1 2BJ, T:01-387 3601 ext 55

Quaker Workcamps run projects lasting one to four weeks each summer which aim to meet the needs of special groups within the community. On most workcamps about half of the volunteers will come from abroad. Projects may involve construction work, conservation, play schemes, community work, study camps or a wide range of other activities asked for and needed by the particular community. Food and accommodation (usually communal) are provided. Volunteers are asked to meet their own travel costs.

Samaritans Incorporated, 17 Uxbridge Road, Slough, Berks SL1 1SN, T:0753-32713

The Samaritans aim to help the suicidal and the despairing. Most of the work is done on the telephone so that while no special qualifications are required, it is important to have good hearing, an ability to listen and an unshockable disposition. Training is given – usually six sessions of about two hours each – and those who qualify will be expected to attend further courses from time to time. The minimum time commitment is of the order of one three-hour session a fortnight, plus four all-night duties a year. Reliability is obviously crucial. No expenses are paid. Apart from this work, there is need for fund-raising help from anyone with a little time and a lot of enthusiasm.

Offenders and the victims of crime

NACRO (National Association for the Care and Resettlement of Offenders), 169 Clapham Road, London SW9 0PU, T:01-582 6500

The Association promotes the care, after-care and resettlement of offenders and the involvement of the public in crime prevention. It also runs innovative and experimental projects and initiates research in this area. Voluntary help is required with inner-city projects for educational schemes and for running leisure activities for young people. The necessary training is provided and the work is under the supervision of professionals. There is no minimum time commitment – any help is welcome. Write to the Assistant Director for more details.

National Association of Victims Support Schemes, 17a Electric Lane, London SW9 8LA, T:01-737 2019

300 local schemes train volunteers to visit, console and advise victims of crime. Advice covers possible compensation available, insurance claims, as well as the availability of local resources, from the right person to speak to at the DHSS to locksmiths and legal help. Contact the nearest scheme either by writing to the London office or via the local police.

The Society of Voluntary Associates, 240a Clapham Road, London SW9 0PZ, T:01-735 4421

The Society encourages volunteers to work with offenders, ex-offenders, their families and young people at risk. It recruits, trains, deploys and promotes the use of volunteer assistance to the probation services. The work may be with children, in the adult literacy scheme, prison visiting or helping ex-offenders.

The necessary training is given by the Society and the volunteer then works with a professional in association with the probation service.

Widows

CRUSE, Cruse House, 126 Sheen Road, Richmond, Surrey TW9 1UR, T:01-940 4818/9047

CRUSE is the national organisation for the widowed and their children. It provides counselling, practical help and organises social programmes to counter loneliness. Volunteers are needed in the branch offices to help in all these areas. Training for counselling is provided and the work involves about half a day a week.

Work after work

Business in the Community, 227a City Road, London EC1V 1LX, T:01-253 3716

For executives and managers who would like to continue to work in business after retirement, the Business in the Community scheme may be the answer. Set up as a partnership between Government, Employers, Trade Unions and the Voluntary Sector it aims to encourage the greater local involvement of businesses in the communities in which they operate. In practice the work will involve advising and helping new small firms at the start-up stage and as they further develop. Time involved is likely to be of the order of one day a week. Expenses are paid. Contact can be made through your nearest local Enterprise Agency (listed in the telephone book) or via the London head office above.

Politics

You may not immediately think of political parties in the context of voluntary work, but they all do use vast numbers of volunteer helpers. Between elections the help is mostly required with fund-raising, with committee work and in manning the constituency offices. At election time activity is obviously intense: delivering literature, addressing envelopes, stuffing envelopes, recording canvas returns, driving the elderly and disabled to the polls, and, for the politically informed, canvassing. Contact your constituency office which will be listed in the telephone book or, if you have difficulty in finding it, contact the national party headquarters. The addresses of the four major parties are:

Conservative Central Office, 32 Smith Square, Westminster, London SW1, T:01-222 9000.

Labour Party Headquarters, 150 Walworth Road, London SE17, T:01-703 0833.

The Liberal Party, 1 Whitehall Place, London SW1, T:01-839 4092.

Social Democratic Party, 4 Cowley Street, London SW1, T:01-222 7999

Long-term volunteering

If you are thinking of a long term, probably residential, commitment there are a number of organisations both in the UK and abroad who are in need of help of this kind. The most complete guides to this sort of work are those produced by the Central Bureau, Seymour Mews House, Seymour Mews, London W1H 9PE. They now publish two handbooks *Volunteer Work Abroad*, price £3 and *Working Holidays*, price £4, but as an indication of the kinds of opportunities that exist we have listed below some of the main bodies in this sector.

Overseas

There are four major groups all of which require a two-year minimum period of service. General conditions are similar for all of them, i.e. travel is paid plus a living allowance/salary which is based on local levels rather than on expatriate rates; couples without dependent children are welcome as long as both have the necessary skills; national insurance contributions are provided and a resettlement grant is paid on completion of the tour.

Voluntary Service Overseas, 9 Belgrave Square, London SW1X 8PW, T:01-235 5191

VSO, the largest organisation in its field, places some 550 volunteers each year in over 40 Third World countries in Africa, Asia, the Pacific and the Caribbean. Its aims are to combat poverty and injustice and by the transfer of skills to enable people to shape their own futures. They are particularly interested in volunteers with agricultural, teaching, medical, technical, business and social development experience. Training is provided.

International Voluntary Service, Ceresole House, 53 Regent Road, Leicester LE1 6YL, T:0533-541862

The IVS provides volunteer help to the Third World — mainly Southern Africa. It recruits about 35 volunteers a year. Postings may be on a wide variety of projects: provision of water supplies or electricity; road and bridge construction; setting up cooperative business enterprises in horticulture, irrigation or building. People with specialist skills in these and similar areas are obviously particularly sought but general business ability may also be of real value.

Catholic Institute for International Relations, CIIR Overseas Programme, 22 Coleman Fields, London N1 7AF, T:01-354 0883

An educational charity providing technical support for community projects which tackle the causes of poverty. It operates in Latin America, Africa and the Yemen. The programme is open to people of any religious belief or none and posts are available for agriculturalists, those with medical experience (midwives/-physiotherapists) and teachers. Most jobs involve teaching local people new skills and some knowledge of Spanish or Arabic would be useful. A preliminary orientation course is arranged with training sessions and thorough briefings.

United Nations Association International Service, 3 Whitehall Court, London SW1A 2EL, T:01-930 0679

UNAIS is a voluntary body which campaigns for disarmament, a fairer world economic order and for human rights. It sends skilled personnel to work in the Third World (Africa, Latin America, West Bank) on projects aiming to achieve a fundamental change in the distribution of wealth and power. Third World and community work experience are an advantage and it is essential to have either knowledge of the local language or the ability and willingness to learn. Recent vacancies have been for people with a wide range of skills from nurses and agronomists to computer operators and social researchers. There is a one-month orientation course plus language training as necessary.

British Executive Service Overseas, 10 Belgrave Square, London SW1 8PH, T:01-235 0991

This, an independent organisation initiated by the Institute of Directors and established with the backing of the Government and the CBI, operates on a rather different, less long-term basis. It aims to improve managerial skills, to promote management science and to advance commercial training and education in developing countries. Volunteers should be retired or seconded executives with successful records in commercial or industrial fields and projects last an average of two to three months with a normal maximum of six months. The scheme allows (and pays for) an accompanying spouse. Travel, insurance and incidentals are paid for by BESO. Accommodation, subsistence and local transportation are paid for by the requesting organisation.

In UK

Although the groups which we have listed in this section are primarily concerned with schemes requiring volunteer help for between two weeks and six months, many of them also do need shorter term help with administration and fund-raising.

Children's Country Holidays Fund, 1 York Street, Baker Street, London W1H 1PZ, T:01-935 8371/3/4. Contact: The Director.

The aim of this scheme is to give underprivileged London children aged 5-13 a two-week holiday in private homes in the country during July or August. The need is for people out of London to act as hosts and to find other families willing to do the same. There are also opportunities for 'Train Marshals', to escort parties of children to and from the holidays, for general fund-raising and for helping to run an exhibition stand at local agricultural shows which explains and promotes the work of the Fund.

The Richmond Fellowship for Community Mental Health, 8 Addison Road, Kensington, London W14 8DL, T:01-603 6373

The Richmond Fellowship runs 'halfway houses' on therapeutic community lines for individuals of all diagnoses. Volunteers are needed to work at headquarters and in the houses. At headquarters there is need for occasional short-term administrative help but in the houses the minimum stay is around six months and here the skills required cover a wide range from clerical/secretarial to cooking, decorating, drama and art. Board and lodging is provided in the houses and pocket money is paid, according to the length of stay.

MENCAP (National Society for Mentally Handicapped Adults and Children), Holiday Services, 119 Drake Street, Rochdale OL16 1PZ, T:0706-54111

Volunteers help on holidays for the mentally handicapped. They work in groups of four or five looking after a similar number of guests, usually for a two week period. After the holiday volunteering can be continued by helping at a Gateway Club, which is a leisure time youth club for mentally handicapped people, or working at weekends at a hostel or subnormality hospital. Board and lodging on the holidays is free for volunteers and a travel allowance up to £15 is also paid.

Sue Ryder Foundation, Sue Ryder House, Cavendish, Suffolk CO10 8AY, T:0787-280252. Contact: Mr K Wilkinson

Sue Ryder Homes cater for the sick and disabled of all ages. They are run fairly informally and as far as possible as family homes in the true sense of the word. Volunteers are asked to work with the patients under the supervision of qualified nursing staff. Others may work in a variety of jobs connected with the general running of the homes. Minimum stay two months. Board and lodging provided.

The Winged Fellowship Trust, Angel House, Pentonville Road, London N1 9XD, T:01-833 2594

Volunteers are required from mid-March to mid-December at the three holiday centres run by the Trust for severely disabled people. Qualifications are not necessary. The work involves helping with routine running of the centres and generally assisting the guests. Stay is for one or two weeks. Board and lodging are provided free and fares are paid.

Further reading

Age Concern, *Health Enhancement: a Directory of Projects for Older People*, 1985
Elizabeth Gundrey, *Spring Time*, Unwin Paperbacks 1981
Elizabeth Gundrey, *Helping Hands: A Guide to Conservation*, Unwin Paperbacks 1981
Health Education Council, *Age Well Ideas Pack*
Judy Kirby, *Work after Work*, Quiller Press 1984
Sheila Moore, *Working for Free*, Pan Books 1977
New Opportunities Press, *Towards a Happier Retirement*, 1981
Thames Television, *Help! Volunteer Book: A Guide to Voluntary Work and how to get involved*, Thames Television 1985
Hilary Blume, *Fundraising*, Routledge. Covers most aspects of fundraising including: sponsored events, press releases, fetes, legal aspects of running lotteries, raising money from firms and businesses, street collections, etc.
The Volunteer Centre, *Crossover Pack* (linking early retired people from industry with voluntary action) 1985
New Society now lists various volunteer opportunities in each issue.
The Information Unit of the Volunteer Centre (see list of national operations) provides pages of information which are broadcast on BBC 2's Ceefax Service. The pages called 'Volunteer' feature items of volunteering news which may be of interest to the general public. They can be found on p.293. There is no charge to the viewer, or the information provider at the Volunteer Centre.

11. Health

How often have you enviously commented when meeting a recently retired friend: 'Goodness, he looks a different man. Fit, relaxed, contented — retirement must suit him.' And why not? Perhaps more than any other period since your twenties, retirement is a time for positive good health!

You have more chance to be out in the fresh air and take up a favourite sport again. You won't have to rush your meals so much and, without the need for business lunches or sandwiches day after day, will probably knock off a few pounds without any effort at dieting. At the same time, there will be less temptation to pop into the pub on the way home so you will feel brighter and more alert at the start of the evening.

A major gain is that there will be no more fighting your way to work on buses and trains, jam-packed with people all coughing and sneezing; or sitting in traffic, raising your blood pressure. Also, once free of the strains and pressures that are part of any job, you will feel less harassed, look better, maybe cut down on smoking and best of all have the energy to devote to new interests and activities.

People can get aches and pains of course as they become older but, as any doctor will tell you, this is far less likely if you remain physically and mentally active. In other words, the days for putting out the carpet slippers and equating retirement with the onset of old age are definitely attitudes of the past. Today's retirement brigade — younger in age, looks and behaviour than any previous generation — can legitimately look forward to many healthy years ahead.

As with anything else, however, bodies do require a modicum of care and attention if they are to function at their best and, just as cars need regular servicing, routine checks such as eye testing and dental apppointments are obviously sensible.

Also moderation, middle-aged as it may sound, is generally a wiser policy than excess. Don't get it wrong! This has nothing to do with treating yourself as a premature geriatric — quite the reverse. It means enjoying small vices without paying the penalty for over-indulgence, keeping trim instead of getting out of shape and looking good when you take exercise rather than puffing like the proverbial grampus.

Keeping fit

Exercise plays an important part in keeping you healthy. It tones up muscles, improves the circulation, reduces flab, helps ward off illnesses such as heart disease and, above all, can be a great deal of fun.

The experts' motto is: little and often. For those not accustomed to regular exercise, it is essential to build up gradually. If you are planning to run a marathon, win the local tennis competition, start playing your son at squash or recapture the sporting feats of your youth, do check with your doctor before jumping into your track suit.

The Sports Council has launched a campaign, aimed at the 50 plus age group, to encourage men and women to get back into the sporting habit. Training in a whole range of activities is available around the country, with beginners particularly welcome. Details of some of the many facilities, together with other keep fit options are listed in Chapter 7.

In addition to some of the more exotic choices, swimming has long been recognised as one of the best forms of exercise of all. Some swear that there is nothing to beat a good brisk walk. Gardening is also recommended.

With the explosion of sports clubs, leisure centres and adult keep fit classes run by local authorities, opportunities have never been better for athletes of all ability levels – and none.

At the very plush end of the market, there are Fitness for Industry Health Clubs run by the Institute of Directors in conjunction with Trust House Forte where, in addition to facilities such as gymnasiums, snooker, swimming pools and squash, qualified staff advise on – and supervise – personal fitness programmes. Information from: **Institute of Directors**, 116 Pall Mall, London SW1, T:01-839 1233.

Similar facilities are provided by commercial organisations up and down the country, often combined with sauna, sunbeds and various beauty treatments. However, at a fraction of the price, many local authority leisure centres offer a marvellous range of sports as well as training classes in everything from self defence to badminton.

Equally, emphasis on more leisurely keep fit is also on the increase and a welcome innovation is the growing number of opportunities for older people as well as the disabled. The town hall should be able to tell you what local provision exists. Additionally, the following organisations may be able to help you.

Extend, 5 Conway Road, Sheringham, Norfolk NR26 8DD.
Extend caters especially for the over 60's and disabled. Exercises, which are performed to music, are gentler than most and are suitable for those with back trouble or a heart condition. Write to the above address for information about their own or recommended classes in your area. (Send sae).

Relaxation for Living, 29 Burwood Park Road, Walton-on-Thames, Surrey KT12 5LH.

A registered charity which aims to promote the teaching of physical relaxation to combat stress, strain and anxiety. There are usually about six to eight in a class and courses vary from a few days to several weeks. Prices are very roughly in the bracket £15 to £40, depending on area, length of course and whether classes are sponsored by the local authority. Correspondence classes with a tape are available for those who prefer to exercise in their own home. For addresses of local teachers, write to the above address enclosing sae.

The Women's League of Health and Beauty, 18 Charing Cross Road, London WC2H 0HR, T:01-240 8456.

A national organisation whose aim is to promote fitness in an atmosphere of 'happy informality'. Emphasis is on dancing and movement to music and classes are organised in three grades: elementary, intermediate and advanced. Additionally, some areas provide special courses for the elderly and disabled. Membership (including joining fee) is about £2.50. Classes cost from 50p upwards.

Yoga

The number of yoga enthusiasts is increasing year by year and it is estimated that over half a million people in Britain regularly practice yoga as a means of improving fitness and helping relaxation. Classes are provided by a great many local authorities. There are also a number of specialist organisations. Two which run courses in many parts of the country are:

Iyengar Yoga Institute, 223a Randolph Avenue, London W9, T:01-624 3080.

Classes fall into three categories: general classes, suitable for all levels; remedial classes for those with serious medical conditions; relaxation classes. Membership is £8 a year. Class fees range from £1.50 to £2.50, according to length of the session.

Yoga for Health Foundation, Icknell Bury, Northill, Nr. Biggleswade, Bedfordshire, T:076 727 271.

This is a registered charity with about 80 clubs and centres around the country. Additionally, at the headquarters near Biggleswade residential courses, lasting from a week-end to a week, are provided. Cost includes full board and for five days would be £110. Additionally, Monday to Thursday 'Bargain Breaks' are offered to Senior Citizens with 4 days costing £54. National membership is £6 a year (£9 for a couple), which includes a journal. A list of local clubs can be obtained from the above address.

Yoga Biomedical Trust, P.O. Box 140, Cambridge CB2 2HP, T:0223 65771.

Older people who practice yoga regularly might like to help with a research project to explore more fully how yoga can benefit the elderly. Those who have not yet started yoga will be able to join at a later stage. Founder membership is £10. The Trust supplies a selection of relaxation cassettes (£6 each incl. p & p). For further information, write to the Trust enclosing sae.

Sensible eating

A trim, well kept body is one of the secrets of a youthful appearance, whereas being fat and out-of-condition adds years to anyone's age. Regular exercise is one half of the equation, sensible eating the other.

Not to put too fine a point on it, more than one in five adults in Britain is obese — in other words, overweight. No one is going to fuss about 2 or 3 pounds but half a stone or more, as well as looking unsightly, starts to become a health risk. In middle-aged men in particular, it increases the possibility of a heart attack, can lead to other illnesses, makes operations more difficult — and, in older people, is one of the causes of restricted mobility.

No one should go on a serious diet without first consulting their doctor. However, medical advice is not necessary for knocking off: sweets, cakes, sticky buns, deep fried foods, alcohol and rich sauces.

Healthy foods which most people (except of course those on a special doctor's diet) can eat in almost unlimited quantities are: fruit, salad, vegetables, fish and white meat such as chicken.

Excessive cholesterol (fatty deposits that collect in the arteries) is another concern and, whereas it often goes with overweight, slimmer people can also be affected. The basic health message is: eat more of the foods listed above; include plenty of roughage such as wholemeal bread in the diet; cut down on dishes with a high sugar, salt and animal fat content — including cream, butter and too much red meat.

As every health magazine advises, crash diets are no solution for long term fitness — not least because, unless individuals re-educate their eating habits the weight creeps back on; or more frequently, gallops back within a few days.

However, most of us need a boost to get ourselves started. One increasingly popular method is sponsored dieting for charity. Another possibility, which some people swear by and others rubbish, is going to a health farm. As opposed to starvation, the emphasis today is on a few days' general fitness eating (but usually enough to avoid being hungry). If nothing else, the experience is very relaxing, albeit expensive, with average costs being in the region of £70 to £90 a day. Magazines such as *Vogue* carry regular advertisements.

Cheaper and arguably more successful for long-term slimmers are Weight Watchers clubs. This is a national organisation, offering approximately 2,100 classes a week across the British Isles. Weight Watchers' aim is to establish a permanent way of healthy eating and to 'lose weight without hunger by eating three balanced meals a day, giving a low calorie intake but being nutritionally good'.

Undoubtedly part of Weight Watchers' success is the help and encouragement received by belonging to a group where everyone else is trying to shed a few pounds. More important than the initial weight loss, the organisation sets store by teaching members how to maintain their desired weight. Initial registration is £4 and classes are £2.60 each. Prices for Senior Citizens are 85p registration; £1.85 per class. For further details and address of local club, contact:

Weight Watchers, 11 Fairacres, Dedworth Road, Windsor, Berks SL4 4UY, T:0753 856 751.

As a rule chubby people tend to be those who enjoy rather too many good meals in the company of others. People living on their own, however, sometimes also get weight problems: either because they cannot be bothered to cook for themselves, so snack off the wrong kinds of food such as jam sandwiches and chocolate biscuits; or because they neglect themselves and do not take enough nourishment.

Elderly ladies, in particular, sometimes quite literally hardly eat enough to keep a bird alive and in consequence not only undermine their health but because of their general frailty are more susceptible to falls and broken bones. An excellent stocking filler for anyone living alone or for couples whose family has flown the nest is *Easy Cooking for One or Two* by Louise Davies. Penguin. £1.50.

Self-help to avoid trouble is one thing. But anyone who suspects that they could have something wrong should not hesitate to consult a doctor.

Drink

Most doctors cheerfully maintain that 'a little of what you fancy does you good'. The majority of healthy adults can enjoy a drink at a party or a glass of wine with dinner without any ill effects and retirement is no reason for giving up these pleasures. Moreover, in small quantities, it can be a very effective nightcap and can also help to stimulate a sluggish appetite. However, where problems begin is when people fancy more than is good for them. Alcoholism is the third greatest killer after heart disease and cancer.

The condition is far more likely among those who are bored or depressed and who, perhaps almost without realising it, drift into the habit of having a drink to cheer themselves up or to pass the time when they have nothing else to do. The trouble is the habit can become insidious and, though at the beginning it does not feel that way, individuals can quite quickly start becoming dependent on drink. Because the early symptoms appear fairly innocuous, the danger signs are apt to be ignored but these include: needing a drink as a confidence boost; having 'just one more' out of misplaced conviviality at the end of a party; drinking in the morning to cure a hangover; drinking on your own; keeping a spare bottle 'just in case'; and having sneak drinks when you think no one is noticing.

Whereas most people are sensible enough to be able to control the habit themselves, others may need held. The family doctor will of course be the first person to check with for medical advice. But additionally, for those who need moral support, the following self-help groups may be the answer.

Drinkwatchers, 200 Seagrave Road, London SW6 1RQ, T:01-381 3157.

Drinkwatchers is for those who want to cut back on their alcohol consumption and drink more sensibly – rather than abstain altogether. It aims to help people develop a healthier lifestyle by acquiring the habit of moderation and by learning to recognise for themselves when 'enough is enough'. Similar to Weightwatchers, groups exist nationwide where individuals can meet, share their experiences and help support each other. Drinkwatchers also publishes a handbook with tops on how to control drinking (£2.25). For further information and addresses of local groups, contact the headquarters above.

Alcoholics Anonymous, P.O. Box 514, 11 Redcliffe Gardens, London SW10, 9BQ, T:01-352 9779.

AA has 1700 autonomous groups all over the country, designed to help those with a serious alcohol problem learn how to abstain. Through friendship and mutual support, sufferers assist each other in trying to kick the habit which is made easier by meeting others with the same problem. Meetings take two forms. Some are for members only, where everyone is anonymous and participants can discuss their feelings in strictest confidence. Others are open to relatives and friends, where discussion of the wider family problems is welcomed. Membership is free, although sometimes a collection is taken towards the cost of renting meeting rooms. For addresses of local groups: either see telephone directory or contact the national headquarters.

Al-Anon Family Groups, 61 Great Dover Street, London SE1 4YF, T:01-403 0888.

Al-Anon is a worldwide fellowship, linked to Alchoholics Anonymous, designed to provide understanding and support for the families of alcohol victims. Regular meetings are held where, in addition to being able to talk to others in the same situation as themselves, families can learn how to help sufferers in trying to overcome their problems. Part of the education is that AA never considers anyone to be 'cured', since as many addicts know sometimes it only takes one drink to slip back into the habit.

Often the greatest stress and anxiety is caused when victims do not recognise that they have a problem and so refuse help. Enquiries are particularly welcome from families with this difficulty. Al-Anon also publishes a range of useful leaflets, priced variously between 20p and 40p. Addresses for Scotland, Northern Ireland and Eire as follows:

Al-Anon Information Centre. 136 Ingram Street, Glasgow G1 1EJ, Scotland, T:041-552 2828; **Al-Anon Information Centre**, Cathedral Building, Room 8, 64 Donegall Street, Belfast BT1 2GT, Northern Ireland. T: Belfast 243489; **Al-Anon Information Centre**, 12 Westmoreland Street, Dublin 2, Eire, T:Dublin 774195.

Alcohol Concern, 305 Gray's Inn Road, London WC1 8QF, T:01-833 3471.

Alcohol Concern is a charity which aims to promote better understanding of alcohol-related problems and to improve services for those in need of help. It publishes a regular journal and can supply addresses of local advice and information centres.

Useful reading

The Facts about Drinking and how to Control it. 85p, from BUPA Medical Centre, Battle Bridge House, 300 Gray's Inn Road, London WC1X 8DU.

Smoking

Any age is a good one to cut back on smoking or preferably give up altogether. The dangers are so well known that only idiots (like this author) continue puffing, when it is obvious lunacy. The gruesome facts are that smokers are twenty times more likely to contract lung cancer. They are at more serious risk of suffering from heart disease, particularly coronary thrombosis; and additionally are more liable to chronic bronchitis as well as various other ailments.

Most people agree that it is easier to give up completely than attempt to cut back since, as every smoker knows after the first cigarette of the day, you can always think of a thousand excuses for lighting another. Aids to will power include: travelling in non-smoking carriages in the train; leaving your cigarettes behind when you go out; not buying cigarettes for guests to smoke in your home, which they leave but you take; and refusing as a personal point of honour to cadge off friends. Working out how much money you could save in a year and promising yourself a holiday or other reward on the proceeds could help. Thinking about your health in years to come should be an even more convincing argument.

Dozens of organisations concerned with health publish leaflets giving the facts, including how unpopular you make yourself with non-smokers. To list just a few, you can obtain literature from:

Coronorary Prevention Group, 60 Great Ormond Street, London WC1.

Chest, Heart & Stroke Association, Tavistock House North, Tavistock Square, London WC1H 9JE.

National Society of Non-smokers, Latimer House, 40-48 Hanson Street, London W1P 7DE.

Bupa Medical Centre, 300 Gray's Inn Road, London WC1X 8DO.

Ash, 5-11 Mortimer Street, London W1N 7RH.

Accident prevention

One of the most common causes of mishap are accidents in the home, including in particular falls and incidents due to faulty electrical wiring. The vast majority could be avoided by taking normal common-sense precautions, such as repairing worn carpets and installing better lighting near staircases. For a list of practical suggestions, see Chapter 6.

Health insurance

An increasing number of people are covered by health insurance or provident schemes during their working lives. If you wish to continue this benefit, and you are unable to remain in your company scheme after retirement, you will be welcomed as an individual client by any of the main groups providing you are under the age of 65. You can then renew your membership when you do reach 65 – so it may be wise to join early.

Terms and conditions of the different schemes vary to some extent but all the major ones offer to pay all or the greatest part of the costs of in-patient accommodation, treatment and medical fees as well as out-patient charges for specialists, X-rays and similar services. They do not normally cover GPs' costs.

Subscription levels depend on area and on the type of hospital to which you choose to be admitted. The top figure is based on the current charges in London teaching hospitals and their independent equivalents; the next is based on teaching hospitals outside London; the lowest rate is for NHS non-teaching hospitals outside London.

Although the NHS has an excellent record in dealing with urgent conditions and accidents, it has in many cases a lengthy waiting list for the less urgent and more routine operations like hip replacements and hernias. By using health insurance to pay for private medical care you will probably get faster treatment as well as greater comfort and privacy in hospital.

The major organisations are:

BUPA, Provident House, Essex Street, London WC2R 3AX, T:01-353 5212.

BUPA is a non profit-making association that welcomes new subscribers up to the age of 65 although fees are increased with age. The current basic BUPACARE annual rates are as shown below. However, as is the case with the other groups listed, it may well be possible to obtain some level of discount either as an ex-member of your company group scheme, through a co-operative buying group or even as a member of the Automobile Association (AA).

		London Teaching £	*Provincial Teaching* £	*Provincial Non-Teaching* £
Age 50-64	Single	491	320	264
	Married	906	590	488
Age 65 plus	Single	724	463	393
	Married	447	927	787

Private Patients Plan, PPP House, Upperton Road, Eastbourne, East Sussex BN21 1LH, T:0323-641155.

PPP operate three different schemes to meet the cost of private treatment. Subscription levels and benefits are somewhat complicated and although we have tried to summarise them below, it is very important to study the company literature thoroughly before making any decision.

Family health plan

This can cover the cost of treatment in hospital, consultants' charges, physiotherapy, radiotherapy and chemotherapy. Subscription levels vary widely depending on the hospital scale selected and the range of benefits you choose to include. It is also possible to opt to pay the first part of the costs of your treatment in any one year. This will result in a 15 per cent reduction in the premium. Subscribers may join up to the age of 65 and renew thereafter at an increased cost. As an indication of charges, the top monthly rates (i.e. the most expensive hospitals, all benefits, full cover) are:

Age	*Single*	*Married*
60 – 64	£73.60	£138.90
65 plus	£99.60	£187.70

Private hospital plan

This is designed especially to meet cases where the NHS has long waiting lists. If you can obtain treatment in an NHS hospital within six weeks, the plan will pay you £26 per night, tax free, to meet any additional expenses. If you cannot be admitted within that time it will meet the costs of private hospital treatment up to £5,000 per year, or £10,000 for open-heart surgery and double those amounts if complications develop during treatment. Once again subscribers may join up to the age of 65 and renew thereafter. Current monthly rates are:

Age	Single	Married
50 – 64	£12.50	£22.45
65 plus	£22.45	£42.25

Retirement health plan

This operates on a similar basis to the Private Hospital Plan but is available to new subscribers up to 75, with renewal thereafter. If NHS hospital treatment is available within six weeks, £17 per night is payable, tax free, for a maximum of 180 nights. If treatment is not available in that time, private hospital charges will be paid up to a total of £4,500 a year or £9,000 for open-heart surgery and double those amounts for complications developing during the treatment. The cost per person per month is:

Up to 64	£11.90
65 – 69	£16.25
70 – 74	£21.90
75 – 79	£29.25
80 plus	£38.60

Western Provident Association Ltd., Culverhouse, Culver Street, Bristol BS1 5JE, T:0272-273 241.

This provident association is smaller than the other two and its rates are rather lower. New applicants can join up to the age of 65 and renew thereafter at an increased premium. If you are treated in a free NHS hospital, WPA will pay you up to £140 per week to a maximum of £2,100 in any one year. Their annual rates for the different kinds of hospital are:

		London Teaching £	Provincial Teaching £	Provincial Non-Teaching £
Subscriber	Single	394	271	228
56-64	Married	778	534	448
	Family	889	610	512
Renewal at	Single	475	324	273
age 65 plus	Married	937	640	539
	Family	937	640	539

Exeter Hospital Aid Society, 5-7 Palace Gate, Exeter. Devon EX1 1UE, T:0392-75361.

EHAS is an old established non profit-making friendly society. Its scheme has three major distinguishing features that may make it particularly attractive to people of retiring age:

- it accepts new subscribers of any age up to 75
- it charges the same premium for people of any age (although if you are over 65 when you join they will ask you for a lump sum payment representing 50 per cent of the premiums that you would have paid since the date of your 65th birthday)
- the subscription rates for older people are accordingly considerably lower than for most other schemes.

Current rates are:

		London Teaching £	Provincial Teaching £	Provincial Non-Teaching £
Age 21-75	Single	292	236	220
	Family	458	366	339

Although some benefits are marginally lower, cover in general is very comparable with the other main schemes and the substantially lower annual subscription may more than compensate for any differences.

Private patients without insurance cover

If you do not have private medical insurance but want to go into hospital as a private patient, there is of course nothing to stop you doing so providing your doctor is willing and you are able to pay the bills. The choice is between the private wings of NHS. hospitals, hospitals run by charitable or non profit making organisations (such as the Nuffield Hospitals) and those run for profit by private companies.

Health screening

Prevention is better than cure and most of the provident associations offer a diagnostic screening service to check general health and to provide advice on diet, drinking and smoking if these are problem areas. These tests show that roughly a quarter of patients aged over 55 have an unsuspected problem which can often be treated quickly and easily. Screening services normally recommend a check-up every two years and centres are usually available to members of insurance schemes and others alike.

BUPA. There are BUPA medical centres in the following cities: London, Bristol, Glasgow, Norwich, Birmingham, Bushey, Leeds, Nottingham, Brentwood, Cardiff, Manchester, Portsmouth and Sutton Coldfield. The cost of a full health screen and consultation is: Men, £185; Women, £210; and a Well Woman check, £75. Discounts are available for members of BUPA and the Institute of Directors. For further details, see relevant telephone directory; or call BUPA on 01-353 5212.

PPP. There are PPP medical centres in London, Southampton, Solihull, Canterbury, Cheadle and Glasgow. Rates are similar to those for BUPA. For further details, call PPP Medical Centre Ltd., 99 New Cavendish Street, London W1M 75A, T:01-637 8941.

WPA. Centres are located in: Bristol, T:0272-273 241; Harrogate, T:0423-622 76; Leicester, T:0533-5513 18; London, T:01-409 0414 and Reading, T:0734-54141.

National Health Service. The NHS offers two different screening services of particular relevance to those aged 50 plus. The first is the well woman check, designed to test for cancer of the cervix and sometimes also breast. The second, offered on a more limited basis, is general screening for all those aged over 65. Ask your local hospital or area health authority for details.

Hospital cash plans

These schemes provide a cash sum for every night the insured person spends in hospital. Premiums range from 30p to £2 a week and payments vary between £8 and £40 a day. By taking out two or three policies, you can build up quite a significant sum which can be used to substitute for loss of earnings or to meet additional bills such as transportation costs for family visits. All benefits are tax free. Most schemes operate strict age limits and the majority will not accept contributions from individuals over the age of 65. The one or two that do, normally reduce the benefits by approximately 33 per cent. About 30 organisations offer such schemes. A full list can be obtained from:

The British Hospitals Contributory Schemes Association, 4th Floor, Refuge Buildings, Baldwin Street, Bristol BS1 1SE, T:0272-273 776.

Aches, pains and other abnormalities

There is nothing about becoming 50, 60 or even 70 that makes aches and pains an inevitability. Age in itself has nothing to do with the vast majority of ailments. However, a big problem is that many people ignore the warning signs when something is wrong, on the basis that this symptom or that is only to be expected as one becomes older. More often than not, treatment when a condition is still in its infancy can either cure it altogether or at least help to delay its advance.

The following should always be investigated by a doctor, to be on the safe side:

- any pain which lasts more than a few days
- lumps, however small
- dizziness or fainting
- chest pains, shortness of breath or palpitations
- persistent cough or hoarseness
- unusual bleeding from anywhere
- unnatural tiredness or headaches
- frequent indigestion
- unexplained weight loss.

National Health Service

Most readers will need no introduction to the National Health Service. However, there are one or two scraps of information that you may not know – or possibly have forgotten – that may come in useful around retirement. One area is the range of professionals, including district nurses and occupational therapists, who can provide invaluable support if you are caring for an elderly relative or if a member of the household requires to go into hospital. Most of what you need to know is described in Chapter 13.

Choosing a GP

If you move to a new area, you will need to find a new doctor. The best way is normally by recommendation but if you do not know whom to ask, you can write to the **Family Practitioner Committee** (see telephone directory) for a list of all NHS doctors practising in the area. The information provided will include: names, addresses, telephone numbers and hours of surgery.

If you would like to know more about a doctor, you can borrow a copy of the *Medical Directory* from the library, where you will find details of his/her training, qualifications and special areas of knowledge. This could be useful if someone in the household has a particular health problem and you would feel happier with a doctor who has more specialised experience.

Additional points you may want to consider are: how close the doctor is to your home; whether there is an appointments system; whether it is a group practice and, if so, how this is organised.

Having selected a doctor, you should take your medical card to the receptionist in order to try to get your name registered. This is not automatic as there is a limit to the number of patients any one doctor can handle. Also, some doctors prefer to meet potential patients before accepting them on their list.

If you want to change your GP, you go about it in exactly the same way by writing to the Family Practitioner Committee. You do not need to give a reason for wanting to change.

Benefits

People over retirement age are entitled to free prescriptions as well as NHS hearing aids and batteries. Those on a low income may also get free dental treatment, glasses and help with fares to hospital. Other assistance for those on Supplementary Pension or Housing Benefit may include: help towards the cost of a special diet, if this is a medical necessity; and also help with laundry or heating bills, if these are particularly heavy because of illness. Contact your local social security office, or, in the case of laundry, speak to the social services department or district health authority. In both cases, a doctor's letter will usually help.

Those below retirement age, who require a lot of prescriptions could save money by purchasing 'a season ticket'. This costs £11 for four months; or £30.50 for a year. Obtain Form FP 95 (EC 95 in Scotland) from a post office, chemist or social security office.

Various *social security benefits* are also available to those with special problems because of illness. These include:

● Invalidity Benefit, see Leaflet NI 16A
● Attendance Allowance, see Leaflet NI 205
● Mobility Allowance, see Leaflet NI 211
● Sickness Benefit, see Leaflet NI 16

All the above leaflets are obtainable from any social security office.

Going into hospital

Stories abound of people who wait months and months for an operation because of shortage of beds. But while waiting lists for a hernia or hip replacement may stretch from here to eternity in one area, hospitals in another part of the country may have spare capacity. Many patients are unaware that they can ask their doctor to refer them to a surgeon anywhere in Britain.

A very helpful booklet, *Guide to Hospital Waiting Lists* (£2.50) has recently been published by the College of Health, giving a district-by-district breakdown of waiting lists in England and Wales. Another useful new publication is *Going into Hospital* (£2). Write to: **The College of Health**, 18 Victoria Park Square, Bethnal Green, London E2 9PF, T:01-980 6263.

Those likely to need help on leaving hospital should speak to the Hospital Social Worker, who will help make any necessary arrangements.

If you go into hospital, you will continue to receive your state pension as normal for eight weeks. After that, it will be reduced.

Complaints

If you have a complaint about the National Health Service, you should contact your local **Community Health Council** (in Scotland, the **Local Health Council**). These councils represent the interests of patients with regard to hospitals and the health service in general.

Alternatively, you can get in touch with **The Patients Association**. This is an independent advice centre which offers guidance and practical help to patients in the event of a problem with the health service and, if necessary, will take up the cudgels on a patient's behalf. The Association also publishes a selection of useful leaflets:

Rights of the Patient	20p
Changing your Doctor	20p
Going into Hospital	40p
Using the NHS	40p
Can I Insist?	40p

The Patients Association, Room 33, 18 Charing Cross Road, London WC2H 0HR, T:01-240 0671.

Alternative medicine

Alternative medicine remains a very controversial subject. Some doctors dismiss it out of hand. Many patients claim that it is of great benefit. We list here some of the better known organisations.

British Acupuncture Association, 34 Alderney Street, London SW1V 4EU, T:01-834 1012.

Treatment, which is by needles, is claimed to be effective for: migraine, lumbago, arthritis, high blood pressure and other conditions. The Association can provide a register of its members (£1.50).

British Chiropractic Association, 5 First Avenue, Chelmsford, Essex CM1 1RX, T:0245-358487.

Practitioners specialise in mechanical disorders of the joints and their effects on the nervous system, especially with regard to the spine. Treatment is mainly by specific manipulation without drugs or surgery. For a register of members, write to the Association enclosing a 9 x 6 sae.

British Homoeopathic Association, 27a Devonshire Street, London W1N 1RJ, T:01-935 2163.

This is the treatment of illnesses and diseases by using natural herbal or mineral substances. In theory, homoeopathy is available on the NHS but not many doctors are trained in this branch of medicine. The Association can supply a list of practising GPs as well as the names and addresses of pharmacies that stock homoeopathic medicines. Patients can only apply to GPs in their catchment area. Some will however treat patients outside their area on a private basis.

British Hypnotherapy Association, 67 Upper Berkeley Street, London W1H 7DH, T:01-723 4443.

Hypnosis is sometimes sought by people with phobias, emotional problems and by those who wish to give up smoking. For address of a suitable registered hypnotherapist in your area, write to the Association stating your age and details of the problem. Charge is £1. Any treatment you have is, of course, extra.

General Council of Osteopaths, 1-4 Suffolk Street, London SW1Y 4HG, T:01-839 2060.

Treatment is sometimes sought by those with back problems, muscle or joint disorders. A Directory of Osteopaths is available at most public libraries. Alternatively, you can write to the Council for a list of their members.

Incorporated Society of Registered Naturopaths, 328 Harrogate Road, Leeds LS17 6PE, T:0532-685 992.

Naturopaths are concerned about the underlying conditions that may cause illness including, for example: diet, general fitness, posture, stress and the patient's mental outlook on life. A list of registered practitioners can be obtained from the Society.

Institute for Complementary Medicine, 21 Portland Place, London W1N 3AF.

This is a charity which aims to promote the use and knowledge of Natural Therapies. It runs an Information Centre with a computerised database, containing details of hundreds of organisations as well as directories of practitioners in the fields of: osteopathy, acupuncture, chiropractice, herbal medicine and homoeopathy. It can also provide information on lectures and classes for interested members of the general public.

Wessex Health Living Foundation, 72 Belle Vue Road, Southbourne, Bournemouth BH6 3DH, T:0202-422087.

Registered as a charity, the Foundation is in effect a 'clinic' for natural therapies, where different treatments are available under one roof. Membership, which includes a newsletter and leaflets, is £4 a year. Consultations are charged extra. For further details, write enclosing sae.

Eyes

It is advisable to have your eyes checked every year or two. Regardless of your age or income, this is an entirely free service. You do not need a doctor's referral. Simply make an appointment with your nearest opthalmic optician or opthalmic medical practitioner.

Normally only children and those on a low income (i.e. in receipt of supplementary benefit or housing benefit) are entitled to free glasses on the NHS. If you are eligible, you should ask the optician you visit for Form F1, which you will need to send to your local social security office. Those with more serious eyesight problems receive extra help. People who are registered blind are entitled to a special tax allowance of £360 a year. Those on a low income may be able to claim a small addition to their supplementary pension. Enquire at the local social security office.

A great deal of very practical help can be obtained by contacting the Royal National Institute for the Blind. In addition to giving general advice and information, it can supply a range of specially adapted equipment as well as help with getting braille added to cooker knobs, clocks, watches and so on. The Institute also publishes a selection of free fact sheets, including *Running Your Own Home* and *Useful Articles Sold in Shops or by Mail Order*, which gives details of electrical appliances, cooking aids, bathroom equipment and garden utensils. For information, contact:

Royal National Institute for the Blind, 224 Great Portland Street, London W1N 6AA, T:01-388 1266.

Another helpful organisation is the National Library for the Blind, which lends books in braille and moon to any blind reader who registers with the service. The library can also provide enlarged music scores for those who are partially sighted. For information, contact:

National Library for the Blind, Cromwell Road, Stockport, Cheshire SK6 2SG, T:061-494 0217.

Other library services include: **Talking Book Service**, Mount Pleasant, Wembley, Middlesex HAO LRR, T:01-903 6666, and **Cassette Library for**

Blind Gardeners, 48 Tolcarne Drive, Pinner, Middlesex HA5 2DQ, T:01-868 4026. Annual subscription £1.

Also worth knowing, all the main banks will provide statements in braille. There is no extra charge for this service.

Feet

Many people forget about their feet until they begin to give trouble. Corns and bunions if neglected can become extremely painful and ideally everyone, especially women who wear high heels, should have chiropody treatment from early middle age or even younger.

One of the problems of which chiropodists complain is that because many women wear uncomfortable shoes they become used to having painful feet and do not notice when something is more seriously wrong. The result can sometimes be ingrowing toenails or infections.

Chiropody is available on the National Health Service without referral from a doctor being necessary but facilities tend to be very over-subscribed, so in many areas it is only the very elderly or those with a real problem who can get appointments.

Private chiropodists are listed in the Yellow Pages. Alternatively, you can write to the Society of Chiropodists which is the professional association of state registered chiropodists, asking for some local names off their list. In addition to keeping a register, the Society can supply a number of free leaflets on foot health plus a booklet called *Care of Your Feet* (30p). The address to contact is:

Society of Chiropodists, 53 Welbeck Street, London W1M 7HE, T:01-486 3381.

Hearing

As they grow older, a great many people suffer some deterioration in their sense of hearing. The main problem is usually not so much medical as the social inconvenience. Should you begin to have difficulty in hearing people speak clearly or find that you are having to turn up the television, it is probably worth having a word with your doctor.

Your GP may well refer you to an Ear, Nose and Throat (ENT) consultant who will advise whether a hearing aid would be helpful and, if so, will prescribe one that is suitable.

You can either obtain a hearing aid and batteries free on the NHS or you can buy them privately. Either way, you may like to read a booklet entitled *General Guidance for Hearing Aid Users*, available free from the **DHSS**, P.O.Box 21, Stanmore, Middlesex HA7 1AY.

There are many other aids on the market that can make life easier. British Telecom, for example, has a variety of special equipment from louder bell tones to flashing light systems. You can either try out the gadgets at one of BT's Aids Centres or dial the operator and ask for Freefone Telecom Sales, who will advise about local shops where you can see the equipment.

The **Disabled Living Foundation**, 380/384 Harrow Road, London W9 2HU, T:01-289 6111, also has a comprehensive display of equipment to assist the hard of hearing and will provide a list of stockists. If you want to try out the different aids, it is a good idea to make an appointment before you go, so that one of their trained advisers can be available to help you.

Additionally, there are a number of specialist organisations that can give you a lot of help, both as regards hearing aids and other matters.

British Association for the Hard of Hearing, 7/11 Armstrong Road, London W3 7JL, T:01-743 1110.

The BAHOH publishes a selection of practical leaflets, including: *Thinking about a Hearing Aid, Lip Reading, Other Aids to Hearing* (for example, adapters for radio and television), as well as leaflets written for the family with advice on how to make hearing easier.

The Association also publishes a newspaper, *Hark*, and has about 230 local clubs throughout the UK with a lively social programme including films, whist drives, dances and many other activities. It also arranges holidays abroad. Membership is £2.50 a year; subscription to *Hark*, £2.

Royal National Institute for the Deaf, 105 Gower Street, London WC1, T:01-387 8033.

The RNID publishes a comprehensive range of leaflets designed to assist deaf or hard-of-hearing people. Titles include:

Current Hearing Aids, a list of hearing aids on the market, giving details of price and performance; *Hearing Aids: Questions and Answers*; *Visual Doorbell Systems*, a list of manufacturers is given.

British Tinnitus Association, 105 Gower Street, London WC1, T:01-387 8033.

Tinnitus is a condition that produces a sensation of noise, rather like a bell ringing in the ear. It can be a great inconvenience to sufferers and in extreme cases can make sleeping more difficult. The BTA can give advice about maskers which help dull the sound and also has many local groups throughout the country.

British Deaf Association, 38 Victoria Place, Carlisle CA1 1HU, T:0228-48844 (Voice) 0228-28719 (Vistel)

The BDA aims to help those who are profoundly deaf, rather than those simply with hearing difficulties. It has branches in most cities and towns that organise social activities. The Association also arranges holidays, both in this country and overseas.

Friends and family can do a great deal to help those whose hearing is less good. The essentials are not to shout but to speak slowly and distinctly. You should always face the person, so they can see your lips; and avoid speaking with your hand over your mouth or with a cigarette in it.

Teeth

Everyone knows the importance of having regular dental check-ups. Many adults, however, slip out of the habit which could result in their having more trouble with their teeth as they become older.

Dentistry is one of the treatments for which you have to pay under the NHS, unless you have a low income. If you are receiving supplementary pension or believe you may be entitled to reduced charges, obtain a copy of Leaflet D 11 from any social security office which explains the eligibility conditions. If you think you qualify, you should ask your dentist for Form F 1D before he treats you. Sometimes, although treatment is not free, you may get help towards the cost of dentures should these be necessary.

Prevention is always better than cure. The British Dental Health Foundation publishes a range of free pamphlets including, among others: *Selecting a Dentist*; *Eating Well*; *Preventive Dentistry and Oral Hygiene*; *Partial Dentures and Bridges*; and a useful booklet – with advice for all ages – called *Tell Me about my Family's Teeth*. Write, enclosing 9 x 6 sae to:

British Dental Health Foundation, 88 Gurnards Avenue, Fishermead, Milton Keynes MD6 2BL, T:0908 667 063.

Despite their somewhat depressing titles, other useful free leaflets are: *Dental Care for the Elderly* from the **Scottish Health Education Group**, Woodburn House, Canaan Lane, Edinburgh EH10 4SQ, and *Dental Problems in Old Age* from **Age Concern**, 60 Pitcairn Road, Mitcham, Surrey CR4 3LL.

Personal relationships

Retirement is a bit like getting married again. It involves a new life style, fresh opportunities and inevitably, as with marriage, a few adjustments for both husband and wife to make. He will have to accustom himself to no longer going to a regular job. She will have to start thinking about another meal to prepare and may possibly feel that she will have to reorganise her domestic or working routine. After years of perhaps hardly seeing each other for more than a few hours a week except for week-ends, suddenly almost the whole of every day can be spent together. He may feel hurt that she does not appear more delighted. She may feel guilty about wanting to pursue her normal activities. Even in the most loving marriages, the first weeks of retirement – for either partner – can produce tensions, which may even affect their sex life, that neither had anticipated.

Normally with good will and understanding on both sides any difficulties are quickly resolved and an even deeper, more satisfying relationship develops. However, for some couples it does not work out so easily and it may be helpful to seek skilled guidance.

National Marriage Guidance Council, Herbert Gray College, Little Church Street, Rugby CV21 3AP, T:0785-73241.

The NMGC offers a counselling service to people who are experiencing difficulties in their marriage or other personal relationships. Their clients are all ages. Some have been married twice or even three times. Many are in the throes of actually seeking a divorce but are trying to prevent the bitterness that can develop. Some come for advice because of upsets with their stepchildren. Others may have sexual problems.

Sometimes couples come together. Sometimes, either the husband or wife comes alone. There are no particular rules and the Council welcomes anyone who feels that it would help to discuss their problems. Often, the emphasis is not on a particular crisis but instead because couples are seeking to make their marriage more positively enjoyable, as at retirement.

The Council has some 400 centres around the country. You can either find the address in the local telephone directory or by contacting the national headquarters above. There is no charge for the service but contributions are very much welcomed.

The address for Scotland is: **Scottish Marriage Guidance Council**, 26 Frederick Street, Edinburgh EH2 2JR, T:031-225 5006.

The Catholic Marriage Advisory Council offers a similar service for those who are having problems with their marriage. Addresses are: **Catholic Marriage Advisory Council** for England/Wales, 15 Lansdowne Road, London W11 3AJ, T:01-727 0141; for Scotland, 18 Park Circus, Glasgow G3 6BE, T:041-332 4914, for Northern Ireland, Cana House, Corry Square, Newry, Co Down BT35 6AW, T:0693-3377.

Two other organisations that may be of interest are:

Westminster Pastoral Foundation, 23 Kensington Square, London W8 5HN. T:01-937 6956.

Counselling is offered to those who are lonely or depressed; having marriage problems or difficulties with family relationships. As the name implies, there is a religious content and service to the community is encouraged. As a rough guide, charges are in the region of £14 per session; or £25 where a couple or family are involved. These may be waived in cases of need.

Albany Trust, 24 Chester Square, London SW1W 9HS, T:01-730 5871.

Offers counselling for people with difficulties in relationships or psychosexual problems. The initial interview which is partially an assessment session is £15, after which fees are determined according to the length of time and frequency of counselling required. As well as London, counselling can be arranged in Birmingham, Surrey and Sussex.

Depression

Depression can be first cousin to marriage and other relationship problems. It is fairly common after bereavement, can be caused by worries or may occur after an operation. Sometimes too, as a number of retired people find, it develops as a result of loneliness, boredom or general lack of purpose. Usually people come out of it on their own accord: either as time heals sorrow or the scars of a relationship that has gone wrong; or in the case of those who are temporarily bored and fed up, as they find new interests and outlets for their talents.

If the condition persists for more than a few days, a doctor should always be consulted as depression can create sleeping difficulties as well as affect the appetite and lead to an overall feeling of physical malaise. The sufferer can be caught in a vicious circle of being too listless to enjoy anything, yet not having done enough during the day to be able to sleep at the proper time.

Another reason for consulting a doctor is that depression may be due to being physically run down, as after 'flu, and all that is required is a good tonic – or perhaps a holiday. Sometimes, however, depression persists and it may be that rather than medicines or the stimulus of a new activity, individuals may feel they need to talk to someone outside the family circle who has a deeper understanding of what they are experiencing. There are several organisations that may be able to help.

Depressives Associated, P.O. Box 5, Castletown, Portland, Dorset DT5 1BQ.

This is a self-help organisation, run by people who themselves have suffered from the effects of depression at some stage of their lives. There are many local groups across the country, where individuals can meet to provide mutual support and advice. Pen-friendships are encouraged, as are friendships by telephone contact. There is also a quarterly newsletter plus a range of leaflets dealing with such subjects as: retirement, divorce, loneliness and helping a depressed relative. For address of a local group and other information, write to the headquarters enclosing sae.

Samaritans, 17 Uxbridge Road, Slough SL1 1SN, T:75-32713

Samaritans are available at any time of the day or night, every single day of the year. They are there to talk or listen for as long as an individual needs or wants to be able to speak to another person. Although most people think of Samaritans as being a telephone service for those who feel they may be in danger of taking their own lives, anyone who would like to can visit their local branch. You do not need to feel positively suicidal before contacting the Samaritans; if you are simply very depressed or lonely, they will equally welcome your call. The service is free and completely confidential. To find your local branch, look in the telephone directory.

Mind, 22 Harley Street, London W1N 2ED, T:01-637 0741.
Mind is a national charity that aims to help both individuals suffering from mental illness and their families. There is a wide network of local groups throughout the country as well as day centres, social clubs, friendship schemes and self-help projects. Services also include counselling and Mind publishes a large range of pamphlets and books. For further information, either contact your local branch (see telephone directory) or the above address.

Useful reading

To Help Cope with Depression, 30p from the Scottish Adult Education Unit, 4 Queensferry Street, Edinburgh EH2 4PA.

Some common afflictions

Quite probably you will be one of the lucky ones and the rest of this chapter will be of no further interest to you. It deals with some of the more common afflictions, such as back pain and heart disease as well as with disability. However, if you are unfortunate enough to be affected, or to have a member of your family who is, then knowing which organisations can provide support could make all the difference in helping you to cope.

Arthritis and rheumatism

Although arthritis is often thought of as an older person's complaint, it accounts for the loss of an estimated 88 million working days a year in Britain.

Arthritis Care, 6 Grosvenor Crescent, London SW1X 7ER, T:01-235 0902.
Arthritis Care is a registered charity and national welfare organisation for arthritis sufferers. It acts as a self help group with over 350 local branches which both offer practical support including transport facilities and a home visiting service for the housebound, and also arrange regular social activities. At national level, Arthritis Care organises holidays and publishes various free

leaflets and booklets. Membership, including quarterly newspaper *Arthritis News* is £2 a year. For address of local branch, contact the headquarters above.

The Arthritis & Rheumatism Council for Research, 41 Eagle Street, London WC1R 4AR, T:01-405 8572.

Although essentially concerned with sponsoring research, the Council publishes a number of free pamphlets including, among others: *A Guide to Arthritis and Other Rheumatic Diseases*; *Marriage, Sex and Arthritis*; *Gout*; *Pain in the Neck*. Send 9 x 6 sae.

Back pain

Four out of five people suffer from back pain at some stage of their lives. While there are many different causes, doctors agree that much of the trouble could be avoided through correct posture, care in lifting heavy articles, a firm mattress and chairs that provide support in the right places. Whether you have problems or are hoping to prevent them, the following two organisations could be helpful.

The Back Shop, 24 New Cavendish Street, London W1M 7LH, T:01-935 9120.

A shop and mail order business that sells medically approved beds, chairs, golf belts and other products that help prevent back trouble or may provide relief for those who suffer. The shop is staffed by qualified nurses with specialised knowledge of back pain and related problems. For a mail order catalogue, send large envelope with 35p stamp.

Back Pain Association, Grundy House, 31-33 Park Road, Teddington, Middlesex TW11 0AB, T:01-977 5474.

The BPA is a registered charity that both encourages research into the treatment of back pain and provides information on how to avoid it. It publishes a range of leaflets including, among others, *The ABC of Moving Things Safely* and *About Preventing Back Problems* (both 50p each) as well as a cassette with exercises to music, called *Back to Mobility* (£5.50). The Association has local branches around the country which organise talks, lectures and social activities as well as fund-raise. Membership which includes copy of the quarterly magazine *Talk Back* is £10. For further information, write enclosing sae.

Cancer

One of the really excellent trends in recent years is a far greater willingness to talk about cancer. Quite apart from the fact that discussing the subject openly has removed some of the dread, increasingly one hears stories of people who have made a complete recovery. Early diagnosis can make a vital difference. Anyone with a lump or swelling, however small, should waste no time in having it investigated by a doctor. There are a number of excellent support groups for cancer sufferers. Rather than list them all, we have only included two as BACUP acts as an umbrella organisation for all related charities.

BACUP (British Association of Cancer United Patients), 121/123 Charterhouse Street, London EC1M 6AA, T:01-608 1661.

BACUP was formed in 1984 with three main aims: to provide information to help cancer patients and their relatives; to offer them emotional support and practical advice; and to help patients talk about their illness with doctors and family. BACUP will deal with both telephone and letter enquiries and additionally publishes a comprehensive range of free booklets, including information about mortgages, insurance and nursing assistance.

Mastectomy Association of Great Britain, 26 Harrison Street, Gray's Inn Road, London WC1H 2JG, T:01-837 0908.

Offers support to women who have had a breast removed, by providing both practical help and the opportunity to meet other women who have had the same operation. The Association can supply a list of manufacturers and stockists of special bras and swim suits and also publishes a number of free booklets.

Chest and heart diseases

The earlier sections on smoking, diet and exercise list some of the most pertinent 'do's and don'ts' that can help prevent heart disease. The statistics make grisly reading. One man in four over the age of 65 is likely to suffer a heart attack and the evidence suggests that women are fast beginning to catch up with men.

Chest, Heart & Stroke Association, Tavistock House North, Tavistock Square, London WC1H 9JE, T:01-387 3012.

This is a registered charity with groups all over the country who offer advice and practical help to sufferers as well as organise social activities through local clubs. The Association also provides a 'Volunteer Stroke Scheme' to help rehabilitate people with speech difficulties. There is an extensive list of publications. Free leaflets, which can be obtained by sending a 9 x 6 sae, include among others: *Bronchitis*; *Get Thin – Keep Alive*; *Reducing the Risk of Coronary*. Additionally, there are a number of booklets (prices, 30p and 40p) and a quarterly magazine *Hope* (annual subscription, £1).

Other useful reading includes *Avoiding Heart Trouble*, £5.95, published by the Consumer Association, P.O. Box 44, Hertford SG14 1SH; *Healthier Eating and Your Heart* and other leaflets, free from the Coronary Prevention Group, 60 Great Ormond Street, London WC1N 3HR, T:01-833 3687 (enclose sae); *Smoking and Your Heart* and other pamphlets free from the British Heart Foundation, 102 Gloucester Place, London W1H 4DH, T:01-935 0185.

Diabetes

Diabetes can very largely be kept under control by diet, although in some cases those affected may need to take insulin.

British Diabetic Association, 10 Queen Anne Street, London W1M 0BD, T:01-323 1531.

The BDA has over 300 local branches who support those with diabetes by providing information to help them adjust to the diabetic regime. There is a comprehensive range of leaflets covering such subjects as: diet and cookery, exercise, travel, insurance and driving. Membership which includes a regular magazine *Balance*, is £5 a year (£1 for Senior Citizens).

Useful reading includes *Life with Diabetes*, 60p plus 15p p & p, from Family Doctor Publications, BMA House, Tavistock Square, London WC1H 9JP.

Migraine

Migraine is thought to be caused by tension, anxiety and possibly also certain foods such as chocolate, cheese and red wine. A bad attack can be very unpleasant and, because other people tend to think of it as just a headache, sufferers often feel that they do not get the sympathy they deserve.

The Migraine Trust, 45 Great Ormond Street, London WC1N 3HD, T:01-278 2676.

As well as furthering research into migraine, the Trust provides advice by post or telephone and publishes a booklet called *Understanding Migraine* (£1.50). It also runs many groups around the country where migraine sufferers can meet and share their problems. Membership is £5 a year and includes a regular newsletter.

The best detailed work on the subject is *Migraine* by the neurologist Oliver Sacks (second edition, Duckworth £14.95), a vividly imaginative account of its history and therapy.

Disability

Disability is mainly covered in Chapter 13; so if you or someone in your family has a problem, you may find the answer you need there. In this section, we list some of the key organisations that can help you and include one or two other points that may be useful for younger people.

Local authority services

Social Services Departments (Social Work Departments in Scotland) provide many of the services which people with disabilities may need, including:

- practical help in the home, perhaps with the support of a home help
- adaptations to your home, such as a ramp for a wheelchair or other special equipment for your safety
- meals on wheels
- provision of day centres, clubs and similar
- issue of orange badges for cars driven or used by a disabled person (in some authorities this is handled by the Works Department; or by the Residents' Parking Department)
- advice about other transport services or concessions that may be available locally.

In most instances, you should speak to a social worker who will either be able to make the arrangements or signpost you in the right direction. He/she will also be able to tell you of any special facilities or other help provided by the authority.

Occupational therapists, who can advise about special equipment and help teach someone with a disability through training and exercise how best to manage, also come within the orbit of the Social Services Department.

Health care

Services are normally arranged either through a GP or the local authority Health Centre. Key professional staff include:

- health visitors: qualified nurses who, rather like social workers, will be able to put you in touch with whatever specialised services are required
- district nurses: will visit patients in their home
- physiotherapists: use exercise and massage to help improve mobility, for example after an operation
- medical social workers: employed at hospitals and will help with any arrangements before a patient is discharged.

Employment

The Disablement Resettlement Officer helps and advises people looking for work and can also give information about any available grants, for example towards the cost of fares to work and for special equipment that may make work life easier. Ask at your nearest jobcentre.

Rates

If someone in the family is disabled, you may be able to claim a reduction on your rates. This is more likely if your home has been specially adapted and the alterations put you in a higher rates bracket. If you have an orange badge on your car, you may get a rebate for a garage. You would normally apply to the *Housing Benefits Officer* but different councils employ different officers to deal with this. Either ask a councillor or enquire at the town hall whom you should approach.

Equipment

If you have temporary need of, say, a wheelchair, you will normally be able to borrow this from the hospital or your local British Red Cross branch. Best source of information for equipment you want on a more permanent basis, including aids for the home, is the Disabled Living Foundation Aids and Equipment Centre where all sorts of equipment can be seen, demonstrated and tried out by visitors. Qualified therapists are available to provide advice and a prior appointment is normally recommended. Contact:

Disabled Living Foundation, 380 Harrow Road, London W9 2HU, T:01-289 6111.
    If it is not possible for you to come to London, the Disabled Living Foundation will be able to recommend a centre nearer your home.

    Another extremely useful organisation to contact for advice on equipment and home adaptations is RADAR – see 'Helpful organisations' below.
    Finally, British Telecom supplies more than 70 aids to enable handicapped people to use the telephone more easily. These are illustrated in a booklet entitled *British Telecom's Guide to Equipment and Services for Disabled Customers*. For further information, dial 100 and ask the operator for Freefone Sales.

Helpful organisations

Fount of all knowledge on almost every topic to do with disability is:

Royal Association for Disability and Rehabilitation (RADAR), 25 Mortimer Street, London W1N 8AB, T:01-637 5400.
    RADAR can give help and advice across a very wide spectrum including:

welfare services, access and mobility issues, holidays, employment and housing. In particular, it welcomes enquiries about the best way of adapting a home and publishes a monthly bulletin with sections on equipment, aids for the disabled and other helpful information. Especially recommended among many other useful publications is *The Directory for Disabled People* (£12.50).

RADAR also helps with the National Key Scheme for Toilets for Disabled People. Over 200 local authorities throughout the country have fitted standard locks to their loos – and issue keys to disabled people – so that the facilities can be used by them, even when these would normally be locked against vandalism. RADAR supplies keys at a charge of £2.50 for those who are unable to obtain an NKS key in their own locality. It also maintains a list of toilets, which is sent out with each key. Copies of the list on its own cost 25p.

For all further information and RADAR's publications list, contact the above address.

Health Education Council, 78 New Oxford Street, London WC2, T:01-631 0930.

The HEC in partnership with Age Concern has launched a national campaign promoting positive attitudes to health in later life. Called the 'Age Well Campaign', it is intended to continue until at least the year 2000. For details of future events and publications, contact the Health Education Unit through your District Health Authority. The HEC also runs 'Look After Yourself' classes around the country, teaching general fitness together with the importance of exercise, sensible eating and so on. These are operated through adult education programmes. For further details, write to: **Look After Yourself Project Centre**, Christ Church College, Canterbury, Kent CT5 JQY.

Disability Alliance, 25 Denmark Street, London WC2 8NJ, T:01-240 0806.

The Disability Alliance is the umbrella organisation for nearly 100 charitable bodies concerned with the welfare of the disabled. It publishes the *Disability Rights Handbook* which is a complete guide to rights, benefits and services for all people with disabilities and their families. Very clearly written and set out, it is an invaluable source of information. Price is £2.60.

Scottish Council on Disability, Princes House, 5 Shandwick Place, Edinburgh EH2 4RG, T:031-229 8632.

The Scottish Council is a national voluntary organisation for all Scotland's disabled people. The Information Department, which offers a 24 hour service, is available to answer queries by letter or telephone or alternatively, visitors are welcome at Princes House. A large range of free leaflets on transport, special equipment, holidays and many other subjects are available.

Northern Ireland Council for the Handicapped, 2 Annadale Avenue, Belfast BT7 3JR, T:0232-640 011.

NICH supplies information and advice for disabled people in Northern Ireland. A wide range of fact sheets are available, single copies free with sae. Full details from the Information Service at the above address.

Wales Council for the Disabled, Information Service, Caerbragdy Industrial Estate, Bedwas Road, Caerphilly, Mid Glamorgan CF8 3SL, T:0222-887 325.
Offers a similar service for people in Wales.

Greater London Association for Disabled People, 336 Brixton Road, London SW9 7AA, T:01-274 0107.
GLAD provides an information service to individuals in the Greater London area, mainly through a network of borough associations. A publications list is available, free with sae.

Disablement Information and Advice Line (DIAL UK), Victoria Buildings, 117 High Street, Clay Cross, Chesterfield S45 9DZ, T:0246-864498.
A national network of 80 local information and advice services.

Disablement Income Group, Attlee House, 28 Commercial Street, London E1 6LR, T:01-247 2128.
DIG is a national charity concerned about the financial consequences of disability. It runs an advisory service for individuals and publishes a quarterly newspaper *Dig Around*. Annual membership is £2.50.

Useful reading

Better Health in Retirement by J.A.Muir Gray, £1.20. Published by Age Concern England, 60 Pitcairn Road, Mitcham, Surrey CR4 3LL.
Door to Door Guide. An official guide to transport for disabled people. Free from the Department of Transport, Freepost, Ruislip, Middlesex HA4 0BR.
Care in the Air. Advice for handicapped airline passengers. Free from the Air Transport Users Committee, 129 Kingsway, London WC2B GNN.
British Rail and Disabled Travellers. Free from mainline stations or Public Affairs Department, British Railways Board, Rail House, Euston Square, London NW1 2DZ.

12. Holidays

Holidays can be even better when you retire! You do not have to plan months ahead in order to fit in with colleagues. You can avoid the peak periods which are almost invariably more expensive and crowded. You can also enjoy real flexibility, in a way that is usually not possible when you are working, by taking several mini breaks when you feel like it or going away for an extended period. Additionally, one of the great things about retirement is the availability of concessionary prices, including in particular the possibility of cheaper fares and reduced charges for hotel accommodation.

Apart from these benefits, the fact of being retired makes very little difference. You can ride an elephant in India, take a caravan around Europe, sail on the Norfolk Broads, go bird-watching in Scotland, combine a holiday with a special interest such as painting or music, enrol for summer school, exchange homes with someone in another country or sign on for a working holiday, such as voluntary conservation activity or home-sitting, for which you get paid.

The choice is literally enormous. The list of suggestions which follows is by no means exhaustive. You can go to any travel agent and collect further ideas by the dozen. However, the two main criteria we adopted in deciding which, among the thousands of possibilities, to include were: variety and holidays which, one way or another, offer some special attraction or specifically cater for those aged 50 and above.

Some of the options verge on the exotic, with prices to match; others are extremely reasonable in cost. There are suggestions which are only suitable for the really fit and active; at the other extreme, there are a number of inclusions which would only be of interest to individuals in need of special care.

Some of the choices may strike you as mad, risky, humdrum, too demanding – or simply not your style. But retirement is a time for experimentation and trying something entirely different is half the fun.

For ease of reference, entries are listed under such headings as 'arts and crafts', 'sport', 'self-catering holidays' and so on. Inevitably some organisations criss-cross several sections but to avoid repetition, the majority are only featured once in what, hopefully, is the most logical place.

At the end of the chapter, there is a general information section with brief details about insurance, concessionary fares and other travel tips. Prices and some of the other detailed information, while accurate at the time of writing, may be slightly out-of-date as programmes change (sometimes at very short notice) and it is impossible to keep track. The intention is to provide an indication of fairly typical events together with an idea of price bracket.

Art appreciation

The choice ranges from a grand tour of the Ottoman Empire to a couple of days' residential seminar on china and porcelain. It also includes the music and drama festivals held in many parts of the country, usually during the summer months.

Christie's Collectors' Tours, 40 Ponton Road, London SW8 5BA, T: 01-627 4801.

These are designed for people 'with an informed interest in the visual arts'. Many are study tours related to events in Christie's Sales Calendar; others cover wider topics. Groups are limited to 25 with an international mix. Tours cover such topics as contemporary decorative arts, Americana in the USA, study of European furniture in British collections, an Ottoman Empire tour through Turkey, Yugoslavia, Hungary and Austria. Information on dates and prices is given in Christie's *International Magazine*.

Geoffrey Godden, 17 Crescent Road, Worthing, Sussex BN11 1RL, T: 0903-35958.

Geoffrey Godden – the 'Chinaman' – arranges residential meetings in various parts of the country on china and porcelain. The lecture charge is £25 and hotel price (full board) is about £55 for 2 nights.

National Association of Decorative & Fine Arts Societies, 36 Ebury Street, London SW1W 0LU, T: 01-730 3041

NADFAS is an association of 150 fine arts societies all over Britain. It organises tours at home and abroad to places of interest to its members. Recent events in Britain have included a Victorian evening in London (£15.50 with supper) and a 4-day visit to Lindisfarne (about £200 with coach travel and accommodation). Some tours abroad have been: 3 weeks in Australia (about £2,400), a Grand Tour of Italy (about £970), 2 weeks in Japan (about £1,900), 9 days' visit to great classical cities of the Middle East (about £740), 8-day musical tour of Austria (about £640), 3-week tour of China (£2,200) and a Christmas party in Vienna (about £500 for 5 days). For a list of local societies, write to NADFAS at the above address.

Prospect Art Tours, 10 Barley Mow Passage, London W4 4PH, T: 01-995 2163.

Prospect designs tours to help people deepen their understanding of the visual arts. The prices include all transport, accommodation with private bath or shower, half board, all commission charges plus the services of tour leaders and lecturers. Recent tours have included: 11 days in Lombardy (£500); 3 days Houses of Derbyshire (£125); 4 days Budapest (£325); 11 days Venice and Florence (£620); a week in Jordan (£560).

Special Tours, 2 Chester Row, London SW1W 9JH, T: 01-730 2297.

Special Tours organises expeditions abroad for the British Museum Society, Folio Society, Friends of the Ashmolean, Courtauld Institute, National Maritime Museums, Royal Academy, National Art Collection Fund and for Scotland's Garden Scheme. The cost of a holiday includes flight, hotel with board, travel within the country, entrance fees, guides and lecturers. The programme includes such holidays as Historic Sicily; Lakeside Gardens of Italy; Moscow and Leningrad and Austrian Baroque. Prices of these are in the range of £700 – £950. Non-members of societies for which tours are arranged can join before going on the tour.

Festivals

A veritable feast of music, drama and the arts. The most famous are those held at Edinburgh and Aldeburgh. Over the years the number of festivals has been growing and these are now a regular feature in many parts of the country. To find out what is going on where, you should contact the Arts Council (see below) or your Regional Arts Association. The **British Federation of Music Festivals** publishes a Yearbook, which should be in your local reference library, listing festivals around the country. The major events, especially at the bigger festivals, tend to get booked well in advance, so early application for tickets is advisable.

Aldeburgh Festival Office, Aldeburgh, Suffolk 1PS5 5AX, T: 072-885 2935.

The Aldeburgh Festival of Music and Arts is held annually in June, and the Benson and Hedges Festival of Chamber Music is held in November. There are also music, opera, ballet and other performances at the Maltings at Snape around the year. Ask for details of programmes and local accommodation from the Festival Office.

Edinburgh International Festival Office, 21 Market Street, Edinburgh EH1 1BW, T: 031-226 4001

The Edinburgh Festival is organised each year during the last three weeks of August. A detailed programme of events, including exhibitions and the tattoo as well as music and drama performances, is available around mid April from the above address.

Arts Council of Great Britain, 105 Piccadilly, London W1, T: 01-629 9495.

For information about established festivals throughout the country.

Arts and crafts

The focus here is on taking courses or just participating for the pleasure, rather than viewing the works of others. The choice includes brass rubbing and other crafts, painting and music. Further suggestions are also given in Chapter 7.

Academy of Monumental Brass Rubbing, Queen Street, Lynton, Devon EX35 6AA, T: 059 85-2529.

Offers diploma courses over two days, out of peak holiday periods. Fee of £30 includes all materials, equipment and course notes. More advanced courses are £75, over four days, and include materials, equipment, advanced methods of teaching and all relevant historical data. Prices do not include accommodation but a list of local hotels, and guest houses can be supplied.

Association of British Craftsmen, 57 Coombe Bridge Avenue, Stoke Bishop, Bristol, Avon BS9 2LT, T: 0272-686417.

If you write saying what particular type of craft interests you, the Association will send you a list of residential courses for your chosen subject. (Please enclose stamp to cover postage.)

Crafts Council, 8 Waterloo Place London W1, T: 01-930 4811

The Council keeps a list of organisations that run their own short craft courses or that can provide information on where similar courses are being held.

Galleon Holidays, 45 Cathedral Place, London EC4M 7PB, T: 01-248 1011 (in Scotland: 369-71 Sauchiehall Street, Glasgow G2 3HX, T: 041-332 3521.)

Galleon runs tutored painting holidays in Britain, Gibraltar, Malta, Austria, France and an art appreciation course in Belgium. The courses include both general painting and special subjects, such as botanical, landscape or portrait painting. Holidays cost from about £170 a week with full board and tuition.

Rural Music Schools Association, Little Benslow Hills, Ibberson Way, Hitchin, Herts SG4 9RB, T: 0462-59446.

The RMSA exists to promote the study and practice of music among students of all ages. This work is centred on the Association's residential centre in Hitchin. There are weekend and other courses all year for amateur players and singers. The programme covers: chamber music, orchestra, choral music, various instruments including recorder and guitar, early music and jazz. Subscription (£7.50 a year) gives members free use of the music library, priority booking for both courses and single rooms and regular mailings of programmes. The standard fee for a weekend course is £40 with full board or £30 non-resident; £110 for a week, £80 non-resident. There are some special weekends for older musicians and a Christmas house party.

Summer Music, 22 Gresley Road, London N19 3JZ, T: 01-272 5664.

Despite its name, Summer Music organises a series of music schools at weekends throughout the year. A typical programme might include: cello playing, guitar, putting over a song and string quartets. There is also a week-long summer school in August and a Christmas house party for singers, string players and others. The charges vary, but a weekend with full board costs about £40.

West Dean College, West Dean, Chichester, West Sussex PO18 0Q2, T: 024-363 301.

West Dean College, housed in a beautiful mansion surrounded by landscaped gardens and parkland, organises short residential courses in arts, crafts and music – variously lasting a weekend, 5 or 7 days. A typical programme includes: stained glass, calligraphy, embroidery, woodcarving, picture framing, music appreciation, photography, upholstery, gemmology, sculpture, landscape sketching, jewellery, cane and rush seating and many more. Prices, which include board and lodging, range from about £68 for a weekend to £200 for a 7-day course. There are also longer courses, including a year's Diploma course run in conjunction with the British Antique Dealers' Association.

Coach and rail holidays

Golden Rail and some of the coach companies organise holidays proper, as distinct from simply offering a mode of transport. Advice note from other holidaymakers: before embarking on a lengthy coach tour, try a few shorter excursions to see how you cope with the journey. Some people swear by the comfort, others find coach travel very exhausting.

Frames National, 97 Southampton Row, London WC1B 4BQ, T: 01-637 4171.

Frames run a wide variety of coach tours in the U.K. and Europe. Prices cover: travel, breakfast and dinner, luggage handling and all rooms with private bath. Examples include: Scottish tour, 7 days, from £273; English Homes and Gardens, 4 days, from £135; Scenic Europe and Paris, 8 days, from £260 covering Belgium, Germany, Austria, Switzerland and France; classic tour of Spain, 14 days, from £385.

National Express, 1 Vernon Road, Birmingham B16 9SJ, T: 021-622 4373

Offers a wide choice of inclusive package holidays in Britain; for example: 3 nights in the Lakeland, 5 days in Wales, 9 day coach tour of Ireland – with prices ranging from approximately £89 to £279. There are also considerably cheaper winter breaks. Holiday prices include: travel, hotels, most meals, insurance cover and often special excursions. Over sixties are entitled to a third discount on most adult fares. For further information, contact the above address or one of the area offices (Cheltenham, Manchester, Liversedge).

Wallace Arnold Tours Ltd., Geldern Road, Leeds LS12 6DH, T: 0532-636456.

Wallace Arnold organise both coach tours and rail holidays in Britain; also activity and short break holidays. Most can be joined at 70 different points, making for easier journeys. Prices include holiday insurance; and in the case of winter breaks, free excursions from the holiday centre. Examples at the time of writing are: modern sequence and ballroom dancing holidays, about £60 for 4 nights with dinner, bed and breakfast; visiting gardens, about £90 for 4 nights; London visits with theatres booked for you; touring Scotland from about £130 a week; 8-day holidays in Bournemouth and other coast towns, about £100. Overseas tours include all the European favourites.

Golden Rail Holidays, P.O. Box 12, York YO1 1YK, T: 0904-28992.

Golden Rail Tempo holidays are designed for the over 55's. They provide: rail travel with seat reservations, dinner, bed and breakfast at hotels in 12 seaside resorts, holiday insurance and three coach tours from your resort. The costs vary from about £130 for a week in the spring to £250 in early autumn, depending on the resort and hotel.

Field studies

The number and variety of courses arranged by National Parks and Field Centres almost deserves a special publication of its own. In addition to wildlife studies, the choice which varies from one centre to another includes: archaeology, landscape painting, spinning and weaving, ecology, folklore, yoga, silk screen printing and many others.

Council for National Parks, 45 Shelton Street, London WC2H 9HJ, T: 01-240 3603.

There are 10 National Parks in England and Wales designated to conserve and enhance areas of natural beauty. They are: Northumberland, Lake District, Yorkshire Dales, North Yorkshire Moors, Peak District, Snowdonia, Pembrokeshire Coast, Brecon Beacons, Exmoor and Dartmoor. The Council is the national voluntary organisation concerned with promoting and protecting these parks. Friends of the National Parks support the work of the Council and keep in touch with national park issues and events. The minimum subscription (£5) entitles you to receive the newsletter which gives visitor information and details of current activities in the parks. To give you a flavour of the different style and types of programme that are on offer, mini descriptions of typical events at National Parks in Brecon and the Peak District follow.

Danywenallt Study Centre, Talybont-on-Usk, Brecon, Powys LD3 7YS, T: 087-487 677.

Courses are based on such topics as: local history, industrial archaeology and landscape painting. There is also a special 'out and about in the National Park' programme for older people, with tours conducted largely by minibus. Courses cost from about £30 for a weekend to £75 for 5 days. Accommodation is in double rooms. Fees include three meals a day and visitors help with the washing up.

Peak National Park Study Centre, Losehill Hall, Castleton, Derbyshire S30 2WB, T: 0433-20373.

Weekend courses include, among others: archaeology, folklore, birds, photography, spinning and weaving, gardening, railways, caves, great houses and gardens. There are also rambling weekends and a special week-long course for over 50's to explore the Peak District. Losehill Hall is set in beautiful country with comfortable accommodation. The cost is £125 for a week and about £50 for a weekend, including full board and lectures.

Field Studies Council, Preston Montford, Montford Bridge, Shrewsbury SY4 1HW, T: 0743-850 674.

The Council runs field centres around the country, offering a wide variety of courses categorised as follows: General Interest, Natural History, Ecology and Conservation, Flowers and Other Plants, Birds and Animals, Geology, Landscape and Climate, History and Architecture, Painting and Drawing, Photography and Crafts. The centres are based near Colchester, Dyfed, Taunton, Settle in North Yorkshire, Shrewsbury, Dorking, Kingsbridge, Betws-y-Coed and Chepstow. Each centre organises its own programme and usually includes one or two courses featuring local attractions. For example, the Flatford Mill Centre in Suffolk offers a Constable weekend, the Juniper Hall Centre in Dorking includes Surrey Churches, while the Preston Montford Centre in Shrewsbury highlights Offa's Dyke. The Council publishes an 'Index', giving a complete list of all courses at their residential centres. Most last for a week (Friday to Friday) and average cost is about £135 including board, lodging and tuition. Weekend courses are around £55.

The Field Studies Council also organises Expeditions Overseas and examples include: Sea Eagles in France (4 days, about £200); Birds of the Gambia (2 weeks, about £800); Flowers and Painting in Andalucia (2 weeks, about £550) and Iceland: Land of Fire (2 weeks, about £770). Enquiries to: **Flatford Mill Field Centre**, East Bergholt, Nr.Colchester, Suffolk CO7 6UI, T: 0206-298 283.

Anyone attending a course is expected to join the Field Studies Council (£3 a year, £6 for families, £60 for life). Members receive the annual report and details of programmes and, for an extra £5 a year, the Council's journal *Field*

Studies. For membership: **Field Studies Council**, 62 Wilson Street, London EC2, T: 01-247 4651.

Scottish Field Studies Association, Kindrogan Field Centre, Enochdhu, Blairgowrie, Perthshire PH10 7PG, T: 0250-81286.

The Centre runs courses through the spring, summer and autumn on such subjects as painting, birds, spiders, flowers and lichens. There are also courses on landscape gardens, photography and rambling weeks. Cost is about £105 for a week including tuition, board and lodging.

Historical holidays

Holidays with a particular focus on history are becoming increasingly popular. The choice includes: battlefield and other overseas tours, exploring historic parts of Britain and the highly imaginative 'production' at Kentwell Hall.

Battlefield Tours, 15 Market Street, Sandwich, Kent, T: 0304-612248.

Battlefield Tours, run by Major and Mrs. Holt, are official organisers of pilgrimages for the Royal British Legion. The prices include accommodation, meals, tour guides, entrance fees, luxury coach and air travel, ferry fares and comprehensive insurance. Recent trips have included: Gallipoli and the Dardanelles (£460 for 11 days): Ypres-Vimy-Somme (£133 for 3 days); Salerno/Monte Casino (£340 for 8 days); Brussels/Waterloo (3 days £130); A Bridge Too Far in Holland (4 days £169); El Alamein Anniversary (16 days £600). The Holts arrange special tours for groups and have an annual reunion. They also organise Good Companion Tours to the Rhineland and to Holland in tulip time. Should you wish to visit a war grave and know the exact location of the cemetery from the Commonwealth War Graves Commission (2 Marlow Road, Maidenhead, Berkshire, T: 0628-34224), Battlefield Tours will help and advise you.

Historical Association, 59a Kennington Park Road, London SE11 4JH. T: 01-735 3901.

The Association brings people together to share their interest in history. It organises tours with expert lecturers. Foreign holidays in 1986 have included: India (2 weeks £1,020), Upper Normandy (a week £250) and Portugal (11 days £580). Home tours included: a week in Cambridge (£122), walking in Yorkshire (£24 plus own accommodation), exploring in North Wales (£213).

Kentwell Hall, Long Melford, Suffolk, T: 0787-310 207.

Every summer Kentwell Hall recreates a living demonstration of what life was like during a certain period of history. Participants are required to provide their own costumes and to enter into the role of a character living at the time:

for example, this could be a 16th century cook or hay-maker. You are expected to prepare yourself by reading and there are Open Days at Kentwell with briefing sessions. The event lasts for three weeks and participants can stay for as long as they like. The only cost involved is the provision of a suitable costume. All meals are free and there is a choice of camping space or dormitory accommodation. Those requiring better accommodation can book into one of the many local bed and breakfast hotels.

Language courses

If you are hoping to travel more when you retire, being able to speak the language when abroad will greatly add to your enjoyment. Quickest and easiest way to learn is in the country itself. There are attractive opportunities for improving your French, German, Italian and Spanish.

The British Institute, Florence, Palazzo Lanfredini, Lungarno Guicciardina 9, Florence, Italy.

The Institute, an officially sponsored joint Anglo-Italian institute of nearly 70 years' standing, runs 4-12 week graded Italian language courses throughout the year for learners of all ages and levels. There are also courses in English on the Italian Renaissance and other subjects. Various events such as lectures and concerts are arranged by the Institute for students and local people. Accommodation is in local homes, pensioni and hotels: cost is from £10 a day. Teaching takes place in a 13th century palazzo. Tuition fees vary according to the length and intensity of the course you choose: for example £190 for 10 lessons a week for 4 weeks; or for 20 lessons a week over a fortnight. The Florentine Renaissance courses (in English) last 3 weeks and cost £105.

En Famille Agency (Overseas), Westbury House, Queen's Lane, Arundel, Sussex BN18 9JN.

The Agency arranges short or long stays with host families for people who want an insider's view of a European country. There is a registration fee of £12 plus a selection fee of £18. You pay travel costs and about £70-£80 a week full board; or £55-£75 demi-pension. En Famille matches your background and interests to the people on their register and sends you details of a selection of families from which to choose. The Agency also runs three centres in France as well as cookery weeks and independent language courses. Older people are especially welcome at these Centres. Costs are from about £70 a week demi-pension.

Eurocentres, 36 Honor Oak Road, London SE23 3SN, T: 01-699 1174.

Eurocentres run language teaching studies in France, Italy, Spain and Germany for students of all levels. The courses last from a couple of weeks to about 3 months and are set in the life and culture of the host country. Most students live with families but Eurocentres will also arrange hotels. A 10-week French course in Paris with accommodation and half board costs about £1,500; a month's Italian course with half board costs about £500. There is a supplementary charge of about £10 a week for a single room. In all cases, fares are additional.

Estudio General Luliano, c/o 24 High Street, Portsmouth PO1 2LS, T: 0705-824095.

The Estudio runs 2-5 week Spanish courses in Majorca for adult English students of all levels of proficiency. Classes are held in the morning in small groups. The fee is about £75 a week, with accommodation in private houses or beach hotels; with full board the cost comes to about £110. Air travel can be arranged.

Goethe Institut, Zentralverwaltung, Rererat 31, Len Bach Platz 3, D-8000 Munchen, Federal Republic of Germany, T: FRG 089-5999-20. For German courses in Britain: **Goethe Institute**, 50 Princes Gate, Exhibition Road, London SW7 2PH, T: 01-581 3344.

The Goethe Institute, through its 4 centres in Britain and 15 in Germany, offers 2, 4 or 6 week part-time courses in German language and culture, for beginners to examination level. The instruction is designed so that you can follow from one level to another in all centres.

Off-beat

A couple of very different suggestions for people seeking an unusual and inexpensive holiday.

Common Cold Research Unit, Coombe Road, Salisbury, Wiltshire SP2 8BW.

The Unit is always looking for volunteers to come and stay for 10-day periods with 2-3 flat mates. You have free board and lodging and pocket money. You may or may not get a cold, but you must not go within 30 feet of anyone but your flat mates and the doctors. A very cheap way to have a quiet holiday in the country! Write to the Unit for further details.

Association for Promoting Retreats, Church House, Newton Road, London W2, T: 01-727 7924.

Some people want to have no more than peace and quiet for a few days. The Association's annual journal gives details of retreats all over the country. Accommodation is simple and costs are low.

Other people's homes

Living in someone else's home for free is one of the cheapest ways of enjoying a holiday. There are two ways of arranging this. You can exchange your home with another person, in this country or abroad. The onus is on you to select a suitable property and to decide whether the person with whom you are swopping is likely to care for your home properly. The alternative is to become a homesitter and, for a modest payment, mind someone else's property while they are away.

Home exchange

Unless you are lucky enough to hear about someone through personal recommendation, probably the easiest method of finding a swop (and of advertising your own home) is through a specialised directory. In most cases, this is not an introduction service as such. The exchanges are normally arranged direct between the two parties concerned, who agree the terms between themselves. Some people even exchange their cars and pets.

Home Interchange, 8 Hillside, Farningham, Kent DA4 0DD, T: 0322-86 4527.

Publishes *The Holiday Exchange Book* twice a year. Thousands of homes in different countries are listed. There are separate sections for those wanting to do a straight let and also for those seeking paying guests. Subscription rates are from £20. If you do not wish to advertise but simply want to buy the book, price is £18.

Worldwide Home Exchange Club, 45 Hans Place, London SW1X 0JZ, T: 01-589 6055.

Publishes a directory of about 750 listings in 30 countries. To be listed you join the Club, pay £15 annual subscription and your property will then be included in the annual directory. For £13 you can receive the directory without listing your home. Specially good for America, as the club has an office in Philadelphia.

Homesitting

Homesitting means that you provide a caretaking service and get paid for doing so. Retired people are generally considered ideal. Duties variously involve: light housework, plant watering, care of pets and sometimes tending the garden. First class references are naturally required.

Homesitters, Moat Farm, Buckland, Aylesbury, Bucks HP22 5HY, T:0296-631289.

Homesitters are looking for mature, responsible people with no children or pets, usually non-smokers and it is useful to have your own car. Assignments may be for short or long periods. Pay is about £20 – £30 a week depending on responsibilities plus travel, expenses and food. With agreement, a homesitter can take their partner. The houses can be anything from a small flat to a mansion.

Universal Aunts, 250 King's Road, London SW3 5UE, T:01-351 5767.

Universal Aunts organise a home sitting service for absent owners and recruit single or pairs of mature, responsible people for this work. They pay £56 a week plus travelling expenses (whether you go alone or with a partner). All applicants for the home sitters panel are interviewed before acceptance on the list.

Overseas travel

Many of the big tour operators make a feature of offering special holidays, designed for the over 55's. For fun, we have also included one or two companies that specialise in arranging cruises; and also details of a time-sharing arrangement with a difference. For up-to-date details, you should check the brochures.

Golden Circle Holidays, 200 Tottenham Court Road, London W1P 0JP, T: 01-323 3266.

These are holidays arranged by Global for the over-55's. Departure dates are from October to April and destinations include: Spain, Portugal, Greece, the Canaries, Malta and the USSR. The programme includes special interest holidays and also holidays for 'singles'. Most of the hotels offer a variety of entertainment.

Golden Days, Intasun House, Cromwell Avenue, Bromley, Kent BR2 9AQ, T: 01-290 1900, or Intasun House, 47 Grattan Road, Bradford, Yorks BD1 2QF, T: 0274-760011.

Golden Days are special Intasun low season holidays for the over-50s. Destinations include: Spain, the Canaries, Malta, Portugal, Morocco, Yugoslavia and Rhodes. Holidays last from a week to six months and departure is possible from 14 UK airports and 20 regional coach centres. Most holidays include a varied programme of entertainment and there is also a choice of special interest holidays.

Horizon Holidays, Broadway, Edgbaston, Birmingham B15 1BB, T: 021-643 2727.

'Home from Home' holidays for the over-55s in Spain, Malta and Cyprus during the winter months. Holidays last from a week to three months. Excursions and other entertainment is provided. Accommodation is either in hotels or rented apartments.

Portland Holidays, 218 Great Portland Street, London W1N 5HG, T: 01-388 3299.
Holidays in Spain and Portugal, for over-55s, arranged under Portland's Travel Trust programme. Entertainments and a sightseeing tour are included in the price.

Thomson Young at Heart, Greater London House, Hampstead Road, London NW1 7SD, T: 01-387 9321.
Winter holidays in warmer climates for people over 55, accompanied by 'Thomson Staff', in hotels and apartments. The resorts are in Spain, Portugal, Madeira, Malta, Tenerife and Tunisia. There are special interest weeks and also holidays especially for 'singles'. Twin room sharing arrangements for people travelling alone.

Cruises

Cruises become more exotic by the year. Among the programmes we particularly liked are those arranged by:

P & O Cruises, Beaufort House, St. Botolph Street, London EC3A 7DX, T: 01-283 8080.

Royal Viking Line, 3 Vere Street, London W1M 9HQ, T:01-734 0774.

Gray Dawes Travel Ltd., 3 Cathedral Place, London EC4M 7DT, T:01-248 6474.
For traditional sea-farers rather than luxury travel seekers. Gray Dawes arranges for passengers to travel on cargo vessels to all parts of the world. Voyages are prone to delays and changes en route, so you must be able to be flexible as to time. Recent voyages have included: Cape Town via Tenerife, St.Vincent and St.Helena (from £1,020 one way); 12-week round trip to Australia £2,923); 8-week round trip to South America £2,115). One way fares are available on round trips and the company will arrange homeward flights.

Time sharing

Time sharing more properly belongs in the section headed 'investment'. And as with other investments, decisions should not be taken lightly. We have made an exception for Hapimag because, although the normal warnings apply when you are parting with considerable money, the scheme avoids some of the well known problems associated with conventional time-shares.

Hapimag of Switzerland, Comser International Ltd., Fairview Road, Timperley, Cheshire WA15 7AR, T: 061-904 9750.

Hapimag is a non-profit making club which buys sites and builds leisure complexes for use by its members. Unlike most time-sharing arrangements, with Hapimag you are not buying into one property but instead are purchasing the right to stay rent free in any of the club's chalets, flats or hotels. These are located in a variety of resorts in eleven countries, so enabling you to choose a different holiday every year. Time shares cost about £1,500 each. You can buy as many or few as you like, depending on the number of weeks you anticipate wanting to spend abroad. There are also cheaper holiday passes, valid for twenty years – in contrast to time shares, which are valid in perpetuity. In both cases, as well as your capital outlay, there is an annual membership charge.

Saga – in a class of its own

Saga Holidays plc, P.O.Box 65, Folkestone, Kent, T: 0303-30030.

Saga specialises in holidays for over-60s and offers a vast choice of options both in Britain and overseas. The list includes: coach tours, cruises, weekend breaks, multi-centre vacations in far-away places plus a huge selection of special interest holidays, featuring everything from bowls and bridge to collecting antiques and retirement planning. There are also special holidays for 'singles' as well as Reunion Flights to Australia, New Zealand, South Africa and North America for people wishing to visit family and friends. All holidays are courier-assisted and travel insurance is included in all overseas prices. Accommodation is variously in hotels, self-catering units and college halls of residence (all single rooms). Prices are too varied to quote, other than the fact that Saga give reductions of 15 per cent (or more) on cruise fares of most of the great lines including P & O, Swan Hellenic and Cunard. The company also operates a savings plan, whereby you can pay for your holiday by instalments. For further information, obtain Saga brochures: *Shortbreaks Review*, *Saga Cruise Book*, *Holidays in Great Britain* and *Worldwide Holidays*, available from the Folkestone address above.

Self-catering and other low budget holidays

If you cannot quite manage to survive on a tenner a day, some of the suggestions in this section need hardly cost you very much more. This applies especially if you are camping, caravanning or renting very simple accommodation with friends. The list includes: farm cottages, hostels, university accommodation, forest cabins and other rentals of varying degrees of sparseness or luxury. There are also one or two hotels that offer specially attractive rates.

British Universities Accommodation Consortium, General Office, University Park, Nottingham NG7 1BR, T:0602-504571.

Many universities provide bed and breakfast and self-catering accommodation during the vacations for individuals and families, and sometimes also group facilities. Prices vary according to size, amenities and location. For example, a flat sleeping 6-8 persons in Sussex costs about £180 weekly; bed and breakfast in Central London, about £9-20 a night per person. BUAC publishes a brochure, *British Universities*, describing facilities, booking periods and rates.

Bournanza Holidays, 4 Westover Road, Bournemouth, Dorset BH1 2BY, T:0202-293569.

Some rail/hotel holidays in Bournemouth offer special rates to anyone over 60 years, between April and June, and September and mid-October. The price includes dinner, bed and breakfast, rail travel, transfer from station and four excursions. Costs range from £70-£110 a week, depending on the time of year. There are also Christmas weekends, dinner dance weekends, and holidays throughout the year, for which holders of Senior Citizens Rail Cards have a £2.50 reduction.

Camping & Caravanning Club, 11 Lower Grosvenor Place, London SW1, T:01-828 1012.

Members may use the network of Club sites all over Britain, listed in the annual *Handbook and Sites List* and receive a free copy of the monthly magazine, *Camping and Caravanning*. The Club also offers insurance and reduced subscription to the Royal Automobile Club. The Foreign Touring Service gives advice and help when you go abroad and arranges activity programmes which include excursions, wine tasting and barbecues at their continental sites. Membership costs £15 a year.

The **English Tourist Board** has recently published a brochure illustrating the 42 caravan parks in England to which it has granted its special 'Rose Award' on the basis of their providing first class holiday facilities in an attractive and well managed setting. The guide is available from travel agents, tourist information centres or direct from the ETC (Department E), Thames Tower, Black's Road, Hammersmith, London W6 9EL.

English Country Cottages Ltd., Claypit Lane, Fakenham, Norfolk NR21 8AS, T:0328-4041; **Welsh Country Cottages**, T:0328-51341; **Country Cottages in Scotland**, T:0328-4011.

The 'cottages' range enormously in size and are variously capable of sleeping between 2 and 16. Many are available all the year round with low out-of-season prices and short break arrangements from November to March. Apply for the brochure which gives full details and pictures of all properties.

Everymann Holidays, 13 Victoria Street, Douglas, Isle of Man, T:0624-29914.

Everymann runs special cheap offer holidays in May, June and September on the Isle of Man for people over 55. They include return fare, full board in hotel or guest house, a coach trip and discount entry to many entertainments. Holidays cost from about £100 a week; second week is cheaper.

Farm Holidays Bureau, National Agricultural Centre, Stoneleigh, Kenilworth, Warwickshire CV8 2L2, T:0203-555100

Many farms let rooms or cottages, or have fields for tents or caravans. The Bureau will give you area lists of organisations and individual farms. You book direct with the farms. FMB publishes *Farm Holidays in Britain* (£1.95), available from bookshops and Tourist Information Centres.

Scottish Farmhouse Holidays, Drumtenant, Ladybank, Fife. KY7 7UG, T:0337-30451.

A pamphlet describes farms and crofts in all areas of Scotland which take guests for 2 nights or longer. The cost is £14 per night for evening meal, bed and breakfast. SFH can offer holiday insurance cover and car rental.

Forestry Commission, 231 Corstophine Road, Edinburgh EH12 7AT, T:031-334 0066.

The Forestry Commission lets modern forest cabins and holiday houses in Scotland, Cumbria, North Yorkshire and Cornwall. These sleep from 2-6 people and cost from about £60 a week in low season. They are also available for shorter periods and weekends. The Commission also runs over 30 camp and caravan sites all over Britain.

Higher Education Accommodation Consortium, 36 Collegiate Crescent, Sheffield S10 2BP, T:0742-683759.

HEAC is a group of 50 colleges and polytechnics that let residential accommodation in the vacation periods. A few rent rooms throughout the year and some have self catering flats. Arrangements can be made for handicapped people. Group facilities can sometimes also be provided. Charges vary but, as a very rough guide, average about £25 a head, self-catering. The basic price may sometimes include full or half board. Some of the centres organise special interest holidays, such as bridge weeks or painting classes. For further details, apply to the Consortium for its brochure.

Holimarine, 171 Ivy House Lane, Bilston, West Midlands WV14 9LD, T:09073-77235.

Holimarine runs self-catering holidays for the over-50s at their seaside holiday villages in England and Wales. The accommodation is in caravan homes, flats, villas or maisonettes, set in attractive grounds. Some are equipped for the handicapped. Facilities normally include: dancing, tennis, putting, darts, boating and fishing, restaurants, cafeterias and shops; and evening entertainment is sometimes arranged. Cost varies according to season, with a flat for two ranging from about £60 to £100 a week.

Landmark Trust, Shottesbrooke, Maidenhead, Berkshire, T:0628-82 5925.

The Trust owns houses of special architectural interest all over Britain. They tend to be quite expensive during the high season but are cheaper the rest of the year, when they can often be rented for less than a week. Sample prices are: £140 for a 6-bed mill in Derbyshire, during April; £170 for a 5-bed castle in Wales, in May or October. For further information, obtain the Landmark Trust book (price £2), which contains illustrations of all the properties.

Lee Abbey, Lynton, North Devon EX35 6JJ, T:0598-52621

Lee Abbey is a Christian Community which cares for the estate. Accommodation is either in the house or in self-catering units and, depending on the time of the year, visitors can stay for either a short break weekend or up to a fortnight. There is a Christian content to the holidays but guests can come and go – and be involved as much or as little – as they please. Costs vary according to season: a week in the summer is from about £110. There are reductions for clergy and their families.

National Trust Holiday Cottages

The National Trust lets some holiday properties in places of exceptional beauty: You write direct to the Organiser for details in the area that interests you.

Cornwall: Cornish Holiday Cottages, Lanhydrock Park, Bodmin.
Devon: The National Trust, Killerton House, Broadclyst, Exeter.
Dorset: Filcombe Farmhouse, Morcombelake, Bridport, Dorset DT6 6EP.
Gloucestershire: Snowshill Manor, Broadway WR12 7JU.
Hereford & Worcester: Hanbury Hall, Droitwich WR9 7EA.
Isle of Wight: The National Trust, 35 St. James Street, Newport.
The Lake District: Fell Foot Park, Newly Bridge, Ulverston, Cumbria LA12 8NN.
West Wales: The National Trust, 22 Alan Road, Llandeilo, Dyfed.
Somerset: Holincote Estate Office, Selworthy, Minehead.
Sussex: Scotney Castle, Lamberhurst.

Severn: The National Trust, 34-36 Church Street, Tewkesbury, Glos.

Yorkshire: Goddards, 27 Tadcaster Road, Dringhouses, York YO2 2OG.

Northern Ireland: The National Trust, Row Allane, Saintfield, Ballynahinch, Co.Down BT24 7LH.

North Wales: Trinity Square, Llandudno, Gwynedd LL30 2DC.

For cottages in Scotland, contact National Trust for Scotland, 5 Charlotte Square, Edinburgh EH2 4DU.

National Trust for the Welfare of the Elderly, 33 Hooke Road, Goole, North Humberside DN14 5JB, T:0405-3149

The Trust owns chalets and mobile homes along the north-east coast, and provides rent-assisted holidays to needy elderly people.

Pontin's Holidays, Compton House, St. Peter's Road, Bournemouth BH1 2NT, T:0202-295600.

Pontin's offer holidays for over-60s in England and Wales in chalets, caravans and self-catering units. These are described in their magazine *Greensleeves*. To give you an idea of price: a seaside chalet for 2 in Dorset costs from about £50-£165 a week depending on season.

Vacances en Campagne, Bignor, Nr. Pulborough, West Sussex RH20 1QD, T:07987-366.

Vacances en Campagne specialise in letting country houses in rural areas of France. Properties vary widely in size, amenities and price: from £77 a week for a studio flat in the low season to over £1,000 for a 4-bedroomed house, sleeping 8-10, with a swimming pool at the height of the summer.

Youth Hostels Association, Trevelyan House, St. Stephen's Hill, St. Albans, Herts, T:0727-55215, **Scottish YHA**, 7 Glebe Crescent, Stirling Central FK8 2JA, T:0786-72821.

Despite the name, most hostels welcome people of all ages. Membership is £5.50 a year or £55 for life membership. This gives you access to 260 hostels in England and Wales and to 5,000 more throughout the world. Hostels are simple and cheap; but also clean, tidy and comfortable. Beds are usually in single sex dormitories with communal washrooms. Most have a lounge and many have recreational facilities and a shop. Some provide meals, others are self-catering. Overnight charges vary according to the grade of hostel and its location; for example, the price range in London is from about £2.30 to £5. The *YHA Handbook* describes the hostels in England and Wales (£1.25). Membership of the Scottish YHA gives you the same access to hostels. To find out about hostelling abroad, contact **YHA Travel**, 14 Southampton Street, London WC2E 7HY.

P.S. Watch the Sunday newspapers. From about early January, the classified section begins to fill up with advertisements for rentals both in this country and overseas. Later in the season, this is the column to watch for slashed prices and other last minute bargains.

Special interest

This is the longest section – and a real mixed bag. It includes weekend courses and more formal summer schools, between them offering a huge range of subjects including: calligraphy, cooking, computer studies, ceramics, car maintenance, bell ringing, creative writing and many others. It also includes holidays in the more conventional sense, both in Britain and abroad, but with the accent on a hobby such as: bridge, folk dancing, chess, antiques, public speaking, model making and other pastimes. There are one or two pre-retirement courses and even religious interest holidays. They are impossible to categorise other than alphabetically because many of the organisations offer a veritable bran-tub of choices.

British Theatre Association, The Darwin Building, Regents Park, London NW1, T:01-387 2666.

The Association runs a summer school for people of all ages with little or no acting experience. Fee (£255 for BTA members, £260 for non-members) includes accommodation, meals and tuition. The course lasts a week. For a booklet on this and other training courses, write to the Association.

Centre for Alternative Technology, Machynlleth, Powys, Wales SY20 9A2, T:0654-2400

The Centre, set in a magnificent slate quarry overlooking Snowdonia National Park, exhibits the possibilities of living with alternative technology. There are displays of solar energy, windmills, water power and an organic vegetable garden. The Centre runs short residential courses including: renewable energy systems, organic and wildlife gardening, birds of Wales, healing herbs, philosophy and practical skills; and summer courses on the theory and practice of alternative technology. Accommodation is in 3-6 person bedrooms (and a few single rooms). Meals are eaten in the whole food restaurant. Fees range from £45 to £120; full board and tuition is included. For pensioners, there is a reduced charge. The courses are generally held at weekends – Friday evening to Sunday mid-day. The Centre also offers opportunities for voluntary work, for example: building, cooking, cleaning, typing and weeding. Volunteers pay £2.50 a day for bed and board in simple accommodation.

The Cookery Centre, 43 Norwich Avenue West, Bournemouth, Dorset BH2 6AJ, T:0202-293321.

The Centre runs 2-week and 11-week cookery courses. Cost is respectively £165 and £875 plus VAT. The 2-week course covers: soups, pate, fish, meat, poultry, vegetarian, pastry making and desserts. Accommodation can be arranged locally by the Centre.

Countrywide Holidays Association, Birch Heys, Cromwell Range, Manchester M14, T:061-225 1000.

Countrywide aims to provide warm hospitality, comfortable accommodation and sensible prices for holidays at home and abroad throughout the year. Many of the British based holidays include walking or offer other activities, such as: folk dancing, bridge, photography, literature, singing and skiing (in Scotland). The cost varies from about £55 for 5 days' winter walking to £96 for a week with coach excursions. There are special Vintage Holidays for people who enjoy more gentle walking and excursions. Holidays at CHA centres without a course cost £80 for a week's full board. These are also open for Christmas and New Year for traditional house parties, from about £90 for 4 days. People of pension age are offered a £10 reduction at the holiday centres, although not for special interest holidays. There are bargain offers on travel for those using British Rail. CHA holidays abroad include walking in Madeira, Christmas in Switzerland, exploring Israel or Cyprus, with prices varying from about £300 to £700.

Cox and King's Special Interest Holidays Ltd., 46 Marshall Street, London W1V 2PA, T:01-734 8291.

Led by qualified lecturers, Cox and King's special interest holidays include: botany and wild flower studies in Malta and the Dolomites; a Dutch garden tour; bird watching in Northern India; and painting in France, Switzerland and Italy. Prices, with travel and full board, vary from roughly £300 to £1,000.

Denman College (National Federation of Women's Institutes), Marcham, Abingdon, Oxfordshire OX13 6NW, T:0865-391219.

Denman College is the NFWI's residential adult education centre. It runs 200 courses for WI members and their husbands each year. These take place from Monday to Friday or over weekends and cost £24 a day with full board. Accommodation is in shared rooms (£4 supplement for single rooms). Courses cover such subjects as: guest house management, architecture, English ceramics, book illustration, caring for dependent relatives, attitudes to retirement, gardening, cookery, crafts, the police and society, music, French, poetry, Elizabethan life, birdwatching, women and money, health.

Earnley Concourse, Earnley, Chichester, Sussex PO20 7JL, T:0243-670392.

A residential centre near Chichester which holds weekend and week-long courses throughout the year on such subjects as: arts and crafts, music, drama, wildlife, computer studies, cookery, keep fit, yoga and others. Charges are about £25 a day for full board and tuition.

Highland Guides, Inverdruie, Aviemore, Inverness-shire PH22 1QH, T:0479-810729.

Organise Retirement Interest Holidays in the Cairngorms introducing outdoor pursuits and hobbies to be followed up at home. These include: bird and wildlife watching; rock, bog and pool gardening; gems and lapidary; and photography.

Highway Holidays, Avon Close, 95 Crane Street, Salisbury, Wiltshire SP1 2PU, T:0722-338733.

Highway Holidays specialise in religious interest holidays. These are organised in the UK, many parts of Europe, the Holy Land, Egypt and Jordan; with Mission Holidays further afield. The programme includes house parties for all ages in Scotland, the Peak District, Rutland, Wales and Lakeland. There are organised walks, coach tours, social activities and a time for shared Christian fellowship. Cost is about £105 a week, with full board. On the overseas front, a two week coach tour in Romania costs about £400 with return air travel and full board. A tour entitled 'In the Steps of St. Paul' across Turkey costs about £650 inclusive for 13 days. There is also a bird watching tour of the Holy Land. Mission Holidays go to such countries as Zambia and Malawi and combine sightseeing with visits to mission centres. Cost is about £1,700 for three weeks.

Holiday Fellowship Ltd., 142-4 Great North Way, London, NW1 1EG. T: 01-203 3381.

Holiday Fellowship organises hobby and special interest holidays at their centres in Britain and abroad. The choice of activities includes, among others: bowls, bridge, chess, scrabble, cycling, keep fit, yoga, fishing, golf, music making, dancing, painting, brass rubbing, china repairing, public speaking, calligraphy, writing, crafts, birdwatching, wildlife study, natural history, British heritage and industrial archaeology. A wine study week in France costs about £250, half board; a landscape painting fortnight in Brittany, around £370. There are also coach and minibus tours; walking holidays; and Special Harmony Weeks, designed as relaxing holidays especially suited to older people. These include some coach excursions and cost from about £90 a week, full board. The walking holidays range from easy walking, under 5 miles a day, to rock scrambling in Britain and abroad. A week on Exmoor costs about £125, full board; a week in Brittany, about £325.

Leisure Learning Ltd., Embassy Hotels, Station Street, Burton on Trent, Staffordshire DE14 1BS, T: 0283-66587.

There are about 50 Leisure Learning weekends each year based in Embassy Hotels in various parts of the country. Subjects include: canals of Britain, country gardens, photography, music, literature and fine china, among many others. Cost is about £75 inclusive for 3 nights.

Marlborough College Summer School, Marlborough, Wiltshire, SN8 1PA, T: 0672-53888.

Open in late July and August, the summer school offers a choice of about 70 weekly courses. Among the subjects are: landscape painting, pottery, textile crafts, picture framing, woodcrafts, public speaking, dancing, music, languages, cookery, computers, chess, bridge, natural history and various sports. Accommodation is in single rooms and dormitories and cost is from about £155 a week with full board. There are reductions for longer stays.

Millfield School Village of Education, Street, Somerset BA16 0XD, T:0458-45823.

The Village of Education operates during August, offering about 95 courses including: painting, pottery, car maintenance, tennis and other sports. There are special evening programmes for people of 55-plus and a pre-retirement course 'Preparation for Freedom'. Price for board and lodging and tuition are from £143 a week. There is a 10 per cent reduction for senior citizens and previous visitors.

National Institute of Continuing Education, 19b De Montford Street, Leicester LE1 7GE, T:0533 551 451.

Special interest weekend and summer school courses are offered by many colleges and universities throughout the country. Choice of subjects is enormous ranging from yoga to astronomy, creative writing to video techniques. Prices vary very roughly from about £20 to £30 a night, including full board and tuition. Probably the easiest way to find out what is available is to obtain a copy of *Residential Short Courses*, published twice a year by the National Institute. Price £1 inc. p&p.

Another very useful source is the **Adult Residential Colleges Association**, which is at the same address as the National Institute.

Old Rectory, Fittleworth, Pulborough, West Sussex RH20 1HU, T:079-882 306.

The programme is especially tilted at those approaching retirement age with the aim of creating new interests and opportunities. Typical courses, which last 3 to 7 days, include, painting, calligraphy, bridge, embroidery, singing, great estates, writing, clock repair, bell ringing, book binding, Spanish, stocks and shares. Prices range from about £35 for 2 nights to £125 for a week, plus VAT.

Pontin's Holidays, Compton House, St. Peter's Road, Bournemouth BH1 2NT, T: 0202-295600.

Organise Hobby and Leisure Holidays at 23 places in the UK and abroad. These include such activities as: Drama, Darts, Snooker, Badminton, Bridge, Bowling, Model Making, Antiques, Music, Dance, and Retirement Planning. Fees range from about £30 for 2 nights in the UK to £145 for a winter get fit week in Spain.

Saga Holidays Plc, P.O. Box 64, Folkestone, Kent. T:0303-30030.

Saga have recently introduced Summer Study holidays. These last a week and offer an attractive mix of lectures, excursions, leisure time and evening entertainment. The programme has included: Genealogy and Heraldry at Canterbury (about £160 with coach travel); Education in Great Britain (about £170 in Oxford); Life in Medieval London (about £185); and Antiques (in Plymouth, about £150). Study holidays with an outdoor theme have been: Mountains and Shores, in Wales; Scotland's Wild Life, in Dundee; and Discovering the West Country. Charges are all inclusive.

Workers' Education Association, Temple House, 9 Upper Berkeley Street, London W1H 8BY, T:01-402 5608.

The WEA runs weekend schools and residential summer schools at home and abroad. Participants are all ages from 18 to 80. Subjects cover a very wide range including: local history, literature, music appreciation and pre-retirement counselling. There are cultural visits to faraway places, for example India and China. Facilities are available on some of the courses for the disabled.

Useful reading

Activity and Hobby Holidays, published by the English Tourist Board, £1.99.

Sport

Holidays with on-site or nearby sporting facilities exist all over the country. However, if sport is the main objective of the holiday, it is often more difficult to know where to apply. The list that follows is limited to organisations that can advise you about organised residential courses or can offer facilities, rather than simply put you in touch with, say, your nearest tennis club. For wider information, see Chapter 7, which lists some of the many national sports associations.

Sports Council, 16 Upper Woburn Place, London WC1H 0QP, T:01-388 1277, **Scottish Sports Council**, 1 St. Colme Street, Edinburgh EH1 3SA, T:031-225 8411.

The Council publishes a list of opportunities for combining holidays with sport. Expert tuition is available on all courses. Some of the centres are suitable for disabled people and many welcome beginners. Cost varies according to accommodation, the activity you choose – and how long you stay. This can be a weekend or longer. All prices quoted are inclusive of full board. The programme covers a huge range. Among the more leisurely suggestions are: 5 nights' archery in Hampshire (£80); 6 nights' fishing, bird watching and fell walking in Cumbria (£115); 5 nights' orienteering, shooting and riding in Dorset (£70); 5 nights' walking, caving and camping in Devon (£90); pool/billiards, table tennis and putting in Suffolk (from about £15 a day). Some of the centres also run arts and crafts courses alongside the more active pursuits.

YMCA National Centre, Lakeside, Ulverston, Cumbria LA12 8BD, T:0448-31758.

Despite the youth connotation, the YMCA runs Adventure Holidays suitable for all ages including the over 60s. The activities include, among many others: sailing, pony trekking, canoeing, orienteering, abseiling, archery, country crafts and fell walking. The Centre is in a superb setting on Lake Windermere. The accommodation is simple with bunk beds and permanent tents. Cost for a week with full board is £105; £75 for 5 days.

Boating

One or two ideas for holidays afloat are included as well as organisations that offer serious sailing instruction.

National Sailing Centre, Arctic Road, Cowes, Isle of Wight, T:0983-295938.

Short sailing and canoeing courses are available from April to November. All standards are welcome, from beginners to those working for the RYA certificate. The cost is about £140 for 5 nights, including full board and tuition.

Royal Yachting Association, Victoria Way, Woking, Surrey GU21 1EQ, T:048-62 5022.

The RYA can supply you with a list of holiday centres, which offer approved courses.

Blakes Holidays Ltd., Wroxham, Norwich NR12 8DH, T:06053-3224.

Blakes hire yachts, cruisers and houseboats for holidays in various parts of Britain, Denmark, Holland and France. Basic tuition is provided for novices. Costs vary according to season, size and type of craft. For example, a week-end break on the Broads during the Spring and Autumn months costs around £100 for a couple; during the high season, prices are roughly double. Boats for 2-4 people in Holland start at about £200 a week. Pets are normally allowed on British holidays, at an extra cost of £12 weekly. For holidays abroad, Blakes will quote an inclusive price with travel arrangements.

Boat Enquiries, 43 Botley Road, Oxford, T:0865-727288.

A useful central point for hiring cruisers or narrow boats for enjoyment on the River Thames and also the Severn and Avon areas. Alternatively, you can book a cabin on a hotel boat complete with crew and catering.

A 2-4 berth cruiser costs from about £145 upwards a week, depending on the season. Hotel boat holidays cost about £195 a week, all inclusive.

British Waterways Board, Hire Cruiser Booking Office, Chester Road, Nantwich, Cheshire CW5 8LB, T:0270 625122.

The office hires boats on the canals around Nantwich and gives you all the necessary instruction before you set off. Will advise on less strenuous routes. Cost for a 4-berth boat is about £360 a week.

French Tourist Office, 178 Piccadilly, London W1, T:01-499 6911.

Can provide information about houseboats and other craft for hire in France.

Cricket

Otterburn Hall, Otterburn, Northumberland NE19 1HE, T:0830-20663.

Offers cricket holidays during August with tuition and matches. Beginners are welcome. £110 for 7 nights with half board.

Cycling

Cyclists' Touring Club, Cotterell House, 69 Meadrow, Godalming, Surrey GU7 3HS, T:04868-7217.

The CTC organises cycling tours in Britain and overseas for members and can also provide a great deal of extremely helpful information for cyclists wishing to organise their own holiday, including advice on accommodation and scenic routes. Organised U.K. cycle tours cost about £125 a week with full board. Overseas tours vary but examples include: about £435 for an 11 day cycle tour of the Holy Land, with an add-on week in Egypt; about £260 for 9 days in rural France. The CTC also offers members: insurance, a club magazine, handbook and introductions to local cycling groups. Membership costs £13 a year.

British Rail

Cycles are carried free on many trains. The service is described in British Rail leaflet *Bike it by Train*. Available from railway stations.

Golf

Many clubs will allow non-members to play on week-days when the course is less busy, on payment of a green fee. A telephone call to the Secretary before arrival is normally advisable. Best source of information for golfing holidays is the **Sports Council**, who run residential courses in conjunction with clubs or hotels, typically lasting 3 days or a week. Examples include **Windermere Golf Club** in Cumbria and **Ashlands House** in Crewkerne, Somerset. The Holiday Fellowship (see 'Special Interest' section above) includes golfing in its holiday programme. Further ideas are given in Tourist Board activity booklets.

Rambling

Rambling features on many special interest and other programmes as one of the options on offer. Two organisations that specialise in rambling holidays are:

Ramblers Holidays Ltd., 13 Longcroft House, Fretherne Road, Welwyn Garden City, Herts AL8 6PQ, T:077073-31133.
   A subsidiary of the Ramblers Association, Ramblers Holidays organise vacations for nature lovers, energetic sightseers and for those whose real interest is the scenery and exercise. Holidays are graded from about 5 hours a day to 9 hours hard mountain walking in, among other places: Austria, China, France, Greece, India, Nepal, New Zealand, Norway, Switzerland and Turkey. Prices start from about £400 for two weeks with full board.

Waymark Holidays, 295 Lillie Road, London SW6 7LL, T:01-385 5015.
   Spring and summer walking holidays graded to your level from about 4 hours a day in Austria, France, Germany, Greece, Greenland, Iceland, Italy, Malta, Norway, Portugal, Spain, Switzerland and Yugoslavia. Accommodation in hotels and guesthouses, mountain huts and, for some, tents. Cost for half board is from about £300 for 2 weeks depending on the country and time of year.

Skiing

Ski Club of Great Britain, 118 Eaton Square, London SW1W 9AF, T:01-245 1033.
   The Ski Club runs skiing holidays in France and Switzerland for over-50's who have some basic skiing experience. The cost is about £500 for 2 weeks for half board and travel. A volunteer leader accompanies each group and will ski with you and offer advice, if wanted.

For other sporting holidays see below under Tourist Boards and Highlands & Islands Development Council. Their publications list scores of suggestions for golfing, sailing and fishing holidays, pony trekking in Wales, skiing in Scotland and many others.

Working holidays

There is scope for volunteers who would like to engage in a worthwhile project during their holidays. Activities vary from, for example, helping with the handicapped to conservation work. In order to avoid repetition, only a couple of suggestions are listed here. For more information and ideas, see Chapter 10.

British Trust for Conservation Volunteers, St. Mary's Street, Wallingford, Oxon. T:0491-39766.

Anyone, from 16 to 75, who is prepared for hard work can become a Conservation Volunteer. The work might be anything from fencing sand dunes in Wales to touching up the chalk of one of the White Horses. Projects last 1-2 weeks and there are also weekend courses in countryside skills and leadership. The cost ranges from £20-£60 a week including board and lodging. Membership fee £8 (£14 for couples); £5.50 for unemployed.

Scottish Conservation Projects Trust, 70 Main Street, Doune, Perthshire FK16 6BW, T:0786-841479.

The Trust runs projects in various parts of Scotland through the summer months for skilled and unskilled volunteers. Type of work varies from conservation proper to jobs such as cooking and driving. The accommodation and food is simple. Cost is generally low and can be as little as £14 a week plus your fare.

TOC H, 1 Forest Close, Wendover, Aylesbury, Bucks HP22 6BT, T:0296-623911.

TOC H organises a number of projects which depend on volunteer help including for example: holidays for handicapped children, conservation work, the running of playschemes and work with the mentally handicapped. There is a £5 registration fee. Accommodation and other charges are generally very low. TOC H also organises special interest holidays near Oxford at an inclusive cost of about £70 a week.

Holidays for those needing special care

Over the past few years, facilities for the infirm and disabled have at last been improving. More hotels are providing wheelchairs and other essential equipment. Transport has become easier. Specially designed self-catering units are more plentiful and of a higher standard. As a result of these improvements, many disabled people can now travel perfectly normally, stay where they please and participate in the entertainment and sightseeing without disadvantage. This section lists general sources of advice plus one or two organisations that arrange special care holidays.

Travel and other information

If you need help getting on and off a train or plane, inform your travel agent in advance. Arrangements can be made to have staff and, if necessary, a wheelchair available to help you at both departure and arrival points. If you are travelling independently, you should ring the airline and/or local station master: explain what assistance you require, together with details of your journey in order that facilities can be arranged at any interim points, for example if you need to change trains.

A couple of useful free leaflets are:

British Rail & Disabled Travellers, available from mainline stations.

Care in the Air – advice for handicapped airline passengers, from: **Air Transport Users Committee**, 129 Kingsway, London WC2B GNN.

Highly recommended are two very comprehensive books, published by RADAR. Both are annual guides to accommodation and facilities available to disabled holidaymakers, one dealing with the UK, the other with travel overseas:

Holidays for Disabled People, £2, and *Holidays and Travel Abroad.* £1. Available from bookshops or direct from: **Royal Association for Disability and Rehabilitation**, 25 Mortimer Street, London W1N 8AB.

Another helpful publication is the *AA Travellers' Guide for the Disabled.* £2.25 from bookshops, free to members at AA Centres.

A useful organisation to contact could be:

The Holiday Care Service, 2 Old Bank Chambers, Station Road, Horley, Surrey RH6 9HW, T:0293-774 535.

This is a central reference point for information and advice on holiday opportunities in the UK and abroad for elderly and disabled people. The service is free. Details are available on accommodation, transport, escort services and possible sources of financial help.

Many local **Age Concern** branches are a mine of information. They can often put individuals in touch with organisations that assist with, say, transport; or that organise special care holidays, as do a number of Age Concern branches themselves. Age Concern also publishes a free fact sheet *Holidays for Elderly People*. See telephone directory for the address of your local branch or write to the headquarters: **Age Concern England**, 60 Pitcairn Road, Mitcham, Surrey.

Another source to contact is your local Social Services department. Some local authorities arrange holidays or give financial help to those in real need.

Examples of special holidays

Many voluntary organisations and others provide special holidays for those with a particular disability.

Arthritis Care, 6 Grosvenor Crescent, London SW1X 7ER, T:01-235 0902.
Runs holiday centres and self-catering flats adapted for people with rheumatism and arthritis. Holiday centres cost about £36 a week; flats, £30-£80 depending on the time of year.

British Association of the Hard of Hearing, Harmony Cottage, Newlandrig, Gorebridge EH23 4NS. T:0875-20278
Organises holidays in various resorts around Britain. Arrangements include: hotel booking, travel, insurance, coach tours or similar.

British Diabetic Association, 10 Queen Anne Street, London W1M 0BD, T:01-323 1531.
Diet and other special needs are catered for at holiday centres in such places as North Wales, the Isle of Wight and the Outward Bound Mountain School in Cumbria. Cost including full board is around £200 for a fortnight.

Out and About, 25 Constable Avenue, Eaton Ford, St. Neots, Cambridgeshire PE19 3RH, T:0480-217234.
Arranges escorted group holidays in UK and abroad which cater for people who have arthritis or have suffered from strokes. Please send sae for details.

Royal National Institute for the Blind, 224 Great Portland Street, London W1N 6AA, T:01-388 1266.
Has several seaside hotels, specially adapted for blind people. Additionally it can provide advice about suitable hotels, self-catering holidays, accommodation in London, outdoor activity holidays and educational holidays.

Threshold Travel, Wrendal House, 2 Whitworth Street West, Manchester M1 5WX, T:061-236 9763.
Specialises in providing world wide travel, including fly-drive and activity holidays – such as a safari in Kenya – for disabled people.

Winged Fellowship Trust, Angel House, Pentonville Road, London N1 9XD, T:01-833 2594.
Caters for people of all ages who would not otherwise have a holiday because of their disability, in well staffed, purpose-built centres. There is plenty of activity including: drama, crafts, music, photography and various sports, as well as theatre outings and other excursions. The Trust also organises holidays abroad. Cost is from about £275.

Other useful organisations

John Grooms Association for the Disabled, 10 Gloucester Drive, London N4 2LP, T:01-802 7272.

Multiple Sclerosis Society of Great Britain & Northern Ireland, 25 Effie Road, London SW6 1EE, T:01-381 4022.

National Trust for the Welfare of the Elderly, 33 Hook Road, Goole, North Humberside, T:0405-3149.

Chest, Heart and Stroke Association, Tavistock House North, Tavistock Square, London WC1H 9JE, T:01-387 3012

Parkinson's Disease Society of the UK Ltd., 36 Portland Place, London W1N 3DG, T:01-323 1174.

Royal National Institute for the Deaf, 105 Gower Street, London WC1E 6AH, T:01-387 8033.

Tourist boards

The English, Scottish and Wales Tourist Boards are the main sources of information for all aspects of holidays in their areas. They can advise about: accommodation, transport, highlights to see, special events and festivals, sporting facilities, special interest holidays – in short, almost everything you could possibly want to know. All produce excellent leaflets and guide books.

English Tourist Board, Thames Tower, Blacks Road, London W6 9EL, T:01-846 9000.
  Activity and Hobby Holidays (£1.99) and *England Holidays* (free).

Scottish Tourist Board, 23 Ravelston Terrace, Edinburgh EH4 3EU, T:031 332 2433.
  Scotland: 1001 Things to See (£2.50). Free brochures include: *Scotland: Where to Go and What to See* and *Surprising Scotland*.

Wales Tourist Board, Brunel House, 2 Fitzalan Road, Cardiff CF2 1UY, T:0222-499909.
  The Wales Holiday Brochure (free).

Highlands & Islands Development Board, Bridge House, 27 Bank Street, Inverness IV1 1QR, T:0463-234 171.

Performs a similar function to the tourist boards, with particular relevance to the Highlands and Islands area. There are Scottish Highland and Island travel passes which give you unlimited travel on public transport by train, bus, postbus and ferry. Cost is about £50 for 8 days off peak; and £70, peak periods.

Long-haul travel

Two organisations that can offer a great deal of practical information and help, as well as assist in obtaining low cost fares, if you are planning to travel independently.

Trailfinders Travel Centre, 42-48 Earls Court Road, London W8, T:01-937 9631.

Will work out an itinerary with you, obtain the necessary visas and arrange comprehensive insurance. Trailfinders also supply maps and travel guides and offer the facilities of a well stocked library.

Wexas, 45 Brompton Road, London SW3, T:01-589 0500.

As well as provide a comprehensive travel service for far distance independent holidaymakers, the World Expeditionary Association also organises Discoverers Trips to such places as the Peruvian Andes, Nile Valley, China and Iceland. Members receive *The Traveller's Handbook* and also regular magazine. Membership costs £17.58 (£21.45 for families).

Insurance

Even the best-laid holiday plans can go wrong. It is therefore only sensible to take out proper insurance cover before you depart. Many tour operators insist that, as a condition of booking, you either buy their inclusive insurance package; or alternatively, make private arrangements which are *at least as good*. While this suggests that they are demanding very high standards, terms and conditions vary greatly; so before signing on the dotted line, you should read the small print carefully to ensure that the package you are being offered meets all the eventualities *and* provides you with adequate cover should you make a claim. If you are travelling independently, if anything it is even more important to be properly insured, since you will not be protected by the normal compensation that the reputable tour operators provide, for claims for which they could be held liable in the event of a mishap. Holiday insurance should cover you for:

● personal accident leading to injury or death.
● medical expenses including: hospital treatment, cost of ambulance, emergency dental treatment plus expenses for a companion, who may have

to remain overseas with you should you become ill (see 'Medical Insurance' note).

- additional hotel and repatriation costs resulting from injury or illness.
- loss of deposit or cancellation: check what emergencies or contingencies this covers.
- cost of having to curtail your holiday because of serious illness in the family.
- compensation caused by travel delays.
- cover for baggage and personal effects and for emergency purchases should your baggage be delayed.
- cover for loss of personal money.
- personal liability cover, should you cause injury to another person or property.
- extra insurance in respect of your car, if you are taking it abroad (see 'Motoring Abroad' note).

When assessing the insurance you are being offered, it pays to do a bit of mental arithmetic. Although at first glance the sums look enormous, the likelihood is that should you have to claim you will end up being out of pocket. £500 or even £750 in respect of lost baggage might well be insufficient if, as well as your clothes, you had to replace your watch, camera and other valuables.

It is essential that you take the insurance documents with you as losses or other claims must normally be reported immediately. You will also be required to quote reference number and/or other details, given on the docket. Failure to report a claim within the specified time limit could nullify your right to compensation.

Be sure to get a receipt for any special expenses you incur – extra hotel bills, medical treatment, long distance phone calls and so on. You may not get all the costs reimbursed but if your insurance covers some or all of these contingencies, you will need to produce evidence of your expenditures.

The **British Insurance Association**, Aldermary House, Queen Street, London EC4N 1TU, publishes a free leaflet on holiday insurance, explaining the key points you should know in simple language.

The **Association of British Travel Agents**, 55-57 Newman Street, London W1P 4AH, operates a code of conduct for all tour operators who are members of ABTA and also runs a conciliation scheme to deal with complaints.

Medical insurance

This is one area where you should never skimp on insurance. Although many countries now have reciprocal arrangements with Britain for medical treatment, these vary greatly both in quality and generosity. Some treatments are free, as they are on the National Health Service; others, even in some EEC countries, may be charged for as if you were a private patient. The DHSS leaflet *Medical Costs Abroad* (SA 30) explains what is entailed and what forms you should obtain (such as certificate E111) before you depart.

However, even the very best reciprocal arrangements may not be adequate in the event of a real emergency; and they certainly will not cover you for any additional expenses you may incur, such as: the cost of having to prolong your stay; extra hotel bills if a companion has to remain with you; special transport home, should you require it, and so on. Additionally, since in an emergency you may need or want private treatment, you would be advised to insure for this – even if you are going to a country where good reciprocal arrangements exist.

As a general rule of thumb, the further from Britain you are going the higher the cover you need. This applies especially to third world countries, where the risk of falling ill is greater and where medical facilities away from the big towns may be basic in the extreme; and also to America, where the cost of medical treatment is literally astronomic.

Most insurance companies impose various terms and let-out clauses as a condition of payment. You should read these very carefully because, whereas some are obviously sensible, others may be very restrictive or, for whatever reason, you may not be able to satisfy the requirements: for example, if you have a chronic heart condition.

Although there is no upper age limit if you want to take out medical insurance, many companies request a note from a qualified medical practitioner stating that you are fit to travel if you are over 75.

Another common requirement is that the insured person should undertake not to indulge in any dangerous pursuits, which is fine in theory but in practice (depending on the company's interpretation of 'dangerous') could debar you from any activity that qualifies as 'strenuous'.

Motoring abroad

If you are taking your car abroad, you should contact your insurance company or broker well ahead of time to arrange special insurance cover. Alternatively, if you are a member of the AA or RAC, contact their overseas travel department who, in addition to providing insurance, have facilities for helping you abroad should you become stranded. Another well recommended organisation is **Europ Assistance**, 252 High Street, Croydon, Surrey.

Travel and other concessions

Buses, coaches, some airline companies and especially the railways offer valuable concessions to people of retirement age. Some of the best value savings which are available to anyone aged 60 are provided by British Rail. These include:

Senior Citizens Railcards. These come at two prices: £12 railcards and £7 railcards:

A £12 railcard entitles you to: ⅓ off saver tickets; ½ off cheap day and standard day returns; 10 per cent off some Golden Rail Holidays; £6 off Golden Rail Short Break Holidays. Additionally, you can travel with up to four children for £1 each.

A £7 railcard entitles you to ½ off cheap day and standard day returns. You can also travel with up to four children for £1 each.

Disabled Persons Railcard. This costs £12 and entitles the holder and companion accompanying him/her to reduced rates by train. Details and conditions are described in the British Rail brochure.

Rail Europe Senior Cards. Available to retired persons, who must be Senior Citizen Railcard holders. Cost is £5 and it entitles you to reductions of either 50 or 30 per cent (this varies from one country to another) on trains in most parts of Europe.

Sealink B & I and Hoverspeed. Reductions of up to 30 per cent are allowed to Senior Citizen Railcard holders.

Other useful train services include: the Intercity Motorail, Rail Rovers and Freedom of Scotland ticket. Senior and other railcards can be obtained from post offices, stations, British Rail travel centres; or, in the case of Rail Senior Europe Cards, also from Europe rail appointed travel agents. For further information, ask at the post office or station for leaflet *Senior Citizen Railcard*.

Overseas

Many countries offer reductions to retired holidaymakers and others, for example, on: internal flights, coach travel, entry to museums and galleries, day excursions, sporting events and other entertainment. As in Britain, provisions are liable to change and for up-to-date information probably the best source to contact is the national tourist office of the country to which you are travelling. Herewith, however, a flavour of reductions current at time of writing.

Austria: 30 per cent reductions on railways and rail buses; most museums and galleries are free at weekends.
Belgium: 50 per cent reductions on rail fares.
Denmark: cheap rate fares for retired people on some transport, when space

allows. Most museums offer pensioner discounts.

Eire: CIE Rambler Tickets give unlimited travel by rail and bus at discounted prices and there are also 50 per cent reductions off standard railway fares. Museums are free and most entertainments offer concessionary prices to people of retirement age.

Finland: There are 50 per cent reductions on both railway fares and on internal weekday Finnish airline flights; and also 30 per cent reductions on coaches for people over 65. Additionally, many museums offer reduced entrance charges.

France: Some rail fare reductions, lower entrance charges at most museums and also at some theatres and cinemas.

Greece: 50 per cent reductions on rail fares.

Hungary: 30 per cent reductions on rail fares.

Italy: 30 per cent reductions on rail fares.

Luxembourg: 50 per cent reductions on coaches, buses and railways.

Netherlands: 50 per cent discount on rail fares and also reduced prices on internal KLM flights; cheaper entrance charges at museums.

Norway: 30 per cent reductions on rail fares.

Portugal: 50 per cent reductions on rail fares.

Spain: 50 per cent reductions on rail fares; also concessionary entrance to museums.

Sweden: 50 per cent reductions on rail fares and some coaches; off peak flat rate fare for internal flights, concessionary entry to museums and entertainment.

Switzerland: 50 per cent reductions on national railway lines; plus various other travel and entrance charge concessions See *Season for Seniors*: details from the Swiss National Tourist Office.

Air Travel Advisory Board, T:01-636 5000; 01-832 2000.

Advises on low cost fares to all parts of the world. If you are looking for good value fares, it is well worth giving them a ring rather than shopping around. The Board can also provide information on hotels, villa rentals and car hire.

Health tips

Most are plain common sense – but worth repeating for all that.

- Remember to pack any regular medicines you require: even familiar branded products can be difficult to obtain in some countries.
- Take a mini first aid kit, including: plaster, disinfectant, tummy pills and so on. If you are going to any under-developed country, it is advisable to consult your doctor as to what pills (and any special precautions) you should take.

- One of the most common ailments among British travellers abroad is an overdose of sun. In some countries, it really burns, so take it easy, wear a hat and apply plenty of protective lotion.
- Travelling is tiring and a sudden change of climate more debilitating than most of us admit: allow plenty of time during the first couple of days to acclimatise before embarking on an activity programme that would exhaust a 17 year old.
- Have any innoculations or vaccinations well in advance of your departure date.
- The other big travellers' woe is 'Delhi belly', which unhappily can apply in most hot countries, including Italy and Spain. Beware the water, ice, salads, seafood, ice cream and any fruit which you do not peel yourself. Check with your doctor.
- When flying, wear loose clothes and above all comfortable shoes as feet and ankles tend to swell in the air. On long journeys, it helps to drink plenty of fruit juice and remember the warning that 'a drink in the air is worth two on the ground'. If you have a special diet, inform whoever makes your booking: most airlines, especially on long distance journeys, serve vegetarian food.
- Finally, the old favourite: don't drink and drive.
- DHSS Leaflet SA 35, *Protect your Health Abroad*, advises on what precautions to take and vaccinations that may be required. Available from any DHSS office.

Keep fit and have a wonderful holiday!

13. Caring for Elderly Parents

Most of us sooner or later have some responsibility for the care of elderly parents. Although an increasing number of people live well into their eighties and beyond, the vast majority manage with a little help to remain in their own homes rather than go into residential care. While there is no hiding the fact that with a very elderly person this can impose strains, most families cope exceedingly well. Moreover since the evidence shows that this is the undoubted preference of most older people themselves, the main bias of this chapter is towards helping aged parents remain as independent as possible.

Knowing what facilities are available, what precautions you can take against a mishap occuring and whom you can turn to in an emergency can make all the difference, both to you and to parents who may fear becoming a burden. Over the last few years provision has enormously improved and ranges from simple gadgets such as alarm systems which can buy peace of mind to full scale nursing care, should this become necessary.

A basic choice for many families is whether parents should move in with them or continue to live on their own. While the decision will depend on individual circumstances, in the early days at least the majority choice on all sides is generally in favour of 'staying put'. Although later in the chapter we cover sheltered housing, which some people see as the best of all worlds, an alternative solution to any move may be simply to adapt the home to make it safer and more convenient.

Ways of adapting a home

Many even quite elderly people will not require anything more complicated than a few general improvements, such as: better lighting, especially near staircases; a non-slip mat and grab-rail in the bathroom; safe heating arrangements; and perhaps the lowering of some kitchen and other units to place them within easy reach.

Another sensible plan worth considering is to convert a downstairs room into a bedroom and bathroom, in case managing the stairs should later become a difficulty. These and other common-sense measures are covered in more detail in Chapter 6.

For some people, however, such arrangements are not really sufficient. In the case of a physically handicapped or disabled person, more radical improvements will usually be required. Far from presenting a major problem as used to be the case, today these are normally fairly easy to organise.

Local authority help

Local authorities have a legal duty to help people with disabilities and, depending on what is required and the individual's ability to pay, may assist with the cost.

Your parents can either approach their GP or contact the Social Services Department direct. A sympathetic doctor will be able to: advise what is needed; supply any prescriptions such as for a medical hoist; suggest which unit or department to approach; and can make a recommendation to the housing department, should rehousing be desirable.

The Social Services Department can supply kitchen, bathroom and other aids for the home, arrange an appointment with an occupational therapist and support an application for a housing grant, should major adaptations be required.

If only relatively small changes are necessary, e.g. a hand-rail on the stairs or ramp for a wheelchair, the occupational therapist may arrange for these to be done by the local authority. This can take months however, so if your parents cannot wait and want the work done privately, the OT will give you names of local firms.

Housing grants

There are two types of grant available, in the event of major adaptations being required: intermediate grant and improvement grant. Council tenants should apply to the Housing Department; owner occupiers and private tenants, to the Environmental Health Department.

Intermediate Grant. In most circumstances, this is available *as of right* if a home lacks one or more basic amenities such as an indoor lavatory, bathroom or running hot water. However, it also applies if an individual's disability prevents them from using an existing amenity, for example, if they cannot get upstairs to the bathroom. In these circumstances, the grant could be applied for to enable major alterations such as the installation of a lift. If approved, the grant will cover up to 90 per cent of the cost of the work, with the following ceilings: London, £3,005 (or up to £4,200 if repairs are involved); elsewhere, £2,275 (or up to £3,000 if repairs are involved).

Improvement Grant. This grant is discretionary and is generally intended to assist with extensive alterations to upgrade property. The local authority has the power to give it for adapting accommodation for disabled people but does not have a duty to do so. Applications that might succeed include: altering doors and windows together with fitting suitable handles; installing fixed ramps or equipment such as an entry phone system; altering electrical switches and sockets and providing suitable fixed heating appliances. The grant covers up to a maximum of 90 per cent of the cost of alterations with the following ceilings: London, £13,800; elsewhere, £10,200. For further information about grants, see Chapter 6.

Other sources of help

The Disabled Living Foundation, 380-384 Harrow Road, London W9 2HU, T:01-289 6111.

This is a charitable trust concerned with all forms of disability and handicap, including infirmities of age. As well as running an advisory service, it has an *Aids and Equipment Centre* on site which is a permanent exhibition where aids of all kinds can be seen, demonstrated and tried out by visitors. The range includes: special equipment for the bathroom, kitchen, bedroom and living room; hoists, wheelchairs and gadgets to assist reading and writing. None of the items are for sale but the Centre can provide leaflets, a list of suppliers and prices. Qualified therapists are available to show visitors round and, although anyone can pop in, it is normally advisable to make a prior appointment if assistance is likely to be wanted. Opening hours are: 9.30am to 5.00pm, Mondays to Fridays.

The Royal Association for Disability and Rehabilitation (RADAR), 25 Mortimer Street, London W1N 8AB, T:01-637 5400.

RADAR can help and give advice across a very wide spectrum, including: welfare services, access and mobility issues, holidays, employment and housing. In particular, it welcomes enquiries about the best way of adapting a home and publishes a useful monthly bulletin.

Both the **British Red Cross** and **Age Concern** (see local telephone directory) can loan equipment in the short term and can usually advise on local stockists. Larger branches of Boots, for example, sell a wide range of special items for the disabled, including: bath aids, tableware, grips and wheelchairs.

Homecraft of London, 27 Trinity Road, London SW17 7SF, T:01-672 7070. Stocks a very wide variety of practical equipment to help older people cope with everyday life including: 'reachers' (to help lift down items beyond reach), stair rails; bed raisers; bath seats and kitchen aids, such as tin openers and tap turners as well as special gardening utensils. There is a also a mail order service.

Another useful organisation to know about is the **Centre on Environment for the Handicapped**, 35 Great Smith Street, London SW1P 3BJ, T:01-222

7980. It runs an architectural advisory service and can recommend local architects with experience of designing for the disabled. When writing, you should give broad details of the type of work required. The Centre can also let you have a set of 9 housing design sheets (£2.50) and a practical consumer guide, *Buying or Adapting a House or Flat* £1.

British Telecom supplies some 70 devices to assist those with hearing difficulties, visual handicap, impaired mobility and other problems that make using a telephone more difficult. For details see *British Telecom's Guide to Equipment and Services for Disabled Customers*, available from local BT offices. A home visit can sometimes be arranged for those who are housebound. For further information, dial 100 and ask the operator for Freefone sales.

Other sources of advice include:

Scottish Council on Disability, Princes House, 5 Shandwick Place, Edinburgh EH2 4RG, T:031-229 8632.

Northern Ireland Council for the Handicapped, 2 Annadale Avenue, Belfast BT7 3JH. Information Service, T:0232-649 555.

Wales Council for the Disabled, Bedwas Road, Caerphilly CF8 3SL, T:0222-887 325.

Useful reading

Equipment for the Disabled. A series of 14 books which give full details of the wide range of available equipment and self-help devices for those with a disability. Available from Mary Marlborough Lodge, Nuffield Orthopaedic Centre, Headington, Oxford OX3 7LD, T:0865-750103. Price £3.95 for each book.

Staying Put, published by Age Concern in association with Anchor Housing Trust, explains how remaining in your own home in retirement has been made easier thanks to various government grants and other help. Staying Put schemes are also listed. Price 55p (inc. p&p) from Marketing Department, Age Concern England, 60 Pitcairn Road, Mitcham, Surrey CR4 3LL.

Alarm systems

Alarm systems have become very much more widespread in recent years. The knowledge that help can be summoned very quickly in the event of an emergency is not only reassuring in its own right but in practical terms can enable many elderly people to remain independent far longer than would otherwise be sensible. Some local authorities have alarm systems that now allow people living in their own homes to be linked to a central control. Types of alarm vary greatly. Some have a telephone link, enabling personal contact to be made; others simply signal that something is wrong. In other areas, a relative or friend who has been nominated will be alerted; or sometimes, the police. To find out whether your parents' local authority operates such a system, contact the Social Services department.

Commercial firms

A number of firms install and operate alarm systems. Price, installation cost and reliability can vary quite considerably. For general advice plus a list of firms, contact the **Disabled Living Foundation**, 380-384 Harrow Road, London W9 2HU.

Piper Lifeline

One system, approved by Help the Aged, is the 'Piper Lifeline'. Manufactured by Tunstall Telecom Ltd., it operates on the public telephone network and can be used by anyone with a direct telephone line. Grants may be available in some cases to meet part of the equipment charges. For further information, contact: **The Lifeline Appeal**, Lifeline Department, Help the Aged, Freepost, London EC1B 1BD. Or telephone 01-253 0253 and ask for the Lifeline Office.

Main local authority services

Quite apart from any assistance with housing, local authorities supply a number of services which can prove invaluable to an elderly person. The two most important are Meals on Wheels and Home Helps. Additionally, there are social workers and various specialists concerned with aspects of health.

Meals on wheels

The meals on wheels service is sometimes run by local authorities direct and sometimes by voluntary organisations, such as the Women's Royal Voluntary Service or the British Red Cross, acting as their agents. As you will know, the purpose is to deliver a hot lunch to individuals in their own home. Different arrangements apply in different areas and schemes variously operate from two to seven days a week. Cost also varies: from 35p to £1.15 a day, with the norm about 65p. For further information, contact the Social Services Department or your local Citizens Advice Bureau.

Home helps

Local authorities have a legal obligation to run a Home Help service to help frail and housebound elderly people with such basic household chores as shopping, tidying up, a little light cooking and so on. In many areas the service is overstretched, so the amount of help actually available varies considerably, as does the method of charging. In some authorities, people are means-tested on their ability to pay; in others the service is free. Sometimes, there is a charge per number of visits; sometimes, a flat rate weekly charge, ranging from 50p to about £2.50. Apply through the Social Services department. Some of the larger authorities have a special telephone number which may be listed either as 'Home Help Services' or 'Domiciliary Services'.

Specialist helpers

Local authorities employ a number of specialist helpers, variously based in the Social Services Department or Health Centre, who are there to assist.

Social Workers. Normally the first people to contact if you have a problem. They can put you in touch with the right person, if you require a Home Help, Meals on Wheels, have a housing difficulty or other query and are not sure whom to approach. Often, even if ultimately it is the responsibility of another department, a social worker may come and discuss the matter with you – or with your parents direct. You should ring the local Social Services Department; in Scotland, this is normally referred to as the Social Work Department.

Occupational Therapists. Have a wide knowledge of disability and can assist a handicapped person via training, exercise, or access to aids, equipment or adaptations to the home. Ring the Social Services Department.

Health Visitors. Qualified nurses with broad knowledge both of health matters and of the various services available through the local authority. Rather like social workers, health visitors can put you in touch with whatever specialised facilities are required. Contact through the local Health Centre.

District Nurses. Fully qualified nurses who will visit a patient in the home: change dressings, attend to other routine nursing matters, monitor progress and help with the arrangements if more specialised care is required. Contact through the Health Centre.

Physiotherapists. Use exercise and massage to help improve mobility and strengthen muscles, for example after an operation or to alleviate a crippling condition. Normally available at both hospitals and health centres.

Medical Social Workers. In the old days, used to be known as almoners. Are available to consult, if patients have any problems – whether practical or emotional – on leaving hospital. MSWs can advise on coping with a disablement, as well as such practial matters as transport, after-care and other immediate arrangements. Work in hospitals and an appointment should be made before the patient is discharged.

Good neighbour schemes

A number of local authorities have an organised system of good neighbour schemes. In essence, these consist of individuals contracting with the authority to act as good neighbours to one or several elderly people living close by. Depending on what is required, they may simply pop in on a daily basis to check that everything is all right; or they may give more sustained assistance such as providing help with dressing, bathing, shopping or preparing a light meal. In some authorities, the service may largely be run by volunteer organisations. In others 'Good Neighbours' are paid by the authority, according to the number of hours they commit. To find out whether such a scheme exists locally, enquire at the Social Services Department or at your Citizen's Advice Bureau.

Key voluntary organisations

Voluntary organisations complement the services provided by statutory health and social services in making life easier for elderly people living at home. The range of provision varies from area to area but can include:

- lunch clubs
- day centres and clubs
- aids such as wheelchairs
- transport
- good neighbour schemes
- advice and information
- holidays and short term placements
- friendly visiting
- odd jobs and decorating
- gardening
- prescription collection
- family support schemes

The particular organisation providing these services depends on where you live but the Citizen's Advice Bureau will be able to advise you whom to contact. The following are the key agencies:

Age Concern Groups may provide any or all of the voluntary services listed above.

Most groups recruit volunteers to do practical jobs and provide friendship. They also give advice and information and when necessary refer enquirers to a more appropriate agency. Their addresses and telephone numbers are in the local phone book. Alternatively you can telephone **Age Concern Greater London**, T:01-737 3456, for London addresses; or contact the national headquarters for addresses outside the capital:

Age Concern England, 60 Pitcairn Road, Mitcham, Surrey CR4 3LL, T:01-640 5431. **Age Concern Scotland**, 33 Castle Street, Edinburgh, T:031-225 5000.
Age Concern Wales, 1 Park Grove, Cardiff, South Glamorgan, T:0222-371821/371566.
Age Concern Northern Ireland, 128 Great Victoria Street, Belfast 2, T:0232 245729.

Women's Royal Voluntary Service runs a number of invaluable services:

- meals on wheels
- lunch clubs
- day centres
- crisis support for 24-48 hours
- day and night sitting
- books-on-wheels
- transport
- home visiting
- shopping outings

Look in the phone book for the address of the local office or contact the national headquarters: **WRVS**, 17 Old Park Lane, London W1, T:01-499 6040.

British Red Cross Society supplies some important services to elderly people free of charge. The principal ones include:

- acting as a link between hospital and home (before admission and after discharge)
- visiting
- escorting sick, handicapped or frail people when travelling
- loaning medical equipment for patients at home, e.g. wheelchairs and commodes
- after care and home visiting (including practical help in such tasks as hair washing, shopping, changing library books)
- sitting-in with elderly and handicapped people
- providing transport for the housebound
- organising stroke clubs
- 'signposting' sick and handicapped people towards the statutory service by which their needs may best be met.

The following activities are also carried out by the Red Cross in co-operation with or on behalf of statutory authorities:

- clubs
- lunch clubs
- day centres
- Christmas shopping
- holiday homes for the handicapped
- short-stay homes
- 19 retirement homes in England and one in Scotland.

To contact your local British Red Cross Society branch, see telephone directory, or write to: **The British Red Cross Society**, 9 Grosvenor Crescent, London SW1X 7EJ, T:01-235 5454.

St. John Ambulance comprises a quarter of a million volunteers who are examined annually in first aid; and sometimes nursing as well. They help in hospitals and will also come to people's homes to assist with various practical tasks such as shopping, staying with an elderly person for a few hours or providing transport to and from hospital. It is emphasised however, that the kind of help which the volunteers can provide (if any) varies enormously from county to county and depends on the local resources available. In some areas loan of equipment, such as wheelchairs, can be arranged. St. John have now started to give advice on caring and run courses locally for carers looking after elderly people. Anyone wishing to enlist the help of St. John Volunteers should contact their *County* headquarters: ask your local Citizens Advice Bureau for the address, see telephone directory or enquire at the London headquarters:

St. John Ambulance, 1 Grosvenor Crescent, London SW1X 7EF, T:01-235 5231.

Other sources of help and advice

Counsel & Care for the Elderly, 131 Middlesex Street, London E1 7JF, T:01-621 1624.

Provides a free confidential advisory and counselling service, which is used by thousands of elderly people and their relatives each year. Some matters can only be dealt with by caseworkers attached to the London office. However, where personal contact is required, CCE will refer enquirers to appropriate local organisations. Grant aid can sometimes be given to elderly invalids in need of nursing care. Additionally CCE supplies free information sheets on accommodation and other subjects. For further details, write to the above address (large sae is appreciated).

Central Council for Jewish Social Services, 212 Golders Green Road, London NW11 9DW, T:01-458 3282.

CCJSS is an umbrella organisation for Jewish Social Services in the country and has 45 affiliated member organisations. Services for elderly Jewish people in London and the South East are carried out by the Jewish Welfare Board, located at the same address. Principal facilities include:

Kosher Meals Service, run by the JWB on the same lines as Meals on Wheels. It operates in: City of Westminster, Tower Hamlets, Muswell Hill and Highgate, Enfield, Barnet, Brent, Chelsea and Kensington, Lambeth and Watford. Charges range from 40p to 90p per meal. Enquire through the local authority Social Services Department.

Day Centres, of which there are four in the London area for elderly or handicapped Jewish people. Individuals are sometimes referred by a hospital but can apply direct and will be invited to be a guest for one or two days. Charges range from 55p to £1.90 a day.

Other services include domiciliary care, hostels and a day care centre for those recovering from mental illness. There are also 12 residential homes in London and the South East.

Outside London, contact: **Leeds Jewish Welfare Board**, 311 Stonegate Road, Leeds LS17 6AZ, T:0532-684211. **Manchester Jewish Social Services**, 12 Holland Road, Manchester M8 6NP, T:061-795 0024. **Brighton & Hove Jewish Welfare Board**, c/o 2 Modena Road, Hove, E. Sussex, T:0273-722523. **Merseyside Jewish Representative Council**, Rex Cohen Court, Liverpool 17, T:051-733 2292.

Help the Aged, St. James's Walk, London EC1R 0BE, T:01-253 0253.

Although primarily a fund-raising organisation to assist projects of benefit to elderly people such as rehabilitation units, minibus services, housing repair schemes and many others, Help the Aged runs a telephone information service and can put enquirers in contact with an appropriate local organisation. Also publishes the monthly magazine *YOURS*, available from bookstalls, 25p.

Civil Service Retirement Fellowship, 1b Deals Gateway, Blackheath Road, London SE10 8BW, T:01-691 7411.

The Fellowship has an extensive network of branches and local groups throughout the country which offer a wide range of social activities for retired civil servants and their families. It also runs a home visiting service for those who are housebound or living alone.

Disability Alliance Era, 25 Denmark Street, London WC2H 8NS, T:01-240 0806.

Provides an advice service by telephone and letter. Also publishes a regularly up-dated *Disability Rights Handbook* which is packed with information on benefits and services for all people with disabilities and their families. Price: £2.60.

Transport

The difficulty of getting around is often a major problem for elderly and disabled people. In addition to the services run by voluntary organisations already mentioned, there are a couple of very useful publications highlighting facilities and services all over the country:

Door to Door, produced by the Department of Transport, includes sections on: individual personal transport schemes, community buses, social care schemes, local and health authority transport, coaches, air and sea travel and many others. Free from the **Department of Transport**, Door to Door Guide, Freepost, Victoria Road, South Ruislip, Middlesex HA4 0NZ; or from your local Social Services Department.

Travelling with British rail: A Guide for Disabled People. Gives details of accessible facilities at over 400 British Rail stations. Published by RADAR (see below) or available from W.H. Smith. Price £2.80.

Radar Mobility Factsheets. There are 10 different factsheets, covering a wide range of topics including: Mobility Allowance, Motoring with a Wheelchair, Motoring Accessories and a list of Hand Control Manufacturers. 17p each with sae from RADAR, 25 Mortimer Street, London W1N 8AB, T:01-637 5400.

London Taxi Card Service. A scheme whereby disabled people can incur taxi fares up to £6 but only pay £1. Leaflets and application forms are obtainable from any London post office.

See also below under 'Mobility Allowance'.

Holidays

Many people in their late seventies and older travel across the world, go on activity holidays, see the great sights in this country and abroad without any more difficulty than anyone else. They will find ideas galore in Chapter 12, including information about how to obtain assistance at airports and railway stations. However, some elderly people, especially those who are in any way disabled, need special facilities if a stay away from home is to be possible. A number of organisations can help.

Holiday Care Service, 2 Old Bank Chambers, Station Road, Horley, Surrey RH6 9HW, T:02934-774 535.
    Runs an information service providing details of holiday facilities, both in the UK and abroad, for people with special needs including the disabled and frail

elderly. Advice on possible sources of financial assistance can also be supplied. The service is free.

John Grooms Association for the Disabled, 10 Gloucester Drive, London N4 2LP, T:01-802 7272.
Owns a range of self-catering accommodation and two seaside hotels (one of which was the winner of the British Tourist Authority Award for Facilities for Disabled Visitors) that are specially adapted to cater for wheelchairs and other requirements of the disabled. Most holidaymakers come with their families or a companion. Special care, although not generally provided, is offered at one or two of the venues.

A number of the specialist voluntary organisations run holiday centres or provide specially adapted self-catering accommodation. In some cases, outings and entertainment are offered; in others, individuals plan their own activities and amusement. Guests needing assistance usually need to be accompanied by a companion, although in a few instances care arrangements are inclusive. Most of the organisations can advise about the possibility of obtaining a grant or other financial assistance. For further details, contact the following:

Arthritis Care, 6 Grosvenor Crescent, London SW1X 7ER, T:01-235 0902.

Multiple Sclerosis Society, 25 Effie Road, London SW6 1EE, T:01-381 4022.

Chest, Heart and Stroke Association, Tavistock House North, Tavistock Square, London WC1H 9JE, T:01-387 3012.

Royal National Institute for the Blind, 224 Great Portland Street, London W1N 6AA, T:01-388 1266.

Royal National Institute for the Deaf, 105 Gower Street, London WC1E 6AH, T:01-387 8033.

Parkinson's Disease Society, 36 Portland Place, London W1N 3DG, T:01-323 1174.

There are also several extremely useful publications, listing a wide choice of holiday venues, where disabled travellers can go in the normal way but with the advantage of having special facilities provided.

AA Travellers' Guide for the Disabled. Lists over 400 hotels, guest houses, inns and other accommodation suitable for those confined to wheelchairs together with details of some European tours suitable for handicapped people. £2.25 from bookshops (free to members at AA Centres).

Holidays for Disabled People. £2.
Holidays and Travel Abroad. £1.
Both available from RADAR, 25 Mortimer Street, London W1N 8AB.

Golden Rail Holidays Brochure indicates a number of hotels with special facilities for physically handicapped guests. Available free from most travel agents, main railway stations and BR travel centres.

Finally, a number of organisations provide rent-assisted (or sometimes, free) holidays for the financially needy. Local **Citizens Advice Bureaux**, **Age Concern** groups and county branches of the **British Red Cross Society** will often know what, if anything, is available to residents in the area. Additionally, the **National Trust for the Welfare of the Elderly** may have space at one of their chalets or mobile homes. Contact the Trust at: 33 Hook Road, Goole, North Humberside, T:0405-3149.

Power of attorney

Around the late 60s, many perfectly fit men and women wonder whether it might be sensible to give power of attorney to someone they trust. This involves authorising another person to take business and other decisions on their behalf, on the basis that any such decisions would reflect the action that they themselves would have taken.

Until very recently, the power was only valid where the individual was *unwilling rather than incapable* of acting for himself. So in effect just at the time when the power was most needed it ceased to exist. However, thanks to a new law, the Enduring Powers of Attorney Act, the power is not automatically revoked by any subsequent mental incapacity but can now continue, regardless of any decline, throughout the individual's life.

To protect the donor and the family, the Act clearly lays down certain principles which must be observed; and furthermore calls for the power to be formally registered, with both sides signing a declaration that they understand the various rights and duties involved.

As any lawyer would explain, the right time to give power of attorney is when the individual is in full command of his or her faculties, so that potential situations that would require decisions can be properly discussed and the donor's wishes made clear.

There are two ways of drawing up a power of attorney: either through a solicitor; or by buying a standard form published by the **Solicitors Law Stationery Society**. Available from the Society at Oyez House, 237 Long Lane, London SE1 4PU, or from Oyez shops. It is sensible for people without a legal background to consult a solicitor.

Temporary living-in help

Elderly people living alone can be more vulnerable to 'flu and other winter ailments. They may have a fall; or, for no apparent reason, may go through a period of being forgetful and neglecting themselves. Equally, as they become older, they may not be able to cope as well with managing their home or caring for themselves. In the event of an emergency or if you have reason for concern – perhaps because you are going on holiday and will not be around to keep a watchful eye – engaging living in help can be a godsend. Most agencies tend inevitably to be on the expensive side, although in the event of a real problem often represent excellent value for money. A more unusual and interesting possibility is to recruit the help of a Community Service Volunteer.

Community Service Volunteers, 237 Pentonville Road, London N1, T:01-278 6601.

The Volunteers are young people, mostly between 18 and 22, involved in community service through a range of nationwide projects. CSV's *Independent Living Scheme* matches full-time helpers with individuals and families who need a high degree of support. The volunteers are untrained and work for periods of four to six months, usually away from home. They take their instructions from the people for whom they are working but are not of course substitutes for professional carers. In general, they provide practical assistance in the home including, for example: shopping, light cooking, tidying up, attending to the garden and sometimes also decorating jobs. Usually a care scheme is set up through a social worker, who supervises how the arrangement is working out. Volunteers are placed on a one month's trial basis. People using the services are invoiced monthly (in case of real financial need, the social worker would assess whether the local authority could pay the costs). Charges include: fares; accommodation; full board or a weekly food allowance of £18.50; pocket money of around £15.25 a week; plus one week's paid holiday, after four months. There is also a monthly placement fee of £68. Contact your parents' local Social Services Department; or approach CSV direct, at the address given above.

Agencies

The agencies listed specialise in providing temporary help, rather than permanent staff. Charges vary, but in addition to the weekly payment, there is normally an agency booking fee. As a rule payment is gross, so your parents will not be involved in having to work out tax or national insurance.

Consultus, 17 London Road, Tonbridge, Kent, T:0732-355231

Country Cousins, 10a Market Square, Horsham, West Sussex RH12 1EU, T:0403-61960

Easymind, 3 Oakshade Road, Oxshott, Surrey, T:037284-2087.

Minders, 33 St.George Street, London W1, T:01-499 8929/4714.

Domestic Aid Services, 32 Pope Road, Bromley, Kent, T:01-464 5317.

Universal Aunts Ltd., 250 King's Road, London SW3 5UE, T:01-351 5767.

For a further list of agencies, see Yellow Pages under 'Domestic' or 'Domestic Staff'.

Nursing care

If one of your parents needs regular nursing care, their doctor may be able to arrange for a community or district nurse to visit them at home. This will not of course be a sleeping-in arrangement but simply involves a qualified nurse calling round when necessary.

If you want more concentrated home nursing you will have to go through a private agency. Both *Consultus* and *Domestic Aid Services* (see above) can sometimes supply trained nurses. Additionally, there are many specialised agencies, which can arrange daily or resident nurses on a temporary or longer term basis. Terms of employment vary considerably. Some nurses will literally only undertake nursing duties – and nothing else; and may even expect to have their meals provided. Others will do light housework and act as nurse-companions. Fees are pretty hefty. The British Nursing Association, which is claimed to be the largest nursing agency in Europe, quotes £4.79 an hour (weekdays) or £259 for a Monday to Sunday week, excluding VAT on the commission. The fees for nursing auxiliaries and care attendants are: £3.87 an hour, weekdays; £217 for a full week. Private health insurance can sometimes be claimed against part of the cost but this is generally only in respect of qualified nurses, not auxiliaries and care attendants. Address of the BNA is:

British Nursing Association, 3rd Floor, 443 Oxford Street, London W1R 2NA, T:01-629 9030.

For other addresses, see Yellow Pages under 'Nursing Agencies'.

Permanent living-in help

There may come a time when you feel that it is no longer safe to allow one of your parents to live entirely on their own. One possibility is to engage a companion or housekeeper on a permanent basis but such arrangements are normally very expensive: the going rate for housekeepers in London is anything between £70 and £150 a week clear. However, if you want to investigate the idea further, many domestic agencies (see the Yellow Pages) supply housekeeper-companions. Alternatively, you might consider advertising in *The Lady*, which is probably the most widely read publication for these kinds of posts.

Au pairs are cheaper: roughly £20 to £25 a week with full board and lodging. A drawback, however, is that most au pairs speak inadequate English (at least when they first arrive); and, as they are technically students living 'en famille', they must by law be given plenty of free time to attend school and study.

An alternative solution for some families is to engage a reliable daily woman who, in the event of illness or other problem, would be prepared to stay overnight.

Although any of these suggestions *can* work extremely well, most families find them either too expensive or haphazard – or both. So sooner or later the decision may come down to a choice between residential care and inviting a parent to live with you. Most families, to their credit, choose to care for an elderly parent in their own home; or sometimes, particularly in the case of a daughter, to move into their parents' home.

Practical help for carers

If your parent is still fairly active – visits friends, does her own shopping, enjoys some hobby which gets her out and about – the strains and difficulties may be fairly minimum. This applies particularly if your home lends itself to creating a 'granny flat', so everyone can retain some privacy and your parent can continue to enjoy maximum independence. However, this is not always possible and in the case of an ill or very frail person far more intensive care may be required.

If you have to go out to work, need time to attend to other responsibilities or quite understandably feel that if you are to remain human you must have time for your own interests, it is important to know what help is available and how to obtain it.

The many services provided by local authorities and voluntary agencies, described earlier in the chapter, apply for the most part equally to an elderly person living with their family as to one living alone. If there is nothing in the list that solves a particular problem you may have, it is sensible to talk to the Citizens Advice Bureau and Social Services department, as there may be some special local facility that could provide the solution.

In particular, you might ask about *day centres and clubs*. Activities and surroundings vary, so you might wish to investigate. However, a responsible person will always be in charge and transport, to and from the venue, is often provided. You could also ask the local Age Concern group and WRVS. These organisations will also be able to tell you about the possibility of *voluntary sitters*: people who come in and stay with an elderly person for a few hours (or sometimes overnight), to prevent them being on their own. Other sources to try include: the local Red Cross, St. John Ambulance and the Volunteer Bureau (see local telephone directory).

Another service well worth knowing about are *Crossroads Care Attendant Schemes*. This is a national organisation which arranges for attendants to care for very frail or disabled people in their own home, while the regular carer is away. They will come in during the day, or stay overnight, and provide whatever practical help is required. Arrangements are planned very much on an individual basis and are tailored to meet particular family circumstances. There is no charge but donations are welcome. Demand for the service is very high, so priority is given both according to the degree of disability and to the strain imposed on the carer. Both the CAB and Social Services department should be able to give you the address of the local branch. Alternatively, you could contact Crossroads direct:

Association of Crossroads Care Attendant Schemes: 94 Coton Road, Rugby, Warwickshire CV21 4LN, T:0788-73653; 24 George Square, Glasgow G2 1EG, T:041-226 3793; Unit 8, Comber Road Industrial Estate, Newtownards, Co. Down, and 87 University Street, Belfast BT7 1DL, T:0232-231105.

Holidays

There are various schemes to enable families with an elderly relative to go on holiday alone or simply to enjoy a respite from their caring responsibilities.

A number of local authorities run *fostering schemes*, on similar lines to child fostering. Elderly people are invited to stay in a neighbour's home and live in the household as an ordinary family member. Lasting relationships often develop. There may be a charge or the service may be run on a voluntary basis (or paid for by the local authority). Schemes are patchy around the country. The CAB and Social Services department will advise you if anything exists.

Some voluntary organisations, in particular the WRVS, Age Concern groups and sometimes the Mothers' Union, organise *holidays for elderly people* to give relatives a break. Different charities take responsibility according to the area where you live: the CAB, Volunteer Bureau or the Social Services department should know whom you should approach. As with most types of provision, priority is given to families in greatest need.

Another solution is a *short stay home*, which is residential accommodation variously run by local authorities, voluntary organisations or by private individuals which cater specifically for elderly people. Style and facilities vary from the very luxurious to the frankly decrepit. The different types of home are described in more detail under the heading 'Residential Homes' below. For information about local authority provision, ask the Social Services department. For information about other names, contact:

National Council for Carers, 29 Chilworth Mews, London W2 3RG, T:01-724 7776.

Counsel and Care for the Elderly (for Greater London area only), 131 Middlesex Street, London E1 7JF, T:01-621 1624.

Grace (for southern England), P.O. Box 71, Cobham, Surrey KT11 2JR, T:0932-62928.

If, as opposed to general care, proper medical attention is necessary, you should consult your parent's GP. *Many hospitals and nursing homes* offer short stay care arrangements as a means of relieving relatives and a doctor should be able to help organise this for you.

Other invaluable organisations

Fount of almost all knowledge on anything to do with caring are two organisations, set up specifically to assist those with responsibility for an elderly dependent relative.

National Council for Carers and their Elderly Dependants, 29 Chilworth Mews, London W2 3RG, T:01-724 7776.

Formerly known as the National Council for Single Women and their Dependants, the NCCED which has branches throughout the United Kingdom, provides a thorough-going information service. It can advise on: the statutory services; sources of financial help; housing adaptations; where to obtain special equipment, holiday and other relief services. Additionally, it keeps a list of volunteers willing to move in with an elderly person while relatives are on holiday. It also runs a pen-friends' club for carers and circulates a bi-monthly newsletter, giving information on up-to-date developments including current rates of grants and allowances. Supporters of the Council can be enrolled as follows: carer or former carer, £2; supporters, £3 a year.

Association of Carers, Medway House, Balfour Road, Rochester, Kent ME4 6QU, T:0634 813 981.

Through its local branches, the Association offers practical support to carers, forges links with both voluntary and statutory bodies, makes a feature of publicising local facilities and provides a setting for carers to meet. Additionally, it supplies informantion on a wide range of topics including finance, housing, equipment and so on, produces a bi-monthly newsletter and sells a number of useful publications, for example: *Help at Hand*, a guide for carers with information about benefits and services, £1; and *Keep Fit While Caring*, safe ways of lifting and handling a disabled person, £3.45 (plus 40p postage). Membership is open to anyone caring for an elderly or disabled person at home, £3 a year.

Benefits and allowances

There are a number of benefits/allowances available variously to those with responsibility for the care of an elderly person and to elderly people themselves.

Entitlements for carers

Home Responsibilities Protection. A means of protecting your state pension if you are unable to work because of the necessity to care for an elderly person. For further details, see Chapter 2 or ask for leaflet NP 27 at any Social Security office.

Dependent Relatives Allowance. An allowance against tax (in contrast to a benefit you receive) if you are contributing at least £75 a year towards the support of an elderly relative,whose income does not exceed the basic state pension, currently £38.70 a week. For further details, obtain leaflet IR 22 from any Inland Revenue (tax) office, see local telephone directory.

Invalid Care Allowance. Until recently, married women were not able to claim ICA. However, the rules have been changed and now all women up to the age of 60 and men up to 65 who do not work because of the need to stay at home to care for a severely disabled person may qualify. To be eligible, it is necessary to spend at least 35 hours a week looking after an invalid. For further details, obtain leaflet NI 212 from any Social Security office.

It was announced in August 1986 that ICA paid to a married woman can be offset against the wife's earned income allowance (currently £2,335 per year). What this means is that ICA will be tax free for most wives.

Entitlements for elderly disabled people

Attendance Allowance. This is paid to people who are severely disabled, either mentally or physically, and have needed almost constant attention for at least six months. There are two rates of allowance: £30.95 a week for those needing

24 hour care; and £20.65 for those needing intensive day or night time care. The allowance is tax free and can help towards the fees of a private nursing home. If the patient enters an NHS hospital or is supported by their local authority in a residential home, the allowance ceases after four weeks. For futher details, obtain leaflet NI 205 from your local Social Security office.

Mobility Allowance. Designed to help severely disabled people be more mobile and can be used towards a car or taxis. The current rate is £21.65 a week, free of tax. Eligibility is restricted to those who become unable to walk before the age of 65. However, recipients continue to receive the benefit until they reach 75. For further information, obtain leaflet N1 211 from your Social Security office.

Housekeeper's Allowance. Widows and widowers can claim a tax allowance of £100 a year towards the cost of someone living with them to act as housekeeper. This could be a relative of either sex but a male in receipt of married man's allowance would not qualify. For further details, obtain IR leaflet No.22 (Income Tax Personal Allowances) from any tax office.

Financial assistance

A number of charities give financial assistance to elderly people in need. These include:

Distressed Gentlefolk's Aid Association, Vicarage Gate House, Vicarage Gate, London W8, T:01-229 9341.
Provides grants to enable people to remain in their own home. Also runs both a nursing and residential home.

Guild of Aid for Gentle People, 10 St. Christopher's Place, London W1M 6HY, T:01-935 0641.
Priority for grants is given to educated people who live in their own home and receive no help from other sources.

Invalids-at-Home Trust, 23 Farm Avenue, London NW2 2BJ, T:01-452 2074.
Aims to help permanent invalids remain in their own home by making grants and providing special equipment to maintain independence. Applications must be made through a social worker. Assistance is normally limited to those who are without entitlement to any equivalent statutory benefit.

Counsel and Care for the Elderly, 131 Middlesex Street, London E1 7JF, T:01-621 1624.

Assistance is primarily for those, in need of nursing care, who wish to remain in their own homes. Single needs payments are sometimes available for holidays, special equipment, telephone installations and other priority items.

SSAFA, (Soldiers', Sailors' and Airmen's Families Association), 27 Queen Anne's Gate, London SW1H 9BZ, T:01-222 9221.

Assistance is restricted to those who have served in the armed forces and their families. Grants (the average is about £100) can be made to meet immediate need including rent, wheelchairs and similar essentials. Contact via the local branch is preferred (address from Citizens Advice Bureaux and main post offices).

The Royal Agricultural Benevolent Institution, Shaw House, 27 West Way, Oxford OX2 0QH, T:0865-724 931.

Assists retired or disabled farmers, farm managers and their families in need. Help may be given in the event of illness or special misfortune.

Wireless for the Bedridden Society, 81b Corbets Tey Road, Upminster, Essex RM14 2AJ, T:04022 50051.

Loans on a permanent basis radios and televisions to elderly housebound people who cannot afford sets. Application should be made through a health visitor, social worker or doctor.

Special accommodation

Retired people who need particular support, assistance or care may choose or need to move to accommodation where special services are provided. This can either be sheltered housing or a residential home. Both terms cover an enormous spectrum, so anyone considering either of these options should make a point of investigating the market before reaching a decision.

An all too common mistake is for people to anticipate old age long before it arrives and to move into accommodation that is either too small or quite unnecessarily 'sheltered', years before they have need of the facilities. By the same token, some individuals buy or rent sheltered housing with a minimum of support services, only to have to move a few months later because they need rather more help than is available.

Choosing the right accommodation is critically important, as it can make all the difference to independence, life style and general wellbeing. It can also of course lift a great burden off families' shoulders to know that their parents are happy, comfortable, in congenial surroundings and with help on tap, should this be necessary.

Sheltered housing

As a general description, sheltered housing is usually a development of independent bungalows or flats with a warden, an alarm system for emergencies and often some common facilities, such as: a garden, possibly a launderette, a sitting room and a dining room with meals provided for residents, on an optional basis, either once a day or several days a week.

The accommodation is often only available at entry to people under the age of seventy, who are able to look after themselves and do not require nursing. However, some sheltered housing developments now have 'extra care' units suitable for the frail elderly.

Residents have access to all the usual range of services – home helps, meals on wheels – in the same way as any other elderly person.

Sheltered housing is available for sale or rental, variously through private developers, housing associations or local authorities. It is occasionally also provided through gifted housing schemes; or on a shared ownership basis.

Sheltered housing for sale

This is a fast growing market for private housebuilders. There are now some 90 companies offering sheltered housing for sale – with standards and facilities varying enormously. Flats and houses are usually sold on long leases (99 years or more) for a capital sum, with a weekly or monthly service charge to cover maintenance and resident care services. Occupiers normally have to enter into a management agreement with the housebuilder and it is important to establish exactly what the commitment is likely to be before buying into such schemes. A particular point to watch is that the service charge tends to rise annually in line with inflation.

Prices

The range of prices is very wide – between approximately £24,000 and £100,000 – depending on size, location and type of property. Weekly service charges vary between roughly £8 and £40, with £12 – £14 being the norm. The service charge usually covers: the cost of the warden, alarm system, maintenance and repair of any communal facilities (external and internal) and sometimes the heating and lighting costs. It may also cover insurance on the building (but not the contents).

A specific saving on warden-aided sheltered accommodation is that the TV licence is a nominal 5p a year. For those on lowish incomes, it may also be possible to get Housing Benefit to meet some or all of the service charge. The local authority Housing Department will advise on this.

Sheltered housing for sale is a relatively new trend and some people are unaware of what questions they should ask when considering a purchase. These include: who the managing agent is; the warden's duties; what the service charge covers; the arrangements for any repairs that might prove necessary; whether there is a residents' association; whether pets are allowed; what the conditions are with regard to reselling the property – and the tenant's rights in the matter.

Lists of builders offering sheltered housing for sale can be obtained from:

New Homes Marketing Board, 82 New Cavendish Street, London W1.

The following also provide information:

Retirement Housing, SAGA Holidays, P.O. Box 65, Folkestone, Kent CT20 3SG.
Has a register of purpose built retirement housing.

Elderly Accommodation Council, 1 Burward House, 31 Kensington Court, London W8, T:01-937 8700.
For a £5 fee, supplies detailed information on accommodation to suit individual requirements, in area of choice and suitable price range.

Useful reading

A Buyer's Guide to Sheltered Housing, published by Age Concern, Price, £1.
Sheltered Housing For Sale, published by the Housebuilders Association. Available from BEC Publications Department, Federation House, 230 Coventry Road, Sheldon, Birmingham B26 3PL. £4 incl. p & p.

Private companies with sheltered housing for sale

Alfred McAlpine Retirement Homes, Caxton House, St. John's Hill, Sevenoaks, Kent TN13 3NP, T:0732-458655.
Houses, bungalows and flats, mainly in southern England.

Barratt, Windgrove House, Ponteland Road, Newcastle upon Tyne NE5 3DP. T:091 286 6811.
Barratt is Britain's biggest housebuilder and has flats and bungalows for people over 50. They will also help you to sell your present property.

English Courtyard Association, 8 Holland Street, London W8 4LT, T:01-937 4511.
Architecturally award-winning luxury accommodation for sale on 150-year leases. 2-bedroom cottages on one of their new estates would cost in the region of £70,000.

McCarthy & Stone (Developments) Ltd., 11 Queensway, New Milton, Hampshire BH25 5NR, T:0425 611129.

Builds approximately 3,000 new sheltered apartments a year. Prices start at around £25,000 for a 99-year lease.

Nationwide Housing Trust Ltd., 57 George Street, Altrincham, Cheshire WA14 1RJ, T:061-941 6245 (or local branches of the Nationwide Building Society).

Evergreen Housing scheme providing sheltered houses (usually 2-bedroom) on 125-year leases. Prices start at around £25,000. The Trust is able to advise on and make available the most suitable type of mortgage.

Retirement Homes Association, Southdowns, South Darenth, Dartford, Kent 9BG 4LG, T:0322-862494.

Village-style communities usually in rural surroundings (but near a town or village). Prices range from £22,000 for a 1-bedroom flat to £57,000 for a 2-bedroom bungalow; service charges, between £1,600 and £3,000 a year.

Retirement Properties of Bath, General Wolfe's House, 5 Trim Street, Bath, Avon, T:0225-338000.

Mainly luxury flats in converted period buildings around the West Country. Also new 'courtyard' development in Winchester. Prices from £53,000 for a 999-year lease.

Country Houses Association Ltd., 41 Kingsway, London WC2B 6UB, T:01-836 1624.

The Association lets 1-3 room apartments in houses of historic or architectural interest. This is expensive property and consequently more likely to be of interest to those who would normally be in the market to buy. Residents loan the Association a fixed sum, based on the apartment chosen, which is refunded – less 3 per cent a year – when they leave. Additionally, there are monthly charges for: heating, rates, cleaning, resident staff and other overheads. Loans range from £18,500, plus monthly charge of £435, for one bedroom and bathroom; to £32,000, plus monthly charge of £650, for a two-room flat.

Housing associations with sheltered housing

Guardian Housing Association, 1st Floor, Hinksy Court, Westway, Botley, Oxford OX2 9LQ, T:0865 249549.

Flats, bungalows and cottages on long leases (99 to 999 years) at prices ranging from £21,000 to £60,000.

Hanover Housing Association, Hanover House, 18 The Avenue, Egham, Surrey TW20 9AB, T:0784-38361.

Most of the property is built by private developers and managed by Hanover. Prices start at about £30,000 for a 99-year lease.

James Butcher Housing Association, Horncastle Drive, Bath Road, Reading, T:0734 413333.

Houses and flats on 99-year leases, starting at around £40,000.

Retirement Lease Housing Association, 2 Grosvenor Road, Aldershot, Hants, T:0252-318181.

Houses and flats on 60-year leases from £36,000 to £70,000.

Royal British Legion Housing Association, P.O. Box 32, Unit 2, St.John's Industrial Estate, Penn, High Wycombe, Bucks HP10 9JF, T:049-481 3771.

New flats for sale (from January 1987) on 60-year renewable leases from around £30,000. Also shared ownership scheme.

Rented sheltered housing

This is normally provided by local authorities, housing associations and certain benevolent societies. As with accommodation to buy, quality varies.

Local authorities. This is usually only available to people who have resided in the area for some time. There is often an upper and lower age limit for admission and prospective tenants may have to undergo a medical examination, since as a rule only those who are physically fit are accepted. Should a resident become infirm or frail, alternative accommodation will be found. Apply to the local Housing or Social Services Department or via a Housing Advice Centre.

Housing associations. Housing associations supply much of the newly built sheltered housing. Rents, which may sometimes be inclusive of service charge, vary very roughly from £25 to £45 a week. In case of need, supplementary benefit may be obtained to help with the cost. Citizens Advice Bureaux and Housing Departments often keep a list of local housing associations. You can look in the Yellow Pages telephone directory. Or alternatively, you can contact either Age Concern or the Housing Corporation, at the following addresses:

Age Concern England, 60 Pitcairn Road, Mitcham, Surrey CR4 3LL.

Has a complete list of housing associations. Letters should be addressed to the Housing Information Officer and a large sae enclosed.

Housing Corporation, 149 Tottenham Court Road, London W1P 0BN, T:01-387 9466.

Will send a list of housing associations for any area of the country. For Scotland and Northern Ireland, contact:

Scottish Federation of Housing Associations Ltd., 42 York Place, Edinburgh EH1 3HU. T:031-556 1435.

Northern Ireland Committee, National Federation of Housing Associations, 123 York Street, Belfast BT15 1AB, T:0232-30446.

Some housing associations

The Abbeyfield Society, 186-192 Darkes Lane, Potter's Bar, Herts EN6 1AB, T:0707-44845; and 3 Howe Street, Edinburgh EH3 6TE, T:031-556 9406.
Abbeyfield has more than 930 sheltered houses nationwide providing bed-sitting room, a resident housekeeper and sometimes communal meals.

Anchor Housing Association, Oxenford House, 13-15 Magdalen Street, Oxford OX1 3SP, T:0865-722261.
Over 500 housing schemes of self-contained flats with communal facilities such as a guest bedroom, laundry and lounge and sometimes communal meals. Applicants must have strong links with the area.

Fellowship House Trust, Clock House, Byfleet, Weybridge, Surrey KT14 7EN, T:093-23 43172.
Sheltered flats, flatlets and bedsitters in Southern England.

Habinteg Housing Association, 10 Nottingham Place, London W1M 3FL, T:01-935 6931; and 3rd Floor, Orient House, Harris Street, Bradford, West Yorks BD1 5HR, T:0274-720328.
Sheltered housing with special provision for the disabled.

Hanover Housing Association, 18 The Avenue, Egham, Surrey, TW20 9AB, T:0784-38361.
Provides sheltered accommodation through its regional offices in Wimbledon, Horsham, St. Neots, Shipley, Nailsea and Cardiff. Applicants must be over 60 and have some connection with the areas to which they are applying.

James Butcher Housing Association, James Butcher House, Horncastle Drive, Bath Road, Reading RG3 2HP, T:0734-413333; and Murray House, Murray Street, Belfast BT1 6DN, T:0232 225175.
Sheltered housing schemes in southern counties and Northern Ireland. Priority given to those with connections in the areas.

JBG Housing Society Ltd., 221 Golders Green Road, London NW11 9DW, T:01-458 3282.

Some 240 warden-controlled flatlets primarily for Jewish people in housing need, in and near London.

Servite Houses Ltd., 125 Old Brompton Road, London SW7 3RP, T:01-370 5466.

Over 2,500 flatlets with resident warden in and around London, the West Midlands, Merseyside and in Scotland. Some communal meals provided.

Benevolent societies

These all cater for specific professional and other groups.

Housing Association for Officers' Families, Alban Dobson House, Green Lane, Morden, Surrey, T:01-648 0335.

Houses and flats to let in Southern England for war disabled, married ex-officers of the three armed services and their widows.

King William IV Naval Foundation, c/o Coutts & Co., 440 Strand, London WC2, T:01-379 6262.

Sheltered unfurnished bungalows to let for widows of naval officers.

Royal Alfred Seafarers' Society, Weston Acres, Woodmansterne Lane, Banstead, Surrey SM7 3HB, T:073-73 52231.

Residential homes for retired naval officers and ratings, and their widows. Some nursing care provided.

Royal British Legion Housing Association, P.O. Box 32, Unit 2, St.John's Industrial Estate, Penn, High Wycombe, Bucks HP10 9JF, T:049-481 3771.

Over 300 sheltered housing schemes for ex-service men and their dependants with nearly 12,000 units.

Soldiers', Sailors' and Airmen's Families Association (SSAFA), 16 18 Old Queen Street, London SW1H 9HP, T:01-222 9221.

Works with the Abbeyfield Society to provide sheltered accommodation for retired ex-service people.

Teachers' Benevolent Fund, Hamilton House, Mabledon Place, London WC1H 9BE, T:01-388 6191.

Sheltered unfurnished accommodation for active retired state school teachers and their dependants. Some meals provided.

'Investment' and gifted housing schemes

Some charities and housing associations operate these schemes (sometimes called 'leasehold schemes'), for which a capital sum is required to obtain sheltered accommodation. This usually takes the form of an interest-free loan, which is returnable on leaving or when the owner dies.

Gifted housing schemes differ in that an individual *donates* his/her property to an association (usually a registered charity) in return for being housed and, if necessary, cared for in either their own home or in one of the charity's sheltered homes. The attraction is that the owner can remain in his or her own property with none of the burden of its upkeep. However, it is advisable to consult a solicitor before signing anything, because such schemes have the big drawback of reducing the value of the owner's estate with consequent loss for any beneficiaries.

One of the better known organisations to offer both kinds of scheme is the charity, Help the Aged. Its investment type accommodation is in: Chester, Luton, Woking, Rustington, Salcombe, Lowestoft, Corbridge, Huddersfield, Colchester and Lindfield.

With the gifted scheme, Help the Aged converts the owner's house into flats and becomes responsible for the building's external maintenance, insurance and rates. Their alternative sheltered accommodation consists of private apartments in large houses; or modern purpose-built flats and bungalows, set in the grounds of the main house. For further information, contact:

Help the Aged, The Court House, 1 Ward Street, Guildford, Surrey, GU1 4LH, T:0483-571772/3.

For further information on such schemes, send for a copy of Age Concern's free factsheet *Housing Schemes for Elderly People Requiring a Capital Sum*, available from: the Information Department, 60 Pitcairn Road, Mitcham, Surrey (enclose sae).

Almshouses

There are some 2,000 groups of almshouses, with around 26,000 units. They variously consist of a cluster of cottages, flats, sheltered schemes or new bungalows which are owned and managed by trustees. Rents are usually on the low side and sometimes the accommodation is rent free. There is no standard way to apply but most trusts determine priority either by residential or occupational qualification. Some housing departments and housing advice centres keep lists of local almshouses. Or write to:

National Association of Almshouses, Billingbear Lodge, Wokingham, Berkshire RG11 5RU, T:0344 52922.

Granny flats

A granny flat or annex is a self-contained unit attached to a family house. A large house can be converted or extended for this purpose, but planning permission is needed. Enquire at your local authority planning department. Some councils have houses to rent with granny flats, particularly New Towns.

Housing for cultural groups

ASRA (Asians' Sheltered Residential Accommodation): Leicester, c/o Stonesby House, 44 Princess Road East, Leicester LE1 7DQ; Lambeth, c/o Asian Community Action Group, 15 Bedford Road, London SW4; Wandsworth, 54 Dafforn Road, London SW17.

Eastwards Trust, Aram House, 217 Romford Road, London E7. Hostel for elderly Asians.

Very sheltered schemes

These are similar to sheltered schemes but have the advantage of extra facilities such as: two to three wardens to give 24-hour coverage, at least one cooked meal provided every day in a central dining room, plus communal areas assigned for the needs of the very frail. Approximate charges are in the range of £50 – £60 a week. A number of organisations which provide this type of accommodation also have '*extra care*' sheltered housing, designed for those who can no longer look after themselves without assistance in their own rooms. Priority would normally be given to tenants of very sheltered schemes but others can apply. Cost is in the region of £120 a week. Although expensive, it is cheaper than most private full-scale residential care. A possible problem is that tenants of some of these schemes do not have security of tenure and could therefore be asked to leave if additional care were required. Among the housing associations that provide these facilities are *Abbeyfield* and *Servite*, (see above). Additional names should be obtainable from the **Housing Corporation**, 149 Tottenham Court Road, London W1P OBN.

Residential homes

There may come a time when it is no longer possible for an elderly person to manage without being in proper residential care.

Sometimes known as rest homes, the accommodation usually consists of a bedroom plus communal dining rooms, lounges and gardens. All meals are provided, rooms are cleaned and staff are at hand to give whatever help is needed. Most homes are fully furnished, though it is usually possible to take small items of furniture. Except in some of the more expensive private nursing homes, bathrooms are normally shared. Proper nursing care is not included. Homes are run by private individuals (or companies), voluntary organisations and local authorities. All private and voluntary homes should be registered with the Social Services to ensure minimum standards. Any unregistered home should not be considered. No home should ever be accepted 'on spec'. It is very important that the individual should have a proper chance to visit it and ask any questions. Before reaching a final decision, it is a good idea to arrange a short stay to see whether the facilities are suitable and pleasant.

Private rest homes

Private rest homes tend to be smaller than those run by councils or voluntary organisations and are usually converted private houses, taking from 5 to 30 people. The degree of care varies. If a resident becomes increasingly infirm, a rest home will normally continue to look after them if possible although it may be necessary at some point to arrange transfer to a nursing home or hospital. Fees cover an enormous range: from £30 a week to £400. The average is about £150. For sources of information, see below.

Voluntary rest homes

These are run by charities, religious bodies or organisations that exist to care for retired members of certain professions, trades and crafts. Eligibility may also be determined by age, background or religion, depending on the criteria of the managing organisation. Income may be a factor, as may general fitness and individuals may be invited to a personal interview before acceptance onto the waiting list. Priority tends to be given to those in greatest need. Homes are often in large converted houses, with accommodation for under 10 people or up to 100. Fees start around the £70 mark with top charges about £120, or £200 for Greater London. In cases of need, the local Social Services department may assist with the fees; if they refuse, individuals can then apply to the Department of Health and Social Security (DHSS) for supplementary benefit. Both Age Concern and Counsel & Care for the Elderly provide factsheets on how to claim.

Sources of information

Key sources of information about voluntary homes are: *The Charities Digest* (available in libraries), Housing Aid Centres and Citizens Advice Bureaux.

Social Services departments keep lists of both voluntary and private homes, as does **Counsel & Care for the Elderly**, 131 Middlesex Street, London E1 7JF, T:01-621 1624. Its real expertise is in the Greater London area, where it visits all homes every year.

A useful publication for advice on private homes is the *Directory of Private Hospitals and Health Services* (available in libraries).

Grace, P.O. Box 71, Cobham, Surrey KT11 2JR, can provide detailed information on private residential accommodation and nursing homes in Southern England (except Greater London).

Local authority homes

These are sometimes referred to as 'Part III Accommodation'. In theory, any local resident who needs care and attention (but not nursing care) is eligible. In practice, there are often waiting lists and, except in an emergency, individuals normally have to wait a few months before being offered a place. If someone does not like the particular accommodation suggested, they can turn it down and wait for another offer. Charges range from £85 to £185. Regardless of income, there is a minimum fee of £30.95. In cases of need, the local authority may pay the balance. Alternatively, it may be possible to claim supplementary benefit. Age Concern publishes a factsheet *Local Authorities and Residential Care*. Also obtain leaflet *Supplementary Benefit for Residential Care and Nursing Homes*, available from any Social Security office.

Nursing homes

Nursing homes provide medical supervision and fully qualified nurses, 24-hours a day. The vast majority are privately run with the remainder being supported by voluntary organisations. All nursing homes must be registered with the District Health Authority who will have a list of what is available in the area.

Private. They normally accommodate between 10 and 40 patients. Average fees are about £240 a week; in London, they *start* at around £250; and throughout the country as a whole, charges can reach £450. In some cases, district health authorities may meet the cost for a patient for whom there is no other suitable facility. For information about private nursing homes in the UK and Republic of Ireland, contact:

The Registered Nursing Homes Association, 75 Portland Place, London W1N 4AN, T:01-631 1524.

Voluntary. There are normally very long waiting lists and beds are often reserved for those who have been in the charity's rest home. Charges in Greater London start around £190. Social Services departments will sometimes help with the fees in an emergency or if there is no other suitable facility. Voluntary organisations which run residential and nursing homes include:

British Red Cross Society, 9 Grosvenor Crescent, London SW9 7EJ.

Catholic Housing Aid Society, 189a Old Brompton Road, London SW5

Catholic Old People's Homes are listed in the Catholic Directory, available in libraries.

Church Army Sunset and Anchorage Homes, CSC House, North Circular Road, London NW10 7UG.

Cecil Houses, 2/4 Priory Road, Kew, Richmond, Surrey TW9 3DG.

Church of England Board for Social Responsibility, Church House, Deans Yard, London SW1.

Crossways Trust Ltd., Grosvenor House, Kings Road, Brighton, Sussex.

Distressed Gentlefolk's Aid Association, Vicarage Gate House, Kensington, London W8 4AG.

Friends of the Elderly and Gentlefolk's Help, 42 Ebury Street, London SW1W 0LZ.

Jewish Welfare Board, 221 Golders Green Road, London NW11.

Methodist Homes for the Aged, 1 Central Buildings, London SW1.

Royal Benevolent Trust, High Street, Gillingham, Kent.

Quaker Social Responsibility and Education, Friends House, Euston Road, London NW1.

Royal British Legion, Pall Mall, London SW1.

Royal UK Beneficent Association, 6 Avonmore Road, London W14.

Salvation Army (for women), 280 Mare Street, Hackney, London E8.

Salvation Army (for men), 110-112 Middlesex Street, London E1.

The SOS Society, 14 Culford Gardens, London SW3.

Women's Royal Voluntary Service, 17 Old Park Lane, London W1.

Some special problems

A minority of people as they become older suffer from special problems which can cause great distress. Because families do not like to talk about them, they may be unaware of what services are available so may be missing out both on practical help and sometimes also on financial assistance.

Hypothermia

Elderly people tend to be more vulnerable to the cold. If the body drops below a certain temperature, it can be dangerous because one of the symptoms of hypothermia is that sufferers no longer actually feel cold. Instead, they may lose their appetite and vitality and may become mentally confused. Instead of doing all the sensible things like getting a hot drink and putting on an extra sweater, they are liable to neglect themselves further and can put themselves at real risk.

Although heating costs are often blamed, quite wealthy people can also be victims by allowing their home to become too cold or not wearing sufficient clothing. For this reason, during a cold snap it is very important to check up regularly on an elderly person living alone.

The Gas and Electricity Boards and the Solid Fuels Advisory Service are all willing to give advice on how heating systems can be used more efficiently and economically. (See telephone directory for nearest branch or ask at the Citizens Advice Bureau).

Insulation can also play a very large part in keeping a home warmer and cheaper to heat. There are various grants available to assist with this. See heating and insulation sections in Chapter 6. Additionally, help with heating costs is available for pensioners on a low budget. For further details, obtain leaflet SB 17 *Help With Heating Costs for People Getting Supplementary Benefit*, available from any Social Security office. In the event of any emergency, such as a power cut, contact the Citizens Advice Bureau or local Age Concern group.

Useful reading
Hypothermia the Facts available free from Age Concern England, Bernard Sunley House, 60 Pitcairn Road, Mitcham, Surrey CR4 3LL. Please enclose large sae.

Incontinence

Incontinence is a problem that can cause deep embarrassment to sufferers as well as inconvenience to relatives. It can occur in an elderly person for all sorts of reasons and a doctor should always be consulted, as it can often be cured or at least alleviated by proper treatment. To assist with the practical problems, many local authorities operate a laundry service which collects soiled linen, sometimes several times a week. In many areas the service is free and the person to talk to is the Health Visitor or District Nurse (telephone your local Health Centre) who will be able to advise about this and other facilities.

The **Disabled Living Foundation** has an advisory service on incontinence and also a couple of useful publications on the subject. For further information, contact: the Incontinence Adviser, Disabled Living Foundation, 380/384 Harrow Road, London W9 2HU, T:01-289 6111.

People on very low budgets, such as those claiming supplementary pension or housing benefit supplement, can obtain financial assistance which may take the form of a single payment or a weekly allowance to help with the laundry and other extra costs. Claim forms are available at Social Security offices. The Health Visitor will be able to advise as to the appropriate leaflet number.

Dementia

Sometimes an elderly person can become confused, forgetful, suffer severe loss of memory or can have violent mood swings and at times be abnormally aggressive. It is important to consult a doctor as soon as possible as the cause may be due to depression, stress or even vitamin deficiency, all of which can be treated and often completely cured. If dementia is diagnosed, there are ways of helping a sufferer to cope better with acute forgetfulness and other symptoms. As well as a doctor, it is usually a very good idea to talk to the Health Visitor, as she will know about any helpful facilities that may be available locally and can also arrange appointments with other professionals, such as the Community Psychiatric Nurse and Occupational Therapist. The charity, Mind, can often also help. Addresses to contact are:

Mind (National Association for Mental Health): for England, 22 Harley Street, London W1N 2ED, T:01-637 0741; for Wales, 23 St. Mary Street, Cardiff CF1 2AA, T:0222-395123.

Scottish Association for Mental Health, Angus House, 67 York Place, Edinburgh EH1 3JB, T:031-556 3062.

Northern Ireland Association for Mental Health, 84 University Street, Belfast BT7 1HE, T:0232-28474.
Another helpful organisation, with local groups throughout the country is:

Alzheimers Disease Society: for England and Wales, Third Floor, Bank Buildings, Fulham Broadway, London SW6 1EP, T:01-381 3177; for Scotland, First Floor, 40 Shandwick Place, Edinburgh EH2 4RT, T:031-225 1453.

Useful reading includes:

The 36-Hour Day – Caring at Home for Confused Elderly People. Co-published with Age Concern by Hodder & Stoughton and available from bookshops, £5.95.

Coping with Caring, by Brian Lodge, published by Mind and available from Mind Bookshop, 155 Woodhouse Lane, Leeds 2, £1.60 incl. p&p.

Forgetfulness in Elderly Persons, Advice for Carers, by Tim Dowdell, published by Age Concern Greater London, 54 Knatchbull Road, London SE5 9QY, 50p incl. p&p.

Mental Health in Old Age: A Collection of Projects. A directory of schemes throughout Britain that offer support for carers and practical help to handicapped and ill people. Published by Age Concern England, 60 Pitcairn Road, Mitcham, Surrey, £1 incl. p&p.

14. No One Is Immortal

In Bali death is celebrated with glorious processions, merry-making and days of feasting. In Western society, we go to the other extreme. Many couples never even discuss death or the financial practicalities, in the subconscious belief perhaps that to do so would be tempting fate. For the same reason, many people put off making a will or rationalise that it does not really matter, since in any case their possessions will eventually go to their family. However, as every widows' organisation would testify, a great deal of heartbreak and real financial worry could be avoided if husbands and wives were more open with each other.

Wills

Anyone who is married or over the age of 35 should make a will. At very least, should anything happen, this will ensure that their wishes are known and properly executed. But also very important, it will spare their family from the legal complications that arise when someone dies intestate. A very major problem if someone dies without leaving a will is that the surviving husband or wife will usually have to wait very much longer for badly needed cash, as the legal formalities are more complex. There will be no executor. Also, the individual's assets will be distributed according to a rigid formula, which may be a far cry from what he or she had intended and may perversely result in their partner's security being quite unnecessarily jeopardised.

Laws of intestacy

The rules if you die without leaving a will are as follows:

- If there are *no surviving children, parents, brothers, sisters or direct nephews or nieces* of the deceased, the widow/widower inherits the whole of the estate.
- If there are *children but no surviving partner*, the estate is divided equally among the children.
- If there is a *partner and children*, the partner receives: all personal possessions (excluding the house), £40,000, plus a life interest in half of the remainder. The other half goes to the children, who will also inherit their mother or father's half on his/her death. Straightforward as this sounds, if the house is in the name of the deceased and is worth more than £40,000,

the surviving partner could be left without a home.

- If there are no children but other close members of the family still living (parents, brothers, sisters, direct nephews or nieces), the surviving partner receives: all personal possessions, £85,000, plus half of the remainder of the estate. The other half is divided between the rest of the family.
- Common law spouses have no legal rights of inheritance (unless it can be proved that they were being supported by the deceased).
- If a couple are separated, but not divorced, they are still legally married and, therefore, the separated partner would in all probability be the major beneficiary.

Making a will

You have three choices: you can do it yourself; you can ask your bank to help you; or you can use a solicitor.

Doing it yourself

Homemade wills are not generally recommended. People often use ambiguous wording, which while perfectly clear to the individual who has written it, may be less patently obvious to others. This could result in the donor's wishes being misinterpreted and could also cause considerable delay in settling the estate.

You can buy forms from W.H. Smith and other stationers which, while helpful, are not perfect and still leave considerable margin for error. Two witnesses are needed and an essential point to remember is that beneficiaries cannot witness a will; nor can the spouses of any beneficiaries. In certain circumstances, a will can be rendered invalid. A sensible precaution for anyone doing it themselves is to have it checked by a solicitor or by a legal expert from the Citizens Advice Bureau.

Banks

Advice on wills and the administration of estates is carried out by the *trustee companies* of most of the major high street banks. In particular, the services they offer are: to provide general guidance, to act as executor and to administer the estate. They will also introduce clients to a solicitor and keep a copy of the will – plus other important documents – in their safe, to avoid the risk of their being mislaid. Additionally, banks can give tax planning and other financial guidance, including advice on inheritance tax. Unless one of the others has very recently introduced the service, the only bank that will actually draw up a will for you is the Midland.

Solicitors

Solicitors offer to: draw up a will, act as executors and administer the estate. Like banks, they will also of course keep a copy of your will in safe keeping. If you do not know a solicitor, you can ask your bank or the Citizens Advice Bureau. Or you can write to the **Law Society**, 113 Chancery Lane, London WC2A 1PL, T:01-242 1222. People on supplementary benefit or who have very little income may qualify for legal aid for assistance in drawing up a will.

Charges

These can vary enormously, depending on the size and complexity of the will. A basic will could be as little or £25 or the cost could run into many hundreds of pounds. Always ask for an estimate before proceeding. Remember too that professional fees carry 15 per cent VAT. Solicitors charge according to the time they spend on a job, so although the actual work may not take very long, if you spend hours discussing your will, or changing it every few months, the costs can escalate very considerably.

Executor

You will need to appoint an executor. This could be a friend whom you trust to act impartially, always providing of course that he/she is willing to accept the responsibility. Or, and this is generally advisable for larger estates, you could appoint your solicitor or bank.

The fees will be additional. They are not paid at the time of making the will but instead come out of the estate. Pretty significant sums could be involved, so the advice on obtaining an estimate is, if anything, even more relevant. In certain instances, banks can be more expensive; in others, solicitors. The only way to discover is to get an estimate from each.

Banks publish a tariff of their charges. Solicitors render bills according to the time involved; so, although it is impossible for them to be precise, they should nevertheless be able to give a pretty accurate assessment – at least at the time of quoting. Both banks' and solicitors' fees may increase during the interval between their being appointed and fulfilling their duties as executor.

Other points

Wills should always be kept in a safe place – and their whereabouts known. The most sensible arrangement is for the solicitor to keep the original and for the bank to have a copy. Wills may need up-dating in the event of an important change of circumstances, for example: a divorce, remarriage or the birth of a grandchild. Partners who wish to leave all their possessions to each other should consider including 'a survivorship clause' in their wills, as an insurance against the intestacy rules being applied were they both to be involved in the same fatal accident.

Useful reading

Wills and Probate. Available from the Consumers' Association, Castlemead, Gascoyne Way, Hertford, £6.95.

Money worries – and how to minimise them

Most people say that the first time they really think about death, in terms of what would happen to their nearest and dearest, is after the birth of their first baby. As children grow up, requirements change but key points that any family man or woman should consider – and review from time to time – include life insurance and mortgage protection relief.

Both husbands and wives should have *life insurance cover*. If either were to die, not only would their partner lose the benefit of their earnings, they would also lose the value of their services: home decorating, gardening, cooking and so forth.

Most banks and building societies urge homeowners to take out *mortgage protection schemes*. If you die, the loan is paid off automatically and the family home will not be repossessed.

Banks also offer *insurance to cover any personal or other loans*. This could be a vital safeguard to avoid leaving the family with debts.

Many people worry about *funeral costs*. The National Association of Funeral Directors has recently launched an imaginative savings plan in conjunction with Windsor Life Assurance. For details, write to: **Windsor Life**, Royal Albert House, Windsor, Berkshire SL4 1BE.

Two other organisations that offer funeral cost policies are:

Independent Order of Odd Fellows, 23 Greek Street, Stockport, Manchester, T:061-480 2796.

Prudential Assurance Co. Ltd., 142 Holborn Bars, London EC1, T:01-405 9222 (or see local telephone directory).

A very real crisis for some families is the need for immediate money while waiting for the estate to be settled. At least part of the problem can be overcome by couples having a *joint bank account*, with both partners having drawing rights without the signature of the other being required. Sole name bank accounts and joint accounts requiring both signatures are frozen.

For the same reason, it is also a good idea for any savings or investments to

CHART 1

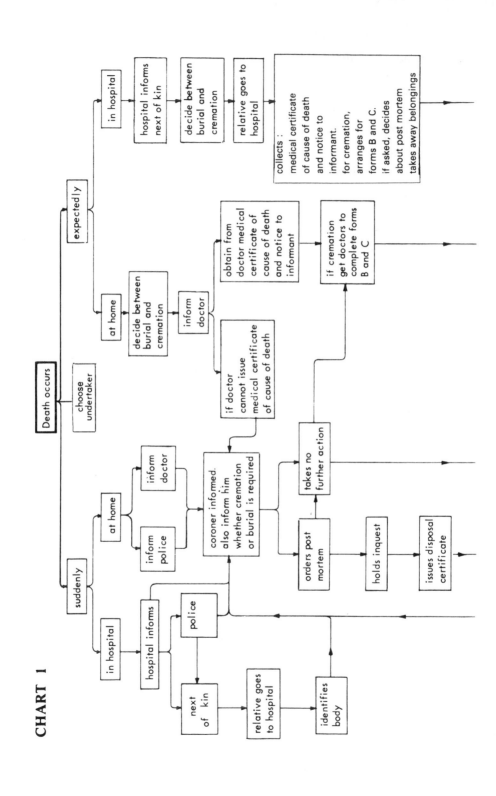

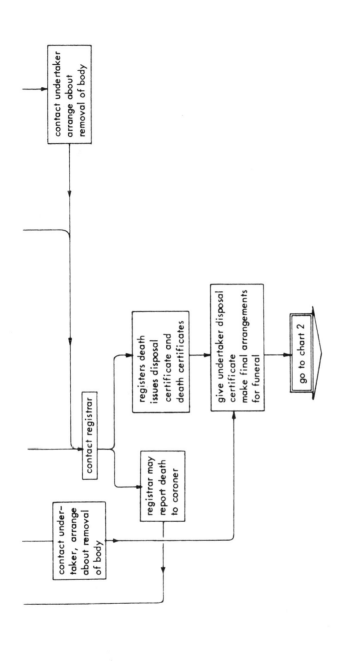

CHART 2

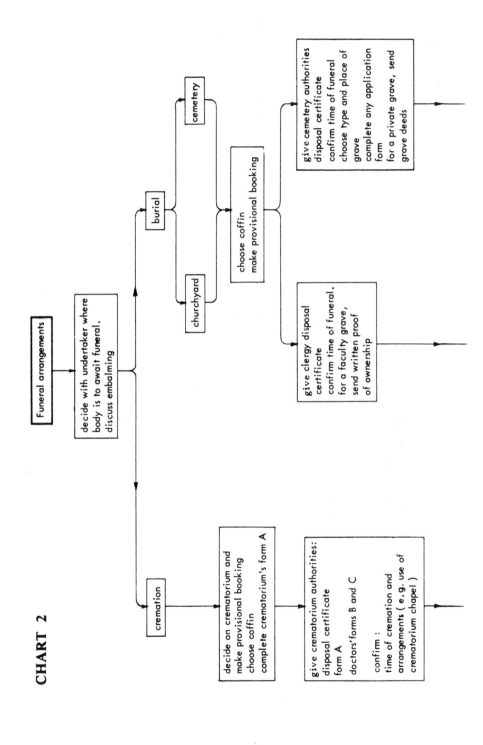

Funeral arrangements

decide with undertaker where body is to await funeral. discuss embalming

cremation

decide on crematorium and make provisional booking
choose coffin
complete crematorium's form A

give crematorium authorities:
disposal certificate
form A
doctors' forms B and C

confirm :
time of cremation and arrangements (e.g. use of crematorium chapel)

burial

churchyard

cemetery

choose coffin
make provisional booking

give clergy disposal certificate
confirm time of funeral.
for a faculty grave,
send written proof
of ownership

give cemetery authorities
disposal certificate
confirm time of funeral
choose type and place of grave
complete any application form
for a private grave, send grave deeds

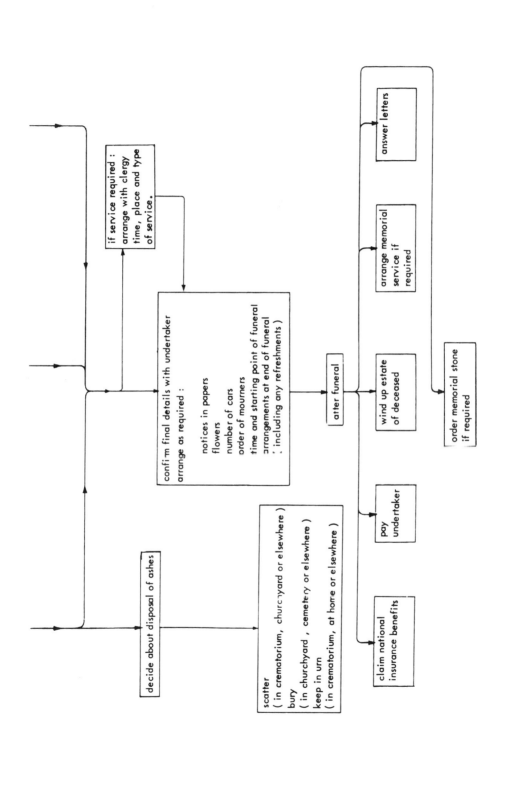

be held in the joint name of the couple. A really essential point is that these and any other *important documents should be discussed together* and understood by the wife as well as by the husband. Even today, an all too common saga is for widows to come across insurance policies and other papers, which they have never seen before and do not understand – often causing quite unnecessary anxiety.

A further common-sense 'must' is for both partners to *know where important papers are kept*. Best idea is either to lock them, filed together, in a home safe; or to give them to the bank to look after.

If someone dies, *the bank manager should be notified as soon as possible*, so he can assist with the problems of unpaid bills and help work out a solution until the estate is settled.

The same goes for the *suppliers of essential services*: gas, electricity, telephone and so on. Unless they know the situation, there is a risk of services being cut off if there is a delay in paying the bill. Add too any credit card companies, where if bills lie neglected, the additional interest could mount up alarmingly.

What to do when someone dies

There are formalities to be observed and arrangements to be made. The two charts on pp.370-3, published by courtesy of the Consumers' Association whose book *What to Do When Someone Dies* provides a fund of practical information, illustrate what action is required.

The first chart deals with the period immediately after death; the second, with the necessary arrangements for a funeral.

Recommended reading

What to Do When Someone Dies. Available from the Consumers' Association, Castlemead, Gascoyne Way, Hertford SG14 1LH, £6.95.
What to Do After a Death. Free leaflet from DHSS, Leaflets Unit, P.O. Box 21, Stanmore, Middlesex HA7 1AY.

State benefits, tax and other money points

Some extra financial benefits are given to widows and widowers. Several take the form of a cash payment. Others come in the form of a relief against tax.

The figures quoted apply until April 1987, at which point at least a number of these benefits are likely to be modestly increased.

Some fairly major changes, mainly affecting younger widows, are planned to take effect in April 1988.

Benefits paid in cash form

All leaflets quoted are obtainable from any social security office.

Death Grant. This is a single payment to assist with funeral expenses. Value of the grant is £30. See leaflet NI 229. This is expected to be abolished in 1987 and replaced by the new social fund discretionary grant.

Widows' Allowance. This is paid during the first 26 weeks of widowhood. Value of the Allowance is £54.20 a week. Those already in receipt of retirement pension are not eligible to claim. See leaflet NP 35.

Widowed Mother's Allowance. This is paid to mothers with at least one child still at school under the age of 19. The value is £38.70 a week. The allowance is usually paid automatically. If for some reason, although eligible, you do not receive it, you should inform your local social security office. See leaflet NP 36.

Child Dependency Addition. This is a payment of £8.05 a week, for each dependent child. It does not affect entitlement to child benefit (£7.10), which continues to be paid in the normal way. Information about the addition is included in both leaflets NP 35 and NP 36.

Widows' Pension. The normal retirement pension for widows is the same as for a single person: £38.70 a week.

Widows over the age of 50 may also receive a widow's pension, when the special 26 weeks' allowance ceases to be paid. See leaflet NP 32A.

Age-Related Widows' Pension. This is a pension for younger widows who do not qualify for a full widow's pension. It is payable to a widow who is aged between 40 and 49 inclusive when her husband dies, or when her children cease to be dependent. Rates depend on age and vary from £11.61 for 40 year olds to £35.99 for those aged 49. See leaflet NP 36.

Particular points to note

- A reduced rate of benefit may be paid if there are any gaps in the husband's National Insurance record.
- A woman widowed under age 40 without dependent children receives no Widows' Pension after the first 26 weeks.

- Widows' benefits are taxable. However, Child Dependency Allowance and Child Benefit are tax free, as are War Widows' Pensions.

- There is no Widowers' Pension. On retirement, an exception could be made in cases where the wife's National Insurance contribution was better than her husband's.

● A widower with dependent children will receive Child Benefit. Single parents who are not eligible for any state benefit are paid an extra £4.60 a week Child Benefit.

● Men and Women widowed after April 1979 will normally be able to inherit their spouse's additional pension rights, if he/she contributed to SERPS; or at least half their guaranteed minimum pension, if they were in a contracted-out scheme. Additionally, where applicable, all widows are entitled to   half the graduated pension earned by their husband. For further information, see Chapter 2.

● Widows who remarry, or live with a man as his wife, cease to receive Widow's Pension. They will, however, continue to receive a retirement pension if they remarry when they are aged 60 or over.

Tax and tax allowances

Widows and widowers are taxed as single persons and receive the normal single person's tax allowance of £2,335 a year. A widower, however, is entitled to continue claiming the Married Man's Allowance until the end of the tax year.

Widow's Bereavement Allowance. This is an extra allowance, worth £1,320 a year at current rates, specially given to widows to assist them over the first difficult period. The only qualification is that a widow's late husband must have been entitled to the married man's tax allowance at the time of his death. The allowance is given from the date of bereavement to the end of that tax year, plus the year following.

Housekeeper's Allowance. Widows or widowers who have someone living with them to act as housekeeper may be able to claim a tax allowance of £100.

Useful Inland Revenue leaflets. These are available from any tax office:

Income Tax and Widows. Leaflet IR 23.
Income Tax: Personal Allowances. Leaflet IR 22.
Income Tax and CGT – What Happens when Someone Dies. Leaflet IR 45.

Organisations that can help

Many people have difficulty in working out exactly what they are entitled to – and how to claim it. The Citizens Advice Bureau is always very helpful.

Additionally, Cruse and the National Association for Widows (see below) can also assist you.

Problems vary. For some, the hardest thing to bear is the loneliness of returning to an empty house. For others, money problems seem to dominate everything else. For many older women in particular, who have not got a job, widowhood creates a great gulf where for a while there is no real sense of purpose. Many widowed men and women go through a spell of feeling enraged against their partner for dying. Most are baffled and hurt by the seeming indifference of friends, who appear more embarrassed than sympathetic.

In time, all these feelings soften, problems diminish and individuals are able to recapture their joy for living with all its many pleasures. Talking to other people who know the difficulties from their own experience can be a tremendous help. The following organisations not only offer opportunities for companionship but also provide an advisory and support service.

Cruse, Cruse House, 126 Sheen Road, Richmond, Surrey TW9 1UR, T:01-940 4818.

This is a national organisation for the widowed and their children, with over 100 branches throughout Britain. It offers a counselling and advice service, including visiting the bereaved in their own home where there is a local branch. Additionally, Cruse publishes a wide range of informative leaflets (mostly 10p each) on such matters as: buying and selling a house, income tax, insurance, state benefits and employment opportunities. The branches organise their own programmes which typically include: meetings with a speaker, theatre outings, rambles and dances. There is a monthly newsletter. National membership is £4 a year. Addresses of local branches can be obtained by contacting the headquarters above.

National Association for Widows, c/o Stafford District Voluntary Services Centre, Chell Road, Stafford ST16 2QA, T:0785-45465.

The Association is a nationwide voluntary organisation which aims to improve the financial status of widows. As well as acting as a pressure group, it operates an advisory service, specialising in financial matters, and has many groups around the country. Membership is £5 initially; £3.50 a year thereafter. Enquiries are also welcomed from non-members.

Many professional and other groups offer a range of services for widows and widowers associated with them. These include:

Civil Service Retirement Fellowship, 1b Deals Gateway, Blackheath Road, London SE10 8BW, T:01-691 7411.

The Forces Help Society, 122 Brompton Road, London SW3 1JE, T:01-589 3243.

The War Widows Association of Great Britain, Low Bank, 81 Gargrave Road, Skipton, North Yorkshire BD23 1QN, T:0756-3719.

The Northern Ireland Widows Association, 137 University Street, Belfast BT7 1HP, T:0232-228 263.

Many local **Age Concern** groups offer a counselling service.

Trade unions are often particularly supportive, as are Rotary Clubs, all the Armed Forces organisations and most Benevolent Societies.

Recommended reading

The Widow's Survival Guide. Available from: Marketing Department, Age Concern, 60 Pitcairn Road, Mitcham, Surrey CR4 3LL. Price is £3.50 including p & p.

Index of Organisations